Informatik aktuell

Herausgeber: W. Brauer
im Auftrag der Gesellschaft für Informatik (GI)

Rüdiger Dillmann   Jürgen Beyerer
Christoph Stiller   J. Marius Zöllner
Tobias Gindele (Hrsg.)

Autonome Mobile Systeme 2009

21. Fachgespräch
Karlsruhe, 3./4. Dezember 2009

Herausgeber

Rüdiger Dillmann
Tobias Gindele
Karlsruher Institut für Technologie - KIT
Institut für Anthropomatik
Adenauerring 4
76131 Karlsruhe
dillmann@kit.edu
gindele@kit.edu
http://his.anthropomatik.kit.edu/

Jürgen Beyerer
Karlsruher Institut für Technologie
Lehrstuhl für Interaktive Echtzeitsysteme
Fraunhofer-Institut für Informations- und
Datenverarbeitung IITB
Fraunhoferstr. 1
76131 Karlsruhe
juergen.beyerer@iitb.fraunhofer.de
http://www.ies.uni-karlsruhe.de

Christoph Stiller
Karlsruher Institut für Technologie
Institut für Mess- und Regelungstechnik
Engler-Bunte-Ring 21
76131 Karlsruhe
stiller@mrt.uka.de
http://www.mrt.uni-karlsruhe.de

J. Marius Zöllner
FZI Forschungszentrum Informatik
Technisch kognitive Assistenzsysteme
Haid-und-Neu-Str. 10-14
76131 Karlsruhe
zoellner@fzi.de
http://www.fzi.de

Bibliographische Information der Deutschen Bibliothek
Die Deutsche Bibliothek verzeichnet diese Publikation in der Deutschen Nationalbibliografie; detaillierte
bibliografische Daten sind im Internet über http://dnb.ddb.de abrufbar.

CR Subject Classification (1998): I.2.9, I.2.10, I.2.11, I.4.7, I.4.8, J.7

ISSN 1431-472-X
ISBN-13 978-3-540-10283-7 Springer Berlin Heidelberg New York

Springer Berlin Heidelberg New York
Springer ist ein Unternehmen von Springer Science+Business Media

springer.de

© Springer-Verlag Berlin Heidelberg 2009
Printed in Germany

Satz: Reproduktionsfertige Vorlage vom Autor/Herausgeber
Gedruckt auf säurefreiem Papier   SPIN: 12796007   33/3142-543210

Vorwort

Das 21. Fachgespräch „Autonome Mobile Systeme (AMS)" findet am 3. und 4. Dezember 2009 in Karlsruhe statt und wird vom Institut für Anthropomatik, Lehrstuhl Prof. Rüdiger Dillmann, dem Fraunhofer-Institut für Informations- und Datenverarbeitung IITB, Lehrstuhl Prof. Jürgen Beyerer, dem Institut für Mess- und Regelungstechnik, Lehrstuhl Prof. Christoph Stiller, und dem FZI Forschungszentrum Informatik, Abteilung Technisch kognitive Assistenzsysteme, Dr.-Ing. J. Marius Zöllner, ausgerichtet.

Das Fachgespräch stellt seit über 25 Jahren ein Forum für Wissenschaftler aus Forschung und Industrie dar, die auf dem Gebiet der autonomen und teilautonomen mobilen Roboter forschen und entwickeln. Es stellt besonders für Nachwuchswissenschaftler eine besondere Möglichkeit dar, die Ergebnisse aktueller Forschungsarbeiten auf diesem Gebiet zu diskutieren. Der Dialog zwischen Grundlagenforschern und der Robotikindustrie sorgt für einen bereichsübergreifenden Wissenstransfer und stellt für beide Seiten eine fruchtbare Bereicherung dar. Die ursprünglich auf den deutschsprachigen Raum ausgerichtete Konferenz findet mittlerweile auch im europäischen Raum regen Anklang. Diese Entwicklung wird durch den wachsenden Anteil englischsprachiger Veröffentlichungen begünstigt.

Inhaltlich finden sich dieses Jahr aktuelle Beiträge, die neueste Ergebnisse und Trends aus dem weiten Bereich der autonomen mobilen Robotik präsentieren. Zu den großen Themengebieten zählen Wahrnehmung und Sensortechnik, Regelung und Robotersteuerung, Lokalisierung und Kartierung, Navigation und Systemarchitekturen sowie Anwendungen von autonomen mobilen Systemen. Speziell die Bereiche humanoide Roboter und Laufroboter sowie Flugmaschinen und intelligente Automobile sind durch eine Vielzahl von Beiträgen vertreten.

Insgesamt wurden für die AMS 48 Beiträge eingereicht. Der Fachgesprächsbeirat hat aus diesen Arbeiten 34 ausgewählt, die in einem Vortrag präsentiert werden. Zusätzlich zu den wissenschaftlichen Präsentationen werden in einer begleitenden Ausstellung Exponate aus den Forschungs- und Anwendungsbereichen vorgestellt. Diese sollen den hohen Leistungsstand solcher Systeme demonstrieren und laden zur persönlichen Diskussion mit den Entwicklern ein.

Die Organisatoren der AMS 2009 möchten sich zunächst beim Fachgesprächsbeirat für die Begutachtung und Auswahl der Beiträge bedanken. Unser herzlicher Dank gilt auch den Autoren für die Einreichung der wissenschaftlichen Arbeiten, die wie in den letzten Jahren von hoher inhaltlicher Qualität sind.

Weiterhin sei auch Prof. Dr. Dr. h.c. Brauer, dem Herausgeber der Buchreihe „Informatik aktuell", sowie dem Springer-Verlag für die erneute Bereitschaft, das Buch herauszugeben, und Frau Glaunsinger für ihre Unterstützung bei der Erstellung des Manuskripts gedankt. Für den unermüdlichen Einsatz möchten

wir den beteiligten Mitarbeitern und Studenten sowie dem Sekretariat des Lehr-
stuhls für Industrielle Anwendungen der Informatik und Mikrosystemtechnik
hiermit herzlich danken. Ohne sie wäre diese Veranstaltung nicht möglich gewesen.

Karlsruhe, im September 2009   Die Herausgeber
                                               Rüdiger Dillmann, Jürgen Beyerer,
                                              Christoph Stiller, J. Marius Zöllner

Inhaltsverzeichnis

Perzeption

Advanced Data Logging in RoboCup 1
Andreas Koch, Adam Berthelot, Bernd Eckstein, Oliver Zweigle,
Kai Häussermann, Uwe-Philipp Käppeler, Andreas Tamke,
Hamid Rajaie, Paul Levi
Institute of Parallel and Distributed Systems, Universität Stuttgart

Data Association for Visual Multi-target Tracking Under Splits, Merges
and Occlusions 9
Michael Grinberg, Florian Ohr, Jürgen Beyerer
Universität Karlsruhe (TH), Lehrstuhl für Interaktive Echtzeitsysteme

Fusing LIDAR and Vision for Autonomous Dirt Road Following –
Incorporating a Visual Feature into the Tentacles Approach 17
Michael Manz, Michael Himmelsbach, Thorsten Luettel,
Hans-Joachim Wuensche
University of the Bundeswehr Munich, Autonomous System Technology

Improved Time-to-Contact Estimation by Using Information from
Image Sequences 25
Maria Sagrebin, Josef Pauli
Fakultät für Ingenieurwissenschaften, Abteilung für Informatik und
Angewandte Kognitionswissenschaft, Universität Duisburg-Essen

Monocular Obstacle Detection for Real-World Environments 33
Erik Einhorn, Christof Schroeter, Horst-Michael Gross
MetraLabs GmbH, Neuroinformatics and Cognitive Robotics Lab,
Ilmenau University of Technology

Stereo-Based vs. Monocular 6-DoF Pose Estimation Using Point
Features: A Quantitative Comparison 41
Pedram Azad, Tamim Asfour, Rüdiger Dillmann
Institute for Anthropomatics, University of Karlsruhe

Probabilistisches Belegtheitsfilter zur Schätzung dynamischer
Umgebungen unter Verwendung multipler Bewegungsmodelle 49
Sebastian Brechtel, Tobias Gindele, Jan Vogelgesang, Rüdiger Dillmann
Institut für Anthropomatik, Universität Karlsruhe (TH)

Regelung

A Computational Model of Human Table Tennis for Robot Application . .   57
Katharina Mülling, Jan Peters
Max Planck Institute for Biological Cybernetics

A Vision-Based Trajectory Controller for Autonomous Cleaning Robots . .   65
Lorenz Gerstmayr, Frank Röben, Martin Krzykawski, Sven Kreft,
Daniel Venjakob, Ralf Möller
AG Technische Informatik, Technische Fakultät, Universität Bielefeld,
Exzellenzcluster Cognitive Interaction Technology, Universität Bielefeld

Automatic Take Off, Hovering and Landing Control for Miniature
Helicopters with Low-Cost Onboard Hardware   73
Karl E. Wenzel, Andreas Zell
University of Tübingen, Department of Computer Science

Foot Function in Spring Mass Running   81
Daniel Maykranz, Sten Grimmer, Susanne Lipfert, Andre Seyfarth
Lauflabor Locomotion Laboratory, University of Jena

From Walking to Running   89
Juergen Rummel, Yvonne Blum, Andre Seyfarth
Lauflabor Locomotion Laboratory, University of Jena

Generisches Verfahren zur präzisen Pfadverfolgung für
Serienfahrzeuggespanne   97
Christian Schwarz, Christian Weyand, Dieter Zöbel
Universität Koblenz-Landau

Learning New Basic Movements for Robotics   105
Jens Kober, Jan Peters
Max Planck Institute for Biological Cybernetics

Nonlinear Landing Control for Quadrotor UAVs   113
Holger Voos
University of Applied Sciences Ravensburg-Weingarten, Mobile Robotics
Lab

Oscillation Analysis in Behavior-Based Robot Architectures   121
Lisa Wilhelm, Martin Proetzsch, Karsten Berns
Robotics Research Lab, University of Kaiserslautern

Variable Joint Elasticities in Running   129
Stephan Peter, Sten Grimmer, Susanne W. Lipfert, Andre Seyfarth
Locomotion Laboratory, University of Jena

Lokalisation und Kartierung

3D-Partikelfilter SLAM 137
Jochen Welle, Dirk Schulz, A.B. Cremers
Fraunhofer FKIE, Institut für Informatik III, Universität Bonn

Absolute High-Precision Localisation of an Unmanned Ground
Vehicle by Using Real-Time Aerial Video Imagery for Geo-referenced
Orthophoto Registration 145
Lars Kuhnert, Markus Ax, Matthias Langer, Duong Nguyen Van,
Klaus-Dieter Kuhnert
University of Siegen, FB 12 - Electrical Engineering and Computer
Science, Institute for Real-Time Learning Systems

An Improved Sensor Model on Appearance Based SLAM 153
Jens Keßler, Alexander König, Horst-Michael Gross
Neuroinformatics and Cognitive Robotics Lab, Ilmenau University of
Technology

Monte Carlo Lokalisierung Fahrerloser Transportfahrzeuge mit
drahtlosen Sensornetzwerken 161
Christof Röhrig, Hubert Büchter, Christopher Kirsch
Fachhochschule Dortmund, Fachbereich Informatik, Fraunhofer-Institut
für Materialfluss und Logistik IML

Using a Physics Engine to Improve Probabilistic Object Localization 169
Thilo Grundmann
Siemens AG Corporate Technology, Information and Communications,
Intelligent Autonomous Systems

Visual Self-Localization with Tiny Images 177
Marius Hofmeister, Sara Erhard, Andreas Zell
University of Tübingen, Department of Computer Science

Navigation

Coordinated Path Following for Mobile Robots 185
Kiattisin Kanjanawanishkul, Marius Hofmeister, Andreas Zell
University of Tübingen, Department of Computer Science

Kooperative Bewegungsplanung zur Unfallvermeidung im
Straßenverkehr mit der Methode der elastischen Bänder 193
Christian Frese, Thomas Batz, Jürgen Beyerer
Lehrstuhl für Interaktive Echtzeitsysteme, Institut für Anthropomatik,
Universität Karlsruhe (TH), Fraunhofer Institut für Informations- und
Datenverarbeitung IITB

Perception of Environment Properties Relevant for Off-road Navigation .. 201
Alexander Renner, Tobias Föhst, Karsten Berns
Robotics Research Lab, Department of Computer Sciences, University
of Kaiserslautern

Architekturen und Anwendungen

Aufbau des humanoiden Roboters BART III 209
Dimitri Resetov, Björn Pietsch, Wilfried Gerth
Institut für Regelungstechnik, Leibniz Universität Hannover

Development of Micro UAV Swarms 217
Axel Bürkle, Sandro Leuchter
Fraunhofer Institut für Informations- und Datenverarbeitung

Die sechsbeinige Laufmaschine LAURON IVc 225
M. Ziegenmeyer, A. Rönnau, T. Kerscher, J.M. Zöllner, R. Dillmann
FZI Forschungszentrum Informatik, Intelligent Systems and Production
Engineering (ISPE)

Dynamic Bayesian Network Library – Ein C++ Framework für
Berechnungen auf dynamischen Bayes'schen Netzen 233
Ralf Kohlhaas, Ferdinand Szekeresch, Tobias Gindele,
Rüdiger Dillmann
Institut für Anthropomatik, Universität Karlsruhe (TH)

Modellgetriebene Softwareentwicklung für Robotiksysteme 241
Andreas Steck, Dennis Stampfer, Christian Schlegel
Hochschule Ulm, Fakultät Informatik

Situation Analysis and Adaptive Risk Assessment for Intersection
Safety Systems in Advanced Assisted Driving 249
Prof. Dr. Jianwei Zhang, Bernd Roessler
University of Hamburg, Faculty of Mathematics, Informatics and
Natural Sciences, Department Informatics, Group TAMS, Ibeo
Automobile Sensor GmbH

Transparente protokollierbare Kommunikation zwischen Funktionen
kognitiver Systeme 259
Matthias Goebl, Georg Färber
Lehrstuhl für Realzeit-Computersysteme, Technische Universität
München

Walking Humanoid Robot Lola – An Overview of Hard- and Software ... 267
Markus Schwienbacher, Valerio Favot, Thomas Buschmann,
Sebastian Lohmeier, Heinz Ulbrich
Institute of Applied Mechanics, Technische Universität München

Advanced Data Logging in RoboCup

Andreas Koch, Adam Berthelot, Bernd Eckstein, Oliver Zweigle,
Kai Häussermann, Uwe-Philipp Käppeler, Andreas Tamke,
Hamid Rajaie and Paul Levi

Institute of Parallel and Distributed Systems,
Universität Stuttgart, 70569 Stuttgart, Germany
kochas@informatik.uni-stuttgart.de,
WWW home page: www.informatik.uni-stuttgart.de

Abstract. In this work an advanced data logging approach for the RoboCup domain using an autonomous camera man is presented. It includes approaches from the field of real-time robot message logging, situation based camera control and 3D video visualisation. Based on the implementation of this work the RoboCup team of the IPVS of the University of Stuttgart won the first price in the scientific challenge of the RoboCup World Championship 2009 in Graz.

1 Introduction

In this work an approach for advanced data logging in the RoboCup domain is presented which includes real-time robot message logging linked to video recording and situation based camera control in combination with 3D rendering algorithms. The RoboCup domain has become an important testbed for robotic applications during the last years. The department Image Understanding of the IPVS - University of Stuttgart is participating with its team 1. RFC Stuttgart in the robotic soccer middle-size league. In this league a team of five autonomous robots is playing together. The robots share and merge information in order to show real team play and cooperative actions. As the robots are communicating data over a wireless network there is the possibility to log, visualize and analyze that data during matches for debug purposes. Due to the rapidly growing complexity of the robots software system, which acts in the real world, it becomes more difficult to debug the system in real-time. As a consequence powerful tools for collecting and analyzing data are very important. Those tools have to work in real-time during a match as well as in the post game analysis. In order to improve the general logging capabilities of such systems and visualize the corresponding data in a way that is easy to understand for humans, the following approach has been implemented and tested. We call the system the *autonomous camera man*. The system consists of a camera, a pan-tilt unit (PTU) and a software for controlling both. The software is connected to a message channel which the robots are using during a match. On this channel they communicate all relevant data like ball positions, strategical decisions etc. The program now uses this data to automatically steer the pan-tilt unit where the camera is mounted on. As a

consequence a whole match can be filmed autonomously without human interfe-
rence. Furthermore the system is rendering all the information gained from the
robots into the live image of the camera. This allows for interpreting all scenes
in a much better way. Moreover it is possible to save the whole video stream

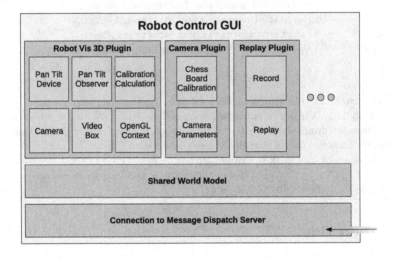

Fig. 1. Architecture of the software.

and data stream from the robots. Consequently the data and video stream can
be replayed and even the kind and amount of information rendered into the
video stream can be changed and adapted. Such a system is based on different
approaches from autonomous systems, 3D visualization and vision. This paper
should give a first overview how such a complex system is working.

The algorithms and concepts described in this paper have been adapted to a
specific software framework, namely the robot control graphical user interface
(RCG). The overall architecture is shown in Figure 1. The software allows to
connect to all of the robots directly and gather their shared world model information with read access.

To mix reality with the communicated data an *OpenGL scene graph* was used.
Four main components are used to bring information together to one view.
Firstly to mention is the *Shared World Model* (Section 3). The second one is
the so called *Action Replay Component* that enables the framework to store
any information including the video frames in a way that allows for very fast
read and write processes. The third part is a *camera framework* (Section 4) that
supports a vast range of different camera types. The fourth component is an *observer* (Section 4.1) that keeps track of the movement of the PTU. All gathered
information is handed to the rendering framework (Section 4.2).

2 Related Work

As the autonomous camera man includes techniques from a lot of different fields, we want to give a short overview over some articles which mainly influenced the development. The information that is exchanged between the robots to generate a common world model [1] is merged to reduce noise in the measurements as described in [2]. The team behavior of the cooperative robot system is a result of negotiations, based on a multi agent system (MAS) [3] and can be compared to [4]. The behaviour can be configured by XABSL [5] and uses methods like selection equations and interaction nets that are described in [6] and [7]. The *autonomous camera man* enables an analysis of the team behavior by visualizing the information that is exchanged between the robots and which leads to the decisions in the teams strategy. The basic approach for the camera location determination problem is based on the work of Bolles and Fischler [8].

3 Shared World Model

All information for the augmented scene is gathered via the communication of the robots using a message dispatch server. The robot control graphical user interface (RCG) holds a copy of all transfered data. Usually the ball is used as an indicator for the most important view frustrum. But in some cases another object might be of interest, e.g. when the ball is shot with high velocity so that it is impossible for the robots to track it, the goal, the attacker or the keeper are chosen as center for the camera direction. The RCG does not only support messages that have been sent by the robots. The same messaging framework can be used internally, when sending information would mean unnecessary network traffic. The flow of information is shown in Figure 2.

4 Camera Framework and PTU

In order to use the same software framework for the camera man and the robots the whole camera framework of the robots was changed, adapted and extended. Since e.g. two cameras of different types should be used to acquire images, but the current filter graph uses a singleton model for each step, a redesign has become inevitable. The new framework consists of three parts. First of all different cameras can be obtained by factory classes and can be decorated by those. All camera parameters are modeled as properties so that a graphical user interface can be generated automatically at runtime. The second essential part is a new filter library, in which the old filters have been reimplemented in a way that also makes use of properties to enable easy generation of user interfaces and serialization of the filters parameters. Filters can be grouped together in one *VisionPipe Object*, that is attached to a specific camera. The distribution of vision results is done via the signal/slot architecture of Qt(c) [9]. The third part of the framework consists of widgets for an easy way of reusing the above mentioned features such as a property editor to parameterize cameras and vision pipes, windows to

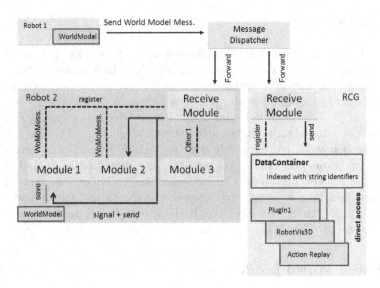

Fig. 2. Flow diagram of information propagated by the shared world model.

display live images from specific cameras and the intermediate results of vision pipes for debugging or parameter adaptation.

4.1   Observer

The PTU is controlled via a serial device, which makes it impossible to steer the device in real-time. The only information available consists of the commands that have been sent to the device. In order to merge the coordinate systems of the video and augmented scene, we have to know precisely the current orientation of the camera. To solve that problem an observer tries to track the angles of the PTU. The update cycle of the observer is depicted in Figure 3. The coordinates of the object of interest are first chosen due to the current state of the shared world model. Those are transformed to the camera frame and the corresponding pan- and tilt angles are calculated. They are sent to both the device and the observer. The visualization process always uses the values of the observer. Correction of the estimated position of the observer is done via *"bang-bang control"*, because the only fact known when reading the values from the device is, whether the observer has already been in position or not. The step of adjustment can be chosen by the time difference between PTU and observer in reaching the wanted position. Experience showed that the acceleration phase of the stepper engines is negligible small. So the observer equation can be obtained as

$$\theta_{n+1} = \theta_n + \text{sgn}(\theta_n - \theta_C)(t_{n+1} - t_n)v_C\delta v_e \;,$$
$$\delta v_e = t_f^{obs} - t_f^{pt} \tag{1}$$

where θ_n is the pan-, resp. tilt-, angle internally calculated in the observer, variables with subscript. C are the values of the latest command that has been

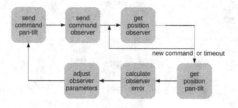

Fig. 3. Update cycle of the observer.

sent to the real PTU. As the communication with the device is done via serial ports, the reading process takes much time, so it is not done in each command cycle.

4.2 Rendering Framework

The grabbed image from the camera is directly mapped on a GL texture, the so called *videobox*, which is displayed as any other ordinary node in the scene graph to enable any 3D mapping of the image. Therefore the field of vision is not limited to the view of the camera. It can be extended to include more information that is exchanged between the robots, which extends the possibilities of analyzing the scene. The GL Thread directly controls the camera device, orders frames and copies them to graphic ram after removing distortions from the image.

5   Camera Pose Framework

In order to overlay the abstract information with the video stream a basic necessity is to find the camera position with respect to the RoboCup game field. The calibration steps have to be done each time the camera is moved. For example, the camera is shifted for a small degree (1 or 2 cm). The calibration is not accurate anymore and has to be done again. The Location Determination Problem is a common problem in image analysis and can be formulated as follows [8] : "Given a set of m control points, whose 3-dimensional coordinates are known in some coordinate frame, and given an image in which some subset of the m control points is visible, determine the location (relative to the coordinate system of the control points) from which the image was obtained". A complete solution to this problem is described by Bolles and Fischler [8]. The problem is simplified into having a tetrahedron, whose three base vertices coordinates are known (3 control points), and where each angle to any pair of the base vertices from top are also known. These angles are computed using the image properties and the location of the control points on this image. Knowing these values, it is possible to solve a biquadratic equation which can give up to four possible solutions. The camera is located near to the field, which makes it impossible to have a sufficient amount of the control points on a single image. Therefore a different way for obtaining the needed angles has to be found. The camera is

Fig. 4. Screenshot of the videobox in the scene, when the view matrix is fixed to the estimated camera position.

attached to a PTU, whose coordinates frame is not known in the soccer field's frame. We know the $3D$-coordinates of the control points, but it's impossible to determine the necessary angles from a single picture. As the camera is attached to the PTU, the idea is to focus the control points step by step, and to measure the angles between the origin position (also called 0-position) and the position heading to each control point as shown in Figure 5(a) and 5(b). Afterwards the camera location can be determined as described by Bolles and Fischler [8].

5.1   Camera Pose Calculation

In order to compute the angles offset of the camera, a new approach is used which differs from the one described by Bolles and Fischler [8]. This new approach consists in comparing the angles used by the pan-tilt unit to focus the control points from the 0-position as shown in orange in Figure 5(b), and the theoretical angles it should have used if there was no angle offset as shown in blue in Figure 5(b). The computation of the theoretical angles is only a geometrical problem: the location of the camera is known since the previous step (see 5) and the coordinates of the control points are known. Assuming that the the sytem is perfectly aligned to the coordinate frame (i.e. the 0-direction perfectly paralllel to one main axis of the coordinate frame), the angles between the 0-direction and the lines formed by the location point and each control point can be easily

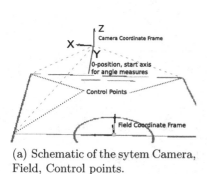

(a) Schematic of the sytem Camera, Field, Control points.

(b) Angles from 0-position up to control points (orange), and angles from center of perspective to any pair of control points(blue)

Fig. 5. Computation of angles for Bolles and Fischler's method.

computed. There are three types of angle offsets for the camera which have to be determined: *pan*, *tilt* and *roll*. The angles previously measured and computed are split for the analysis in the *pan* and *tilt* directions, and we consider these angles as 2-dimensional points with *pan* as x-coordinate and *tilt* as y-coordinate, so that the pan offset and tilt offset are equivalent to a translation (*pan* and *tilt* are the only two angles which are driven by the PTU).

The roll offset is equivalent to a rotation with the origin of the frame as center of rotation (the PTU is mounted in a way that the 0-position is also the axis of rotation for *roll*). Then the roll offset has to be compensated for computing the other offsets (which are simple translations) as depicted in Figure 6 and equation (2).

$$
\begin{pmatrix} cos(\phi_{roll_{offset}}) & -sin(\phi_{roll_{offset}}) \\ sin(\phi_{roll_{offset}}) & cos(\phi_{roll_{offset}}) \end{pmatrix} \cdot \begin{pmatrix} \theta_p \\ \theta_t \end{pmatrix}_{measured} + \begin{pmatrix} \phi_{pan_{offset}} \\ \phi_{tilt_{offset}} \end{pmatrix} = \begin{pmatrix} \theta_p \\ \theta_t \end{pmatrix}_{theoretical}
$$
$$(2)$$

6   Summary and Future Work

In this work we presented a first introduction into the basic techniques of the autonomous camera man as a powerful data logging tool in the RoboCup environment. Experimental results showed that the approach for logging game data in a RoboCup match makes it much easier for the developers to debug the robot software as the visualization is easy to interpret and much more user friendly than a simple graphical representation of the actions taking place on the field. This approach can not only be used for the RoboCup environemnt but also for a lot of other domains where the systems can provide relevant information about

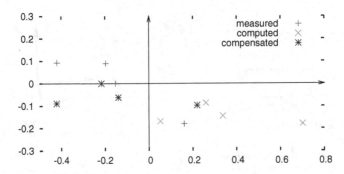

Fig. 6. Example of angles (pan,tilt) in radians. The difference from measured to theoritical angles is a rotation and a translation.

their state. Merged with a camera stream and a 3D visualisation, debugging in all kind of robotic applications becomes much easier and intuitive. As a further step the system should use the panorama camera LadyBug II, which is able to create 360degree images. Transfering the camera location determination problem to such a system will be a new challenge.

References

1. T. Buchheim, G. Kindermann, and R. Lafrenz. A dynamic environment modelling framework for selective attention. In *IJCAI Workshop: Issues in Designing Physical Agents for Dynamic Real-Time Environments: World modeling, planning, learning, and communicating.* IJCAI, 2003.
2. Benkmann et al. Resolving Inconsistencies using Multi-agent Sensor Systems. In *Proceedings of the 8th Conference on Autonomous Robot Systems and Competition: Robotica 08; Portugal,* pages 93–98. Universidade de Aveiro, April 2008.
3. K.M. Muscholl. *Interaktion und Koordination in Multiagentensystemen.* Dissertation, Universität Stuttgart, 2000.
4. M. Tambe. Towards flexible teamwork. *Journal of Artificial Intelligence Research,* 7:83–124, 1997.
5. M. Lötzsch, J. Bach, H.-D. Burkhard, and M. Jüngel. Designing agent behavior with the extensible agent behavior specification language xabsl. In *7th International Workshop on RoboCup 2003,* 2003.
6. Lafrenz et al. Evaluating coupled selection equations for dynamic task assignment using a behavior framework. *Autonome Mobile Systeme 2007,* 1(1), 2007.
7. Zweigle et al. Cooperative agent behavior based on special interaction nets. In *Intelligent Autonomous Systems 9,* 2006.
8. Martin A. Fischler and Robert C. Bolles. Random sample consensus: a paradigm for model fitting with applications to image analysis and automated cartography. *Commun. ACM,* 24(6):381–395, June 1981.
9. Qt web page http://doc.trolltech.com.

Data Association for Visual Multi-target Tracking Under Splits, Merges and Occlusions

Michael Grinberg, Florian Ohr and Jürgen Beyerer

Universität Karlsruhe (TH), Lehrstuhl für Interaktive Echtzeitsysteme
`grinberg@ies.uni-karlsruhe.de`

Abstract. In this contribution we present an algorithm for visual detection and tracking of multiple extended targets which is capable of coping with merged, split, incomplete and missed detections. We utilize information about the measurements' composition gained through tracking dedicated feature points in the image and in 3D space, which allows us to reconstruct the desired object characteristics from the data even in the case of detection errors due to limited field of view, occlusions and sensor malfunction. The proposed feature-based probabilistic data association approach resolves data association ambiguities in a soft threshold-free decision based not only on target state prediction but also on the existence and observability estimation modeled as two additional Markov chains. This process is assisted by a grid based object representation which offers a higher abstraction level of targets extents and is used for detailed occlusion analysis.

1 Introduction

Most of the vision-based vehicle detection and tracking systems presented in the field of driver assistance systems in the last few decades were focusing on the front-looking applications and particularly on highway driving applications. Many of them make use of various presumptions and restrictions regarding possible objects' motion profiles and their lateral position (e.g. relative to the tracked lane markings), as well as assumptions about symmetrical appearance, shadows etc. In many other applications such as intersection assistance systems or side-looking pre-crash systems, most of those restrictions and assumptions do not apply any more. Many different object orientations have to be taken into account. Combined with a large variety of object types and large region of interest, this makes it extremely challenging to detect and track objects based on their appearance in real time. For the realization of such applications that are capable of a robust and reliable object detection, a generic approach has to be chosen. Object hypotheses are often generated from the range data that are the result of binocular stereo or motion stereo processing. Finding corresponding structures in two video images and reconstructing their depth using knowledge of mutual orientation of both viewpoints, delivers range data, the so-called depth maps. After extracting a depth map, road location is estimated and points belonging to the ground plane are removed. Spatial clustering of the remaining three-dimensional points delivers point clouds which are used as an input in the data association step.

Due to the noisy range estimation process, combined with the well known problems of stereo vision systems such as difficulties of depth estimation in homogeneous image regions and gross depth errors in regions with regular patterns, the results of clustering may vary from frame to frame leading to incomplete, split, merged or missing object measurements as well as to phantom objects. Further problem are incomplete measurements due to partial occlusions and limitations of the field of view (FoV) of the sensors. Visible dimensions of objects entering or leaving FoV or becoming occluded may change rapidly, which combined with a centroid-based object tracking approach leads to strongly biased object position and dynamics estimation.

In this contribution we propose a data association scheme which provides and utilizes information about the affiliation of stably tracked points to the tracked objects and allows for an effective handling of such cases. Using a six-dimensional state estimation of dedicated feature points and point-to-object affiliation probabilities together with knowledge about the spatial relationship between tracked points and the objects' centroids we can perform correct update of the object's position and dynamics in spite of partial occlusions, splits and merges. Image data based track existence probability modeling along with the Integrated Probabilistic Data Association Scheme (JIPDA) [1] and point-to-object affiliation based composition of measurements from point clouds allows for a globally optimal threshold-free probabilistic data association without hard decisions. Additionally, we propose an observability treatment scheme utilizing a grid-based object representation with occupancy and occlusion modeling for each cell. This allows for a dedicated observability and occlusion handling.

2   Overall System Description

The video-based object tracking system used in this work has been built in the course of the EU funded project APROSYS [2]. The goal was detection of imminent side collisions to enable timely activation of novel occupant protection systems [3]. The sensor system under consideration here is a side-looking stereo video camera. Ego-motion estimation and compensation is done using vehicle odometry data. Detection and tracking of the feature points is realized similar to the system proposed in [4]. Up to 3000 feature points are tracked simultaneously in 3-D space using Kalman Filters. Their six-dimensional state vectors $[x, y, z, v_x, v_y, v_z]^T$ are estimated from their image coordinates and displacement (optic flow) as well as stereo depth measurements. The measurement vector is thus $[u, v, d]^T$ with image coordinates (u, v) and feature depth d.

After elimination of the ground points, the remaining points are clustered to the point clouds which give measurements for object tracking. For performing the association between the point clouds and the tracks and for the track state propagation we propose to use the Feature-Based Probabilistic Data Association algorithm (FBPDA) which is described in the following sections. FBPDA consists of four major steps: time forward prediction, association between detections and tracks, reconstruction of composite measurements from associated point clouds and innovation. These four steps are described in Sections 3, 4, 5 and 6 respectively. For effective noise handling as well as for handling of split and merged point clouds FBPDA provides affiliation probabilities of each point to the current tracks. These affiliation probabilities are exploited in the course of updating tracks' position, dynamics and dimensions. Object parameters are estimated using an Extended Kalman Filter. Internally, objects are modeled as cuboids with a centroid (x, y, z), dimensions (l, w, h), geometrical orientation ϕ, motion orientation φ, speed v, acceleration a and yaw rate $\dot{\varphi}$. This corresponds to the Constant Yaw Rate Model with Acceleration, which has proved to deliver the best performance in the case of a side-looking system [5]. Due to the fact that often only a part of an object is visible to the sensors, orientation of the object's motion may differ from the estimated geometrical orientation. Object's geometric orientation and dimensions are updated taking into account the occlusion information as described in Section 5.

3   Time Forward Prediction

At each time step, after the ego-motion compensation, we start by predicting the new track attributes. This includes prediction of the track's dynamic state as well as prediction of it's existence and observability probabilities. The FBPDA state prediction of a track is identical to the common Extended Kalman Filter prediction. The time forward prediction equations for the existence and non-existence probabilities $p^{\mathbf{x}}_{k|k-1}(\exists)$ and $p^{\mathbf{x}}_{k|k-1}(\nexists)$ of a track $\mathbf{x}$ are:

$$p^{\mathbf{x}}_{k|k-1}(\exists) = p^{\mathbf{x}}(\exists \rightarrow \exists) \cdot p^{\mathbf{x}}_{k-1|k-1}(\exists) + p^{\mathbf{x}}(\nexists \rightarrow \exists) \cdot p^{\mathbf{x}}_{k-1|k-1}(\nexists) \qquad (1)$$

$$p^{\mathbf{x}}_{k|k-1}(\nexists) = 1 - p^{\mathbf{x}}_{k|k-1}(\exists) \qquad (2)$$

with $p^{\mathbf{x}}_{k-1|k-1}(\exists)$ being the a-posteriori existence probability from the last frame and $p^{\mathbf{x}}(\exists \rightarrow \exists)$ and $p^{\mathbf{x}}(\nexists \rightarrow \exists)$ denoting the persistence and the birth probabilities of a track $\mathbf{x}$. The last two factors are used for modeling the spatial distribution of the target birth and death probabilities. This makes it possible to account e.g. for the fact that at the borders of the field of view and at far distances the birth probability is higher than right in front of the sensors.

For the computation of the observability probability and for the reconstruction of occluded measurements we use a grid-based 3-D representation of the targets. For each track $\mathbf{x}_i$, we define a 3-D grid with the origin at its centroid. The orientation of the grid is aligned with the track's orientation. Using this representation of predicted objects it is possible to calculate their appearance masks in the camera image $M^{\mathbf{x}_i}_A(u, v) \in \{0, 1\}$ by projecting the occupied grid cells into the image. The Appearance Probability Mask $M^{\mathbf{x}_i}_{p(A)}(u, v)$ for each track is given by

$$M^{\mathbf{x}_i}_{p(A)}(u, v) = p(A^{\mathbf{x}_i}(u, v)) = M^{\mathbf{x}_i}_A(u, v) \cdot p^{\mathbf{x}_i}_{k|k-1}(\exists) \qquad (3)$$

where $A^{\mathbf{x}_i}(u,v)$ is the event of the track $\mathbf{x}_i$ appearing at the image position (u,v) and $p_{k|k-1}^{\mathbf{x}_i}(\exists)$ is the predicted existence probability of the track $\mathbf{x}_i$. By overlaying the appearance probability masks of all the objects lying in front of the object $\mathbf{x}_i$ we get the occlusion probability map for the respective object in the new frame. The occlusion probability $p^{\mathbf{x}_i}(\not\supset, u, v)$ at each pixel (u,v) is calculated as

$$p^{\mathbf{x}_i}(\not\supset, u, v) = p(\bigcup_{\mathbf{x}_r \in X_O^i} A^{\mathbf{x}_r}(u,v)) \tag{4}$$

with X_O^i being set of the objects lying at the pixel position (u,v) in front of the object $\mathbf{x}_i$. After the occlusion probability map for an object is built, we can estimate the occlusion probability $p^{\mathbf{x}_i}(\not\supset, c)$ of the object's grid cells. This is done by projecting the cell centers into the image and grabbing the corresponding value of the occlusion probability map. Based on these probabilities we can calculate the observability transition probabilities $p^{\mathbf{x}_i}(\supset \to \supset)$, $p^{\mathbf{x}_i}(\supset \to \not\supset)$, $p^{\mathbf{x}_i}(\not\supset \to \supset)$ and $p^{\mathbf{x}_i}(\not\supset \to \not\supset)$ of a track and predict it's observability probability and occlusion probability in the new frame:

$$p_{k|k-1}^{\mathbf{x}}(\supset) = p^{\mathbf{x}}(\supset \to \supset) \cdot p_{k-1|k-1}^{\mathbf{x}}(\supset) + p^{\mathbf{x}}(\not\supset \to \supset) \cdot p_{k-1|k-1}^{\mathbf{x}}(\not\supset) \tag{5}$$

$$p_{k|k-1}^{\mathbf{x}}(\not\supset) = 1 - p_{k|k-1}^{\mathbf{x}}(\supset) . \tag{6}$$

4   Data Association Between Detections and Tracks

Given multiple active tracks and multiple detections, there are often several assignment possibilities being more or less probable. Unlike other methods such as GNN, FBPDA does not choose one of these hypotheses for the innovation of a track, but considers all assignment possibilities in a soft decision. For this aim we define the set $X=\{X', \mathbf{x}_B, \copyright\}$ as the aggregation $X'=\{\mathbf{x}_1, \mathbf{x}_2, ..., \mathbf{x}_n\}$ of the n current tracks plus two special elements $\mathbf{x}_B$ representing a so far not known object and $\copyright$ representing a clutter source and the set $Z=\{Z', \mathbf{z}_\varnothing, \mathbf{z}_{\not\supset}, \mathbf{z}_{\not\exists}\}$ as the aggregation $Z'=\{\mathbf{z}_1, \mathbf{z}_2, ..., \mathbf{z}_m\}$ of the m current point clouds plus three special elements $\mathbf{z}_\varnothing$, $\mathbf{z}_{\not\supset}$ and $\mathbf{z}_{\not\exists}$. The element $\mathbf{z}_\varnothing$ stands for erroneously missed detection caused by sensor failure, $\mathbf{z}_{\not\supset}$ represents the correct absence of a detection because of occlusion of the target and $\mathbf{z}_{\not\exists}$ the correct absence of a detection because of the target non-existence (death). The association between point clouds and tracks is modeled as a bipartite graph with edges $e : (\mathbf{x} \in X \mapsto \mathbf{z} \in Z)$ between elements of X and elements of Z. Assignments between two special elements are prohibited. A valid assignment hypothesis can thus contain six types of edges e:

- $\mathbf{x}_i \mapsto \mathbf{z}_j$: assumption that point cloud $\mathbf{z}_j$ has been caused by the track $\mathbf{x}_i$
- $\mathbf{x}_B \mapsto \mathbf{z}_j$: point cloud $\mathbf{z}_j$ has been caused by a so far not known object
- $\copyright \mapsto \mathbf{z}_j$: assumption that point cloud $\mathbf{z}_j$ has been caused by clutter
- $\mathbf{x}_i \mapsto \mathbf{z}_{\not\supset}$: track $\mathbf{x}_i$ did not cause a point cloud because it is not observable
- $\mathbf{x}_i \mapsto \mathbf{z}_{\not\exists}$: track $\mathbf{x}_i$ did not cause a point cloud because it does not exist
- $\mathbf{x}_i \mapsto \mathbf{z}_\varnothing$: track $\mathbf{x}_i$ did not cause a point cloud because of a sensing error

The probabilities of the six edge types are calculated in analogy to [6]:

$$p(e =(\mathbf{x}_i \mapsto \mathbf{z}_j)) = p^{\mathbf{x}_i}_{k|k-1}(\exists) \cdot p^{\mathbf{x}_i}_{k|k-1}(\supset) \cdot p^{\mathbf{z}_j}(TP|\mathbf{x}_i) \cdot (1 - p^{\mathbf{z}_j}(FP)) \tag{7}$$

$$p(e =(\mathbf{x}_i \mapsto \mathbf{z}_{\not\supset})) = p^{\mathbf{x}_i}_{k|k-1}(\exists) \cdot (1 - p^{\mathbf{x}_i}_{k|k-1}(\supset)) \tag{8}$$

$$p(e =(\mathbf{x}_i \mapsto \mathbf{z}_{\varnothing})) = p^{\mathbf{x}_i}_{k|k-1}(\exists) \cdot p^{\mathbf{x}_i}_{k|k-1}(\supset) \cdot p^{\mathbf{x}_i}(FN) \tag{9}$$

$$p(e =(\mathbf{x}_i \mapsto \mathbf{z}_{\not\exists})) = (1 - p^{\mathbf{x}_i}_{k|k-1}(\exists)) \cdot p^{\mathbf{x}_i}_{k|k-1}(\supset) \cdot (1 - p^{\mathbf{x}_i}(FN)) \tag{10}$$

$$p(e =(\mathbf{x}_B \mapsto \mathbf{z}_j)) = (1 - \sum_i p^{\mathbf{z}_j}(TP|\mathbf{x}_i)) \cdot (1 - p^{\mathbf{z}_j}(FP)) \tag{11}$$

$$p(e =(\text{\textcopyright} \mapsto \mathbf{z}_j)) = (1 - \sum_i p^{\mathbf{z}_j}(TP|\mathbf{x}_i)) \cdot p^{\mathbf{z}_j}(FP) \tag{12}$$

with $p^{\mathbf{z}_j}(FP)$ being the probability that a clutter-caused point cloud appears at the position of $\mathbf{z}_j$, $p^{\mathbf{x}_i}(FN)$ the false negative probability for the track $\mathbf{x}_i$ and $p^{\mathbf{z}_j}(TP|\mathbf{x}_i)$ being the likelihood function obtained from the Kalman filter.

With (7)-(12) it is now possible to calculate the probability of an assignment hypothesis $E = \{e_1, .., e_q\}$ by:

$$p(E) = \prod_{a=1}^{q} p(e_a) \tag{13}$$

The association probabilities $\beta^{\mathbf{x}_i}_{\mathbf{z}_j}$ are calculated as the sum of all assignment hypothesis probabilities including the edge $e = (\mathbf{x}_i \mapsto \mathbf{z}_j)$ divided by the sum of the probabilities of all assignment hypotheses assuming track $\mathbf{x}_i$ as existent:

$$\beta^{\mathbf{x}_i}_{\mathbf{z}_j} = \frac{\sum_{\{E|e=(\mathbf{x}_i \mapsto \mathbf{z}_j) \in E\}} p(E)}{\sum_{\{E|e=(\mathbf{x}_i \mapsto \mathbf{z}_{\not\exists}) \notin E\}} p(E)} . \tag{14}$$

$\beta^{\mathbf{x}_i}_{\mathbf{z}_0}$ is the probability of the event that no point cloud originated from track $\mathbf{x}_i$. It is calculated analogously to (14).

5   Handling of Split and Merge Effects and Reconstruction of Compatible Object Measurements

For the handling of the possibility of split and merge events in the course of data association, one option is to allow the assignment of a set of point clouds to one track or a set of tracks to one point cloud, respectively [7]. This would make it possible to identify splits and merges but would not allow to make an appropriate update since there is a one-to-one association necessary for doing so. Another possibility would be to create virtual measurements from the original measurements by splitting and merging them using predicted states of the tracked objects as proposed in [8]. This approach would maintain one-to-one matchings between objects and associated point clouds and would allow to update the track's state after creation of compatible state measurement. The disadvantages of the method are ambiguous partitioning of original measurements in case of merging targets and exploding number of feasible associations. Furthermore, when using a centroid-based tracking approach, in the case of split and merged targets the resulting measurement's center of gravity (CoG) might not lie inside the gating ellipse of the targets' tracks. Another problematic case is the position update of a target which is partially occluded (due to either other objects in the scene or restricted field of view of the sensors). If target position is updated based on the CoG of the point cloud, it will cause a shift of the track's centroid and induce an impulse which will introduce bias to the estimated track's state.

To avoid such problems we reconstruct for each detection-to-track association the track's centroid and orientation using stably tracked points. We hereby utilize information about the affiliation of the tracked points to the tracks independently of the currently occurred splits and merges. The reconstructed centroids can then be used instead of the CoGs of the corresponding point clouds for the computation of the state measurement for each track.

5.1   Determination of the Point-to-Track Affiliation Probabilities

The affiliation probability $p(\mathbf{x}_i \mapsto \mathbf{p}_q)$ of a point $\mathbf{p}_q$ to a tracked object $\mathbf{x}_i$ is determined based on the association probability $\beta_{\mathbf{z}}^{\mathbf{x}_i}$ of the point cloud $\mathbf{z}$ containing $\mathbf{p}_q$ to that object. For the realization of a memory effect we filter the affiliation probabilities using a gain constant $g \in [0, 1]$:

$$p_k(\mathbf{x}_i \mapsto \mathbf{p}_q) = g \cdot \beta_{\mathbf{z}}^{\mathbf{x}_i} + (1 - g) \cdot p_{k-1}(\mathbf{x}_i \mapsto \mathbf{p}_q). \tag{15}$$

5.2   Point Cloud Based Reconstruction of the Track's Position and Orientation

For the reconstruction of the track centroid $\mathbf{p}_O$ from an associated point cloud we first calculate the CoG $\mathbf{p}_{CoG}$ of the stably tracked points of this point cloud both in the current and previous frame. Hereby we are weighting the points' 3-D positions with their track affiliation probability (known from the previous frame). Having computed $\mathbf{p}_{CoG}$ in both current and previous frames, we can for each tracked point $\mathbf{p}_q$ reconstruct the vector $(\overrightarrow{\mathbf{p}_{CoG}\mathbf{p}_O})_q$ pointing from the $\mathbf{p}_{CoG}$ to the object centroid $\mathbf{p}_O$ in the current frame using knowledge about the relative orientation of this vector regarding the vector $\overrightarrow{\mathbf{p}_{CoG}\mathbf{p}_q}$ in the previous frame. Building a weighted sum of the resulting vectors $(\overrightarrow{\mathbf{p}_{CoG}\mathbf{p}_O})_q$ according to the affiliation probability of the respective points $\mathbf{p}_q$ we get the new position of the track's centroid with respect to the considered point cloud. The track's new orientation can be obtained in the same way. Together those parameters form the reconstructed measurement of the point cloud. All these measurements weighted according to the association probabilities of the corresponding point clouds build a composed measurement which is then used for the innovation of the Kalman Filter responsible for the track's dynamics.

5.3   Grid-Based Reconstruction of the Track's Extent

The extent of a track is obtained in a similar way. We create one composite measurement from all point clouds associated to the track. This is done using the grid representation of the track which is aligned according to its new position and orientation gained through the innovation of the track's dynamics. The points of each associated point cloud are sorted into the grid. Thereby points of a point cloud contribute to the occupancy value of the grid cell according to their affiliation probability to the track and the association probability of the point cloud. For each cell c its current occupancy value o at time step k with respect to the track $\mathbf{x}_i$ is computed according to

$$o_k^{\mathbf{x}_i}(c) = \sum_{j=1}^{m} \left(\beta_{\mathbf{z}_j}^{\mathbf{x}_i} \cdot \sum_{q=1}^{l} p(\mathbf{x}_i \mapsto \mathbf{p}_q) \right) \tag{16}$$

with m being current number of point clouds and l being the number of points $\mathbf{p}_q$ belonging to the point cloud $\mathbf{z}_j$ and falling into the cell c. The grid is updated using this occupancy values. To avoid an update of the occupancy value of an occluded cell with 0, we filter the occupancy values of the cells using their occlusion probability. For each cell c its filtered occupancy value $\bar{o}_k(c)$ at time step k is given by

$$\bar{o}_k^{\mathbf{x}_i}(c) = p_k^{\mathbf{x}_i}(\supset, c) \cdot o_k^{\mathbf{x}_i}(c) + p_k^{\mathbf{x}_i}(\not\supset, c) \cdot \bar{o}_{k-1}^{\mathbf{x}_i}(c) \tag{17}$$

with $p^{\mathbf{x}_i}(\supset, c) = 1 - p^{\mathbf{x}_i}(\not\supset, c)$.

Object's geometric orientation and dimensions are obtained using a RANSAC based estimation of the main visible object surface in the top view and fitting a rectangle with this orientation into the ground projection of the occupied grid cells. Together, these parameters form the resulting composite measurement which is then used for the innovation of the track's geometric orientation and its dimensions.

6   State, Existence and Observability Innovation

In the innovation step, all three Markov chains are updated. The innovation of the target's physical attributes corresponds to the standard Extended Kalman Filter innovation. For maintaining the centroid position obtained from the grid based object extent computation as the reference point to be tracked, we switch to this point as a new reference point at the end of each frame. This prevents the object dimensions from jittering due to the one-sided changes of the visible object extent (e.g. in the case of a target entering the field of view). The a-posteriori probability of the track existence is calculated as the sum of the probabilities of all assignment hypotheses assuming track $\mathbf{x}_i$ as existent divided by the sum of the probabilities of all possible hypotheses:

$$p_{k|k}^{\mathbf{x}_i}(\exists) = \frac{\sum_{\{E|e=(\mathbf{x}_i \mapsto \mathbf{z}_{\not\exists}) \notin E\}} p(E)}{\sum_{\{E\}} p(E)} . \tag{18}$$

The observability update is done analogously to the existence innovation.

7   Experimental Results

The algorithm has been validated with both simulated and real data. For our simulations we used a tool which generated point clouds with pre-defined parameters and behavior. We modeled several scenarios that caused problems for the standard approach such as splitting and merging point clouds, objects entering and leaving the FoV and occlusion scenarios. Compared to the standard association and tracking scheme which lead to considerable corruption of the position and velocity estimation and even to the termination and re-initialization of the tracks, FBPDA managed to correctly update tracks' parameters through multiple merges, splits and occlusions.

8   Conclusion

In this contribution we have presented an algorithm for visual detection and tracking of multiple extended targets which is capable of coping with noisy, split, merged, incomplete and missed detections. The proposed approach resolves data association ambiguities in a soft decision based not only on target state prediction but also on the existence and observability estimation modeled as two additional Markov Chains. For the correct estimation of the desired object parameters, low-level information about measurement composition is utilized which is gained through tracking dedicated feature points in the image and 3D space. Along with the occlusion analysis, spatial and temporal relationship between the set of stably tracked points and the object's centroid is exploited which allows for the reconstruction of the desired object characteristics from the data even in case of detection errors due to limited FoV, occlusions, noise and sensor malfunction.

References

1. D. Mušicki and R. Evans, "Joint Integrated Probabilistic Data Association - JIPDA," in *Proc. of the 5th Int. Conf. on Information Fusion*, 2002, pp. 1120–1125.
2. APROSYS - Advanced PROtection SYStems: An Integrative Project in the 6th Framework Programme. Available at http://www.aprosys.com
3. J. Tandler, E. Zimmerman et al., "A new pre-crash system for side impact protection," *Int. Journal of Crashworthiness*, vol. 13, no. 6, pp. 679–692, 2008.
4. U. Franke, C. Rabe et al., "6D Vision: Fusion of Motion and Stereo for Robust Environment Perception," in *DAGM Symp. Pattern Recogn.*, 2005, pp. 216–223.
5. S. Rühl, M. Grinberg et al., "Empirical evaluation of motion models for a side-looking driver assistance system," *5th Int. Workshop on Intel. Transportation*, 2008.
6. M. Mählisch, M. Szcot et al., "Simultaneous Processing of Multitarget State Measurements and Object Individual Sensory Existence Evidence with the JIPDA," in *Proc. of the 5th Int. Workshop on Intelligent Transportation*, 2008.
7. P. Kumar, S. Ranganath et al., "Cooperative Multitarget Tracking With Efficient Split and Merge Handling," in *IEEE Trans. on Circuits and Systems for Video Technology*, vol. 16, 2006.
8. A. Genovesio and J.-C. Olivo-Marin, "Split and Merge Data Association Filter for Dense Multi-Target Tracking," in *Proc. of 17th Int. Conf. on Pattern Recogn.*, 2004.

Fusing LIDAR and Vision for Autonomous Dirt Road Following

Incorporating a Visual Feature into the Tentacles Approach

Michael Manz[1], Michael Himmelsbach[1], Thorsten Luettel[1] and
Hans-Joachim Wuensche[1]

University of the Bundeswehr Munich, Autonomous System Technology,
Werner-Heisenberg-Weg 39, 85577 Neubiberg, Germany

Abstract. In this paper we describe how visual features can be incorporated into the well known tentacles approach [1] which up to now has
only used LIDAR and GPS data and was therefore limited to scenarios
with significant obstacles or non-flat surfaces along roads. In addition
we present a visual feature considering only color intensity which can be
used to visually rate tentacles. The presented sensor fusion and color based feature were both applied with great success at the C-ELROB 2009
robotic competition.

1 Introduction

Autonomous driving on forest tracks and dirt roads with faulty GPS localization, more or less no geographical maps and complex lighting condition is still
a challenging task for intelligent vehicles. In the past we used the tentacle approach, utilizing a LIDAR based occupancy grid and GPS-Waypoints to handle
such difficult autonomous driving missions. But up to now the road following capabilities of the tentacles approach without using dense GPS-Points are limited
to scenarios with significant obstacles or non-flat surfaces along what humans
would otherwise easily recognize as roads. To overcome these limitations we extend the tentacles approach to also incorporate visual features. Compared to
other work we do not fuse the sensors on the data level [2] or try to generate
a fused world map [3]. Instead we rate the tentacles independently in a way
adequate to each sensor. The gathered information is subsequently fused during
the process of tentacle selection.

The proposed procedure for visual tentacle evaluation is inspired by the work
of [4] and is able to handle weighted pixel images form various color or texture
segmentation algorithms. In addition it utilizes camera gaze control as well as
compensation of vehicle's pitch and roll movements in a model based manner.

In order to drive through forest and across fields we have developed a fast-
to-compute visual feature based only on the saturation channel of the HSI color
space and is therefore quite robust against difficult lighting conditions and shadows. In addition, the proposed feature does not rely on the knowledge of past

road locations and is therefore best suited to the reactive tentacle approach. Before we explain the visual tentacle evaluation and the proposed visual feature in more detail we briefly introduce the tentacles approach.

2   Driving with Tentacles

Our basic intention underlying the tentacles approach is to let our robot move within an unknown environment similarly to how a beetle would crawl around and use its antennae to avoid obstacles. Indeed, in our approach the analogue to an insects antennae are target trajectories representing the basic driving options of the vehicle given the current vehicle state. These driving options that we named "tentacles" then probe an occupancy grid (built from LIDAR data in a way similar to [5]) to determine drivability and other properties of the corresponding target trajectory. The main loop of the approach is as simple as follows: In each cycle, first select a subset of tentacles according to the vehicle state. Then, by inspecting the occupancy grid, assign properties to each tentacle and select one of the tentacles as the target trajectory for the vehicle to drive. Smooth transitions between selected tentacles can be achieved by temporal filtering or some kind of hysteresis.

2.1   Tentacle Evaluation and Selection

As said, a tentacle basically represents a target trajectory defined in the reference frame of the vehicle. These are represented as point samples p_i on arbitrarily shaped line sequences and denoted by $t_{lsq} = \{p_1, \cdots, p_N\}$. Fig. 1 shows the tentacle geometries we use at the C-ELROB 09. We will now give a brief description of the properties we evaluate for a tentacle and how a tentacle gets selected for execution based on these properties. The interested reader is referred to [1] for more details on this topic.

Drivability. The most important of all tentacle properties for sure is its drivability, $t_{drivable}$. Indeed, all other properties of a tentacle are only evaluated

(a)   (b)

Fig. 1. (a) Some of the tentacles we used at C-ELROB 09. Every image shows one set of tentacles to be selected according to robot velocity. Every set contains 1000 tentacles, discretizing a subspace of curvatures, lateral offsets and headings. (b) Tentacles selected according to current vehicle state shown on top of the occupancy grid they relate to.

if the tentacle was considered drivable. For evaluating this property, we only have a look at the cells near to the skeleton line of a tentacle. If this set does not contain a cell that is within the crash distance of the vehicle and itself considered an obstacle, the tentacle is classified drivable.

Distance to Obstacles. This property is closely related to the drivability of a tentacle. However, of all drivable tentacles, we would prefer to select the one which can be driven for longer time, keeping the vehicle away from threatening obstacles. This is reflected by the property $t_{clearness}$, which is just the longitudinal length to the bin where an obstacle was detected (or infinity if there is no obstacle along the tentacle).

Flatness. Especially in offroad scenarios, a tentacle should be assigned a value reflecting the flatness of the ground it would lead the vehicle to. Assigning a flatness $t_{flatness}$ to a tentacle is a simple matter of computing the weighted sum of absolute z-coordinate differences of all cells within the tentacle support area.

With all drivable tentacles being assigned their properties, it now remains to select one of the drivable tentacles for execution. To be able to fine-tune the influence of individual properties, we decided to combine them all in a weighted sum, choosing the one tentacle minimizing this sum. As a prerequisite, we require all properties be normalized to uniform range. Again, we refer to [1] for details on how the properties are best normalized. Formally, selecting a tentacle is described by

$$t_{selected} = \underset{\{t|t_{drivable}=1\}}{argmin} \quad a_1(1 - t_{clearness}) + a_2 t_{flatness} \tag{1}$$

where the a_i denote the weights allowing fine-tuning the resulting behavior.

Please refer to [1] for more details and an extensive description of how high-level knowledge based on GPS sensors and a geographical map can be incorporated into the tentacle approach. In the following of the paper, we will show how properties derived from a camera system can be incorporated via the introduction of new summands into this last equation.

3   Evaluating Tentacles by Visual Appearances

In this section we propose a possibility to incorporate the visual appearance of a tentacle into the tentacles rating process described in Sec. 2.1. The evaluation process deals with weighted pixel value images such as produced from road color (e.g. [6]) or road texture segmentation (e.g. [7]) algorithms. Furthermore it utilizes gaze control as well as vehicle pitch/roll stabilization in a model based manner. To avoid problems arising from fusing data from different times the camera device is triggered by the LIDAR sensor.

3.1   Perspective Mapping and Gaze Control

As described in Sec. 2.1 each tentacle is defined in the vehicle coordinate system and represents a possible road geometry given by its line sequence. Homogeneous transformation matrices are used to do the perspective projection of the currently active tentacles into the camera frame coordinates. In order to compensate severe disturbances in vehicle pitch and roll angle while driving along dirt roads we consider the measurements of an on board IMU within the perspective projection equation. The IMU measurements of the vehicle's pitch and roll angle are split into two different frequency ranges. At the one hand the high frequencies are considered as disturbances due to rough terrain and directly compensated within the image with the aid of the mapping equations and the low frequencies on the other hand are interpreted as orientation changes of the road surface and therefore considered as a zero shift of the vehicle orientation.

As we want to drive along dirt roads with large horizontal curvatures we have to do gaze control. To this purpose we implemented to different algorithms. The first algorithm takes the current steering angle of the autonomous vehicle as well as a predefined lookahead distance and uses the Ackermann steering geometry and a pinhole camera model to calculate the gaze direction. The second algorithm takes the skeleton line of the last selected tentacle and also uses a predefined lookahead distance and the pinhole camera model to determine the camera platform yaw angle.

3.2   Determine Visual Quality

To determine the visual quality of a tentacle all that is needed is an image of weighted pixel values as input into the evaluation process. Weights should correspond to the probability of a pixel being a "'road"' or a "'non road"' pixel, and numerous algorithms for road color or texture segmentation can be used. In Ch. 4 we introduce such a color feature that is highly convenient for usage within the tentacle approach. A tentacle will be assigned individual properties t_{vis_i}, one by each different pixel weighting method used. Then, a tentacle's visual quality t_{visual} is the combination of all different color or texture features used, given by

$$t_{visual} = \sum_i b_i t_{vis_i} \qquad (2)$$

contributing another summand to (1) when fusing LIDAR and vision for tentacle selection. Here, the b_i allow fine-tuning the influence of single visual features.

The evaluation process starts with first transforming the sample points of each tentacle's skeleton line $t_{lsq} = \{p_1, \cdots, p_N\}$ into the camera image coordinates. If 70% of the points in the line sequence are within the image boundaries, the tentacle is declared as visible. Otherwise, the tentacle is declared as non-visible and all single visual qualities t_{vis_i} are set to a fix value of 0.6. This is simply because we can not blame tentacles for getting out of sight of the camera, a point to which we return later.

The 3D support area boundaries of visible tentacles however are sampled and projected into the camera frame, as shown in Fig. 2 (a). The projected support area is split in two sub-areas on the left and on the right of the tentacle. This is done to account for grass strips in the middle of the road like they often

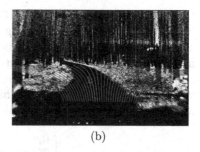

(a)   (b)

Fig. 2. Image of a single tentacle's skeleton line (green) and support area placed between the blue lines on the right and left of the skeleton line) (a), Rating a sparse tentacle set according to the introduced visual feature (red encodes non drivable) (b)

appear on field paths. Subsequently if a tentacle is declared as visible we sum all weighted pixel within the projected support areas for a feature i (see Fig. 2) symbolised by $s_i(x_t, y_t)$ and normalize the sum by the number of considered pixels N_t.

$$w_{vis_i} = \frac{1}{N_t} \sum_j^{N_t} s_i(x_{t_j}, y_{t_j}) \tag{3}$$

To speed up the summing process we use line-oriented integral images like [4] to evaluate the weighted sum w_{vis_i} for each tentacles. In order to make the visual quality values t_{vis_i} comparable to other features, they are normalized to the range $[0,...,1]$, where a value of 0 designates a preference for such a tentacle. The value is calculated by the sigmoid-like function

$$t_{vis_i}(w_{vis_i}) = \frac{2.0}{1.0 + e^{-c_{vis} \cdot w_{vis_i}}} - 1 \tag{4}$$

where the constant c_{vis_i} is calculated by (5) to yield $t_{vis_i}(w_{vis_i\,0.5}) = 0.5$. The value $w_{vis_i\,0.5}$ can be adjusted according to the considered visual feature:

$$c_{vis_i} = \frac{ln1/3}{-w_{vis_i\,0.5}} \tag{5}$$

4   Rating Tentacles by Color Intensity Feature

There is a vast number of works on road detection and following algorithms. Basically, all these works try to identify the road according to visual features special to roads, like road boundaries [8], texture [7] and color [6]. The visual feature we propose goes the other way around: Instead of trying to recognize a road in an image, we try to segment non-drivable pixels in an image.

In numerous video streams of non-urban scenarios, we discovered that one of the best and efficient ways to segment non-drivable terrain is to utilize the saturation channel of the HSI color space. The feature we propose makes use of the knowledge we gained - that the road surface may show all kinds of colors but there will be only a vanishing amount of brightly colored pixels on a road's surface. In the opposite, this means that almost all brightly colored areas will most likely correspond to non-drivable area. This is especially true in dirt road and forest scenarios where the road is typically surrounded by some kind of vegetation. To further enhance this effect we transform the saturation value of each pixel $s(x, y)$ according to the dynamic weighting function,

$$s_w(x, y) = \begin{cases} 0, & s(x, y) \leq \mu_s \\ \frac{255(s(x,y)-\mu_s)}{s_{off}}, & \mu_s < s(x, y) < (\mu_s + s_{off}) \\ 255, & s(x, y) \geq (\mu_s + s_{off}) \end{cases} \tag{6}$$

where μ_s represents the temporally low-pass filtered mean saturation value in the lower image parts excluding the engine hood and s_{off} is a parameter to adapt the weighting transition. The mean value μ_s is subject to constraints to cope with special scenarios like paved areas (almost all image pixels are non colored pixels) or grassland (almost all pixels are colored). To speed up the process we use look up tables to evaluate equation (6). Fig. 3 shows the weighting of pixels according to the proposed visual feature.

One additional advantage of the feature is that, for a good segmentation result on country roads, no online learning algorithm is required. Thus the feature's performance does not depend on any earlier measurements of the road in front of the car. For example, the online learning approach based on the famous histogram back-projection algorithm used in [4] for road detection relies on the vague assumption that if the vehicle was well positioned on the road some successive steps of time before, then, at time t, exactly those pixels will belong to the road that show the same color statistics as those believed to belong to the road several successive time steps earlier. Obviously, such approaches can easily fail if the vehicle leaves the road without the algorithm taking notice of it or if the visual appearance of the road suddenly changes.

This is important because even if there are a thousand tentacles no tentacle might actually fit precisely into the road boundaries. This is due to the fact that tentacles only represent a limited set of driving primitives and will never cover all real-world road geometries. As a consequence, it is most likely that none of the pixel sets associated with any tentacle will fit the true pixel value distribution of

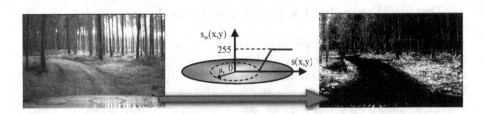

Fig. 3. RGB image of a dirt road scene (left), transformation by the weighting function for the saturation channel (middle) and resulting image (right).

the road. Therefore, knowledge about which pixels really belong to the road is even more incomplete compared to approaches based on more fine-grained road geometry hypotheses, such as the 4D approach for road tracking [8]. Hence, no serious statistics can be done.

Summarizing, compared to all approaches incorporating some kind of history, our feature for road segmentation allows the vehicle to recover from any wrong decision previously taken. Of course there may be more non-drivable terrain which is not recognized by the proposed visual cue (see upper part of Fig. 3), but in combination with a geometric road hypotheses and an obstacle avoidance system such as the tentacles approach it becomes a powerful additional feature. Evaluation of a sparse tentacle set according to the described color intensity feature and the rating process explained in Ch. 3 using $w_{vis0.5} = 70$ is shown in Fig. 2 (b). Incorporating the Intel Performance primitives libraries, we are able to evaluate as much as 1000 different tentacles within the cycle time of the system of 0.1s, corresponding to one LIDAR revolution.

5   Results and Conclusions

The proposed tentacle based LIDAR and vision fusing as well as the explained visual feature were used successfully during the C-ELROB 2009 in Oulu/Finland within the "Autonomous navigation" scenario. The scenario consisted of a round track with a length of approx. 2.6 km, which had to be passed twice, totaling 5.2 km (see Fig. 4 (b)). As most parts of the track led through a dense forest, reliable GPS information was not available. Despite the tough conditions (see also Fig. 4 (a)) the proposed enhanced tentacle approach enabled our autonomous vehicle MuCAR-3 to drive 95 % of the complete distance fully autonomously undercutting the time limit of 1 h by far with 43 min.

Problems due to fusion only arose at crossings, where both the LIDAR and the vision tentacle evaluation tend to go straight on even if the target track suggests to go left or right. With its 360 degree field of view, only the LIDAR is able to sense the right branch, whereas vision might fail sometimes. This is because of the limited field of view of the visual sensor and the fact that if there was no tentacle selected leading into the branch there will be no gaze control for visually focussing the branch. Thus, MuCAR-3 will go straight on and miss the branch even if non-visible tentacles are not rated as completely non drivable (see Sec. 3.2). Nevertheless there are by far more advantages then disadvantages using the described fusion process. An exemplary situation where tentacle navigation benefits from visual information is shown in Fig. 4 (b). Here, without using visual tentacle qualities, MuCAR-3 decided to go right in front of a narrow road surrounded by dense vegetation at both sides, and drove over the flat grassland on the right. In contrast, with the aid of the proposed tentacle evaluation process fusing LIDAR with vision, MuCAR-3 was able to stay on the road and drove through the dirt road section similarly to a human driver.

(a)   (b)   (c)

Fig. 4. Visual tentacle rating facing complex lighting conditions during C-ELROB 2009 (a), comparison between LIDAR based tentacle driving (red), fused LIDAR and vision based tentacle driving (blue) and a human driven trajectory (yellow)(b), aerial image of the C-ELROB track (c)(blue encodes autonomously driven parts)

6   Acknowledgements

The authors gratefully acknowledge funding by DFG excellence initiative research cluster COTESYS, partial support of this work by DFG within the SFB TR 28 *Cognitive Automobiles*, as well as generous funding by the Federal Office of Defense Technology and Procurement (BWB).

References

1. F. von Hundelshausen, M. Himmelsbach, F. Hecker, A. Müller, and H.-J. Wünsche, "Driving with Tentacles - integral structures of sensing and motion," *International Journal of Field Robotics Research*, 2008.
2. C. Rasmussen, "Combining laser range, color, and texture cues for autonomous road following," *IEEE Inter. Conf. on Robotics and Automation*, 2002.
3. A. Broggi, S. Cattani, P. P. Porta, and P. Zani, "A laserscanner- vision fusion system implemented on the terramax autonomous vehicle," *IEEE Int. Conf. on Intelligent Robots and Systems*, 2006.
4. U. Franke, H. Loose, and C. Knöppel, "Lane Recognition on Country Roads," *Intelligent Vehicles Symposium*, pp. 99–104, 2007.
5. S. Thrun, M. Montemerlo, and A. Aron, "Probabilistic terrain analysis for high-speed desert driving," in *Proceedings of Robotics: Science and Systems*, Philadelphia, USA, August 2006.
6. C. Tan, T. Hong, T. Chang, and M. Shneier, "Color model-based real-time learning for road following," *IEEE Intelligent Transportation Systems Conference*, 2006.
7. J. Zhang and H.-H. Nagel, "Texture-based segmentation of road images," *IEEE Symposium on Intelligent Vehicles*, pp. 260–265, 1994.
8. E. D. Dickmanns and B. D. Mysliwetz, "Recursive 3-d road and relative ego-state recognition," *IEEE Transaction on Pattern Analysis and Machine Intelligence*, vol. 14, pp. 199–213, February 1992.

Improved Time-to-Contact Estimation by Using Information from Image Sequences

Maria Sagrebin and Josef Pauli

Fakultät für Ingenieurwissenschaften,
Abteilung für Informatik und Angewandte Kognitionswissenschaft,
Universität Duisburg-Essen, Germany
maria.sagrebin@uni-due.de, josef.pauli@uni-due.de
http://www.uni-due.de/is/

Abstract. Robust time-to-contact (TTC) calculation belongs to the most desirable techniques in the field of autonomous robot navigation. Using only image measurements it provides a method to determine when contact with a visible object will be made. However TTC computation by using feature positions in the last two images only, is very sensitive to noisy measurements and provides very unstable results. The presented work extends the approach by incorporating also the information about the feature positions in the previous image sequence. The achieved results testify the better performance of this method.

1 Introduction

Robot obstacle and hazard detection is an important task within the field of robot navigation. It is fundamental to applications where collision free robot navigation is required. To solve this task successfully 3D information of the surrounding environment has to be obtained.

This paper proposes an approach for 3D reconstruction in the case where the robot sensor system consists of one video camera only. It is also assumed that the camera is oriented towards the robot movement direction. Under these circumstances the usual stereo based algorithms as shown by Hartley et al. [6] give poor reconstructions.

In 1976, Lee [1] presented a technique to estimate the remaining time to contact with the surrounding objects. Using only image measurements, and without knowing robot velocity or distance from the object, it is possible to determine when contact with a visible object will be made. However this approach is very sensitive to noisy measurements of feature positions in an image. As shown by Souhila et al.[8] this results in very unstable time-to-contact values and thus has a direct impact on the practicability of this technique.

To resolve this problem much of the past research had been focused on developing algorithms for extracting outstanding features and for tracking them robustly ([2], [3], [7], [5]). However depending on the hardware used, image resolution and environmental conditions the required high accuracy of the measurement of the feature position can usually not be warranted.

The approach presented in this paper follows a different strategy. It is based on our previous work presented in [9] where image measurements of each feature are used to adapt model equations, which describe how a respective feature diverges from a focus of expansion over a sequence of consecutive images. Using these equation a better estimation of a true feature position in an image can be made. It was shown that time-to-contact values which have been computed based on these estimated feature positions are much more stable and allow more reliable statements about the time to contact. However the approach suffers from several drawbacks, which will be addressed in the presented paper.

First the use of the stochastic gradient descent algorithm to adapt the model equations of the respective feature is problematic. The performance of it strongly depends on the appropriate choice of the step size. Experiments have shown that for some sequences of feature positions a wrong choice led to strong oscillations of the corresponding time-to-contact curve. To overcome these difficulties a different iterative technique has been developed.

The second issue are the strong preconditions under which the previously mentioned model equation can be used to estimate true feature positions in an image. A strict forward motion with a constant velocity is assumed. Since within an usual robot navigation task such assumptions can not be tolerated, this paper presents several procedures to adapt the parameters of the model equations according to the rotational movements and movements with varying velocities. All procedures require information about the odometry data of the robot.

2   Time-to-Contact Calculation

This section discusses briefly the theory behind the time-to-contact calculation and gives a short explanation about the model equations which have been introduced in our previous work.

2.1   Theory of Time-to-Contact Calculation

To estimate the remaining time-to-contact the displacements of feature positions in two consecutive images are considered. Figure 1 describes the optical geometry for time-to-contact.

A point of interest P at coordinates (X, Y, Z) is projected onto the point p in the image plane. The focus of projection is centered at the origin of the camera coordinate system $(0, 0, 0)$. In physical space P is fixed and does not move. The image plane is fixed at a distance z in front of the origin. The focus of expansion (FOE) is a point toward which the camera is moving. In the image plane it is the only point which does not change its position during the forward movement of the camera. As seen in figure 1 the position of a projected point p does change. It diverges from the focus of expansion toward the image borders.

The corresponding TTC value is computed according to the following procedure: pick a feature in the image, and divide its distance from the FOE by its divergence from the FOE. The divergence of a feature is computed as the length of the disparity vector formed by the feature positions in two consecutive images.

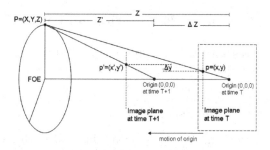

Fig. 1. Optical geometry for TTC.

In figure 1 the disparity vector of an image feature p is depicted as Δy.
It is important to note that the resulted value is actually the number of images, the robot can take before it runs into the respective obstacle. Having the time interval between the two image acquisitions, it is then possible to compute the remaining time and with robot actual velocity the remaining distance.

In simulation environment, where the projected feature positions in an image can be measured precisely, this algorithm provides exact estimates of the remaining time. However in practical applications the required high accuracy of feature measurement can usually not be warranted. As will be shown later the resulting TTC values strongly oscillate around the true values.

2.2   TTC Estimation Using Model Equations

To obtain a smooth TTC curve, the approach proposed in [9] uses, additionally to image measurements also predictions about where the feature position should be, depending on its previous positions. To compute such predictions the following model equations have been derived:

$$x\left(n\right) = \frac{x_1 \cdot x_2}{((n-1) \cdot x_1 - (n-2) \cdot x_2)} \ , \quad y\left(n\right) = \frac{y_1 \cdot y_2}{((n-1) \cdot y_1 - (n-2) \cdot y_2)}$$

where $p_1 = (x_1, y_1)$ and $p_2 = (x_2, y_2)$ correspond to the feature positions in the first two images of a given image sequence and $p_{pred}^n = (x\left(n\right), y\left(n\right))$ defines the predicted position of a respective feature in the n−th image. The accuracy of the predictions depends strongly on how precise the coordinates of a feature can be measured in the first two images.

Because of this drawback, the above equations have been transformed to:

$$x\left(n\right) = \frac{a_x \cdot b_x}{((n-1) \cdot a_x - (n-2) \cdot b_x)} \ , \quad y\left(n\right) = \frac{a_y \cdot b_y}{((n-1) \cdot a_y - (n-2) \cdot b_y)} \quad (1)$$

The parameters a_x, b_x, a_y and b_y have been then adapted using the stochastic gradient descent algorithm. As an input served the newly measured positions $p_{meas}^n = (x_{meas}, y_{meas})$ of a respective feature. The corresponding TTC values have been computed by using the predicted feature positions in the current and the previous image. As stated above these adaptation procedure succeeded only, if the step size parameter of the gradient descent algorithm was chosen appropriately. In a different case the calculated TTC values started to oscillate at some point. To overcome this problem a different adaptation procedure is presented in the next section.

3   Adaptive Parameter Estimation and Its Effect

This section introduces a new iterative technique to adapt the equation parameters for each feature sequence. The presented results show that its performance allows a computation of more precise TTC values.

3.1   Iterative Parameter Estimation

The most relevant insight in the development of this algorithm was that not the exact values of the parameters a_x, b_x and a_y, b_y have most influenced the accuracy of the predicted feature positions but instead the differences between a_x and b_x and between a_y and b_y. Hence the parameters a_x and a_y have been initialised with first measured coordinates of·a feature position x_1 and y_1 respectively and were never changed hereafter. The parameters b_x and b_y were initialised with the second measured position of a feature and have been adjusted every time the next feature position was measured.

First the midpoint $m(n) = (m_x^n, m_y^n)$ between the newly measured feature position and the predicted position was calculated. The predicted position for the current timestamp n was computed using the equations 1 which were parametrised with the old values for b_x and b_y. Next the parameters b_x and b_y have been adjusted to the new values:

$$b_x = \frac{(n-1)\, a_x \cdot m_x^n}{a_x + (n-2)\, m_x^n} \qquad b_y = \frac{(n-1)\, a_y \cdot m_y^n}{a_y + (n-2)\, m_y^n}$$

The above equations have been obtained by rearranging the equations 1 and by replacing $x(n)$ and $y(n)$ by m_x^n and m_y^n respectively. Using these newly computed parameters and again the equations 1 new estimates for the feature position at the actual and the previous timestamp have been calculated. The estimated positions and the previously determined FOE were then used to compute the time-to-contact value at the actual timestamp n.

3.2   Results of the Proposed Estimation Procedure

First the proposed method was tested in a simulation environment along with the adaptation procedure introduced in [9]. Gaussian noise with variance 0.75 was applied to the projected points on the image plane. The left image in figure 2 shows the resulted trajectory of one feature while the camera was moved forward. The origin of the coordinate system of the image plane was shifted to the FOE. The right image shows the corresponding TTC values. Since the camera is moved forward, true values are represented through straight line in this image. The other two curves show TTC values which were computed with the proposed approach and the one introduced in [9]. One can clearly see, that both methods require a short adaptation phase, during which both curves approach the true TTC values. However after an image number 24 the values of the method presented in [9] start to oscillate while the other curve still runs along the straight line. Similar observations were made also with other feature sequences and with increased noise rate.

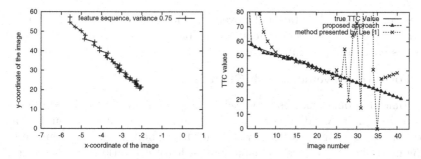

Fig. 2. left image: trajectory of one feature while the camera was moved forward; right image: TTC values computed with the proposed approach and the one presented in [9].

Figure 3 shows exemplary some TTC curves which were computed during the robot movement in the laboratory environment. In this experiment SIFT features, Scale Invariant Feature Transform [7], were used. FOE was set to a previously calibrated value. Again the straight line represents the true TTC

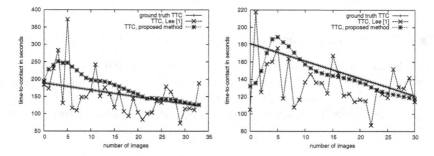

Fig. 3. Each graphic shows calculated TTC values for one respective feature.

values. The curve, marked with (×) shows the TTC values which have been computed using the original approach presented by Lee. The curve, marked with (∗) shows TTC values which were calculated using the proposed approach. The same noisy data were used as an input to both methods. In contrast to the (×)-curve the (∗)- curve is more smooth and avoids sudden jumps. Moreover it approximates the true values up to a variance from 5 to 7 sec. This makes up ca. 5% deviation from the true remaining distance.

Although the results are promising, the main drawback of this approach is the requirement of a constant forward movement. The next section explains how to overcome these assumptions.

4   Extension of the Approach to General Movements

The extension of the approach to arbitrary robot movements evolves from an appropriate update of the parameters of the model equations. This section introduces three update procedures for the following cases: forward movement with varying velocity, simple rotational movement and cornering. The distinction between the different movements is carried out based on the odometry data of the robot, its heading angle and velocity.

4.1   Forward Movement with Changing Velocity

Every time the robot changes its velocity, the parameters are updated in such a way, so that the new values correspond to the hypothetical situation, in which the robot was moving with the new velocity from the beginning of a process.

Figure 4 shows a typical development of feature positions in an image sequence when the robot doubles its velocity between the fifth and the sixth image. In this example, updating the parameters according to the new velocity implies the parameters b_x and b_y to correspond to the feature position in a third image. The new hypothetical sequence of feature positions is denoted through rhom-

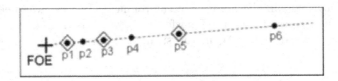

Fig. 4. Feature sequence resulting from forward movement with changing velocity.

buses. Because of the doubled velocity the number of feature positions in a hypothetical sequence is less then in the old sequence. Thus the image index has also to be updated appropriately. The new index n_{new} depends on the ratio of an old and new velocity, which are denoted through v_{old} and v_{new} respectively:

$$n_{new} = \left((n_{old} - 1) \cdot \frac{v_{old}}{v_{new}} \right) + 1$$

Since only the ratio is relevant, the two velocities can also be replaced by corresponding distances driven between the two timestamps of an image acquisition. In the above example the values would be: $\frac{v_{old}}{v_{new}} = 1/2$, $n_{old} = 5$ and $n_{new} = 3$. The parameters b_x and b_y are updated as follows:

$$b_x^{new} = \frac{(n_{new} - 1)\, a_x \cdot m_x}{a_x + (n_{new} - 2)\, m_x} \quad , \quad b_y^{new} = \frac{(n_{new} - 1)\, a_y \cdot m_y}{a_y + (n_{new} - 2)\, m_y}$$

where $m = (m_x, m_y)$ is the midpoint from the previous update. Once the parameters are updated according to the new velocity, a new prediction of a feature position can be computed and with a new image measurement the parameters can be updated again according to the procedure described in section 3.

4.2   Simple Rotational Movement

In the case of a pure rotational movement the parameters have to be updated according to the angle of the rotation. First the parameters, which can be interpreted as the first two positions of a feature sequence, are multiplied with the inverse intrinsic calibration matrix M_{int}^{-1} to obtain a corresponding vector in a camera coordinate system. Multiplication with the rotation matrix R and subsequent multiplication with the inverse intrinsic matrix M_{int} finally results in a new parameter vector:

$$a_{new} = M_{int}RM_{int}^{-1} \cdot a_{old} \ , \quad b_{new} = M_{int}RM_{int}^{-1} \cdot b_{old}$$

where $a_{old} = \left(a_x^{old}, a_y^{old}, 1\right)^T$ and $b_{old} = \left(b_x^{old}, b_y^{old}, 1\right)^T$ are the homogeneous coordinates of the corresponding points. Again after the parameters are updated the method presented in section 3 can be applied as usual.

4.3   Cornering

The cornering movement is defined as a composition of a rotational and translational movement. In figure 5 the change of the heading angle is denoted as β,

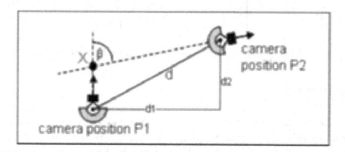

Fig. 5. Graphical representation of a turning movement.

and the displacement of the camera between the two timestamps corresponds to the vector d. The update procedure is composed of the following three steps:

1. Parameter update according to a forward motion to the virtual point X.
2. Parameter update according to simple rotational movement.
3. Parameter update according to the forward motion from the virtual point X to the second camera position $P2$.

The lengths of the distances $\overline{P1\ X}$ and $\overline{X\ P2}$ can be computed as follows:

$$\overline{P1\ X} = d_2 - \frac{d_1}{tan\,(\beta)} \ , \quad \overline{X\ P2} = \frac{\frac{d_1}{tan(\beta)}}{cos\,(\beta)}$$

with the displacement vector $d = (d_1, d_2)$. For an appropriate update of the parameters the methods presented in the previous two sections can be used.

4.4   Results

Figure 6 shows exemplary three trajectories of the robot. The contour of each graphic indicate the corresponding floor plan. For the robot to be able to extract some features the white walls of the floor were partly covered with colored photographs. In the conducted experiments the robot robustly avoided several crashes with the walls and recognised confidently obstacles when they were placed in front of him.

The experiments have shown that by using the presented approach a simple web cam is sufficient to obtain the required 3D information about the robot environment. In contrast to other methods where authors propose to combine the TTC results with additional sensory information, no other equipment was necessary in the conducted experiments.

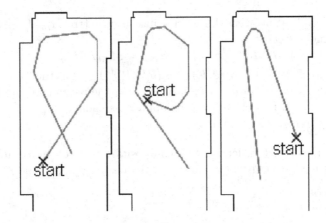

Fig. 6. Several trajectories driven by the robot.

5   Conclusions

To obtain a better and more stable estimation of TTC values, this paper presented a new iterative technique to adapt the parameter of the model equations. Additionally several procedures have been developed to extend the applicability of the approach presented in [9] also to arbitrary movements. The approach was successfully tested in an indoor environment with a robot which was equipped with a simple web cam. The results presented here testify the stability and the robustness of this approach.

References

[1] Lee D.: A Theory of Visual Control of Braking Based on Information about Time-to-Collision. Perception, 1976, 5, 437–459
[2] Harris, C., Stephens, M.: A combined corner and edge detector. In 4th Alvey Vision Conference, 1988, 147–151
[3] Shi, J., Tomasi, C.: Good features to track. IEEE Conference on Computer Vision and Pattern Recognition (CVPR), 1994, 593–600
[4] Camus, T.: Calculating Time-to-Contact Using Real-Time Quantized Optical Flow. Max-Planck-Institut fuer biologische Kybernetik, Arbeitsgruppe Buelthoff, 1995
[5] Mikolajczyk, K., Schmid, C.: An affine invariant interest point detector. In European Conference on Computer vision (ECCV), 2002, 1, 128–142
[6] Hartley, R., Zisserman, A.: Multiple View Geometry in Computer Vision. Cambridge University Press, 2003
[7] Lowe D. G.: Distinctive image features from scale-invariant keypoints. International Journal of Computer Vision, 2004, 2, 60, 91–110
[8] Souhila, K., Karim, A.: Optical Flow based robot obstacle avoidance. International Journal of Advanced Robotic Systems, 2007, 4, 1, 13–16
[9] Sagrebin M., Noglik A., Pauli J.: Robust Time-to-Contact Calculation for Real Time Applications. In Proceedings of 18th International Conference on Computer Graphics and Vision, 2008, 128–133

Monocular Obstacle Detection for Real-World Environments

Erik Einhorn[1,2] and Christof Schroeter[2] and Horst-Michael Gross[2]

[1]MetraLabs GmbH, Germany
[2]Neuroinformatics and Cognitive Robotics Lab
Ilmenau University of Technology, Germany

Abstract. In this paper, we present a feature based approach for monocular scene reconstruction based on extended Kalman filters (EKF). Our method processes a sequence of images taken by a single camera mounted in front of a mobile robot. Using various techniques we are able to produce a precise reconstruction that is almost free from outliers and therefore can be used for reliable obstacle detection and avoidance. In real-world field tests we show that the presented approach is able to detect obstacles that can not be seen by other sensors, such as laser range finders. Furthermore, we show that visual obstacle detection combined with a laser range finder can increase the detection rate of obstacles considerably, allowing the autonomous use of mobile robots in complex public and home environments.

1 Introduction and Related Work

For nearly ten years we have been involved with the development of an interactive mobile shopping assistant for everyday use in public environments, such as shopping centers or home improvement stores. Such a shopping companion autonomously contacts potential customers, intuitively interacts with them, and adequately offers its services, including autonomously guiding customers to the locations of desired goods [1]. Currently, we are developing an interactive assistant that can be used in home environments as companion for people with mild cognitive imparments (MCI) living at home alone. However, both public environments, like home improvement stores, as well as home environments, contain a large variety of different obstacles that must be detected by an autonomous robot.

For obstacle detection our robot is equipped with an array of 24 sonar sensors at the bottom and a laser range finder SICK S300 mounted in front direction at a height of 0,35 meter. Using these sensors, many obstacles can be reliably detected. However, during the field trials it became apparent that many obstacles are very difficult to recognize. Some obstacles are mainly located above the plane that is covered by the laser range finder. Also small obstacles are difficult to perceive since they lie below the laser range finder and can hardly be seen by the sonar sensors, due to their diffuse characteristics and low precision. Therefore, it turned out to be necessary to use additional methods for robust and reliable obstacle detection. Vision-based approaches are suitable for this purpose since they provide a large field of view and supply a large amount of information about the structure of the local surroundings.

Recently, time-of-flight cameras have been used successfully for obstacle detection [2]. Similar to laser range finders, these cameras emit short light pulses and measure the time taken until the reflected light reaches the camera again. Another alternative is to use stereo vision for obstacle detection as described in [3] and many others. However, a stereo camera is less compact than a single camera. Furthermore, a monocular approach that uses one camera only is more interesting from a scientific point of view.

In [4], a monocular approach for depth estimation and obstacle detection is presented. Information about scene depth is drawn from the scaling factor of image regions, which is determined using region tracking. While this approach may work well in outdoor scenes, where the objects near the focus of expansion are separated from the background by large depth discontinuities, it will fail in cluttered indoor environments like home improvement stores or home environments. In [5] we propose an early version of a feature-based approach for monocular scene reconstruction. This shape-from-motion approach uses extended Kalman filters (EKF) to reconstruct the 3D position of the image features in real-time in order to identify potential obstacles in the reconstructed scene. Davison et al. [6,7] use a similar approach and have done a lot of research in this area. They propose a full covariance SLAM algorithm for recovering the 3D trajectory of a monocular camera. Both, the camera position and the 3D positions of tracked image features or landmarks are estimated by a single EKF. Another visual SLAM approach was developed by Eade and Drummond [8]. Their graph-based algorithm partitions the landmark observations into nodes of a graph to minimize statistical inconsistency in the filter estimates [9].

However, Eade's and Drummond's "Visual SLAM" as well as Davison's "Mono-SLAM" are both mainly focusing on the estimation of the camera motion, while a precise reconstruction of the scenery is less emphasized. As we want to use the reconstructed scene for obstacle detection, our priorities are vice versa. We are primarily interested in a precise and dense reconstruction of the scene and do not focus on the correct camera movement, since the distance of the objects relative to the camera and the robot respectively is sufficient for obstacle avoidance and local map building. Actually, we are using the robot's odometry to obtain information on the camera movement. In contrast to Eade and Davison who generally move their camera sidewards in their examples, our camera is mounted in front of the mobile robot and mostly moves along its optical axis. Compared to lateral motion, this forward motion leads to higher uncertainties in the depth estimates due to a smaller parallax. This fact was also proven by Matthies and Kanade [10] in a sensitivity analysis.

The main contribution of this paper is a monocular feature-based approach for scene reconstruction that combines a number of different techniques that are known from research areas like visual SLAM or stereo vision in order to achieve a robust algorithm for reliable obstacle detection that must fulfill the following requirements:

1. A dense reconstruction to reduce the risk of missing or ignoring an obstacle
2. The positions of obstacles that appear in the field of view should be correctly estimated as early as possible to allow an early reaction in motion control
3. Outliers must be suppressed to avoid false positive detections that result in inadequate path planning or unecessary avoidance movements

The presented algorithm is based on our previous work [5] and was improved by several extensions. In the next sections, we describe our approach in detail and show how it can be used for visual obstacle detection. In section 4 we present some experimental results and close with an outlook for future work.

2   Monocular Scene Reconstruction

As stated before, we use a single calibrated camera that is mounted in front of the robot. During the robot's locomotion, the camera is capturing a sequence of images that are rectified immediately according to the intrinsic camera parameters. Thus, different two-dimensional views of a scene are obtained and can be used for the scene reconstruction. In these images distinctive image points (image features) are detected. For performance reasons we use the "FAST" corner detector [11] since it is superior to SIFT or SURF in terms of computation time. The selected features are then tracked in subsequent frames while recovering their 3D positions.

Davison et al. [6,7] use a single EKF for full covariance SLAM that is able to handle up to 100 features. As we require a denser reconstruction of the scene for obstacle detection, we have to cope with a large number of features which cannot be handled by such an approach in real-time. Therefore, we decouple the EKF and use one EKF per feature to recover the structure of the scene similar to [12], i.e. each feature i is associated with a state vector $\mathbf{y}_i$ that represents the 3D position of the feature and a corresponding covariance matrix Σ_i.

2.1 State Representation

Various parametrizations for the 3D positions of the features have been proposed in literature. The most compact representation is the XYZ-representation where the position of each feature is parameterized by its Euclidean coordinates in 3-space. Davison et al. [7] have shown that this representation has several disadvantages since the position uncertainties for distant features are not well represented by a Gaussian distribution. Instead, they propose an inverse depth representation, where the 3D position of each feature i can be described by the vector $\mathbf{y_i} = (\mathbf{c}_i, \theta_i, \varphi_i, \lambda_i)^\top$, where $\mathbf{c}_i \in \mathbb{R}^3$ is the optical center of the camera from which the feature i was first observed, and θ_i, ϕ_i is the azimuth and elevation of the unit ray that points from $\mathbf{c}_i$ to the 3D point of the feature. This ray is given by $\mathbf{m}(\theta_i, \phi_i) = (\cos\theta_i \cos\phi_i, \cos\theta_i \sin\phi_i, -\sin\theta_i)^\top$. The last element λ_i of the state vector denotes the inverse of the features depth $d_i = \lambda_i^{-1}$ along the ray.

2.2 Feature Tracking

While the robot is moving, the image features are tracked in subsequent frames. In [5] we used a feature matching approach that finds correspondences between homologous features in subsequent frames based on a bipartite graph matching. While that approach is suitable for SIFT or SURF features it has some shortcomings with less complex feature descriptors like image patches, because of an increased level of ambiguity. Therefore, we now use a guided active search for tracking the features through the image sequence. As descriptor we utilize a 16×16 pixel image patch around each feature. First, the image position $\mathbf{x}_i^-$ of each feature is predicted by projecting the current estimate of its 3D position $\mathbf{y}_i$ onto the image plane using $\tilde{\mathbf{x}}_i^- = h(\mathbf{y}_i, \mathbf{P})$ with the measurement function[1]:

$$h(\mathbf{y}_i, \mathbf{P}) = \mathbf{P}\left(\lambda \tilde{\mathbf{c}_i} + \begin{pmatrix} \mathbf{m}(\theta_i, \phi_i) \\ 0 \end{pmatrix}\right). \tag{1}$$

Here $\mathbf{P} = \mathbf{KR}[\mathbf{I} \mid -\mathbf{c}]$ is the projection matrix containing the current orientation $\mathbf{R}$, the current position $\mathbf{c}$ and the intrinsic calibration matrix $\mathbf{K}$ of the camera, which captured the current image (see [13] for details). The current camera pose is obtained from the robot's odometry data.

---

[1] For better differentiation we notate homogeneous vectors as $\tilde{\mathbf{x}}$ and Euclidean vectors as $\mathbf{x}$, where $\tilde{\mathbf{x}} = (\mathbf{x}^\top, 1)^\top \cdot s$, $s \in \mathbb{R}$

For each feature i, the corresponding image point is searched in the current image around the predicted image position $\mathbf{x}_i^-$ by computing the sum of absolute differences (SAD) with the image patch that is stored as descriptor of the feature. The image point that yields the lowest SAD is chosen. To achieve sub-pixel precision we fit a 2D parabola into the computed SAD error surface around the chosen image point and use the coordinate of the apex as position of the corresponding image point. The search is restricted to an elliptical region that is defined by the covariance matrix of the innovation that is computed in the EKF.

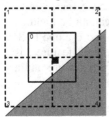

Fig. 1. The correlation window is split into 5 sub-windows.

One major problem of patch-based approaches for feature matching are occlusions near object edges where the patch covers two different objects with large depth discontinuities. During the matching, this leads to a decision conflict since the part of the patch that belongs to the background object moves in a different way than the foreground object. As a result, the reconstructed 3D points along object borders are blurred in different depths. For stereo matching various adaptive window approaches have been proposed to reduce this problem.

We apply a variation of the multiple window approach presented in [14] and [15]. Instead of using a single 16×16 pixel correlation window, the window is split into five sub-windows as shown in Figure 1. The SADs are computed for each sub-window C_i. The final correlation value C is formed by adding the correlation value C_o of the central 8×8 sub-window and the values of the two best surrounding correlation windows C_b and C_s. This measure of similarity performs better near object boundaries since at least two sub-windows are located on a single object in most cases. Depending on the dominant image structure the correspondence is either attached to the foreground or the background object reducing the blur along the reconstructed object borders[2]. Besides the correlation value, we compute an occlusion score C_{occ} by adding the correlation values of the two worst matching surrounding sub-windows. Both the correlation value C and the occlusion score C_{occ} are normalized by the number of pixels in the used sub-windows.

2.3 Descriptor Update

Davison el al. [7] also use the image patch around the feature as descriptor. While they capture this descriptor only once when the feature is first observed, we used a contrary philosophy in [5], where we update the descriptor every time the feature is tracked in a new image. Both variants have pros and cons. If the descriptor is never updated, the feature cannot be tracked over long distances since the appearance changes too much due to affine and perspective deformations, especially when using a forward moving camera or robot. If, on the other hand, the descriptor is updated every frame, tracking errors might be accumulated over several frames, and the descriptor might move along the edges of object boundaries and does not represent a single fixed feature. This usually occurs near occlusions and leads to incorrect estimates.

Therefore, we use the aforementioned occlusion score C_{occ} to determine whether updating the descriptor is reasonable or not. If the normalized occlusion score C_{occ} lies below a certain threshold the descriptor is replaced using the corresponding patch in the current image, otherwise the descriptor remains unchanged. Using this technique,

---

[2] Using the SSE2 processor instruction PSADBW the correlation values can be computed efficiently and splitting the window into 5 sub-windows results in very little computational overhead compared to a single correlation window. This performance improvement is a major reason for choosing the SAD as measure of similarity

most features can be tracked over long distances while the projective deformations are compensated by permanent descriptor updates. Feature descriptors near occlusions are not updated to allow stable tracking along object boundaries.

After the features are tracked and the camera pose is refined, the 3D positions of the features will be updated using the usual EKF update equations leading to a more precise reconstruction of the scenery.

2.4 Feature Initialization

Lost features that left the camera's field of view or that could not be tracked in the previous step are replaced by new features. Different methods for initializing the state of new features have been proposed in related literature. In [5] we have shown how to use a multi-baseline stereo approach for initializing new features. The approach uses the images that were captured *before* the feature was first detected and searches along the epipolar line for corresponding image regions by computing the SAD. By accumulating the SAD error over multiple images, a reliable initial inverse depth estimate is obtained. Additionally, we treat the SAD error along the epipolar line as probability distribution and fit a Gaussian distribution near the minimum in order to obtain a variance of the initial estimate that is used for initializing the error covariance matrix Σ_i.

3   Obstacle Detection

For obstacle detection, we perform the described monocular scene reconstruction for 200-300 salient features of the scene simultaneously. Afterwards, a post-processing step is applied to the reconstructed features in order to remove outliers and unreliable estimates. From all reconstructed features, we only use those that meet the following criteria:

- the estimated height must be above 0.1m; obstacles below this threshold cannot be detected safely and are assumed to be lokated on the ground
- the variance of the estimated inverse depth taken from the error covariance matrix must lie below a threshold of 0.005
- the distance to the camera must have been smaller than 3m when the feature was observed for the last time

The last criterion mainly removes virtual features that arise where the boundaries of foreground and background objects intersect in the image. These features do not correspond to a single 3D point in the scene and cannot be estimated properly.

The features that pass the above filters may still contain a few outliers. Therefore, we examine the neighborhood of each feature. Features that contain less than 4 neighbors within a surrounding sphere with a radius of 0.3m are regarded as outliers and will be rejected. The remaining features are inserted into an occupancy map by projecting them on the xy-plane. This occupancy map is merged with a laser map by choosing the highest obstacle probability for each cell in both maps. Finally, the merged map is used for both local path planning and obstacle avoidance.

4   Results

Figure 2 shows such a map where laser and visual information is merged. The occupancy map that is created using the laser range finder is colored in blue where the different shades of blue correspond to the probability that a cell is occupied. The position of the features that were reconstructed using visual information and the approach presented in this paper are colored in red. In the map, a total number of about 8,200 visual features is shown. While creating the map a total number of 15,400 points was

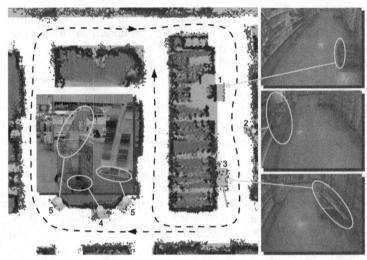

Fig. 2. Map created by combining visual information (red dots) and laser range finder (blue). The robot's trajectory and moving direction is denoted by the dashed line. The ground truth is highlighted in gray. The visual map consists of about 8,200 reconstructed points. Obstacles detected using vision only are labeled using numbers. The images on the right show the obstacles as seen by the front camera. The image on the left was taken using a handheld 8 megapixel camera.

reconstructed, where 6,000 features where filtered due to a bad variance, 1,000 features were classified as belonging to the ground and 100 where detected as outliers. For image acquisition a 1/4" CCD fire-wire camera is installed on the robot that is mounted at a height of 1.15m and tilted by 35° towards the ground.

For better evaluation and for visualization purposes a ground truth map was created and is highlighted in gray in the background of Figure 2. For building the ground truth, we took images of the scene using a hand held Canon EOS 350D 8.0 megapixel camera and used a bundle adjustment tool[3] for creating a precise reconstruction of the scene which finally was edited and labeled manually.

The map covers an area of 14m × 12m within a home improvement store where our tests were conducted. This test area contains typical obstacles that we identified as problematic during the field test since they cannot be detected by the laser range finder due to their reflection properties, their form, or too low height. Some of these obstacles are numbered from 1 to 5 in Figure 2. In detail these obstacles are: 1. an empty Euro-pallet with a height of 11cm, 2. a ladder, 3. a low shopping cart with goods that jut out at both ends, 4. a high shopping cart, and 5. shelves that extend into the scene.

All of these obstacles cannot be seen by the laser range finder and, therefore, might result in collisions. However, using our visual approach these obstacle can be detected safely. In Table 1 we try to quantify this result. For each obstacle, we have manually labeled those parts of the outline that are relevant for navigation and obstacle avoidance during the above test run using the ground truth map. The statistics in Table 1 show the percentage of the relevant obstacle boundaries that were detected by our visual

---

[3] Bundler: http://phototour.cs.washington.edu/bundler/

approach, the laser range finder and a combination of vision and laser. These results show that major parts of the above mentioned obstacles can be detected. Furthermore, it can be seen that the detection rate for all relevant objects in the scene can be increased significantly by 20% compared to obstacle detection using a laser range finder only.

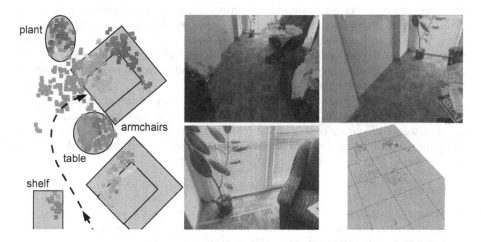

Fig. 3. left: top view of our test area, the reconstructed features are shown as colored dots, where the color indicates the estimated height of each feature (green: < 0.10m, yellow-red: 0.10m-1.15m), **right:** images of the scene superimposed by highlighted features, **lower right:** synthetic 3D view of the estimated features.

Additional tests were carried out in a special test area of our lab that contains typical elements of a living room as well as a floor with repetitive texture. Figure 3 shows a top view of this test area. The reconstructed features are shown as colored dots, where the color indicates the estimated height of each feature. All obstacles that were covered by the camera are detected robustly, while features on the floor are estimated correctly and classified as free and passable. The images on the right of Figure 3 show three images of the scene taken by the front camera as well as a synthetic three-dimensional view of the reconstructed features.

obstacle	visual	laser	visual+laser
1	63%	-	63%
2	71%	-	71%
3	71%	-	71%
4	68%	10%	68%
5	82%	-	82%
others	85%	78%	96%
total	**83%**	**72%**	**93%**

Table 1. Percentage of obstacle boundaries that can be detected using the presented visual approach, a laser range finder and a combination of both for the 5 labeled obstacles and the rest of the scene shown in Figure 2.

All tests were conducted on an Intel Core 2 Duo, 2 GHz CPU. In spite of utilizing one core only we are able to process up to 30 frames per second while reconstructing 200-300 features simultaneously. Depending on the robot's driving speed, we only need to process 10-15 frames per second leaving enough CPU resources for other applications like map building, navigational tasks, user tracking and human-machine interaction.

5 Conclusion and Future Work

In this paper, we have presented an algorithm for monocular scene reconstruction and shape from motion. We have described some improvements that make the reconstruction more reliable and help to reduce outliers. These techniques allow the approach to be used for robust real-time obstacle detection. In realistic field tests, we have shown that some obstacles that are not visible to sensors like laser range finders can be safely detected by the vision based approach. Furthermore, we were able to show that visual obstacle detection combined with a laser range finder can increase the detection rate of obstacles considerably. During the next months we will carry out long-term tests to evaluate how much the number of collisions or near-collisions can be decreased during the daily usage of the robots.

Currently, we are developing a method to estimate the position of moving objects. However, since the position of moving objects can be reconstructed up to a scaling factor only, we will focus on obstacles that reach to the ground. At the moment, features along moving objects are rejected during feature tracking and filtered after the reconstruction due to their high variance in the position estimate.

References

1. H.-M. Gross, H.-J. Böhme, Ch. Schröter, St. Müller, A. König, Ch. Martin, M. Merten, and A. Bley. ShopBot: Progress in Developing an Interactive Mobile Shopping Assistant for Everyday Use. In *SMC*, pages 3471–3478, Singapore, 2008.
2. T. Schamm, S. Vacek, J. Schröder, J.M. Zöllner, and R. Dillmann. Obstacle detection with a Photonic Mixing Device-camera in autonomous vehicles. *International Journal of Intelligent Systems Technologies and Applications*, 5:315–324, Nov. 2008.
3. P. Foggia, J.M. Jolion, A. Limongiello, and M. Vento. Stereo Vision for Obstacle Detection: A Grap-Based Approach. *LNCS GbRPR*, 4538:37–48, 2007.
4. A. Wedel, U. Franke, J. Klappstein, T. Brox, and D. Cremers. Realtime Depth Estimation and Obstacle Detection from Monocular Video. *DAGM*, pages 475–484, 2006.
5. E. Einhorn, Ch. Schröter, H.-J. Böhme, and H.-M. Gross. A Hybrid Kalman Filter Based Algorithm for Real-time Visual Obstacle Detection. In *ECMR*, pages 156–161, 2007.
6. A.J. Davison, I.D. Reid, N.D. Molton, and O. Stasse. MonoSLAM: Real-Time Single Camera SLAM. *IEEE Trans. on PAMI*, 29(6):1052–1067, 2007.
7. J. Civera, A.J. Davison, and J. Montiel. Inverse Depth Parametrization for Monocular SLAM. *IEEE Trans. on Robotics*, 24(5):932–945, Oct. 2008.
8. E. Eade and T. Drummond. Monocular SLAM as a Graph of Coalesced Observations. In *IEEE Int. Conference on Computer Vision, ICCV*, pages 1–8, 2007.
9. E. Eade and T. Drummond. Unified Loop Closing and Recovery for Real Time Monocular SLAM. In *Proc. of the British Machine Vision Conference, BMVC*, 2008.
10. L. Matthies, T. Kanade, and R. Szeliski. Kalman filter-based algorithms for estimating depth from image sequences. *International Journal of Computer Vision*, 3:209–238, 1989.
11. E. Rosten and T. T. Drummond. Machine learning for high-speed corner detection. In *Proc. of the European Conference on Computer Vision*, volume 1, pages 430–443, 2006.
12. Y. Yu, K. Wong, and M. Chang. A Fast Recursive 3D Model Reconstruction Algorithm for Multimedia Applications. In *ICPR*, volume 2, pages 241–244, 2004.
13. R. Hartley and A. Zisserman. *Multiple View Geometry in Computer Vision*. Cambridge University Press, ISBN: 0-521-54051-8, second edition, 2006.
14. H. Hirschmüller, P. Innocent, and J. Garibaldi. Real-Time Correlation-Based Stereo Vision with Reduced Border Errors. *International Journal of Computer Vision*, 47:229–246, 2002.
15. W. van der Mark and D.M. Gavrila. Real-time dense stereo for intelligent vehicles. In *IEEE Transactions on Intelligent Transportation Systems*, 2006.

Stereo-Based vs. Monocular 6-DoF Pose Estimation Using Point Features: A Quantitative Comparison

Pedram Azad, Tamim Asfour, Rüdiger Dillmann

Institute for Anthropomatics, University of Karlsruhe, Germany

Abstract. In the recent past, object recognition and localization based on correspondences of local point features in 2D views has become very popular in the robotics community. For grasping and manipulation with robotic systems, in addition accurate 6-DoF pose estimation of the object of interest is necessary. Now there are two substantially different approaches to computing a 6-DoF pose: monocular and stereo-based. In this paper we show the theoretical and practical drawbacks and limits of monocular approaches based on 2D-3D correspondences. We will then present our stereo-based approach and compare the results to the conventional monocular approach in an experimental evaluation. As will be shown, our stereo-based approach performs superior in terms of robustness and accuracy, with only few additional computational effort.

1 Introduction

Accurate pose estimation of objects in 3D space is an important computer vision task, in particular for robotic manipulation applications. For a successful grasp, in particular accurate estimation of the depth is crucial. In the recent past, the recognition and pose estimation of objects based on local point features has become a widely accepted and utilized method. The most popular features are currently the SIFT features [10]; followed by the more recent SURF features [5], and region-based features such as the MSER [13]. Object recognition frameworks using such features usually operate on a set of computed feature correspondences, either by simply counting feature correspondences or by also exploiting the spatial relationships of the feature points, as proposed in [10].

Operating on the 2D localization result of such a framework, the common approach for 6-DoF pose estimation of objects computes the rotation and translation of the object in 3D space on the basis of 2D-3D point correspondences. The traditional method for this is the POSIT algorithm [7]. A more recent method for estimating a 6-DoF pose on the basis of 2D-3D point correspondences, which also succeeds for coplanar point sets, is presented in [11], and was used throughout our comparative experiments. Monocular approaches are popular for augmented reality applications as presented e.g. in [9].

Such methods all have in common that the full pose of the object is computed on the basis of a monocular image. This means that in particular the distance of the object to the camera, namely the z-coordinate in the camera coordinate system, is derived from the scaling i.e. the size of the object in the image. Furthermore, the computation of out-of-plane rotations on the basis of 2D-3D correspondences is sensitive to small errors in the 2D feature positions.

One possibility for improving the accuracy of a pose estimate is the application of an edge-based optimization step exploiting the projected contour of the object. Such an optimization utilizes essentially the same methods as applied for edge-based rigid object tracking (e.g. [12]). A hybrid approach fusing texture, edge, and color information in an Iterated Extended Kalman Filter (IEKF) is proposed in [14]. However, an edge-based improvement of an object pose estimate always requires the projected contour of the object to be prominent in the image, which is often not the case.

In order to overcome the abovementioned problems, we have developed an approach that exploits the benefits offered by a calibrated stereo system, operating on top of the 2D recognition and localization result based on feature correspondences, as introduced in [3]. In this paper, we will show in theory and in practice that our stereo-based approach is more robust and more accurate compared to conventional monocular approaches based on 2D-3D point correspondences. Note that it is neither an accepted fact nor obvious that monocular pose estimation based on 2D-3D point correspondences performs inferior compared to stereo-based pose estimation[1].

In [6], related work on 3D object tracking is presented, which uses the KLT tracker [15] for tracking features in order to save computation time. A monocular approach using 2D-3D point correspondences and a stereo-based pose estimation method using 3D-3D point correspondences are presented. Although it is experimentally shown that the stereo-based approach is more accurate, a thorough analysis is not performed. Our measurements will show, when monocular and stereo-based pose estimation achieve comparable results and when the monocular approach deteriorates. In particular, we will show that the monocular approach suffers from instabilities for planar objects in the presence of skew and that the stereo-based approach achieves a significantly greater depth accuracy at far distances of the object. Furthermore, our stereo-based approach achieves maximum accuracy by exploiting model fitting rather than relying on point correspondences only.

In Section 2, the maximally achievable accuracy of monocular and stereo-based pose estimation is compared in theory. Our stereo-based 6-DoF pose estimation method is explained in detail in Section 3. The two approaches are compared in simulation and in real-world experiments in Section 4, ending with a conclusion in Section 5.

---

[1]Also note that not any stereo-based approach performs superior. For instance, performing 2D localization in the left and right camera image independently and then fusing the results is a – theoretically and practically – suboptimal approach in terms of accuracy.

2   Accuracy Considerations

In this section, the theoretically achievable accuracy of pose estimation methods based on 2D-3D correspondences will be compared to 3D calculations using stereo triangulation. As an example, values from a real setup on the humanoid robot ARMAR-III [1] are used. The task of localizing an object at a manipulation distance of approx. 75 cm for subsequent grasping is considered. Lenses with a focal length of 4 mm are assumed, resulting in approx. $f = f_x = f_y = 530$ (pixels) computed by the calibration procedure. The stereo system has a baseline of $b = 90$ mm; the principal axes of the cameras are assumed to run parallel.

As shown in [2], a pixel error of Δ pixels leads to a relative error in the estimated z_c-coordinate of:

$$\frac{z_c(u)}{z_c(u + \Delta)} - 1 = \frac{\Delta}{u}. \tag{1}$$

This shows that the error depends – in addition to the pixel error – on the projected size of the object: The greater the projected size u, the smaller the error. For the calculation of the pose on the basis of feature points, u is related to the farthest distance of two feature points in the optimal case. For an object whose feature pair with the farthest distance has a distance of 100 mm, it is $u = \frac{f \cdot x_c}{z_c} \approx 70$, assuming the object surface and the image plane run parallel. A pixel error of $\Delta = 1$ would already lead to a total error of the z_c-coordinate of 75 cm $\cdot \frac{1}{70} \approx 1$ cm under in other respects perfect conditions.

In a realistic scenario, however, objects often exhibit out-of-plane rotations, leading to a skewed image. This skew not only causes a smaller projected size of the object but also a greater error of the feature point positions. A projected size of 50 pixels and an effective pixel error of $\Delta = 1.5$ would already lead to an error greater than 2 cm. Note that the depth accuracy not only depends on the pixel errors in the current view, but also in the learned view, since the depth is estimated relative to the learned view.

In contrast, when exploiting a calibrated stereo system, the depth is computed on the basis of the current view only. As shown in [2], a disparity error of Δ pixels leads to a relative error in the estimated z_c-coordinate of:

$$\frac{z_c(d)}{z_c(d + \Delta)} - 1 = \frac{\Delta}{d}, \tag{2}$$

where d denotes the disparity between the left and right camera image. Eq. (2) shows that the error does not depend on the projected size of the object, as it is the case in Eq. (1), but instead depends on the disparity d: The greater the disparity, the smaller the error. For the specified setup, the disparity amounts to $d = \frac{f \cdot b}{z_c} \approx 64$. For typical stereo camera setups, the correspondences between the left and the right camera image for distinctive feature points can be computed with subpixel accuracy. For this, usually a second order parabola is fitted to the measured disparity/correlation pairs and the two neighbors. In practice, a subpixel accuracy of at least 0.5 pixels is achieved easily by this approach. Together with Eq. (2) this leads to a total error of only 75 cm $\cdot \frac{0.5}{64} \approx 0.6$ cm.

Judging from the presented theoretical calculations, the position accuracy that can be achieved by stereo vision is higher by a factor of approx. 2–3. Although for fine manipulation of objects, e.g. grasping the handle of a cup, the lower estimated accuracy of methods relying on 2D-3D correspondences is problematic, for many other applications it might be sufficient.

However, the real errors arising from pose estimation on the basis of 2D-3D point correspondences can hardly be expressed by theoretic formulas. The accuracy and stability of such approaches dramatically depends on the spatial distribution of the feature points and their accuracy.

3   6-DoF Pose Estimation

Conventional approaches to 6-DoF pose estimation, which are based on 2D-3D point correspondences, cannot achieve a sufficient accuracy and robustness. In particular, they tend to become instable when the effective resolution of the object decreases and thereby also the accuracy of the 2D feature point positions (see Section 4 and [2]). In this section, we present our approach, which exploits the benefits of a calibrated stereo system. As will be shown, this leads to a significantly higher robustness and accuracy, and succeeds also at lower scales of the object.

The idea is to compute a sparse 3D point cloud for the 2D area that is defined by the transformation of the contour in the training view by means of the homography estimated by the 2D recognition and localization procedure (see [4,2]). Given a 3D model of the object, this model can be fitted into the calculated point cloud, resulting in a 6-DoF pose. The general approach is summarized in Algorithm 1.

Algorithm 1 CalculatePoseTextured(I_l, I_r, C) $\rightarrow R, t$

---

1. Determine the set of interest points within the calculated 2D contour C of the object in the left camera image I_l.
2. For each calculated point, determine a correspondence in the right camera image I_r by computing the *Zero Normalized Cross Correlation* (ZNCC) along the epipolar line.
3. Calculate a 3D point for each correspondence.
4. Fit a 3D model of the object into the calculated 3D point cloud and return the resulting rotation R and the translation t.

Essentially, two variants of Step 4 in Algorithm 1 are possible: Fit an analytically formulated 3D representation (or a high-quality mesh) of an object into the point cloud, or perform an alignment based on 3D-3D point correspondences. For applying the first variant, the object or a substantial part of the object, respectively, must be represented as a geometric 3D model.

For applying the second variant, 3D points must be calculated for the feature points from the training view in the same manner as throughout recognition, i.e. by computing stereo correspondences and applying stereo triangulation. A set of 3D-3D point correspondences is then automatically given by the filtered set of 2D-2D point correspondences resulting from the homography estimation. If applicable, the first variant should be preferred, since it does not rely on the accuracy of the feature point positions. However, even the second variant is expected to be more robust and more accurate than the conventional approach, since it does not suffer from the instabilities that are typical for pose estimation based on 2D-3D point correspondences.

In the case of cuboids – as used throughout the comparative experiments from Section 4 – a 3D plane is fitted into the sparse 3D point cloud, which is obtained by computing stereo correspondences for the interest points within the 2D contour of the object in the left camera image (details are given in [2]). Then, the intersection of the 3D plane with the estimated 2D contour is calculated to obtain 3D contour points. In the case of a cuboid, this can be easily achieved by intersecting the 3D straight lines through the corner points and the projection center of the left camera with the computed plane. To provide the result as a rigid body transformation, finally the rotation R and the translation t must be computed that transform the points of the 3D object model from the object coordinate system to the world coordinate system. When using 3D-3D point correspondences without fitting a 3D primitive, this transformation is calculated automatically. Otherwise, the searched rigid body transformation can be computed on the basis of 3D-3D point correspondences between the calculated 3D contour points and the corresponding 3D model points. For this, the minimization method from [8] is used. In the case of a rectangular planar surface, it is sufficient to use the four corner points.

4   Experimental Evaluation

In this section, the accuracies of monocular and stereo-based pose estimation are compared in several experiments. For recognition and 2D localization, the features and the recognition pipeline presented in [4] were used. The system was implemented using the Integrating Vision Toolkit (IVT)[2]. The company keyetech[3] offers highly optimized implementations (e.g. Harris corner detection within less than 5 ms).

In the first experiments, the wide angle stereo camera pair of the humanoid robot ARMAR-III (as specified in Section 2) was simulated, allowing to measure the estimation errors under perfect conditions and having accurate ground truth information. The errors of the z-coordinate are shown in Fig. 1, as they show the weak points of the monocular approach. For this purpose, the object of interest was moved along (resp. rotated around) a single degree of freedom for each plot. In addition, 1,000 random poses were evaluated; the results are shown in Fig. 2.

---

[2] http://ivt.sourceforge.net
[3] http://www.keyetech.de

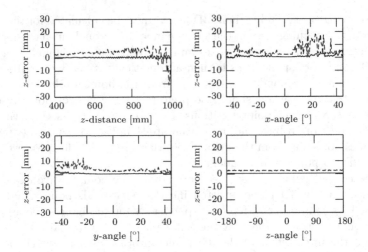

Fig. 1. Results of the simulation experiments. The z-errors are plotted depending on changes in a single degree of freedom. The solid line indicates the result of the proposed method, the dashed line the result of monocular pose estimation.

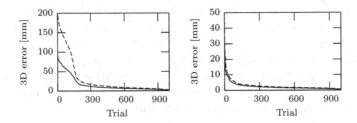

Fig. 2. Accuracy of 6-DoF pose estimation for 1,000 random trials; the errors are sorted in decreasing order. The solid line indicates the average error, the dashed line the maximum error. The 3D error was measured on the basis of sampled 3D surface points. Left: using the monocular method. Right: using the proposed stereo-based method. Note the different scaling of the vertical axis.

In Fig. 3, a situation is shown in which the monocular approach becomes instable. In Table 1, the standard deviations over 100 frames for experiments with a static object are given. As can be seen, the standard deviation of the z-coordinate amounts to 1.52 mm using the monocular approach, in contrast to 0.39 mm when using the stereo-based approach.

The runtime of the 6-DoF pose estimation procedure amounts to approx. 6 ms for a single object using the specified stereo setup (3 GHz single core CPU). The only computational expensive task here is the correlation procedure for the interest points belonging to the object. The runtime can be reduced easily by taking into account the correlation results of neighbored interest points.

Fig. 3. Result of 6-DoF pose estimation. Left: using the conventional monocular approach. Right: using the proposed stereo-based approach.

	x	y	z	θ_x	θ_y	θ_z
Proposed method	0.23	0.42	0.39	0.066	0.17	0.10
Conventional method	0.24	0.038	1.52	0.17	0.29	0.13

Table 1. Standard deviations for the estimated poses of a static object. The standard deviations have been calculated for 100 frames. The units are [mm] and [°], respectively. Note that a situation was chosen in which the monocular approach does *not* become instable.

5   Discussion and Outlook

We have compared monocular 6-DoF pose estimation based on 2D-3D point correspondences to our stereo-based approach. After discussing both approaches, it was shown that our stereo-based approach is significantly more robust and more accurate. The greatest deviations between the two approaches could be observed in the z-coordinate.

Various grasping experiments with the humanoid robot ARMAR-III have proved the applicability of our stereo-based pose estimation method [16].

In the near future, we plan to investigate the performance of our stereo-based approach for objects of arbitrary shape, in particular evaluating the improvement that can be achieved by the fitting of 3D primitives in addition to pose estimation using 3D-3D point correspondences.

Acknowledgment

The work described in this paper was partially conducted within the EU Cognitive Systems projects PACO-PLUS (IST-FP6-IP-027657) and GRASP (IST-FP7-IP-215821) funded by the European Commission, and the German Humanoid Research project SFB588 funded by the German Research Foundation (DFG: Deutsche Forschungsgemeinschaft).

References

1. T. Asfour, K. Regenstein, P. Azad, J. Schröder, N. Vahrenkamp, and R. Dillmann. ARMAR-III: An Integrated Humanoid Platform for Sensory-Motor Control. In *IEEE/RAS International Conference on Humanoid Robots (Humanoids)*, pages 169–175, Genova, Italy, 2006.
2. P. Azad. *Visual Perception for Manipulation and Imitation in Humanoid Robots.* PhD thesis, Universität Karlsruhe (TH), Karlsruhe, Germany, 2008.
3. P. Azad, T. Asfour, and R. Dillmann. Stereo-based 6D Object Localization for Grasping with Humanoid Robot Systems. In *IEEE/RSJ International Conference on Intelligent Robots and Systems (IROS)*, pages 919–924, San Diego, USA, 2007.
4. P. Azad, T. Asfour, and R. Dillmann. Combining Harris Interest Points and the SIFT Descriptor for Fast Scale-Invariant Object Recognition. In *IEEE/RSJ International Conference on Intelligent Robots and Systems (IROS)*, St. Louis, USA, 2009.
5. H. Bay, T. Tuytelaars, and L. Van Gool. SURF: Speeded Up Robust Features. In *European Conference on Computer Vision (ECCV)*, pages 404–417, Graz, Austria, 2006.
6. C. Choi, S.-M. Baek, and S. Lee. Real-time 3D Object Pose Estimation and Tracking for Natural Landmark Based Visual Servo. In *IEEE/RSJ International Conference on Intelligent Robots and Systems (IROS)*, pages 3983–3989, Nice, France, 2008.
7. D. F. DeMenthon and L. S. Davis. Model-Based Object Pose in 25 Lines of Code. In *European Conference on Computer Vision (ECCV)*, pages 123–141, Santa Margherita Ligure, Italy, 1992.
8. B. K. P. Horn. Closed-form Solution of Absolute Orientation using Unit Quaternions. *Journal of the Optical Society of America*, 4(4):629–642, 1987.
9. V. Lepetit, L. Vacchetti, D. Thalmann, and P. Fua. Fully Automated and Stable Registration for Augmented Reality Applications. In *International Symposium on Mixed and Augmented Reality (ISMAR)*, pages 93–102, Tokyo, Japan, 2003.
10. D. G. Lowe. Object Recognition from Local Scale-Invariant Features. In *IEEE International Conference on Computer Vision (ICCV)*, pages 1150–1517, Kerkyra, Greece, 1999.
11. C.-P. Lu, G. D. Hager, and E. Mjolsness. Fast and Globally Convergent Pose Estimation from Video Images. *IEEE Transactions on Pattern Analysis and Machine Intelligence (PAMI)*, 22(6):610–622, 2000.
12. E. Marchand, P. Bouthemy, F. Chaumette, and V. Moreau. Robust Real-Time Visual Tracking using a 2D-3D Model-based Approach. In *IEEE International Conference on Computer Vision (ICCV)*, pages 262–268, Kerkyra, Greece, 1999.
13. J. Matas, O. Chum, M. Urban, and T. Pajdla. Robust Wide Baseline Stereo from Maximally Stable Extremal Regions. In *British Machine Vision Conference (BMVC)*, volume 1, pages 384–393, London, UK, 2002.
14. G. Taylor and L. Kleeman. Fusion of Multimodal Visual Cues for Model-Based Object Tracking. In *Australasian Conference on Robotics and Automation (ACRA)*, Brisbane, Australia, 2003.
15. C. Tomasi and T. Kanade. Detection and Tracking of Point Features. Technical Report CMU-CS-91-132, Carnegie Mellon University, Pittsburgh, USA, 1991.
16. N. Vahrenkamp, S. Wieland, P. Azad, D. Gonzalez, T. Asfour, and R. Dillmann. Visual Servoing for Humanoid Grasping and Manipulation Tasks. In *IEEE/RAS International Conference on Humanoid Robots (Humanoids)*, Daejeon, Korea, 2008.

Probabilistisches Belegtheitsfilter zur Schätzung dynamischer Umgebungen unter Verwendung multipler Bewegungsmodelle

Sebastian Brechtel, Tobias Gindele, Jan Vogelgesang und Rüdiger Dillmann

Institut für Anthropomatik
Universität Karlsruhe (TH), 76128 Karlsruhe
Email: {brechtel | gindele | dillmann}@ira.uka.de, jan.vogelgesang@googlemail.com

Zusammenfassung. In dieser Arbeit wird eine Erweiterung des zellbasierten Belegtheitsfilters BOFUM[1] um Objektgruppen zum BOFUG (Bayesian Occupancy Filtering using Groups) vorgenommen. Diese ermöglicht die Einteilung und Klassifikation der Gruppenzugehörigkeit von Belegtheit, allein auf Basis von statischen Belegtheitsmessungen. Exemplarisch wird für Fußgänger und Fahrzeuge gezeigt, dass die Definition unterschiedlicher Dynamikmodelle ausreicht, um auf Objektinformationen zu schließen und das Filterergebnis nachhaltig zu verbessern. Die implizite Gruppeninferenz stellt einen ersten Schritt zur Vereinigung von Objekt- und Zellebene dar.

1 Einleitung

Wie der Mensch, braucht auch ein Roboter ein Modell seiner Umwelt, um sich kollisionsfrei in ihr bewegen zu können. Sensoren liefern Hinweise auf den realen Zustand der Umgebung. Die Messungen können aber niemals vollständig, eindeutig und sicher sein. Für eine präzise Schätzung muss daher Hintergrundwissen über die Bewegung von Objekten mit den Messungen zu einer Umgebungsschätzung fusioniert werden.

Die herkömmliche Herangehensweise an diese Problematik – das Multi Object Tracking (MOT) – erfordert nicht nur die explizite Erkennung aller umliegenden Objekte, sondern auch die Zuordnung der unsicheren Sensordaten zu unsicheren Objektschätzungen [1]. Dieses Datenassoziationsproblem ist im allgemeinen Fall NP-hart. In [2] findet sich eine Zusammenfassung existierender Methoden zur Behandlung dieser Probleme.

Die Betrachtung der Umwelt als Zellfeld umgeht mit der Objektperspektive einhergehende Probleme. Neuere Ansätze wie z. B. das in [7] beschriebene BOFUM erlauben darüber hinaus das Schließen der Umgebungsdynamik ohne auf Geschwindigkeitsmessungen angewiesen zu sein. Der entscheidende Vorteil ist eine probabilistische und jederzeit vollständige, konservative Schätzung auch von bewegten Hindernissen und unabhängig von deren Typ und Anzahl bei konstanter Problemkomplexität.

Probabilistische Belegtheitskarten werden in der Robotik oft zur Beschreibung der Umgebung und Sensordatenfusion verwendet [5]. In ihrer einfachsten Form diskretisieren sie die Umwelt in ein zweidimensionales, äquidistantes Gitter. Jede Zelle des Gitters

---

[1] Bayesian Recursive Estimation for Cells handling Transition Knowledge

enthält Informationen über die Belegtheit. Diese sagt aus, ob sich ein Objekt innerhalb einer Zelle befindet oder nicht. Um die Komplexität niedrig zu halten, werden die einzelnen Zellen häufig als unabhängig betrachtet. Dies stellt für viele Anwendungen eine ausreichende Approximation der Umwelt dar. Bei der Wegplanung eines Roboters muss beispielsweise nur der Freiraum geschätzt werden. Belegheitskarten werden aufgrund ihrer einfachen Interpretation und Handhabbarkeit auch oft im Bereich der simultanen Lokalisierung und Kartografierung (SLAM) eingesetzt [10].

Diese einfache Darstellung funktioniert gut für statische Umgebungen, liefert aber im Falle von bewegten Szenen nur mäßige Ergbnisse. Um dieses Manko auszugleichen, wurden in den letzten Jahren verschiedene Erweiterungen vorgeschlagen [4] [3] [6] [9] [7]. Durch die Aufnahme von Geschwindigkeitsinformationen in den Zustandsraum, wird es möglich, die Bewegungen von Belegtheit vorher zu sagen. Die einzelnen Verfahren unterscheiden sich hauptsächlich in der Formulierung des Zustandsraums und den verwendeten Prozessmodellen. In [7] konnte gezeigt werden, dass die Verwendung von Hintergrundinformationen über die Straßeninfrastruktur die Genauigkeit der Schätzung maßgeblich verbessern kann. Die Prädiktion des BOFUM beachtete räumliche Unsicherheit im Bewegungsmodell und kann Belegtheit verfolgen, die sich nicht mit konstanter Geschwindigkeit bewegt. Das Konzept der Belegtheitserhaltung sowie die Verknüpfung der Belegtheit mehrerer Ausgangszellen über eine Oder-Relation erlauben eine physikalisch realistische Modellierung (vgl. [7]). Offene Probleme dieser Ansätze sind die Ungenauigkeit durch die Diskretisierung und die Abstraktion von der Objektzusammengehörigkeit.

Im Bereich des MOT kann die Verwendung von verschiedenen Bewegungsmodellen je nach Objekttyp und -Manöver die Prädiktion nachhaltig verbessern [8]. Diese Arbeit überträgt die Interacting Multiple Model (IMM) Idee auf die Zellperspektive.

2   Probabilistische Belegheitsfilterung mit Gruppen

2.1   Zellfeldrepräsentation

N: Menge aller n Zellindizes. Die Dimension des zweidimensionalen, quadratischen Feldes beträgt $\sqrt{n} \times \sqrt{n}$. $N = \{1, \ldots, n\}$

O: Vektor für die Belegtheit aller Zellen. Zellen, in denen sich ein oder mehrere Objekte befinden, gelten als „belegt" (*occ*) , freie Zellen als „nicht belegt" (*nocc*). Daraus ergibt sich die Menge der möglichen Belegheitszustande $\mathcal{O} = \{occ, nocc\}$.

V: Vektor für die Geschwindigkeiten $V_i = (\dot{x}_i, \dot{y}_i)$ in jeder Zelle. Die beiden Komponenten enthalten die Geschwindigkeiten als Zellen pro Zeitschritt Δt in X- sowie in Y-Richtung. $\mathcal{V} = \{\mathbb{Z} \times \mathbb{Z}\}$.

G: Vektor für den zugrunde liegenden Typ einer Zelle, der im Folgenden als „Gruppe" bezeichnet wird. In dieser Arbeit werden exemplarisch zwei Gruppen, nämlich Fußgänger und Fahrzeuge, modelliert : $\mathcal{G} = \{ped, car\}$.

T: Vektor für die Transition. $T_i = j$ drückt aus dass sich die Belegtheit der Zelle i im nächsten Zeitschritt in die Zielzelle j bewegen wird.

$$O = \begin{pmatrix} O_1 \\ \vdots \\ O_n \end{pmatrix} \in \mathcal{O}^n, V = \begin{pmatrix} V_1, \\ \vdots \\ V_n \end{pmatrix} \in \mathcal{V}^n, G = \begin{pmatrix} G_1, \\ \vdots \\ G_n \end{pmatrix} \in \mathcal{G}^n, T = \begin{pmatrix} T_1 \\ \vdots \\ T_n \end{pmatrix} \in N^n$$

X: Zusammengefasste Zustandsmatrix für alle Zellen zum Zeitpunkt t und $t-1$:
$X = (O, V, G)$ und $X^- = (O^-, V^-, G^-)$

R: Matrix, die für eine Gruppe beschreibt, ob ein Zellindex vom einem anderen aus erreichbar ist. $P(R_{a,c} = reach|G)$ ist die Wahrscheinlichkeit, mit der sich ein Objekt der Gruppe G von Zelle a zu Zelle c bewegen kann. $R \in \{reach, nreach\}^{n \times n}$

Z: Vektor mit Zellmessungen. In dieser Arbeit werden sensorbedingt nur Belegtheitsmessungen Z_O vorgenommen.
$Z = (Z_O, Z_V, Z_G), Z_O \in \mathcal{O}^n, Z_V \in \mathcal{V}^n, Z_G \in \mathcal{G}^n$

2.2 Dekomposition der Verbundwahrscheinlichkeit

Aus der Verbundwahrscheinlichkeit aller beteiligten Variablen lässt sich durch Marginalisierung der A-posteriori-Zustand des Zellfeldes berechnen. Der erste Schritt der Herleitung besteht darin, diese in definierbare Elemente zu faktorisieren. Im Folgenden wird die Dekomposition unter Ausnutzung von Unabhängigkeiten erläutert.

$$
\begin{aligned}
P(X, X^-, R, T, Z) &= P(X, X^-, R, T)P(Z|X, X^-, R, T) \\
&= P(X, X^-, R, T)P(Z|X) \\
&= \prod_{c \in N} \underbrace{P(X_c, X^-, R, T)}_{\text{Prädiktion}} \underbrace{P(Z_c|X_c)}_{\text{Korrektur}}
\end{aligned}
$$

$$
P(X_c, X^-, R, T) = \underbrace{P(X^-, R, T)}_{\text{Transitionsmodell}} \underbrace{P(X_c|X^-, R, T)}_{\text{Kombination von Belegtheit}}
$$

$P(X^-, R, T)$ beschreibt die Zusammenhänge zwischen dem Zustand der Zelle zum Zeitpunkt $t-1$ sowie der Erreichbarkeit und der Transition. Anschaulich werden hier die einzelnen voneinander unabhängigen Bewegungen der Belegtheit modelliert. Ob eine Zelle a priori belegt ist, hat keinen Einfluss auf die Transition.

$$
\begin{aligned}
P(X^-, R, T) &= P(O^-, V^-, G^-, R, T) \\
&= P(O^-)P(T, V^-, G^-, R) \\
&= \prod_{i \in N} P(O_i^-) \prod_{j \in N} P(T_j, V^-, G^-, R)
\end{aligned}
$$

Das eigentliche Prozessmodell beschreibt die Kombination von Zelltransitionen:

$$
\begin{aligned}
P(X_c|X^-, R, T) &= P(O_c|O^-, T)P(V_c, G_c|O^-, T, G^-) \\
&= P(O_c|O^-, T) \sum_{\hat{V}_c} P(V_c|\hat{V}_c, G_c)P(G_c|G^-, \hat{V}_c)P(\hat{V}_c|O^-, T)
\end{aligned}
$$

$P(\hat{V})$ ist die rauschfreie Geschwindigkeitsverteilung und stellt eine Zwischenstufe im Inferenzprozess der Geschwindigkeitsverteilung $P(V)$ dar. Die Unsicherheit im Bewegungsmodell wird durch eine Unsicherheit in der Beschleunigung modelliert und kommt erst beim Schließen von $P(\hat{V})$ auf $P(V)$ zum tragen (s. Abschnitt 2.3).

In die Transitionswahrscheinlichkeit $P(X^-, R, T)$ gehen nunmehr nicht nur die a priori Geschwindigkeit und Erreichbarkeit ein, sondern auch die Gruppe. Um zu gewährleisten, dass die Transitionswahrscheinlichkeitsverteilung $P(T_a)$ einer Zelle a in der Summe über alle möglichen Nachfolgerzellen m eins ergibt, wird der Normalisierungsfaktor μ eingesetzt. Diese Normierung sorgt anschaulich dafür, dass sich die gesamte Belegtheit einer Ausgangszelle auf ihre Nachfolgerzellen verteilt.

$$P(T_a = c, V^-, G^-, R) = \frac{P(T_a = c, V_a^-, G_a^-, R_{a,c})}{\sum_{m \in N} P(T_a = m, V_a^-, G_a^-, R_{a,m})}$$
$$= \mu_a \, P(V_a^-, G_a^-) P(R_{a,c}|G_a^-) P(T_a = c|V_a^-, R_{a,c})$$

Das sich ergebende Bayes'sche Netz ist in Abb. 1 zu sehen.

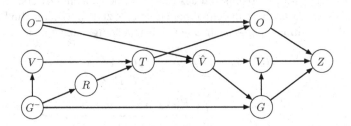

Abb. 1. Bayes'sches Netz des Belegheitsfilters

2.3   Modellierung der Gruppen

Ein Gros der Modellierungen bezüglich dem Verhalten von Belegtheit können aus [7] übernommen werden. Insbesondere das Messmodell bleibt unverändert, da angenommen wird, dass die Sensorik keine Erkennung von Objekttypen erlaubt. Es ergaben sich mehrere Abhängigkeiten zu den eingeführten Gruppen. Die Geschwindigkeitsinferenz in $P(X_c|X^-, R, T)$ wird durch die Gruppenzugehörigkeit beeinflusst, da die Beschleunigungsunsicherheit für Fahrzeuge größer angenommen wird als für Fußgänger. Der Zusammenhang zwischen v_c und $\hat{v}_c$ wird folgendermaßen modelliert:

$$v_c = \hat{v}_c + w_g \Delta t \quad \text{mit} \quad w_g \sim \mathcal{N}(0, \Sigma_g)$$

Das additive Rauschen w_g entspricht einer mittelwertfreien Normalverteilung mit gruppenspezifischer Kovarianz Σ_g. $P(V_c|\hat{V}_c, G_c)$ wird hierbei als Integral über die resultierende Normalverteilung mit Integrationsgrenzen entsprechend der Zelldiskretisierung berechnet.

Für das Schließen der Gruppen selbst wird in $P(G_c|\hat{V}_c, G_c^-)$ eine geringe Wechselwahrscheinlichkeit formuliert, welche sich bei hohen Geschwindigkeiten zugunsten von Fahrzeugen verschiebt.

In der Berechnung der Transition ergeben sich ebenfalls Neuerungen. Die Erreichbarkeit wird anhand der gegebenen Gruppe selektiert. Dies differenziert die Bewegungsmuster der Gruppen voneinander und stellt somit den entscheidenden Faktor für die Verbesserung der Prädiktion und Inferenz der Gruppenzugehörigkeitsinformation dar. $P(R_{a,c}|G_a^- = ped)$ erlaubt Fußgängern das Spazieren auf dem Gehweg und das Überqueren von Straßen. Dass sich Fußgänger entlang der Fahrbahn bewegen wird als unwahrscheinlich angenommen (vgl. Abb. 2a). Dies ist ein typisches Verhalten von Fahrzeugen und wird in $P(R_{a,c}|G_a^- = car)$ modelliert (vgl. Abb. 2b). Letztere verlassen außerdem selten die Straße und wenn sie dies, z. B. beim Einparken tun, beschreibt sie das Fußgängermodell besser. In den Abbildungen darunter sind die Auswirkungen zu sehen: Die als Fahrzeuge inferierten Zellen werden entlang der Straße und mit hoher Geschwindigkeit, der Fußgänger dagegen senkrecht zur Fahrbahn prädiziert.

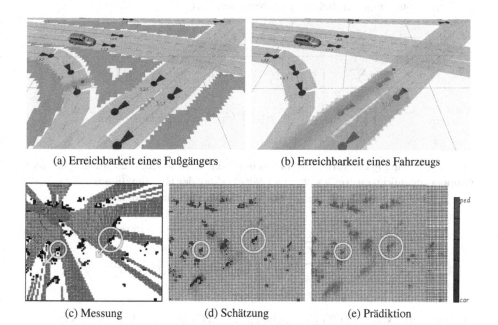

(a) Erreichbarkeit eines Fußgängers   (b) Erreichbarkeit eines Fahrzeugs

(c) Messung   (d) Schätzung   (e) Prädiktion

Abb. 2. Beispiel für die Erreichbarkeit von Zellen für verschiedene Gruppen und deren Auswirkung auf die Filterschätzung. Die Erreichbarkeit ist grün dargestellt. In der Messung sind der Fußgänger und das Fahrzeug, für das die Erreichbarkeit berechnet wurde, gekennzeichnet. Die geschätzten Gruppen sind farblich markiert.

2.4 Berechnung der Filtergleichungen

Die Berechnung des A-posteriori-Zustandes erfolgt durch Marginalisieren:

$$P(X_c|Z) = \frac{\sum_{X^-,R,T} P(X_c, X^-, R, T, Z)}{\sum_{X^-,R,T,X_c} P(X_c, X^-, R, T, Z)} \propto \sum_{X^-,R,T} P(X_c, X^-, R, T, Z)$$

Neben der Aufspaltung in *Prädiktion* und *Korrektur* kann die Berechnung des Transition freigestellt werden.

$$\sum_{O^-,V^-,G^-,R,T} P(X_c, X^-, R, T, Z) =$$

$$\underbrace{P(Z_c|O_c)}_{\text{Korrektur}} \underbrace{\sum_{O^-,V^-,G^-,R,T} \underbrace{P(V^-,G^-,R,T)}_{\text{Transitionsmodell}} P(O^-)P(O_c|O^-,T)P(V_c,G_c|O^-,T,G^-)}_{\text{Prädiktion}}$$

Die Transitionswahrscheinlichkeit wird berechnet über:

$$P(T=t) = \sum_{V^-,G^-,R} P(T=t,V^-,R,G^-) =$$

$$= \sum_{V^-,G^-,R} \prod_{i\in N} \mu_i P(V_i^-,G_i^-)P(R_{i,t_i}|G_i^-)P(T_i=t_i|V_i^-,R_{i,t_i})$$

$$= \prod_{i\in N_{G_i^-}} \mu_i P(V_i^- = v(i,t_i),G_i^-)P(R_{i,t_i} = reach|G_i^-)$$

Für die Berechnung der Verbundwahrscheinlichkeit von Zwischengeschwindigkeit und Gruppenzugehörigkeit ergibt sich, unter Verwendung der Hilfsfunktion $v : N \times N \to \mathbb{Z} \times \mathbb{Z}$ zur Umrechnung von Zellindices in Geschwindigkeiten, Folgendes:

$$P(\hat{V}_c = v(a,c), G_c = g) = \sum_{O^-,T,G^-} P(O^-)P(T)P(G_c|G^-,\hat{V}_c)P(\hat{V}_c = v(a,c)|O^-,T)$$

$$= \sum_{G_a^-} P(O_a^- = occ)P(T_a = c)P(G_c|G_a^-,\hat{V}_c)$$

Die endgültige Verteilung für Geschwindigkeit und Gruppe berechnet sich über:

$$P(V_c,G_c) = \sum_{\hat{V}_c} P(V_c|\hat{V}_c,G_c,)P(\hat{V}_c,G_c)$$

Die neue Belegtheit der Zellen wird von den Gruppen nur indirekt beeinflusst und kann weiterhin effizient über die Veroderung der Vorgängerzellen ermittelt werden:

$$P(O_c = occ) = 1 - \prod_{a\in N} [1 - P(O_a^- = occ)P(T_a = c)]$$

Die Erweiterung des Zustandsraums zieht keine fundamentalen Veränderungen der Modelle gegenüber dem BOFUM nach sich. Da die Bewegungsmodelle der Gruppen weitestgehend orthogonal gewählt wurden, müssen bei einer Monte-Carlo-Sampling Berechung nicht mehr Stichproben gezogen werden als beim BOFUM. Die Vergrößerung des Zustandsraums hat deshalb praktisch keine Auswirkungen auf die Rechenzeit.

3 Evaluierung

Zur Beurteilung der BOFUG-Schätzungen wurden Experimente in einer realen Straßenszene durchgeführt. Für die Messungen wurde eine 360°-Laserscanner (Velodyne HDL-64E) herangezogen (vgl. Abb. 3). Das Messfahrzeug fährt auf einer innerstädtischen, vierspurigen Straße (siehe Abb. 3d). Die Eigenbewegung über Grund ist durch eine IMU gekoppelt mit zwei DGPS-Sensoren bekannt und fließt in die Berechnung des BOFUG ein. Aus diesem Grund wird für statische Objekte, wie etwa geparkte Fahrzeuge oder Häuserfronten, die Geschwindigkeit $0\frac{m}{s}$ und nicht die Relativgeschwindigkeit inferiert. Aus den LIDAR-Daten wurde mit dem in [7] beschriebenen Verfahren die Belegtheitsmessung Z_O erzeugt. Geschwindigkeiten oder Gruppen können mit dem Sensor nicht gemessen werden und wurden somit nur durch das BOFUG inferiert.

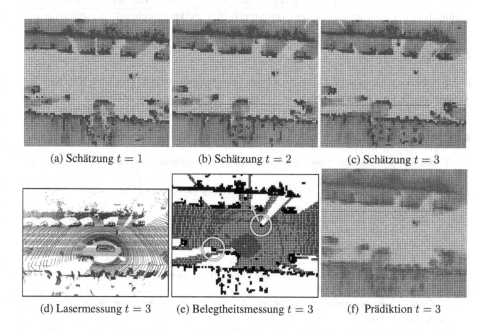

(a) Schätzung $t = 1$ (b) Schätzung $t = 2$ (c) Schätzung $t = 3$

(d) Lasermessung $t = 3$ (e) Belegtheitsmessung $t = 3$ (f) Prädiktion $t = 3$

Abb. 3. BOFUG-Ergebnisse für eine Straßenszene. In (a)–(c) ist das Ergebnis des Korrekturschritts relativ zum Messfahrzeug für die Zeitschritte $t = 1$ bis 3 dargestellt. Belegtheit der Gruppe *car* ist blau dargestellt, Belegtheit der Gruppe *ped* rot.

Bei den in Abbildung 3e markierten Objekten handelt es sich um einen Fahrradfahrer (links) und einen Fußgänger (rechts). Die Filterergebnisse werden relativ zum Messfahrzeug ausgegeben. Der Fahrradfahrer bewegt sich entlang der Fahrbahn. Die durch ihn verursachte Belegtheit wird deswegen der Gruppe *car* zugeordnet. Der Fußgänger überquert die Fahrbahn leicht schräg und wird deshalb der Gruppe *ped* zugeordnet. Obwohl sich beide Objekte auf der Straße befinden wird ihre Belegtheit aufgrund ihrer Bewegungshistorie korrekt klassifiziert.

4   Zusammenfassung und Ausblick

Zur Zustandsschätzung in dynamischen Umgebungen wurde ein Filter auf Basis erweiterter probabilistischer Belegheitskarten vorgestellt. Das BOFUG ergänzt den Zellzustandsraum des BOFUM aus [7] um Objektgruppeninformationen. Das erlaubt es die Belegtheit in Zellen einer zugrunde liegenden Objektgruppe zuzuordnen. Somit kann gruppenspezifisch prädiziert und die Schätzung präziser gestaltet werden. Die Gruppen unterscheiden sich nur in ihrem Bewegungsmodell. Die Schätzung der Gruppenzugehörigkeit erfolgt einzig aufgrund der Bewegungshistorie, da nur Messungen für die Zellbelegtheit und Karteninformationen gegeben sind. Im Rahmen eines Anwendungsszenarios aus dem Bereich der kognitiven Automobile wurden die Fähigkeiten des Verfahrens in mehreren Experimenten anhand realer Daten gezeigt.

Das beschriebene Verfahren stellt einen ersten Schritt zur Kombination von Objekt- und Zellebene dar. Ein Verfahren, das die Präzision eines MOT mit der Robustheit eines probabilistischen Belegtheitsgitters vereint eröffnet vielversprechende Perspektiven.

5   Danksagung

Diese Arbeit wurde von der Deutschen Forschungsgemeinschaft (DFG) im Rahmen des Sonderforschungsbereiches "SFB/TR-28 Kognitive Automobile" gefördert.

Literaturverzeichnis

1. Y. Bar-Shalom. Multitarget-multisensor tracking: Applications and advances. Volume III. *Norwood, MA: Artech House*, 2000.
2. S. Blackman and R. Popoli. *Design and analysis of modern tracking systems.* Norwood, MA: Artech House, 1999.
3. C. Chen, C. Tay, K. Mekhnacha, and C. Laugier. Dynamic environment modeling with gridmap: a multiple-object tracking application. *Control, Automation, Robotics and Vision, 2006. ICARCV'06. 9th International Conference on*, pages 1–6, 2006.
4. C. Coue, C. Pradalier, C. Laugier, T. Fraichard, and P. Bessiere. Bayesian Occupancy Filtering for Multitarget Tracking: An Automotive Application. *The International Journal of Robotics Research*, 25(1):19, 2006.
5. A. Elfes. Using occupancy grids for mobile robot perception and navigation. *Computer*, 22(6):46–57, 1989.
6. C. Fulgenzi, A. Spalanzani, and C. Laugier. Dynamic Obstacle Avoidance in uncertain environment combining PVOs and Occupancy Grid. *Robotics and Automation, 2007 IEEE International Conference on*, pages 1610–1616, 2007.
7. Tobias Gindele, Sebastian Brechtel, Joachim Schröder, and Rüdiger Dillmann. Bayesian Occupancy Grid Filter for Dynamic Environments Using Prior Map Knowledge. *Proceedings of the IEEE Intelligent Vehicles Symposium*, 2009.
8. E. Mazor, A. Averbuch, Y. Bar-Shalom, and J. Dayan. Interacting multiple model methods in target tracking: a survey. *Aerospace and Electronic Systems, IEEE Transactions on*, 34(1):103–123, 1998.
9. MK Tay, K. Mekhnacha, M. Yguel, C. Coué, C. Pradalier, C. Laugier, T. Fraichard, and P. Bessière. The Bayesian occupation filter. Technical report, INRIA, 2008.
10. S. Thrun, W. Burgard, and D. Fox. *Probabilistic Robotics (Intelligent Robotics and Autonomous Agents).* MIT press, Cambridge, Massachusetts, USA, 2005.

A Computational Model of Human Table Tennis for Robot Application

Katharina Mülling and Jan Peters

Max Planck Institute for Biological Cybernetics

Abstract. Table tennis is a difficult motor skill which requires all basic components of a general motor skill learning system. In order to get a step closer to such a generic approach to the automatic acquisition and refinement of table tennis, we study table tennis from a human motor control point of view. We make use of the basic models of discrete human movement phases, virtual hitting points, and the operational timing hypothesis. Using these components, we create a computational model which is aimed at reproducing human-like behavior. We verify the functionality of this model in a physically realistic simulation of a Barrett WAM.

1 Introduction

Human ability to perform as well as learn motor tasks has long awed researchers in robotics. On the other hand, insights into robotics have helped biologists and neuroscientists to understand how humans perform motor tasks. As a result, biomimetic approaches have become highly interesting for both communities. In this paper, we focus on modeling a specific human motor skill, i.e., Table Tennis, which has all basic components of a complex task: it requires accurate control, it is based on several elemental movements or motor primitives (e.g., different forehands and backhands), the goal functions based on perceptual context determine the behavior and even higher level strategies using opponent models can play a role. Thus, it is an ideal task to model human functionality and testing the resulting model in robotics. For robotics, it offers an understanding where the basic components need to be improved in order to create a general, human-like framework for skill representation and control.

In this paper, we will proceed as follows. Firstly we present our problem statement in Section 1.1 and briefly review previous work on robot ping-pong in Section 1.2. Secondly, we present relevant knowledge on modeling human table tennis in Section 2 so that we will be able to obtain a computational model of human table tennis in Section 3. In Section 4, we present the simulation of our real setup and show that the proposed model works well in simulation. In Section 5, we discuss the lessons for motor skill learning in robotics which can be concluded from this framework.

1.1 What Can We Learn from Human Table Tennis?

While current robots rely heavily on high-gain feedback, are not backdrivable and rely on well-modeled environments in order to perform simple motor skills, humans are able to perform complex skills relying on little feedback with long latencies, inaccurate sensory information, and are very compliant. It is clear that many of the properties which humans exhibit are essential for the safe operation of future robots in human inhabited environments. Understanding how humans perform a complex game such as table tennis can yield essential lessons for skill execution and learning in robotics. For such quick and forceful movements as required in table tennis, the human central nervous system has little time to process feedback about the environment and has to rely largely on feedforward components [18] such as accurate task models as well as predictions on the opponent and the environment (i.e., ball, net and table).

It is our goal to build a model of human table tennis which verifies that a concert of known hypotheses on the human motor control in striking sports will in fact yield a viable player and, thus, reconfirming these independent studies.

1.2 A Review of Robot Table Tennis

Table tennis has long fascinated roboticists as a particularly difficult task. Work on robot Ping Pong started with robot table tennis competitions initiated by Billingsley in 1983 [3]. Several early systems were presented by Hartley [7], Hashimoto [8] and others. Early results were often discouraging as fast vision methods were a major bottleneck.

A major breakthrough was achieved in 1988 by Andersson [2] at AT&T Bell Laboratories who presented the first robot ping pong player capable to play against humans and machines. Andersson used the simplified robot table tennis rules suggested by Billingsley.[1] His achievement was made possible by designing a high-speed video system and by elongating a 6 DoF PUMA 260 arm with a stick. He implemented an expert system controller which chooses the strategy as a response to the incoming ping pong ball and employs an exception handling algorithm for special cases. In 1993, the last robot table tennis competitions took place and was won by Fassler et al. [6] of the Swiss Federal Institute of Technology. Nevertheless, interest in robot table tennis did not wane and a series of groups has pursued the shortcomings exhibited by the competitions. Acosta et al. [1] constructed a low-cost robot showing that a two-paddle can already suffice for playing if the paddles only reflect the ball at the right angle. Miyazaki et al. [13,12] were able to show that a slow 4 DoF robot system consisting of two linear axes and a 2 DoF pan-tilt unit suffices for basic table tennis can fully suffice if the right predictive mappings are learned. They employ locally weighted regression (LWR) to predict the impact point and time given the speed and position of the ball as well as an inverse mapping to determine where the racket should be in order to move the ball to a pre-specified position.

In this paper we describe the construction of a robot ping pong player with seven degrees of freedom that is cabable of returning a ball on a human sized table served by a ping pong launcher. We concentrate on modeling the system after human table tennis with a strong focus on prediction while we make use of an anthropomorphic arm. The later requires task appropriate redundancy solution as full table tennis requires only 5 DoFs [2] but using all 7 can lead to significant speed advantages.

---

[1] In contrast to human ping pong rules, the table is only 0.5 m in width and 2 m in length. The net has a high of 0.25 m. Wire frames were attached at each end of the table and the net where the ball has to pass this frame to be a valid shoot.

2   Modelling Human Table Tennis

In the following part of the paper, we are going to present background on modeling table tennis from a striking sports perspective. In particular, we will focus on movement phases, movement selection and parametrization as well as movement generation.

2.1   Movement Phases

Table Tennis exhibits a very regular, modular structure which was studied by Ramant-soa and Durey [14]. They analysed a top player and proposed a spatial adjustment with reference to certain ball events (bouncing, net crossing and stroke). According to Ra-mantsoa, the following four stages can be distinguished during playing of expert players and, to make them more understandable, we named them according to their function:

Awaiting Stage. The ball is moving towards the opponent who hits it back towards the net. In order to prepare during this stage, the racket is moving downwards. At the end of this phase the racket will be in a plane parallel to the table surface.

Preparation Stage. The ball is coming towards the player, has already passed the net and will hit the table during this stage. The racket is moving backwards in order to prepare to strike.

Hitting Stage. The ball is moving towards the point where the player intercepts it. The racket is moving towards the ball until he hits it in a circular movement. For expert players the duration of this phase is constant and lasts exactly 80 ms.

Finishing Stage. After having been hit, the ball is on the return path to the opponent while the racket is moving upwards to a stopping position.

Furthermore they suggested that a virtual hitting point that is the point where the racket intercepts the ball in space and time is chosen in the beginning of the hitting stage.

2.2   Movement Primitive Selection and Parametrization

As humans appear to rely on motor programs or motor primitives [15], it is likely that pre-structured movement commands are employed for each of these four stages. For this a motor primitive needs to be chosen based upon the environmental stimuli at the beginning of each stage.

Motor primitives determine the order and timing of the muscles contraction and, by doing so, define the shape of the action produced. Sensory information can modify motor primitives to generate rapid corrections in the case of changing environmental demands as found in table tennis by Bootsma and van Wiering [4]. The system is only altering the parameters of the movement such as movement duration, movement ampli-tude or the final goal position of the movement [15]. In Table Tennis, the expert players show very consistent stroke movements with very little variation over trials [9,17] in-dicating that motor primitives could be used. The experiments of Tildesley and Whiting supported a consistent spatial and temporal movement pattern of expert players in table tennis. They concluded that a professional player just have to choose a movement pri-mitive for which the execution time is known from their repertoire and to decide when to initiate the drive. This hypothesis is known as operational timing hypothesis [17].

The problem of what information is used to decide when to initiate the movement. Most likely we use the so called *time to contact* that is the time until an object reaches the observer to control the timing. Lee [11] suggested that we determine the time to contact by an optic variable *tau* that is specified as the inverse of the relative rate of dilation of retinal image of an object. Using the operational timing hypothesis we have just to initiate the chosen movement primitive when tau reaches a critical value.

2.3 Movement Generation

Assuming that movement phases, selection and initiation are known, we need to discuss how the different strokes are generated. There are infinitely many ways to generate racket trajectories and, due to redundancies, there also exist many different ways to execute the same task-space trajectory in joint-space. In order to find generative principles underlying the movement generation, neuroscientists often turn to optimal control [16]. One approach is the use of cost functions which allow the computation of trajectory formation for arm movements. Most focus primarily on reaching and pointing movements where one can observe a bell-shape velocity curve and a clear relationship between movement duration and amplitude. However, this does not hold for striking sports. The cost function for the control of the human arm movement suggested by Cruse et al. [5] is based on the comfort of the posture. For each joint, the cost is induced by proximity to a rest joint position, i.e., a function has a minimum at the angles close to the rest posture and increases with the extreme angles. For movement generation, the sum of all comfort values is minimized. We employ this cost function in Section 3.3.

3   Computational Realization of the Model

In this section, we will discuss how the steps presented in Section 2 can be implemented using a physical model as replacement for the learned components of a human counterpart. For doing so, we proceed as follows: first, we discuss all required components in an overview. Subsequently, we discuss how the the details of the goal determination can be realized in Section 3.2 and how the movements need to be generated in order to be executable on a robot in Sections 3.3.

3.1   Overview

We assume the movement phases of the model by Ramanantsoa et al. [14] and use a finite state automaton to represent this model. In order to realize each of these four stages, the system has to detect the presence of the ball and sense its position p_b. Due to noise in the vision processing, the system needs to filter this position.

Movement goal determination is the most complex part to realize. While desired final joint configurations suffice for the awaiting, preparation and finishing stages, the hitting stage requires a well-chosen movement goal. For doing so, the system has to first choose a point on the court of the opponent where the ball should be returned. Similarly, making use of Ramanantsoas [14] virtual hitting point hypothesis, the hitting point p_e can be determined by the location where the ball hits the robots task space. Based on the choice of this point, the necessary batting position, orientation and velocity of the racket are chosen as goal parameters for the hitting movement. More details of the computations involved are given in Section 3.2.

Movement initiation is triggered in accordance to the movement phases and using the movement goals, i.e., the time of the predicted ball intersecting the virtual hitting point p_e is less than a threshold t_e before hitting, the hitting movement is initiated. This step requires the system to predict when the ball is going to reach the virtual hitting plane in the workspace of the robot and the current time to hit can be determined by predicting the trajectory of the ball using a Kalman predictor [10] with exception handling for ball collision. Following [4] suggestion that some online adaptation of the movement can take place, we update the virtual hitting point if its estimate changes drastically, e.g., if the difference between the estimates exceeds a threshold d.

For the movement program determination we use a spline-based trajectory representation. More details of these computations are given in Section 3.3.

3.2   Determining the Goal Parameters

After determining the virtual hitting point, the system can freely choose the height z_{net} at which the returning ball passes the net as well as the positions x_b, y_b where the ball will bounce on the opponents courts. The choice of these three variables belongs to the higher level functions and is not covered in this model, we instead draw from a distribution of plausible values. As goal parameters, we have to first calculate the desired outgoing vector O of the ball which should result from the movement, and, directly from it, we can determine the rackets velocity and orientation.

Desired outgoing vector. Assuming little air resistance, one obtains the straightforward relationship $\dot{x}_o = x_{net}/t_{net} = x_b/t_b$ between the speeds at the net at location x_{net} and at the bouncing point on the opponent court at time t_b. From this, the linear relationship $t_{net} = \alpha t_b$ with $\alpha = x_{net}/x_b$ can be obtained. As the height of the ball after hitting is governed by the equation $z = z_o + \dot{z}_o t - 0.5g \cdot t^2$, inserting and solving for t_b will yield the time of impact

$$t_b = \frac{\sqrt{h_n - 2(\alpha - 1)2gz_o}}{\alpha(\alpha - 1)}. \tag{1}$$

Given the time t_b, we can now calculate the components of the desired outgoing velocity vector of the ball by $\dot{z}_o = 0.5gt_b^2 - z_o/t_b$, $\dot{x}_o = x_b/t_b$ and $\dot{y}_o = y_b/t_b$.

Racket goal orientation. Now it is possible to calculate the orientation of the racket and the end-effector. The attitude of the racket is determined through the normal of the racket. If we assume only a speed change $O - I$ in normal direction n_r, we obtain

$$O - I = n_r(O_{||} - I_{||}) \tag{2}$$

where $O_{||}$ and $I_{||}$ denote the component of O and I, respectively, which is parallel to the normal. Note, that $\|O - I\| = O_{||} - I_{||}$. In order to compute the orientation of the end-effector, we need to proceed in three steps. First, we calculate a quaternion $q_{rd} = (\cos(\theta/2), u\sin(\theta/2))$ with $\theta = n_e^T n_{rd}/(\|n_e\|\|n_{rd}\|)$ and $u = n_e \times n_r/\|n_e \times n_r\|$ to transform the normal of the endeffector n_e to the racket n_r. Second, we multiply the conjungate of the quaternion of the rotation $q_{rot} = (\cos(-\pi/4), u_2 \sin(-\pi/4))$ (where

u_2 denotes the unit vector) from endeffector to racket to get the quaternion $q_{hd'}$. The resulting quaternion of the hand q_{hd} is then determined through $q_{hd} = q_{rot\_rd} \times q_{hd'}$. As there exist infinitely many racket orientations which have the same racket normal, we need to determine the final orientation depending on a preferential end-effector position. For this purpose the orientation of the endeffector is rotated around the normal of the racket. The orientation whose corresponding joint values yield the minimum distance to the comfort position is used as a desired racket orientation.

Required racket velocity. In the next step, we calculate the velocity vector for the end-effector at the time of the ball interception. As $-I_{\parallel}, O_{\parallel} > 0$, and $-I_{\parallel} - O_{\parallel} \neq 0$ we can solve for $O_{\parallel}$ and obtain

$$O_{\parallel} = -\varepsilon_R I_{\parallel} + (1 + \varepsilon_R)v \tag{3}$$

where ε_R denotes the coefficient of restitution of the racket and v the speed of the racket. Note, we assume that $O_{\parallel}$, $-I_{\parallel}$ and v all have the same direction. Equation (3) can be solved for v yielding the desired output velocity $O = I + n_r[(1 + \varepsilon_R)v - (1 + \varepsilon_R)I_{\parallel}]$.

3.3   Trajectory Generation

For the execution of the movements, we need a representation which yields position $q(t)$, velocity $\dot{q}(t)$ and accelerations $\ddot{q}(t)$ of the joints of the manipulator at each point in time t so that it can be executed based on feedforward inverse dynamics models. Based on the four stage model of Durey et al. [14], we can determine for different spline phases consisting splines interpolating between fixed initial and final positions.

We are planning our trajectory in joint space as high velocity movements can be executed better than in the workspace.

To compute the arm trajectory, we have to specify an initial joint configuration $q_i = q(0)$, the initial joint velocity $\dot{q}_i = \dot{q}(0)$, the initial acceleration $\ddot{q}_i = \ddot{q}(0)$, the final position $q_f = q(t_f)$, the final velocity $\dot{q}_f = \dot{q}(t_f)$, the final acceleration $\ddot{q}_f = \ddot{q}(t_f)$ and the duration of the movement t_f. We used fifth order polynomial $q = \sum_{j=0}^{5} a_j t^j$ to represent the trajectory for all phases as it is the minimal sufficient representation, generates very smooth trajectories and can evaluated fast and easily. The trajectories of the hitting and finishing stages are calculated at the beginning of the hitting phase and are recalculated every time the the virtual hitting point has to be updated.

The joint space position of the virtual hitting point is determined using inverse kinematics. The inverse kinematics calculations for the redundant are performed numerically by minimizing the distance to the comfort posture in joint space while finding the racket position & orientation which coincides with the desired posture.

4   Evaluations

In this section, we demonstrate that this model of human table tennis can be used effectively for robot table tennis in a ball gun setup. For this propose, we will first present the simulated setup of the robot table tennis task and discuss its physically realistic simulation using the SL framework (developed by Stefan Schaal at Univ. of Southern California) including a realistic simulation of a Barrett WAM. We show the resulting end-effector trajectories and discuss the accuracy of the system in striking a ball such that it hits a desired point.

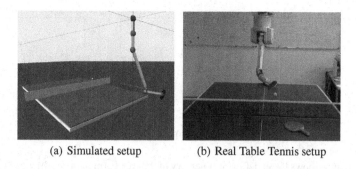

(a) Simulated setup   (b) Real Table Tennis setup

Fig. 1. This figure shows the Barrett WAM arm used for evaluation.

4.1 Simulated Setup

In Figure 1 (a), the simulated environment of the table tennis task is illustrated together with the physical setup in Figure 1 (b). We employ a simulated Barrett WAM^{TM} arm with seven degrees of freedom that is capable of high speed motion. A racket with 16 cm in diameter is attached to the endeffector. The robot arm interacts with a human sized table and a table tennis ball according to the international rules of table tennis. The ball is served randomly with a ping pong ball launcher to the forehand of the robot. That effects an area of 1.24 by 0.7 meters. For this purpose, we have defined a virtual plane which the ball has to pass. The virtual hitting point is determined as the intersection point of the ball and the virtual hitting plane. The ball is visually tracked by using vision system with a sampling rate of 60 frames per second.

4.2 Performance of the Model

The table tennis system is capable of returning an incoming volley to the opponents court which was served randomly by a robot ball launcher. In an evaluation setup with 10 000 random trials, the system was able to return 98,5 % of the balls. In 70 % the ball was returned successfully to the opponent court. The mean deviation of the position of the racket mid point to the ball at the moment of contact is 1.8 cm. This result could be futher increased by optimizing the trajectory generation in joint space. Figure 2 shows the endeffector trajectory of one stroke beginning and ending in the Awaiting Stage.

5 Conclusion

Using the body of knowledge on human table tennis, we have formed a phenomenological model of human table tennis. This model is realized in a computational form using analytical counterparts. We show that the resulting computational model can be used as an explicit policy for returning incoming table tennis balls to a desired point of the opponents court in a physically realistic simulation with a redundant seven degree of freedom Barrett WAM arm. The biological model with its four stages of the table tennis stroke and the the goal parametrization using virtual hitting points and pre-shaping of the orientation has proven successful in operation. In tests, the robot could return 73 % of the balls served by the ping pong ball launcher.

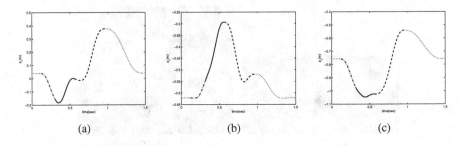

(a)   (b)   (c)

Fig. 2. This figure shows the endeffector trajectory of the robot arm in (a) x , (b) y and (c) z direction. The distinct phases are marked as follows, the Awaiting Stage dotted line, the Preparation Stage dash-dot line, the Hitting Stage solid line and the Finishing Stage dashed line.

References

1. L. Acosta, J.J. Rodrigo, J.A. Mendez, G.N. Marchial, and M. Sigut. Ping-pong player prototype. *Robotics and Automation magazine*, 10:44–52, december 2003.
2. R.L. Andersson. *A robot ping-pong player: experiment in real-time intelligent control.* 1988.
3. J. Billingsley. Robot ping pong. *Practical Computing*, May 1983.
4. R.J. Bootsma and P.C.W. van Wieringen. Timing an attacking forehand drive in table tennis. *Journal of Experimental Psychology: Human Perception and Performance*, 16:21–29, 1990.
5. H. Cruse, M. Brüwer, P. Brockfeld, and A. Dress. On the cost functions for the control of the human arm movement. *Biological Cybernetics*, 62:519–528, 1990.
6. H. Fassler, H.A. Vasteras, and J.W. Zurich. A robot ping pong player: optimized mechanics, high performance 3d vision, and intelligent sensor control. *Robotersysteme*, 1990.
7. J. Hartley. Toshiba porgress towards sensory control in real time. *The Industrial robot*, 14-1:50–52, 1987.
8. H. Hashimoto, F. Ozaki, K. Asano, and K. Osuka. Development of a ping pong robot system using 7 degrees of freedom direct drive. *Industrial applications of Rootics and machine vision*, pages 608–615, November 1987.
9. A.W. Hubbard and C.N. Seng. Visual movements of batters. *Research Quaterly*, 25, 1954.
10. R.E. Kalman. A new approach to linear filtering and prediction problems. *Transactions of the ASME–Journal of Basic Engineering*, 82(Series D):35–45, 1960.
11. D.N. Lee and D.S. Young. *Visual timing of interceptive action*, pages pp. 1–30. Dordrecht, Netherlads: Martinus Nijhoff, 1985.
12. M. Matsushima, T. Hashimoto, M. Takeuchi, and F. Miyazaki. A learning approach to robotic table tennis. *IEEE Trans. on Robotics*, 21:767 – 771, August 2005.
13. F. Miyazaki, M. Matsushima, and M. Takeuchi. Learning to dynamically manipulate: A table tennis robot controls a ball and rallies with a human being. In *Advances in Robot Control*. Springer, 2005.
14. M. Ramanantsoa and A. Durey. Towards a stroke contruction model. *International Journal of Table Tennis Science*, 2:97–114, 1994.
15. R.A. Schmidt and C.A. Wrisberg. *Motor Learning and Performance.* Human Kinetics, second edition, 2000.
16. E. Todorov. Optimality principles im sensorimotor control. *Nature Neuroscience*, 7, 2004.
17. D.A. Tyldesley and H.T.A. Whiting. Operational timing. *Journal of Human Movement Studies*, 1:172–177, 1975.
18. D. Wolpert, C. Miall, and M. Kawato. Internal models in the cerebellum. *Trends in Cognitive Science*, 2, 1998.

A Vision-Based Trajectory Controller for Autonomous Cleaning Robots

Lorenz Gerstmayr[1,2], Frank Röben[1], Martin Krzykawski[1],
Sven Kreft[1], Daniel Venjakob[1] and Ralf Möller[1,2]

[1] AG Technische Informatik, Technische Fakultät, Universität Bielefeld
[2] Exzellenzcluster Cognitive Interaction Technology, Universität Bielefeld

Abstract. Autonomous cleaning robots should completely cover the accessible area with minimal repeated coverage. We present a mostly vision-based navigation strategy for systematical exploration of an area with meandering lanes. The results of the robot experiments show that our approach can guide the robot along parallel lanes while achieving a good coverage with only a small proportion of repeated coverage. The proposed method can be used as a building block for more elaborated navigation strategies which allow the robot to systematically clean rooms with a complex workspace shape.

1 Introduction

Autonomous cleaning robots are supposed to completely cover the whole accessible area. Due to the limited battery power it is important to keep the proportion of repeated coverage as small as possible. How this objective is achieved depends on whether the robot was designed to operate in large buildings or in a domestic environment [1,2].

Robots for large buildings are large and heavy-weight machines which can carry a considerable payload and are usually equipped with strong batteries, large computational power, and sophisticated sensor systems [1,2]. For path planning, complete coverage path planning methods [3] can be used. These methods are computationally demanding and — although some online methods exist [4,5] — usually require the footprint of the workspace to be known beforehand.

In order to clean an apartment, domestic cleaning robots need to be small and agile [2]. Their price should be comparable to the price of a standard vacuum cleaner. For this reason, domestic cleaning robots can only be equipped with little battery power, low computational power, and a small number of cheap sensors. Currently available cleaning robots use a mixture of pre-programmed movement patterns and random walk strategies for navigation [2]. With their limited sensor equipment they cannot build up a representation of the environment. Therefore, they cannot localize in the environment and cannot distinguish between places which have already been cleaned and places which still need to be cleaned. However, these abilities are necessary to systematically cover the robot's workspace.

In this paper, we describe a vision-based controller for the systematic exploration of an area by meandering lanes. The method is in line with the computational power of an embedded system and is based on local visual homing and on topological maps, two concepts from the field of biologically-inspired visual navigation. These concepts are introduced in Sec. 2. The proposed controller is described in Sec. 3; real robot experiments are presented in Sec. 4. In Sec. 5, the paper is summarized, and future working directions are pointed out.

2   Biologically Inspired Visual Navigation

2.1   Local Visual Homing

Local visual homing is the ability of a robot to return to a previously visited place under visual control [6,7]. Most visual homing methods are inspired by the snapshot hypothesis of insect navigation [8,9]: Homing can be achieved by bringing the currently perceived camera image (referred to as current view, CV) into accordance with an image previously stored at the home position (referred to as snapshot, SS). By comparing current view and snapshot, a movement direction (represented by the home vector) is computed, which guides the robot closer towards the goal position. Due to erroneous estimates, the home vector has to be iteratively recomputed until the agent reaches its goal. Homing methods can also be used to take the bearing of a snapshot w.r.t. the robot's current position without approaching the snapshot localization. Thus, previously visited places can be used as landmarks. The trajectory controller presented in this paper uses this type of landmark reference.

Local visual homing methods can be classified depending on how they process the visual information to derive the home direction [10]: Correspondence methods (e.g. [11]) explicitly solve the correspondence problem between image features whereas holistic methods use the image as a whole. From the class of holistic homing methods, the warping methods have shown to be both accurate and robust. Originally developed for 1D images taken along the horizon [12], the method was recently extended to operate on 2D images [13,14].

Depending on a set of movement parameters (distance, direction, change of orientation), all warping methods pre-compute the views the agent would perceive if it moved according to the considered movement parameters (warp views). The resulting warp views are compared to the snapshot, and the movement parameters resulting in the best match are used to determine the home vector. The time-consuming computation of the warp views can be circumvented by pre-computing image distances for all possible pairings of columns in the current view and the snapshot (distance image). Each combination of movement parameters defines which columns from current view and snapshot have to be matched (warp curve); thus, the overall image distance can be computed by accumulating the columnwise distances stored in the distance image along the warp curve. In order to compensate for scale changes, distance images are computed for several scale levels. For the experiments of this paper, a variant of 2D warping (min-warping, [14]) is used which eliminates the equal landmark-distance assumption inherent to earlier warping methods [12,13]. The main advantage of warping methods is that they do not require snapshot and current view to be aligned w.r.t. a common reference direction as it is the case for many other homing methods (e.g. methods based on local optical flow [11]). As a consequence, warping methods also provide an estimate of the relative orientation between current view and snapshot (compass estimate).

The advantage of local visual homing is that an accurate measurement of the bearing of the snapshot location is possible even with small images (here only 335×40 pixels). Due to the size of the images our algorithms are computationally cheap and can be implemented on the onboard hardware of a domestic cleaning robot. The main limitation of local visual homing methods is most of the image features characterizing the snapshot position have to be visible in order to return to this position [6,7].

2.2 Topological Navigation

Long-range navigation capabilities can be achieved by integrating several snapshots into a topological map [7]. A topological map (Fig. 1) is a sparse representation of the environment: Places are represented by vertices annotated with sensory information (e.g. snapshots), and edges link places that can be directly reached from each other [15]. For navigation from place to place, local visual homing methods are used; for path planning, standard graph algorithms can be applied. In a purely topological map, no metrical information is considered. Our method only stores the distance between subsequent snapshot localizations. In the trajectory controller described in Sec. 3, the snapshots associated with vertices on a straight lane are used to drive the next lane parallel to the previous one.

Topological maps differ from standard simultaneous localization and mapping (SLAM) approaches [16,17] as they (i) characterize places by sensory information and not by a metrical position, (ii) use snapshot images taken at former robot positions as landmarks instead of features detected in the environment, and (iii) do not update the landmark position whereas SLAM approaches update the landmark's position according to the estimate of the robot's position.

3 Trajectory Controller

In this section, we describe a trajectory controller for covering an area by meandering parallel lanes [18,19]; long-range navigation capabilities are obtained by building a topological map. While the robot is moving (Fig. 2), snapshots are successively added to the map every 10 cm. At the end of each straight lane (when an obstacle is encountered or after traveling a fixed distance), the robot turns by 90°, moves forward for a short distance (in our case 30 cm), turns again by 90°, and starts a new lane. The inter-lane distance should be chosen to be the width of the robot's cleaning unit in order to achieve optimal coverage. The

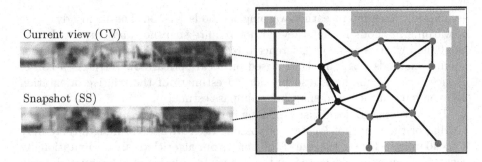

Fig. 1. Topological mapping and local visual homing: A topological map is a graph-like representation. Places are characterized by sensory information (here snapshot images) attached to vertices (dots); edges (lines) connect places which are reachable from each other. For navigation from place to place, local visual homing (Sec. 2.1) can be used. Homing methods compute a vector (arrow) pointing from the robot's current position (represented by the current view) to its goal position (represented by the snapshot).

first lane can be kept straight by wall following or by taking the bearing of a visual feature.

From the second lane on, the proposed controller keeps the robot on a trajectory parallel to the previous lane. In order to control the robot's distance to the previous lane, the bearings α_1 and α_2 of two snapshots SS_1 and SS_2 along the previous lane are taken by visual homing. The two home angles α_1, α_2 and the distance d between the snapshots (measured by the robot's odometry) uniquely specify a triangle. The triangle's height h is used as an estimate for the robot's current distance to the previous lane. This approximation is valid as long as the robot moves along a straight line between the two considered snapshots. If the robot does not move along a straight line or in case of erroneous home vectors, the estimate h deviates from the true distance to the previous lane. In order to obtain a more reliable estimate, several triangles (with identical current view and different snapshot pairings along the previous lane) are used. As an estimate h for the robot's current distance to the previous lane, the median height of all considered triangles is used. Based on the deviation e of h from the desired inter-lane distance, a movement vector m is computed which minimizes the deviation e from the desired inter-lane distance. This procedure is repeated for each current view. These images are also added as snapshots to the topological map and are later used by the controller to adjust the distance of the next lane.

4   Experiments

4.1   Setup

Experiments were performed with a custom-built differential drive robot (Fig. 3 left). With a diameter of 33 cm and a height of 9 cm, its dimensions are comparable to commercially available cleaning robots. As an omnidirectional vision

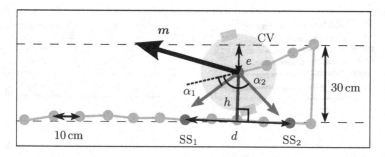

Fig. 2. Proposed trajectory controller to keep the robot on a lane parallel to the previous one. For details see text.

Fig. 3. Left: Custom-built cleaning robot with omnidirectional vision sensor (center) and tracking target (colored disc on top). Middle and Right: Footprint of our lab (furniture depicted in light gray) with ideal lanes (white) and ideal covered areas (dark gray) of experiments 1 (middle) and 2 (right).

sensor, a panoramic annular lens [20] (Tateyama, PAL S25G 3817-27C) is used. Compared to standard catadioptric sensors, the used panoramic annular lens is more compact and only sticking out of the robot by approximately 3 cm which is important while cleaning underneath low furniture such as beds. For wall following, the robot is equipped with IR sensors (Sharp, GP2D120).

In order to analyze the robot experiments, a custom-built visual tracking system is used. On top of the robot, a red disk (not visible in the robot's camera image) is mounted. The robot's workspace is observed by three static cameras. The red disk is detected in each of the camera images, and from its center of gravity, an estimate for the robot's world position is computed by direct linear transformation [21]. The estimates of all cameras are fused by a weighted average depending on the agent's distance to the camera. The resulting tracking accuracy is approximately 1 cm. This position estimate is used solely for data evaluation and not for the trajectory controller of the robot.

In order to assess the quality of the proposed controller, we ran experiments from two different start positions in our lab (Fig. 3, middle and right). For each start position, a total of 10 trials were recorded. In order to keep the first lane straight, wall following along an artificial wall of 7 cm height was used as our lab does not offer a free wall of such length. The robot's motion controller

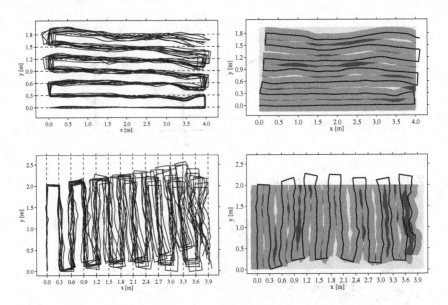

Fig. 4. Results of experiments 1 (upper row) and 2 (lower row). The left column shows the trajectories of all the trials, the right column shows the result of the coverage analysis for a representative run (white: not considered as outside ideally cleaned area; light gray: uncleaned areas; medium gray: areas covered exactly once; dark gray: overlap between consecutive lanes; black lines: trajectories).

was disturbed by a systematical error of 10% which simulates differences in the diameters of the robot's wheels; in order to keep the robot parallel to the previous lane, the controller has to compensate for this error. As the robot's onboard odometry is able to measure this disturbance, a simulated odometry based on undisturbed wheel velocities is used to measure the distance between the snapshots. For each start position, half of the trials were performed with a systematical error resulting in a trajectory curved to the left; for the other half the disturbance caused a curve to the right. Experiment 1 consisted of seven lanes each of 4 m length; experiment 2 consisted of 14 lanes with a lane length of 2 m. In both experiments, the robot was moving with 5 cm/s, and the inter-lane distance was 30 cm.

4.2   Results

The trajectories resulting from experiments 1 and 2 are shown in the left column of Fig. 4. For up to five lanes, consecutive lanes are clearly separated and show only little deviation from the ideal trajectory. With increasing number of lanes, the trajectories deviate stronger from the ideal trajectories. This deviation is due to accumulating errors: Since the controller keeps the robot on a course parallel to the previous lane, the robot also follows the oscillations of the previous lane. Due to additional controller errors on the current lane, these deviations accumulate over time. Nevertheless, consecutive lanes of one trial do not cross each other even for ten or more lanes.

To assess the quality of the resulting cleaning trajectories, we analyzed the covered area. For this purpose, a simulated cleaning unit of 5 cm length and 30 cm width was moved along the robot's trajectory and we computed the area covered exactly once, the overlap between consecutive lanes, and the uncovered area. All percentages are measured w.r.t. the area covered by an ideal cleaning run; lane changes are ignored. Thus, a perfect trial would yield 100.0 % coverage, 0.0 % overlap (repeated coverage), and 0.0 % uncovered area. The right column of Fig. 4 shows the result for an example trial of experiment 1 and 2, respectively. With increasing lane number, the gaps or the overlap between consecutive lanes increase. Averaged over all 10 trials of experiment 1, the coverage is 86.4 %, the overlap is 6.5 %, and the uncovered area is 7.4 %. For experiment 2, we obtained a mean coverage of 75.2 %, a mean overlap of 8.9 %, and a mean uncovered area of 15.9 %.

4.3   Discussion

The results show that the proposed controller is capable of guiding the robot along parallel lanes while achieving good coverage of the robot's workspace with only small overlap and a small proportion of uncleaned area. The main limitation are oscillating deviations from the desired lane which accumulate over time: As the method is purely topological and does not provide any metrical position estimate, the robot's desired trajectory solely depends on the previous lane. We do not think that this drawback limits the applicability of our method: As real apartments are usually more cluttered, the area which can be covered by parallel lanes is often much smaller than in the presented experiments.

5   Summary and Outlook

In this paper, we presented a mostly vision-based navigation strategy which guides the robot along meandering trajectories. The method achieves a good coverage of the accessible area with only a small proportion of overlap or gaps between consecutive lanes. As the controller relies on concepts from the field of biologically-inspired visual navigation (local visual homing and topological maps) it is in line with the computational power of embedded systems. Although we see the greatest benefit of the method in the field of domestic cleaning robots, it can also be applied to cleaning of large buildings or to outdoor applications such as lawn mowing or demining.

As the proposed method is only capable to cover a rectangular area, we are currently developing further strategies which allow the robot to systematically clean an entire apartment. This requires obstacle detection and avoidance, detection of areas which need to be cleaned, and path planning for approaching uncleaned regions or the charging station. Further working directions include topological mapping with metrical position estimates provided by a Kalman-filter framework [22].

References

1. Prassler, E., Ritter, A., Schaeffer, C., Fiorini, P.: A short history of cleaning robots. Autonomous Robots **9** (2000) 211–226
2. Prassler, E., Kosuge, K.: Domestic Robotics. In: Springer Handbook of Robotics. Springer (2008) 1253–1281
3. Choset, H.: Coverage for robotics — a survey of recent results. Annals of Mathematics and Artificial Intelligence **31** (2001) 113–126
4. Gabriely, Y., Rimon, E.: Spanning-tree based coverage of continuous areas by a mobile robot. Annals of Mathematics and Artificial Intelligence **31** (2001) 77–98
5. Hazon, N., Mieli, F., Kaminka, G.: Towards robust on-line multi-robot coverage. In: Proceedings of the ICRA 2006. (2006) 1710–1715
6. Trullier, O., Wiener, S., Berthoz, A., Meyer, J.: Biologically-based artificial navigation systems: Review and prospects. Progress in Neurobiology **51** (1997) 483–544
7. Franz, M., Mallot, H.: Biomimetic robot navigation. Robotics and Autonomous Systems **30** (2000) 133–153
8. Cartwright, B., Collett, T.: Landmark learning in bees. Journal of Comparative Physiology A **151** (1983) 521–543
9. Cartwright, B., Collett, T.: Landmark maps in honeybees. Biological Cybernetics **57** (1987) 85–93
10. Möller, R., Vardy, A.: Local visual homing by matched-filter descent in image distances. Biological Cybernetics **95** (2006) 413–430
11. Vardy, A., Möller, R.: Biologically plausible visual homing methods based on optical flow techniques. Connection Science **17** (2005) 47–89
12. Franz, M., Schölkopf, B., Mallot, H., Bülthoff, H.: Where did I take that snapshot? Scene-based homing by image matching. Biological Cybernetics **79** (1998) 191–202
13. Möller, R.: Local visual homing by warping of two-dimensional images. Robotics and Autonomous Systems **57** (2009) 87–101
14. Möller, R.: Three 2D-warping schemes for visual robot navigation. Autonomous Robots (2009) *submitted*.
15. Filliat, D., Meyer, J.: Map-based navigation in mobile robots: part I. Cognitive Systems Research **4** (2003) 243–282
16. Thrun, S., Burgard, W., Fox, D.: Probabilistic Robotics. MIT Press (2005)
17. Chen, Z., Samarabandu, J., Rodrigo, R.: Recent advances in simultaneous localization and map-building using computer vision. Advanced Robotics **21** (2007) 113–126
18. Kreft, S.: Reinigungstrajektorien mobiler Roboter unter visueller Steuerung. Diploma thesis, Bielefeld University, Faculty of Technology, Computer Engineering Group (2007)
19. Möller, R., Vardy, A., Gerstmayr, L., Röben, F., Kreft, S.: Neuroethological concepts at work: Insect-inspired methods for visual robot navigation. In: Biological Approaches for Engineering. (2008) 91–94
20. Greguss, P.: Panoramic imaging block for three-dimensional space. US Patent No. 4,566,763 (1986)
21. Hartley, R., Zisserman, A.: Multiple View Geometry in Computer Vision. Cambridge University Press (2003)
22. de Jong, J.: Kalmanfilter zur Positionsbestimmung auf mäandrierenden Bahnen. Diploma thesis, Bielefeld University, Faculty of Technology, Computer Engineering Group (2008)

Automatic Take Off, Hovering and Landing Control for Miniature Helicopters with Low-Cost Onboard Hardware

Karl E. Wenzel and Andreas Zell

University of Tübingen, Department of Computer Science, Sand 1, 72076 Tübingen

Abstract. This paper details experiments for autonomous take off, hovering above a landing place and autonomous landing. Our visual tracking approach differs from other methods by using an inexpensive Wii remote camera, i.e., commodity consumer hardware. All processing is done with an onboard microcontroller and the system does not require stationary sensors. The only requirements are a stationary pattern of four infrared spots at the start and landing site and a roll and pitch attitude estimation of sufficient quality, provided by an separate inertial measurement unit.

1 Introduction

Considerable progress in high capacity batteries and energy efficient brushless motors allows for smaller and smaller miniature flying robots (MFRs). Valavanis constitutes in [1] that unmanned aerial vehicles (UAVs) should become smaller and smarter. As MFRs are a relatively new type of UAVs, they require innovative technologies in sensors and sensing strategies.

Most onboard vision-based tracking and navigation research was done on UAVs of significant size and weight using comparatively expensive industrial cameras and high performance control boards [2], [3], [4], [5]. Recent research copes with tracking and landing of MFRs, but often depends on base stations [6], [7], [8]. The accuracy achieved by tracking systems are comparable to our results [9], [10].

We demonstrated in [11] how a infrared camera can be used as main sensor for stable quasi-stationary flight control. In this paper we show how the same system can be used for autonomous take off, hovering and landing. The system works with onboard sensors only and does not require a ground station, as the entire control is achieved on an onboard microcontroller. The small positioning deviations allow for operations in narrow indoor environments.

After autonomous take off, our UAV moves to a hovering position for high-level behaviours like mapping or surveillance, which could be performed by optional controllers. After returning to the landing area, the aircraft lands autonomously on the docking station.

The aircraft we use is an miniature quadrocopter. The camera, the primary sensor in our configuration, is part of the Wii remote controller, distributed by

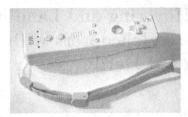

(a) The Nintendo Wii remote controller.

(b) The internal camera sensor in its original frame.

Fig. 1. The main sensor of the system comes with the Wii remote.

Nintendo (Fig. 1). The integrated circuit provides the pixel position of tracked blobs at a high frequency. The key idea of our approach is to track a T-shaped pattern of infrared spots located at the landing place. The camera is attached to the center of the quadrocopter frame, looking downwards. This guarantees clear sight to the pattern when the robot is above the landing place.

By analyzing the image of the pattern, the system is able to calculate the distance (z) and yaw angle (ψ) directly from geometric information. If the inertial measurement unit (IMU) of the aircraft provides accurate roll and pitch angles, the x and y positions can also be estimated. These four degrees of freedom are the inputs for the flight control loop.

Experiments with over 50 autonomous flight cycles were performed, in which the UAV autonomously took off, hovered for 15 seconds at 60 cm height and landed again. The standard deviation of positioning in the air is approximately 1.5 cm in x and y, below 3 cm in z position and 3° in yaw.

2 Features of the Wii Remote Infrared Camera

Size and weight are very important characteristics for miniature flying robots. The very lightweight camera we use was detached from a Wii remote controller and provides special functionalities. The sensor dimension of $8 \times 8 \times 5$ mm^3 at a weight of 0.4 g makes it an ideal MFR onboard sensor. The Wii remote (informally known as the Wiimote) is a Bluetooth-compatible controller, designed for interfacing with the Nintendo Wii game console. The price of 40 € is relatively inexpensive considering the internal components. The internal camera is capable of blob tracking of up to four infrared (IR) sources. By eight times subpixel analysis, the native resolution of 128×96 pixels is scaled up to 1024×768 pixels. The sensor supports different modes, which differ in sensitivity and information about the IR blobs. The complete information includes dot size, intensity and bounding box. For our use, the basic mode is sufficient, providing only pixel positions. The horizontal field of view is approximately 45° and the refresh rate of 100 Hz in Bluetooth mode is adequate for fast optical tracking. When operating in I^{2}C bus mode, 250 Hz can be achieved. Just a few electronic components

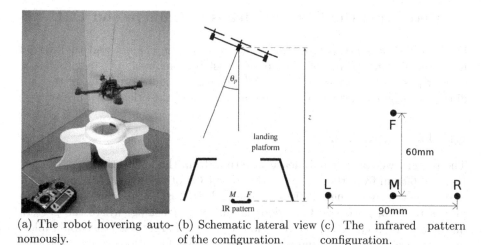

(a) The robot hovering auto- (b) Schematic lateral view (c) The infrared pattern
nomously.   of the configuration.   configuration.

Fig. 2. The robot autonomously hovers above the landing pad. The pattern is placed below the landing platform.

are required to integrate the detached sensor in a microcontroller circuit. The camera runs at 3.3 V and requires an external synchronisation of 24 Mhz.

3 The UAV System

Our quadrocopter system is an AscTec Hummingbird AutoPilot. Its diameter of 53 cm at a weight of 0.475 kg permits to fly indoor. The flight time of up to 23 minutes depends on additional payload and the flight maneuvers. (Fig. 2(a))

The AutoPilot platform provides a three-axis gyroscope, an accelerometer, a compass module, a GPS sensor and a pressure sensor. The sensors, the microcontroller and the flight control algorithm are running at 1 kHz. This ensures fast stabilisation of the quadrocopter.

The ability to connect additional devices via two serial ports also permits high level applications to control the flight. The pressure sensor allows for keeping a specific height in the range of decimeters. The compass and GPS sensors are used for autonomous starting, keeping a given orientation and position in the air or to fly to waypoints. As GPS is for outdoor use only, other solutions must be found for indoor autonomy.

Our flight control processing is done onboard on an Atmel AVR 644P microcontroller. The board also acts as a gateway receiving information from the UAV and sending data to an optional base station. The base station is used for monitoring the current pose estimation and control status and can be used for varying the control loop parameters.

The camera is fixed in the center of the quadrocopter frame, so the position of the aircraft can easily be calculated without additional translations.

4   Retrieving the Pose by Means of Camera and IMU

For accurate pose estimation, the information of the camera and the inertial measurement unit (IMU) of the aircraft must be combined. This results in the current position vector $p = (x, y, z, \psi)^T$. The Cartesian coordinates of the landing place origin, relative to the camera x, y, z and the orientation in yaw ψ.

4.1   Pattern Analysis

The pattern we constructed measures 90 mm from the left to the right IR spot (s_1) and 60 mm from the middle to the front IR spot (s_4) (Fig. 2(c)). Each spot is represented by a single 940 nm wavelength IR LED. This configuration has proven to be of good size for indoor landing pad tracking, where the pattern must be recognized at a relatively close distance. Larger patterns would allow more precise tracking at a larger distance, but would no longer fit in the field of view when getting closer. Our pattern can be completely captured by the camera from a distance larger 15 cm. So, this vertical offset was chosen for the final landing position.

To get unambiguous position information, the disordered points F (front), L (left), M (middle) and R (right) have to be identified first. Our approach focuses on fast processing on a microcontroller, which means that we need to avoid floating point operations as well as trigonometric functions. After identifying the points, the position vector $p = (x, y, z, \psi)^T$ of the aircraft, representing the position error of the UAV against the pattern, is calculated.

The x and y position relative to the center of the pattern can only be estimated when the camera orientation is known. When the quadrocopter is tilted with respect to the pattern, as shown in Fig. 2(b), the pattern appears in a displaced position in the camera image. By combining the geometric and the physical roll and pitch angles, the real x and y values can be calculated with respect to the current z value. This is described in detail in [11].

5   Flight Control

The idea of our approach is to automatically take off and hover the helicopter, so that a high-level behavior can take over control. After returning to the hovering spot above the landing place our controller lands the aircraft automatically. This behavior is achieved by varying the expected altitude over time, until the desired position is reached. Fast controllers ensure sufficient position hold.

The only variable in our controller is the desired height z above the target. All other elements of p should remain zero. The control algorithms are inspired by [10], where four independent controllers were operated.

The control loop is currently performed at a frequency of 20 Hz. The controller requires a recent pose estimate from the IMU. This request lasts approximately 30 ms in total. Additional 10 ms are required to send sensor information to the base station, where the current status is monitored. The remaining 10 ms are available for retrieving sensor information, running the control algorithm and receiving configuration data from the base station. A considerably higher control frequency would be possible with an accelerated IMU request.

5.1   Height Controller

The height controller is divided into three parts. The first part adjusts the current altitude. If the robot is about to land, the desired height is decreased by 25 mm every 100 ms. This avoids the robot "falling down". When starting, the desired height is increased every 100 ms. In both cases, the altitude is only adjusted if the difference between current and desired height is less than 45 mm.

The second and third part controls the thrust value, transmitted to the Hummingbird. The thrust control value needed to hover at a desired height has to be adjusted while flying, as it depends on the actual payload and battery charge. We obtained good results by counting the thrust value up whenever the robot is below the desired height for some cycles, and down otherwise. A fast controller is implemented as a proportional-integral-derivative (PID) loop with K_D being the major component.

5.2   Roll/Pitch and Yaw Controller

The x and y controllers are identical and were harder to derive, since the behavior response is not proportional to horizontal speed but to rotational velocities. A predictive control is required to achieve a stable position hold. By designing a cascaded control loop, where not only the speed but also the acceleration is highly weighted, the behavior obtains the desired prognostic ability.

By designing the landing pad center slightly concave, smooth landing and accurate positioning are guaranteed. The yaw controller is implemented as a PID loop with a high K_P and a small K_I. The quadrocopter provides an integrated compass for controlling the coarse orientation. By measuring the angle relative to the pattern, the orientation can be kept very accurately during flight.

6   Experimental Results

In our experiments, the robot started the motors and performed autonomous take off, hovered at a distance of 60 cm above the ground for 15 seconds, then landed again and turned off the motors. Each cycle needed an average of 23 seconds. A reliable accumulator allows to repeat this procedure about 15 times. This is considerable less than our usual flight time of 15 minutes of the Hummingbird, probably due to higher power requirements for take off and permanent control maneuvers.

The Hummingbird quadrocopter offers a GPS position controller and an air pressure sensor for height control. These functions were disabled during our indoor experiments. The yaw angle is controlled by the internal magnetic compass

Table 1. Controller timing of 50 autonomous flights (in seconds)

	Mean	Std. deviation (RMSD)	Minimum	Maximum
Taking off	5.45	1.76	3.05	13.32
Hovering	15.12	0.07	15.00	15.36
Landing	2.19	0.02	1.88	2.60

Table 2. Controller characteristics of 50 autonomous flights

	Mean	Std. deviation (RMSD)	Minimum	Maximum
Δx (mm)	0.01	14.46	-68	74
Δy (mm)	0.68	15.48	-68	90
Δz (mm)	-5.05	27.42	-78	90
$\Delta\psi$ (°)	0.09	2.90	-17	20

of the quadrocopter. The results were generated with assistance of the internal yaw controller of the quadrocopter.

The following experimental results demonstrate the performance of the system. All position are measured using the Wii camera. Experiments with manual positioning have proven, that the position estimation achieved with the Wii camera is satisfactory and thus can be used as ground truth.

Table 1 shows the timing of the flight. One can notice that take off needs more than twice the time of landing. Take off also shows a larger root mean square deviation (RMSD). While the robot only reduces the thrust when landing, the robot has to adjust the thrust value for hovering when starting. Especially the first take off, when the accumulator charge is unknown, needs more time, leading to a large standard deviation.

Table 2 shows the controller characteristics of autonomous take off, hovering and landing without the time of standing still.

A detailed record of approximately one minute of flight is shown in Fig. 3. The plots show the position estimation sent to the base station while performing two test cycles. The sensor data is smooth and nearly noise-free. Outliers caused by external influences as infrequent reflective lights, can be filtered out easily.

Some oscillations with different frequencies still remain in the control sequence in hovering flight. A deviation in one axis leads to displacements in other directions, so accurate position hold can only be achieved by a combination of stable controllers for each axis.

The standard deviations of Δx and Δy position control are comparable. This was expected, as the controllers are identical. A greater standard deviations of Δz is obvious, as height deviations are induced in the take off and landing phases. However, a standard deviation of 3 cm and a maximum deviation below 10 cm allow for autonomous flights in narrow indoor environments. The orientation of the aircraft changed slightly during take off and is affected by balancing maneuvers and thus depends on the position changes in x-, y- and z-directions.

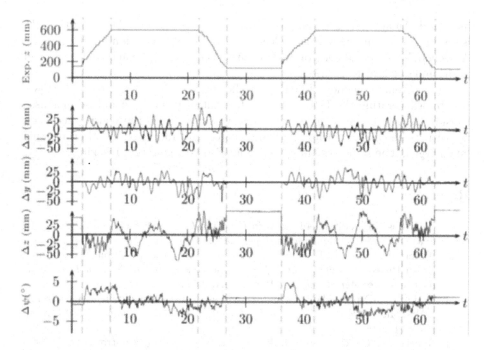

Fig. 3. Expected height (top curve) and position errors (lower four curves) of two take off, hover and landing phases.

One problem which we encountered are reflections of sunlight leading to wrong pattern interpretation, as sunlight contains a notable fraction of infrared light. A better contrast, achieved by using stronger infrared sources should allow for outdoor usage, as long as there are no specular reflections of sunlight on or around the landing pad.

7   Conclusion and Future Work

Experiments have proven that our approach offers repeatable, accurate control of a miniature unmanned aerial vehicle. The Wiimote camera provides well conditioned infrared source information. By using the Wiimote camera as main sensor, an onboard microcontroller provides sufficient processing power for pattern recognition and stable flight control. The small standard deviation of approximately 1.5 cm in x and y, below 3 cm in z position and 3° in yaw allows for safe take off, hovering and landing in narrow indoor environments. High-level autonomy tasks can be initiated from the hovering position.

The field-of-view of the Wiimote camera is large enough for tracking, even at small distances. Most disturbances caused by external light sources, except sunlight, are avoided by the infrared filter. The distance to the target is limited by the dimension of the pattern and the IR light emission. However, by using multiple IR LEDs per point or stronger IR sources, the operating distance can be increased. An accurate roll and pitch estimation, provided by the aircraft's IMU, is essential. A small angular error leads to inadmissible position approximation. A second Wiimote camera or fusion with other sensors would yield a better positioning at larger distances.

The current frequency of 20 Hz is sufficient for robust flight control. However, by accelerating the IMU request, the control fequency could be increased considerably. A higher control frequency would advance the control accuracy. By tilting the camera during hovering, the control radius of the aircraft could be enlarged. The same system could be used for stable target tracking.

References

1. Valavanis K.P., editor. *Advances in Unmanned Aerial Vehicles. State of the Art and the Road to Autonomy.* Springer, 2007.
2. Andert F., Adolf F.M., Goormann L. and Dittrich J.S. Autonomous Vision-Based Helicopter Flights through Obstacle Gates. In *UAV'09 2nd Intl. Symp. on Unmanned Aerial Vehicles*, Reno, USA, 2009.
3. Hrabar S. 3D path planning and stereo-based obstacle avoidance for rotorcraft UAVs. In *IEEE Intl. Conf. on Intelligent Robots and Systems (IROS)*, pages 807–814, 2008.
4. Roberts J., Corke P. and Buskey G. Low-cost Flight Control System for a Small Autonomous Helicopter. In *IEEE Intl. Conf. on Robotics and Automation (ICRA)*, pages 546–551, Taipai, Taiwan, September 2003.
5. Saripalli S., Montgomery J.F. and Sukhatme G.S. Vision-based autonomous landing of an unmanned aerial vehicle. In *IEEE Intl. Conf. on Robotics and Automation (ICRA)*, pages 2799–2804, Washington, DC, USA, 2002.
6. Lange S., Sünderhauf N. and Protzel P. Autonomous Landing for a Multirotor UAV Using Vision. In *SIMPAR 2008 Intl. Conf. on Simulation, Modeling and Programming for Autonomous Robots*, pages 482–491, Venice, Italy, 2008.
7. Herisse B., Russotto F.X., Hamel T. and Mahony R.E. Hovering flight and vertical landing control of a VTOL Unmanned Aerial Vehicle using optical flow. In *IEEE Intl. Conf. on Intelligent Robots and Systems (IROS)*, pages 801–806, 2008.
8. Guenard N. and Hamel T. A Practical Visual Servo Control for an Unmanned Aerial Vehicle. In *IEEE Intl. Conf. on Robotics and Automation (ICRA)*, pages 1342–1348, 2007.
9. Mak L.C. and Furukawa T. A 6 DoF Visual Tracking System for a Miniature Helicopter. In *2nd Intl. Conf. on Sensing Technology (ICST)*, pages 32–37, 2007.
10. Gurdan D., Stumpf J., Achtelik M., Doth K.M., Hirzinger G., and Rus D. Energy-efficient Autonomous Four-rotor Flying Robot Controlled at 1 kHz. In *IEEE Intl. Conf. on Robotics and Automation (ICRA)*, pages 361–366, Roma, Italy, 2007.
11. Wenzel K.E., Rosset P. and Zell A. Low-Cost Visual Tracking of a Landing Place and Hovering Flight Control with a Microcontroller. In *UAV'09 2nd Intl. Symposium on Unmanned Aerial Vehicles*, Reno, USA, 2009.

Foot Function in Spring Mass Running

Daniel Maykranz*, Sten Grimmer, Susanne Lipfert and Andre Seyfarth

Lauflabor Locomotion Laboratory, University of Jena,
Dornburger Str. 23, D-07743 Jena, Germany

Abstract. The leg function in human running can be characterized by spring-like behaviour. The human leg itself has several segments, which influence the leg function. In this paper a simple model based on spring-mass-running but with with a compliant ankle joint is introduced to investigate the influence of a rigid foot segment. The predicted force-length-curve explains changes in leg stiffness as well as changes in leg length during stance phase similar to what is observed in human running.

1 Introduction

The foot function in human running is characterized by a shift of the center of pressure (CoP) from heel to toe. In running, however, different foot strategies are possible, such as heel-toe running and forefoot running.

Specific functions and basic advantages of the human foot during locomotion are not well understood. So far, there is no simple theory or model explaining the observed strategies on foot placement. As of today, most foot models consist of a detailed description of the viscoelastic elements or deformable elements based on the finite element method ([1],[2],[3]).

Recently, in a simple model the function of the foot was described by a translation of the center of pressure during contact at constant speed [4]. Based on this foot model, it was shown that it is possible to achieve similar basic running mechanics with and without the translation of the center of pressure.

In contrast to this model, the CoP in human running does not shift forward at constant speed; e.g. when the heel is lifted the CoP location remains rather constant. Therefore, we aim at developing a model representing the foot as an element with geometrical and mechanical properties resembling the function of the human foot during the ground contact including the heel-off phase.

As the spring-mass model is accepted as general template for both walking and running ([5],[6]), we describe the leg as a telescopic spring. This leg spring is extended by a rigid foot segment, which is coupled to the leg spring by an elastic ankle joint. We will demonstrate how such a combination of a telescopic and a rotational spring can effect the overall leg function during locomotion. Therefore we will focus on the force-length-curve during stance to investigate the adaptation in leg stiffness and leg length during stance phase.

---

* corresponding author. E-Mail: DanielMaykranz@web.de

2   Methods

2.1   Spring-Mass-Model with Foot-Segment

The dynamics of the center of mass (CoM) in running can be modeled by a spring-mass system ([5],[6]). This model consists of a point mass and a single leg spring. We extended the leg spring with an additional massless rigid foot element establishing the foot-spring-model. The foot element is attached to the distal end of the leg spring via a rotational spring at the ankle joint (Fig. 1). The resulting leg forces on the CoM for single support are:

$$F_x = k\left(L_{S0} - L_S\right)\cos\varphi_2 + \frac{c}{L_S}\left(\varphi_0 - \varphi\right)\cos\left(\varphi_2 + \frac{\pi}{2}\right) \tag{1}$$

$$F_y = k\left(L_{S0} - L_S\right)\sin\varphi_2 + \frac{c}{L_S}\left(\varphi_0 - \varphi\right)\sin\left(\varphi_2 + \frac{\pi}{2}\right) \tag{2}$$

$$L_S = \sqrt{\left(x - f\cos\varphi_1\right)^2 + \left(y - f\cos\varphi_1\right)^2} \tag{3}$$

The leg spring produces forces proportional to the difference between resting length L_{S0} and actual length L_S corresponding to the leg stiffness k. Similarly, the ankle spring creates forces proportional to the excursion from the resting angle φ_0 to the actual angle φ depending on the ankle stiffness c. In the simulations, the foot is always flat on the ground at touchdown. Here, the resting angle of the ankle spring φ_0 is chosen as π minus the angle of attack α_0.
During flight phase the CoM follows a parabolic trajectory.
The first terms in eq. 1 and eq. 2 describe the force of the leg spring. The second terms describe the effect of the foot with a linear ankle joint stiffness c. These equations can not be solved analytically and are therefore integrated numerically.

2.2   Analyzing Periodic Solutions

As the system energy E remains constant, the model is conservative. To compare solutions of different system energies a reference velocity is defined, which corresponds to a CoM height of $y = L_{S0}$ (eq. 4).

$$v_{ref} = \sqrt{\frac{2}{m}\left(E - gL_{S0}\right)} \tag{4}$$

At the apex the vertical velocity is zero. Because of the conservation of energy any periodic solution can be characterized by only one state parameter (e.g. the apex height). Therefore periodic solutions can easily be analyzed with the help of apex return maps as described in [10]. With this method, the apex height from one stride (y_i) to the next stride (y_{i+1}) is plotted defining the apex return map. Solutions with $y_{i+1} = y_i$ are called fix points and characterize periodic solutions.

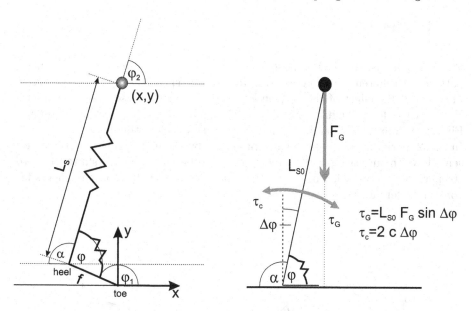

Fig. 1. Left: The foot-spring-model consists of a leg spring extended by a foot segment and an elastic ankle joint; Right: During stance the torque τ_c counteracts the gravity induced torque τ_g.

2.3   Dimensionless Ankle Stiffness

To minimize the number of parameters of the model, a dimensionless ankle stiffness is introduced. The basic idea behind dimensionless stiffness is the requirement for a stable stance. Two legs with a parallel foot placement on the ground can span an area where the CoM lies over this area. In lateral direction the leg can compensate any disturbances out of the equilibrium. In sagittal direction a minimal ankle joint stiffness is required to ensure stable stance (Fig. 1). The two ankle joints have to produce a torque τ_c, which counteracts the gravitational force. For small excursions $\sin \Delta\varphi$ can be approximated by $\Delta\varphi$. In this case the resulting torques are simplified to

$$2c\Delta\varphi = L_{S0}mg\Delta\varphi \tag{5}$$

$$c = \frac{1}{2}L_{S0}mg \tag{6}$$

$$\tilde{c} = \frac{c}{\frac{1}{2}mgL_{S0}} \tag{7}$$

The dimensionless stiffness is normalized to this minimal required stiffness (eq. 7). For a stable stance, the dimensionless ankle joint stiffness has to fullfill the requirement $\tilde{c} \geq 1$. The values selected for the ankle stiffness $\tilde{c} = 1\dots2$ in the model are based on experimental data ($\tilde{c} = 1.1\dots1.4$) on human running [7].

3   Results

We will demonstrate how several values of $\tilde{c}$ will effect the periodic running patterns at different speeds compared to a simple spring-mass model. To better understand the effect of the foot on leg function, we will describe the characteristics of the force length curve during the different phases in ground contact. Finally, we analyze the adaptation in leg length and leg stiffness.

In Fig. 2, periodic running solutions predicted by the foot-spring-model are presented. With increasing values for $\tilde{c}$ the periodic solutions are shifted toward steeper angle of attack with only minor changes in the shape of the curves for constant reference velocity.

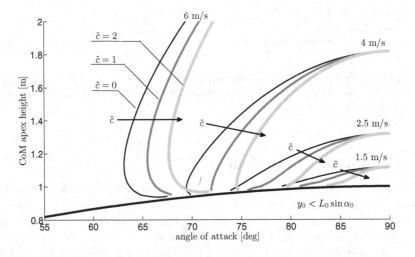

Fig. 2. Apex height y_{Apex} and angle of attack α_0 of periodic solutions with constant reference velocity v_{ref} (eq. 4) for different dimensionless ankle stiffness $\tilde{c}$; parameters: $m = 80kg$, $L_{S0} = 1m$, $k = 20kN/m$, $g = 9.81\frac{m}{s^2}$

This model is able to predict heel-toe running. The CoP is defined by the resulting leg force during stance phase. As the leg force always crosses the CoM, the intersection point of the force with the ground defines the CoP predicted by the model. The CoP excursion predicted by the model slowly starts at the beginning of the stance phase and accelerates until the toe is reached. At the instant where the CoP reaches the toe the heel lifts off and the CoP remains at the toes for the remaining stance phase (Fig. 3).

Due to the geometry of the leg stance is divided into two different phases: the first phase with heel contact and the second phase with heel-off.

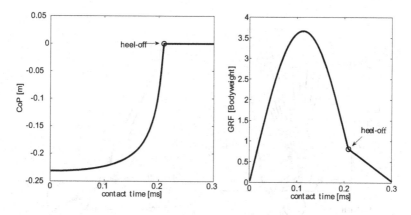

Fig. 3. Left: Shift in CoP; Right: ground reaction force of a periodic solution $y_{Apex} = 1.1m$, $v_{Apex} = 1.99\frac{m}{s}$ with parameters: $m = 80kg$, $L_0 = 1m$, $k = 20kN/m$, $g = 9.81\frac{m}{s^2}$ $\alpha_0 = 80deg$, $g = 9.81\frac{m}{s^2}$

As a consequence of this asymmetric foot function during stance phase, the effective leg length is increased (Fig. 4). The effective leg length at touchdown is the distance from hip to heel. At take-off the effective leg length is the distance from hip to toe. For this increased leg length no additional energy for expanding the leg is required. This can be solved by passive elements.

The foot-spring-model predicts a leg stiffness modulation during contact. At heel contact there is a higher leg stiffness than at heel-off (Fig. 4).

In the spring-mass-model the pivot point equals the foot point. In the foot-spring-model there is no explicit pivot point. The intersection point of the forces moves during the stance phase. This virtual pivot point is located underneath the foot and creates an increase in effective leg length (Fig. 4).

4 Discussion

In this paper the function of the foot is embedded into the spring-mass model for running with a combination of a telescopic leg spring and a rotational ankle spring.

The resulting foot-spring-model exhibits similar periodic solutions (i.e. running patterns) as the original spring mass model with slightly steeper angles of attack (Fig. 2). Hence, the foot-spring-model inherits basic properties of the simple leg spring concept characterized by a linear force-length-relationship. The ankle torque results in additional breaking forces at the beginning of the stance phase. For periodic running, steeper angles of attack are found, which counteract these breaking forces.

This shift of the angle of attack is comparable to the effect of point of force translation (POFT) concept [4], which prescribes a forward translation of CoP

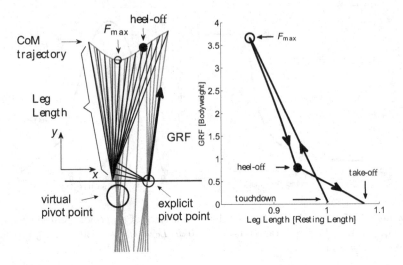

Fig. 4. Left: Leg kinematics and direction of GRF (grey lines) during stance phase; Right: leg stiffness modulation of a periodic solution $y_{Apex} = 1.1m$, $v_{Apex} = 1.99\frac{m}{s}$ with parameters: $m = 80kg$, $L_0 = 1m$, $k = 20kN/m$, $g = 9.81\frac{m}{s^2}$ $\alpha_0 = 80deg$, $g = 9.81\frac{m}{s^2}$

during contact with constant speed. In the foot-spring-model the CoP is a result of leg mechanics and thus is closer to human running than a CoP translation with constant speed.

4.1   Leg Stiffness Modulation

During heel contact both springs (leg spring and ankle spring) are acting separately. The leg spring reflects the longitudinal compression of the leg, while the ankle joint follows the change in leg angle. Due to the structure of the model, these two springs are loaded independently from each other during heel contact. This can be compared to two springs acting in parallel. After heel-off, the ankle joint is lifted leading to an additional degree of freedom, which is defined by an equilibrium minimizing the sum of the stored energies in both springs. In this phase, leg function can be compared with two springs acting in series.

The changed leg configuration between loading and unloading results in a modulation of leg stiffness, namely high leg stiffness during heel contact and low leg stiffness during heel-off. A similar change in leg stiffness is found in human running with higher values at the beginning of stance phase [8]. Although impacts are not simulated in this model, there is still higher leg stiffness in loading than in unloading. This is a consequence of the geometrical arrangement of both the telescopic and the rotational spring. With the combination of two springs it is possible to achieve an adjustable leg stiffness, which depends on the individual

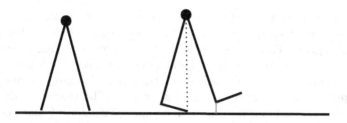

Fig. 5. Leg lengthening during contact supports ground clearance of the swing leg

timing of loading and unloading of both springs due to the heel contact (Fig. 4). The change in leg stiffness also results in an asymmetry of the ground reaction force (GRF). The descending branch of the pattern appears to be flatter than the ascending part both in the model and in experimental data on human running [8].

4.2   Leg Lengthening

The drop in leg stiffness during contact is counteracted by an increase of the effective leg length (Fig. 4) from touchdown (CoM to heel) to take-off (CoM to toe). Therefore, the periodic running solutions are characterized by higher take-off positions compared to the touchdown. With this increased leg length at take-off ground clearance of the swing leg is facilitated (Fig. 5). This can also be observed in human running, where an increased ankle angle (angle between foot and lower leg) at take-off enlarges the effective leg length further improving ground clearance [9]. In the foot-spring-model ground clearance is achieved merely by passive elements requiring no additional energy for leg lengthening.

The increase in effective leg length at take-off results in longer ground contacts. As a result, the vertical excursions of the CoM and the changes in horizontal velocity are reduced. With the foot-spring-model, the leg angle and the corresponding leg force at touchdown are more vertical, which reduces the risk of slipping (Fig. 4). Thus, the foot enhances the comfort and safety during locomotion.

4.3   Shortcommings of the Model

The function of the human foot during locomotion includes viscoelastic deformations and is only partially represented in the model. Also the foot consists of many segments coupled with joints (e.g. metatarsal joint). As a consequence the CoP movements and the force-length-curves are smoother in humans than predicted by the model. A model with an elastic foot segment or a foot segment with additional joints could smoothen the CoP movement.

In human running the knee and ankle joint show an almost synchronous release of the stored energy. This is not found in the foot-spring-model due to the missing coordination between leg spring and ankle spring. To achieve this, a model would be necessary, in which the unloading of the leg spring influences the extension of the ankle spring. This can be realized by a structure coupling knee and ankle joint. With this, knee extension would also support ankle extension.

In the foot-spring-model, the interplay of a relatively simple arrangement of a telescopic and a rotational spring is addressed. The characteristics induced by the rotation spring on overall leg function are significant and may help to interpret results from human running experiments.

Despite of its simplicity this model revealed how the foot of the leg can modify leg stiffness and leg length without the need of active or nonconservative elements.

References

1. Gilchrist, L. A. & Winter, D. A.: A two-part, viscoelastic foot model for use in gait simulations. J Biomech, 29, 795-798, 1996
2. Carson, M. C.; Harrington, M. E.; Thompson, N. et. al.:Kinematic analysis of a multi-segment foot model for research and clinical applications: a repeatability analysis. J Biomech, 34, 1299-1307, 2001
3. Camacho, D. L. A.; Ledoux, W. R.; Rohr, E. S. et. al.: A three-dimensional, anatomically detailed foot model: a foundation for a finite element simulation and means of quantifying foot-bone position. J Rehabil Res Dev, 39, 401-410, 2002
4. Bullimore, S. R. & Burn, J. F.: Consequences of forward translation of the point of force application for the mechanics of running. J Theor Biol, 238, 211-219, 2006
5. Geyer, H.; Seyfarth, A. & Blickhan, R.: Compliant leg behaviour explains basic dynamics of walking and running. Proc Biol Sci, 273, 2861-2867, 2006
6. Blickhan, R.: The spring-mass model for running and hopping, J Biomech, 22, 1217-1227, 1989
7. Günther, M. & Blickhan, R.: Joint stiffness of the ankle and the knee in running. J Biomech, 35, 1459-1474, 2002
8. Lipfert, S. W.; Günther, M.; Grimmer et. al.: Spring and catapult produce a kinematic criterion to distinguish between human walking and running; Proc Roy Soc B, submitted
9. Peter, S.; Grimmer, S.; Lipfert, et. al.: Variable joint elasticities in running. Autonome Mobile Systeme, 2009, submitted
10. Seyfarth, A.; Geyer, H.; Günther, M. et. al.: A movement criterion for running. J Biomech, 35, 649-655, 2002

From Walking to Running

Juergen Rummel, Yvonne Blum and Andre Seyfarth

Lauflabor Locomotion Laboratory, University of Jena,
Dornburger Straße 23, D-07743 Jena, Germany,
juergen.rummel@uni-jena.de, www.lauflabor.uni-jena.de

Abstract. The implementation of bipedal gaits in legged robots is still a challenge in state-of-the-art engineering. Human gaits could be realized by imitating human leg dynamics where a spring-like leg behavior is found as represented in the bipedal spring-mass model. In this study we explore the gap between walking and running by investigating periodic gait patterns. We found an almost continuous morphing of gait patterns between walking and running. The technical feasibility of this transition is, however, restricted by the duration of swing phase. In practice, this requires an abrupt gait transition between both gaits, while a change of speed is not necessary.

1 Introduction

A common field in robotics research is the development of autonomous systems that move like humans on two legs. Such bipedal robots impressively illustrate the progress in engineering science and bring further light into the nature of human bipedalism. A way of implementing locomotion in a biped robot is to imitate human-like leg dynamics which could result in a reduced control effort [1,2]. Dynamically, human legs show a compliant behavior in walking and running with a simple linear spring representing fundamental leg characteristics [3,4,5]. These findings support the idea of simulating legged locomotion with a highly reduced leg template, the bipedal spring-mass model with massless legs [5]. The spring-mass model can be used as a framework to investigate general control strategies for gait stabilization [6,7] or for understanding how leg design, e.g. leg segmentation [8], influences system dynamics in locomotion.

Before implementing control strategies, e.g. swing-leg control [9,7], a periodic gait pattern is required. For identifying such a gait pattern a Poincaré map [10] is applied and a single walking or running step is simulated. Here, start and end point of the simulation are equally defined and form the Poincaré section which reduces the number of independent state variables. Common events used as Poincaré section are the apex, i.e. a maximum height of the center of mass trajectory, and the touch down [10]. Both events, apex and touch down, require definitions dependent on the investigated gait. The apex in running occurs during flight phase while in walking the apex is during stance. Taken into account that more than one apex could exist within a single step [5], this event is not unique which could lead to incorrect Poincaré maps. A unique event within a single step is the touch down, however, the number of independent state variables differs between walking and running. As in walking a double support phase (both legs have ground contact at the same time) exists, the position of the previous leg is required while in running it is not (assuming that the swing leg has no influence on dynamics).

In this paper we present a Poincaré section, based on events that are unique within each step, i.e. the midstance during single support. This Poincaré section is equally defined for both walking and running. Since the term midstance is differently used in literature, we clearly define this Poincaré section as the instant where the supporting leg is oriented vertically. Using this novel map we will investigate walking and running based on purely periodic patterns. Taken into account that periodicity of gait is the basis for stabilizing swing-leg control, we believe that each of the gaits could be stabilized by a combination of swing-leg retraction and leg stiffening [7], and leg lengthening as observed in running birds [11].

The bipedal gaits have already been investigated with highly reduced models. It was discovered that walking and running are optimal at low and high speeds, respectively, due to energy expenditure [12] and self-stability [5]. However, humans can walk and run at the same speed. The purpose of this study is to explore the speed gap between walking and running as predicted by the bipedal spring-mass model. We assume that the speed gap can be smaller when not restricting to self-stability. We will investigate the technical relevance of the observed gait patterns. Here, the time required for swinging the leg forward is an important aspect limiting the realization of gaits in a robot.

2   Methods

The bipedal spring-mass model shown in Fig. 1 describes the action of the stance legs supporting a point mass m against gravity in locomotion. Both legs are represented by linear massless springs of rest length L_0 and leg stiffness k. The legs exert forces F_1 and F_2 on the point mass when in ground contact. The force of one leg directs from it's foot point $r_{fp} = (x_{fp}, y_{fp})$ to the center of mass (COM) $r = (x, y)$. During swing phase the leg does not influence system dynamics due to it's massless representation.

The equation of motion representing the system in the sagittal plane is

$$m\ddot{r} = F_1 + F_2 + mg \tag{1}$$

where $g = (0, -g)$ is the gravitational acceleration with $g = 9.81\text{m/s}^2$. The force of leg 1 is

$$F_1 = k \left(\frac{L_0}{|r - r_{fp1}|} - 1 \right) (r - r_{fp1}) \tag{2}$$

as long as this leg has ground contact. If the leg length reaches it's resting length L_0 the transition from stance to swing phase occurs and the leg force is set to

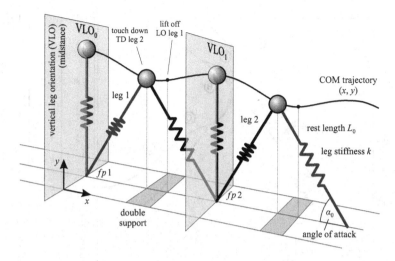

Fig. 1. Walking of the bipedal spring-mass model starting at the instant of VLO (vertical leg orientation).

zero. The transition from swing to stance happens when the landing condition $y_{TD} = L_0 \sin(\alpha_0)$ is fulfilled, where α_0 is the angle of attack.

The system parameters are based on human dimensions, i.e. body mass $m = 80\text{kg}$ and leg length $L_0 = 1\text{m}$. The model can be compared with other bipeds using dimensional analysis. Due to the models simplicity, Geyer et al. [5] showed that it has only three fundamental parameters, i.e. the dimensionless leg stiffness $\tilde{k} = kL_0/(mg)$, the angle of attack α_0, and the dimensionless system energy $\tilde{E} = E/(mgL_0)$. The energy E is the constant total energy of the conservative model.

The model shows walking and running in a steady-state manner which means that strides are periodically repeated. Such a gait pattern is completely described by the selected system parameters (k, α_0, E) and initial conditions $(x_0, y_0, v_{x0}, v_{y0})$. In this study the initial conditions are chosen such that one leg has ground contact and is vertically orientated. Clearly, the COM is orientated vertically above center of pressure $x = x_{fp1}$. A single step of a gait is completed when the counter leg has single support and is vertically orientated where $x = x_{fp2}$ is valid. The instant of Vertical Leg Orientation (VLO) exists in both gaits, walking and running, hence, it is independent on gait. With these definitions we investigate locomotion by analyses of VLO return maps, i.e. Poincaré maps with VLO as Poincaré section (visualized in Fig. 1).

Using VLO as starting point we can reduce the number of independent initial conditions to y_0 and v_{y0} due to the following reasons. The horizontal position x_0 is always zero with respect to the center of pressure x_{fp} and only one leg has ground contact. Since the system is conservative, the horizontal velocity v_{x0} at VLO depends on height y_0 and vertical velocity v_{y0}:

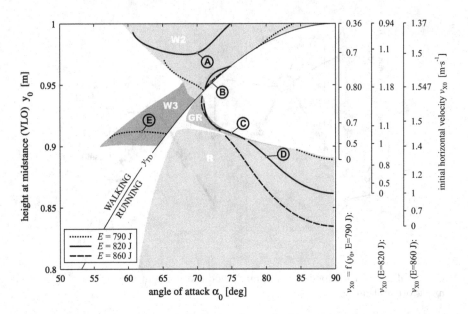

Fig. 2. Initial conditions (systems state at VLO y_0, $v_{x0} = f(y_0, E)$) of symmetric gait patterns ($v_{x0} = 0$) for three selected system energies E and one leg stiffness $k = 15\,\text{kN/m}$. Each point on the thick lines represents a periodic gait solution. Five representative gait patterns (A-E) are shown in detail in Fig. 3. The gray areas indicate the regions where running (R), grounded running (GR), and walking (W2 and W3) were found for $750\text{J} < E < 2000\text{J}$. W2 and W3 represent regions where the ground reaction force has normally two and three humps, respectively. The thin black line represents the landing height $y_{TD} = L_0 \sin(\alpha_0)$ where touch down (TD) takes place.

$$v_{x0} = \sqrt{\frac{2}{m}\left(E - m\,g\,y_0 - \frac{k}{2}(L_0 - y_0)^2 - \frac{m}{2}v_{y0}^2\right)} \qquad (3)$$

In this paper we investigate symmetric gaits only. Here, the COM trajectory can be mirrored about midstance and VLO is identical to midstance while v_{y0} is zero. A Newton-Raphson algorithm is used to find periodic gait solutions.

3 Results

With the VLO return map we found several solutions of periodic gaits (Fig. 2). We distinguish between walking and running gaits by observing the vertical excursion during stance phase. In case of walking the COM is lifted during single stance phase, as can be suggested by a VLO height y_0 above touch down level y_{TD}. In running gaits the COM is lowered during stance as illustrated with pattern D in Fig. 3. Here, the VLO height is below y_{TD} (Fig. 2).

We categorized walking patterns by counting maxima in the ground reaction force (GRF) of representative solutions. However, in some cases the gait patterns

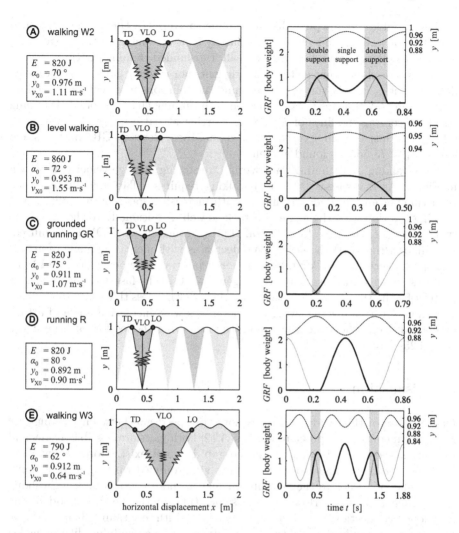

Fig. 3. Representative gait patterns of the bipedal spring-mass model related to the selected initial conditions in Fig. 2. The left column shows leg positions at touch down (TD), VLO, and lift off (LO). The graphs on the right side show vertical ground reaction forces (GRF) and the vertical excursion of the COM (dotted lines) during a complete gait cycles (two steps).

slightly transform into patterns with less maxima. Here, the larger number of maxima was taken into account for the categorization. An example is pattern B which has a single peak in the GRF while it's directly connected with patterns having two maxima.

For running we found only one significant maximum of the GRF. Normally, running is defined as a gait including flight phases (pattern D). However, there exists a neighboring gait with the same vertical excursion of the COM trajectory having a double support phase like in walking (pattern C). Due to the mentioned definition of walking and running we classify it as a running gait, and since the system has always ground contact we call it grounded running (GR).

In Fig. 2 is shown that neither walking gaits nor running gaits cross the touch down height $y_{TD} = L_0 \sin(\alpha_0)$. Examining the solutions more carefully, we find that walking (W2) seems to be connected with running (R) via grounded running (GR). Observing the lines of $E = 860J$ starting at pattern B and following to GR we find just a small vertical gap at $\alpha_0 \approx 71$deg. Between GR and R a small gap at $\alpha_0 \approx 73.5$deg is found as well.

The walking and running gait overlap, regarding average velocity, is shown in Fig. 4. At low speeds (≈ 1m/s) walking requires a flatter angle of attack than running and grounded running. With increasing speed both, walking and running, overlap with the angle of attack as well. Additionally to the speed the swing time (i.e. the time from lift off (LO) to touch down (TD)) is visualized. In walking (Fig. 4(a)) the swing time decreases with increasing angle of attack and speed. Very slow walking, having more than two force peaks (W3 and W4), contains swing durations that are longer than 0.7s. In fast walking (e.g. gait pattern B) the time between lift off and touch down is less than 0.2s. In contrast to walking, in running the swing time increases with increasing angle of attack and speed. Here, the system has more time to swing the leg forward, i.e. more than 0.25s.

4   Discussion

One purpose of this study was to explore the speed gap between walking and running. In contrast to previous studies [5,12] both gaits are possible at low and medium speeds (Fig. 4), hence, a speed gap does not exist. Moreover, walking is almost directly connected with running via grounded running alias jogging. This connection leads to the assumption that a smooth transition from walking to running is possible. However, the swing time in the neighborhood of the mentioned connection (◇ in Fig. 4) is very low. With less than 0.3s it might be technically not applicable and the natural dynamics of a pendulum-like swing leg cannot be used. Hence, the robot should jump over this parameter region when changing from walking to running. This model prediction supports the need of an abrupt gait transition within one or two steps as observed in humans. As walking shows a smaller vertical amplitude of the COM trajectory compared to running (Fig. 3), the COM has to be lowered and lifted significantly within the transition step(s) to match the aimed running pattern. This might be achieved by a softer leg spring at the transition step(s).

The model predicts that walking can be faster than the preferred gait transition speed (≈ 2m/s). This gait shows almost no vertical motion (pattern B in Fig. 3) which relates to 'level walking' [13]. Due to the very short swing duration with less than 0.1s above 2m/s it is neither technically nor biologically feasible (in humans a swing time of ≈ 0.3s is observed [14]). The limitation of walking speed might be caused by the linear force-length relationship of the leg spring.

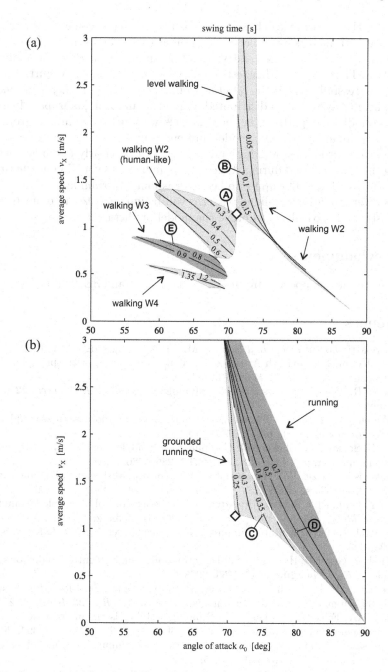

Fig. 4. Average speed and swing time (isolines) of selected gaits. Due to coexistence in similar regions, walking and running gaits were separated into two diagrams, (a) and (b), respectively. The symbol ◇ is a landmark representing a bifurcation inside W2 and connects the region of W2 with that of grounded running. The patterns A-E correspond to gait solutions in Fig. 2 and 3.

We assume that another leg characteristic is needed to overcome this drawback. Here, a leg with increasing or decreasing stiffness function [8] might help.

In this study we presented the VLO return map as a method for analyzing locomotion. This map is neither restricted to gait nor to symmetry. Furthermore, we have successfully tested the VLO as Poincaré section in higher dimensional models, i.e. in a system with distributed body mass and in a quadruped. In order to find periodic gait patterns in these models we inherited solutions from the lower dimensional spring-mass model, presented here. Due to the presentation in Cartesian coordinates, walking and running can be clearly distinguished. In walking the body is lifted during stance phase, indicated by a VLO height above the touch down level. The opposite behavior is found in running.

In further studies the walking patterns will be implemented into our bipedal robot testbed (PogoWalker) to prove the model predictions.

Acknowledgments

This research was supported by the DFG (SE1042/1 and SE1042/7).

References

1. Raibert MH: *Legged robots that balance*. MIT Press, Cambridge, MA, 1986
2. Iida F, Rummel J, Seyfarth A: Bipedal walking and running with spring-like biarticular muscles. *J. Biomech.* **41**: 656–667, 2008
3. Blickhan R: The spring-mass model for running and hopping. *J. Biomech.* **22**: 1217–1227, 1989
4. McMahon TA, Cheng GC: The mechanics of running: how does stiffness couple with speed? *J. Biomech.* **23**(Suppl. 1): 65–78, 1990
5. Geyer H, Seyfarth A, Blickhan R: Compliant leg behaviour explains basic dynamics of walking and running. *Proc. R. Soc. B* **273**: 2861–2867, 2006
6. Poulakakis I, Grizzle JW: Monopedal running control: SLIP embedding and virtual constraint controllers. *IEEE/RSJ Int. Conf. Intell. Robots Syst.*: 323–330, 2007
7. Blum Y, Rummel J, Seyfarth A: Advanced swing leg control for stable locomotion. *Autonome Mobile Systeme 2007*, Springer, Berlin, Heidelberg: 301–307, 2007
8. Rummel J, Seyfarth A: Stable running with segmented legs. *Int. J. Robot. Res.* **27**: 919–934, 2008
9. Seyfarth A, Geyer H, Herr H: Swing-leg retraction: a simple control model for stable running. *J. Exp. Biol.* **206**: 2547–2555, 2003
10. Altendorfer R, Koditschek DE, Holmes P: Stability analysis of legged locomotion models by symmetry-factored return maps. *Int. J. Robot. Res.* **23**: 979–999, 2004
11. Daley MA, Felix G, Biewener AA: Running stability is enhanced by a proximo-distal gradient in joint neuromechanical control. *J. Exp. Biol.* **210**: 383–394, 2007
12. Srinivasan M, Ruina A: Computer optimization of a minimal biped model discovers walking and running. *Nature* **439**: 72–75, 2006
13. Srinivasan M: *Why walk and run: Energetic costs and energetic optimality in simple mechanics-based models of a bipedal animal*. PhD Thesis, Cornell Univ., 2006
14. Nilsson J, Thorstensson A, Halbertsma J: Changes in leg movements and muscle activity with speed of locomotion and mode of progression in humans. *Acta Physiol. Scand.* **123**: 457–475, 1985

Generisches Verfahren zur präzisen Pfadverfolgung für Serienfahrzeuggespanne

Christian Schwarz, Christian Weyand und Dieter Zöbel

Universität Koblenz-Landau, Universitätsstraße 1, 56070 Koblenz
{chrschwarz,weyandc,zoebel}@uni-koblenz.de

Zusammenfassung. In Anbetracht der fortschreitenden Automatisierung im Güterverkehr ist auch der Einsatz von Serienfahrzeugen erstrebenswert. Aus wissenschaftlicher Sicht besteht diesbezüglich ein Bedarf an präzisen und echtzeitfähigen Regelungsverfahren, die auch für Fahrzeuge mit einachsigem Anhänger ein exaktes Abfahren vorgegebener Pfade insbesondere bei rückwärtsgerichteten Fahrmanövern gewährleisten. In diesem Beitrag wird ein zweistufiges Regelungsverfahren vorgestellt, das diese Kriterien erfüllt und sich generisch auf verschiedene Fahrzeuge des gleichen Gespanntyps übertragen lässt. Darüber hinaus kann das vorgestellte Verfahren als Grundlage für das autonome oder assistierte Fahren fungieren.

1 Einleitung

In den letzten Jahrzehnten wurde die Automatisierung im innerbetrieblichen Warenverkehr aus wirtschaftlichen Gründen nachdrücklich vorangetrieben. Diesbezüglich hat die Wissenschaft eine Vielzahl von Konzepten und Verfahren in den Bereichen Planung, Überwachung und Regelung (vgl. [6]) entwickelt, die in der Praxis gewöhnlich unter Einsatz von Fahrerlosen Transportsystemen (FTS) realisiert werden. Bei den FTS handelt es sich i. d. R. um Spezialfahrzeuge (vgl. [8]), die eigens für die jeweilige Transportaufgabe konzipiert sind und sich durch ein einfaches kinematisches Bewegungsverhalten auszeichnen.

Aus industrieller Sicht besteht darüber hinaus auch im außerbetrieblichen Warenverkehr ein hohes Potential, durch die Automatisierung bestimmter Abläufe deren Effizienz und Sicherheit erheblich zu erhöhen. Hier wird der Fokus vornehmlich auf die Automatisierung solcher Abläufe gelegt, die noch auf dem Werksgelände (z. B. Speditionshöfen) selbst anfallen. Im Gegensatz zum innerbetrieblichen Warenverkehr muss die Automatisierung in diesem Kontext jedoch auf der Basis von Serienfahrzeugen erfolgen. Bereits heute kann die Automatisierung von Serienfahrzeugen unter technischen Gesichtspunkten als realisierbar eingestuft werden.

Die zusätzlichen kinematischen Einschränkungen von Fahrzeugen mit Anhänger führen insbesondere beim Rückwärtsfahren zu einem äußerst instabilen Bewegungsverhalten. Infolgedessen wird die Problematik der Fahrzeugregelung beim Abfahren vorgegebener Pfade erheblich erschwert, da bereits geringe

Abb. 1. Modell eines Lkw mit einachsigem Starrdeichselanhänger beim rückwärtigen Unterfahren einer Wechselbrücke.

Störungen zu signifikanten Pfadabweichungen führen können. Für die Automatisierung ist jedoch beim Rückwärtsfahren ein exaktes Regelungsverfahren zur Pfadverfolgung unerlässlich, da verschiedene rückwärtsgerichtete Fahrmanöver, wie z. B. das Andocken an eine Laderampe und das Umsetzen einer Wechselbrücke, eine hohe Fahrpräzision erfordern.

In diesem Beitrag wird für Fahrzeuggespanne mit einachsigem Starrdeichselanhänger ein zweistufiges Regelungsverfahren zur Pfadverfolgung vorgestellt. Das Regelungsverfahren basiert auf der Kinematik des jeweiligen Fahrzeugs und zeichnet sich insbesondere dadurch aus, dass es auf beliebige Fahrzeuge dieses Gespanntyps übertragbar ist. Empirische Untersuchungen mit einem Modellfahrzeug (siehe Abb. 1) haben gezeigt, dass die Abweichungen hinsichtlich aller Freiheitsgrade in der Größenordnung der Mess- und Stellgenauigkeit liegen. Für beide Verfahrensstufen kann darüber hinaus die lokale Konvergenz des Regelungsverfahrens formal nachgewiesen werden.

2   Stand der Technik

In der Vergangenheit wurde eine Vielzahl von Ansätzen für die Pfadverfolgung von Fahrzeuggespannen vorgestellt. Die meisten Arbeiten beschäftigen sich jedoch wie z.B. [5] mit Spezialfahrzeugen mit im Vergleich zu Serienfahrzeugen relativ einfach zu handhabendem kinematischem Verhalten.

Bolzern et. al. beschreiben in [3] einen Ansatz, mit dem diese Verfahren auf Serienfahrzeugen übertragen werden können. Sie nähern das reale Fahrzeug durch eines an, das einfachere kinematische Eigenschaften hat und berechnen mithilfe dieses Modells die Steuergrößen. Daraus resultiert die Problematik, dass der Regelungsalgorithmus nun neben den tatsächlichen Störungen auch noch die Modellfehler ausgleichen muss und das Verfahren deshalb weniger robust ist.

Astolfi et al. beschreiben in [2] eine Lösung, die auf Lyapunov-Stabilität basiert. Ihr Ansatz stellt hohe Anforderungen an die Manövrierfähigkeit des Fahrzeuges, die reale Fahrzeuge selten erfülle. Weiterhin setzt es aufwändige

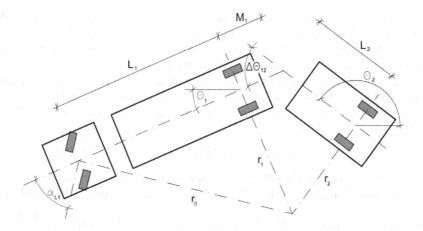

Abb. 2. Einspur-Modell eines *general-2-trailers* bei der stabilen Fahrt.

numerische Berechnungen voraus und benötigt eine Vielzahl von Parametern, die keine intuitive Bedeutung haben und deren Bestimmung sich schwierig gestaltet.

Daneben existieren Ansätze, die auf Maschinenlernen basieren (z. B. [4]). Diese lassen sich jedoch aufgrund des folgenden Problems nicht praktisch einsetzen: Wenn sie an Modellfahrzeugen lernen, lässt sich keine Aussage über ihr Verhalten auf realen Fahrzeugen treffen. Wenn sie hingegen an realen Fahrzeugen lernen, ist die Lernphase i. d. R. mit nicht aktzeptierbaren Risiken verbunden.

Ein interessantes, zweistufiges Verfahren für die Rückwärtsfahrt stellen Predalier und Usher in [7] vor. Im ersten Schritt wird der Einknickwinkel bestimmt, der dann im zweiten Schritt mithilfe eines Reglers erreicht werden soll. Beide Schritte werden durch die vorliegende Arbeit durch andere Verfahren ersetzt. Zur Berechnung des Einknickwinkels wird nur noch einer anstelle von drei Parametern benötigt und der neue Einknickwinkelregler kommt ohne Integralanteil aus, da er keinen Linearisierungsfehler aufweist.

3   Kinematisches Modell

Basierend auf der von *Altafini* in [1] eingeführten Klassifizierung von mehrgliedrigen Gespannfahrzeugen wird ein Lkw mit einachsigem Starrdeichselanhänger (siehe Abb. 2) der Kategorie der *general-2-trailer* zugeordnet. Das kinematische Bewegungsverhalten eines general-2-trailer kann abhängig von der momentanen Konfiguration und den beiden Steuergrößen v_1 und $\dot{\alpha}_{L_1}$ durch die folgende Funktion beschrieben werden:

$$\begin{pmatrix} \dot{x}_1 \\ \dot{y}_1 \\ \dot{\theta}_1 \\ \Delta\dot{\theta}_{12} \\ \dot{\alpha}_{L_1} \end{pmatrix} = \begin{pmatrix} \cos(\theta_1) & 0 \\ \sin(\theta_1) & 0 \\ \tan(\alpha_{L_1})/L_1 & 0 \\ -\frac{\tan(\alpha_{L_1})}{L_1} - \frac{\sin(\Delta\theta_{12})}{L_2} - \frac{M_1\cos(\Delta\theta_{12})\tan(\alpha_{L_1})}{L_1 L_2} & 0 \\ 0 & 1 \end{pmatrix} \begin{pmatrix} v_1 \\ \dot{\alpha}_{L_1} \end{pmatrix} \quad (1)$$

Die Steuergröße v_1 entspricht dabei der Geschwindigkeit eines Hinterrads des Zugfahrzeugs. Das kinematische Bewegungsmodell spiegelt die Nonholonomie-Eigenschaft dieser Fahrzeuge wieder, die die Bewegungsfreiheit erheblich einschränkt und unmittelbare Konfigurationsänderungen ausschließt.

In der in Abbildung 2 dargestellten Situation bewegen sich alle Fahrzeugglieder stabil zueinander auf konzentrischen Kreisen. In diesem Fall wird der Zusammenhang zwischen dem Einknickwinkel $\Delta\theta_{12}$ und dem Lenkwinkel α_{L_1} durch folgende Funktion beschrieben:

$$\alpha_{L_1,stable} = \arctan\left(L_1 \sin\left(\Delta\theta_{12}\right) / \left(L_2 + M_1 \cos\left(\Delta\theta_{12}\right)\right)\right) \tag{2}$$

Ferner besteht zwischen dem Radius r_2 des Kreises, auf dem sich die Hinterachse des Anhängers bewegt, und dem Einknickwinkel $\Delta\theta_{12}$ folgende Abhängigkeit:

$$\Delta\theta_{12,stable} = -\arctan\left(M_1 \left/ \left(r_2\sqrt{\left(L_2^2 - M_1^2\right)/r_2^2 + 1}\right)\right.\right) - \arctan\left(\frac{L_2}{r_2}\right) \tag{3}$$

Ein Lkw mit einachsigem Starrdeichselanhänger konvergiert gegen diesen stabilen Zustand, wenn er mit einem festen Lenkwinkel in Vorwärtsrichtung fährt. Obwohl auch ein Sattelzug der Kategorie der general-2-trailer angehört, unterscheidet er sich diesbezüglich in seinem Bewegungsverhalten. Im Unterschied zu einem Lkw mit einachsigem Starrdeichselanhänger kann für einen Sattelzug ab einem fahrzeugspezifischen Lenkwinkel α_{turn} keine Konvergenz beobachtet werden. Abhängig von dem Verhältnis der Distanzen L_1, M_1 und L_2 erreicht das Fahrzeuggespann in diesem Fall keinen stabilen Zustand. Diese Problematik und das spezifische Bewegungsverhalten von Sattelzügen im Allgemeinen werden in [10] eingehend untersucht.

4   Das zweistufige Regelungsverfahren

Aufgrund der kinematischen Zwangsbedingungen kann weder die Position noch die Ausrichtung des Fahrzeuges direkt beeinflusst werden. Beim Vorwärtsfahren lässt sich lediglich der Radius, auf dem sich das Fahrzeug bewegt, durch die Änderung des Lenkwinkels sofort verändern. Beim Rückwärtsfahren beeinflusst der Einknickwinkel den Radius, auf dem sich der Anhänger bewegt.

Das Verfahren ist deshalb in die folgenden beiden Stufen gegliedert: Erstens die Bestimmung des Radius des Kreises, auf dem sich ein Referenzpunkt bewegen soll, um den Sollpfad zu erreichen. Zweitens die Bestimmung des Lenkwinkels, durch den dieser Radius erreicht wird. Als Referenzpunkt X für die Vorwärtsfahrt wird der Mittelpunkt der Hinterachse des Zugfahrzeuges und für die Rückwärtsfahrt der Mittelpunkt der einzigen Achse des Anhängers ausgewählt. Durch diese Wahl der Referenzpunkte kann die erste Stufe des Verfahrens weitgehend unabhängig von der Bewegungsrichtung durchgeführt werden.

4.1   Bestimmung des Soll-Radius

Um den Soll-Radius zu bestimmen, wird zunächst – analog zur menschlichen Herangehensweise – ein Punkt auf dem Pfad ausgewählt, den man versucht zu erreichen. Dieser Punkt wird im Weiteren als Treffpunkt T bezeichnet. Anschließend wird der Kreis bestimmt, auf dem sich das betrachtete Fahrzeugglied bewegen müsste, um diesen Punkt zu erreichen.

Der Treffpunkt wird bestimmt, indem zunächst der Referenzpunkt X auf den Pfad projiziert und dieser Projektionspunkt dann um eine feste Länge c_v entlang des Pfades verschoben wird. Ein geeigneter Wert für den Parameter c_v hängt zum Einen von der Geometrie des Fahrzeuges und zum Anderen vom Parameter c_p, der im folgenden Abschnitt eingeführt wird, ab. Eine Möglichkeit zur experimentellen Bestimmung eines solchen Wertes ist die, eine Gerade als Soll-Pfad vorzugeben und das Fahrzeug zu Beginn parallel dazu zu positionieren. Wird der Parameter zu klein gewählt, dann führt dies beim Verfolgen des Pfades zu einem zu steilen Auffahren auf die Gerade, so dass der Einknickwinkel nicht schnell genug geändert werden kann und der Sollpfad später erreicht wird. Zu große Werte führen zu einem zu flachen Auffahren auf die Gerade und damit ebenfalls zu einem späteren Erreichen des Sollpfades. Durch Anpassen des Wertes und Wiederholung des Versuches kann man so einen geeigneten Wert finden.

Im Folgenden werden Lösungen für die Berechnung des Treffpunktes für eine Gerade und einen Kreis angegeben. Die Beschränkung auf diese beiden Wegtypen stellt aber keine echte Einschränkung des Verfahrens dar, weil sich jeder Pfad beliebig genau mit Kreisbögen und Geradenstücken annähern lässt.

Gerade: Sei der Sollpfad eine Gerade und durch $g : \mathbb{R} \rightarrow \mathbb{R}^2 : g(\lambda) := \overrightarrow{P} + \lambda \cdot \overrightarrow{PQ}$ gegeben. Der Vektor $\overrightarrow{PQ}$ sei normiert und gebe die Sollfahrtrichtung des Fahrzeuges an. Dann gilt für den Teffpunkt:

$$\overrightarrow{T} = \left(\left\langle \overrightarrow{PX}, \overrightarrow{PQ} \right\rangle + c_v \right) \cdot \overrightarrow{PQ} + \overrightarrow{P} \tag{4}$$

Kreis: Sei der Sollpfad ein Kreis und durch $k : \mathbb{R} \rightarrow \mathbb{R}^2 : k(\phi) := \overrightarrow{M} + r \cdot (\cos\phi, \sin\phi)^T$ gegeben. Die Rotationsmatrix für den Winkel τ werde mit R_τ bezeichnet. Dann gilt für den Treffpunkt:

$$\overrightarrow{T} = r \cdot R_{c_v/r} \cdot \overrightarrow{XM} / |XM| + \overrightarrow{M} \tag{5}$$

Wie in Abb. 2 zu sehen, liegt der Bewegungsmittelpunkt beider Fahrzeugglieder jeweils auf einer Geraden, die senkrecht auf der jeweiligen Längsachse steht und durch den Referenzpunkt verläuft. Der Mittelpunkt des gesuchten Kreises muss also auf eben dieser Geraden liegen. Des Weiteren soll der Kreis durch den Treffpunkt verlaufen. Folglich ist die Strecke zwischen Treffpunkt und aktueller Position eine Sehne des gesuchten Kreises, dessen Mittelpunkt somit auf der Mittelsenkrechten dieser Strecke liegen muss. Diese beiden Bedingungen sind hinreichend, um den Korrekturkreis und damit seinen Radius zu bestimmen. Für diesen gilt:

$$r_k = |TX|^2 \Big/ \left(2 \cdot \left\langle (-\sin\theta, \cos\theta)^T, \overrightarrow{TX} \right\rangle \right) \tag{6}$$

Durch die wiederholte Anwendung dieser Prozedur wird nicht nur der Fehler in der Position des Referenzpunktes minimiert, sondern auch die Krümmung des

Sollpfades wird schließlich erreicht. Genauer gesagt konnte in [9] bewiesen werden, dass das Verfahren bei Kreisen und Geraden lokale, asymptotische Stabilität aufweist, also für eine Umgebung um den Pfad gegen diesen konvergiert.

4.2 Bestimmung des Soll-Lenkwinkels

Mithilfe des im letzten Abschnitt berechneten Radius lässt sich nun der Soll-Lenkwinkel für das Fahrzeug berechnen. Beim Vorwärtsfahren kann dies direkt geschehen, hingegen wird beim Rückwärtsfahren zunächst der Soll-Einknickwinkel bestimmt, der dann als Führungsgröße für einen Regler dient, dessen Stellwert der Soll-Lenkwinkel ist.

Vorwärtsfahrt: Bei der Vorwärtsfahrt ist der Bezugspunkt der Mittelpunkt der Hinterachse des Zugfahrzeuges. Der berechnete Radius entspricht also dem Radius r_1. Aus Abb. 2 folgt damit für den Soll-Lenkwinkel:

$$\alpha_{Soll} = \arctan\left(L_1/r_1\right) \tag{7}$$

Rückwärtsfahrt: Bei der Rückwärtsfahrt entspricht der berechnete Radius dem Radius r_2. Mithilfe von Gl. 3 lässt sich damit der Soll-Einknickwinkel berechnen.

Um einen Lenkwinkel zu erhalten, der diesen Einknickwinkel einstellt, wird ein Regler eingeführt. Der Entwurf dieses Reglers basiert auf der Beobachtung, dass sich der Einknickwinkel bei der Vorwärtsfahrt stets dem stabilen Wert annähert und sich bei der Rückwärtsfahrt von diesem Wert entfernt.

Soll der der Einknickwinkel vergrößert werden, so wählt man also einen Lenkwinkel, der zu einem kleineren Einknickwinkel gehört. Daraus resultiert folgender Proportionalregler mit nicht-linearem Anteil:

$$\alpha_{Soll} = c_p \cdot \left(\Delta\theta_{12,Soll} - \Delta\theta_{12,Ist}\right) + f\left(\Delta\theta_{12,Ist}\right) \tag{8}$$

Dabei bezeichnet f die Funktion, die einem Einknickwinkel den zugehörigen Lenkwinkel bei der stabilen Fahrt zuordnet (siehe Gl. 2), und c_p einen Parameter, der die Geschwindigkeit der Lenkwinkeländerung beeinflusst. Ein geeigneter Wert für c_p hängt von der maximalen Lenkgeschwindigkeit, der Geometrie des Fahrzeuges und von der gewählten Periode des Steuerungsprozesses ab. Zu kleine Werte führen zu langsamer Konvergenz des Einknickwinkelreglers, zu große zu Überschwingen. Es ist möglich, nur diesen Regler isoliert zu betrachten, indem man einen festen Soll-Einknickwinkel vorgibt. Deshalb kann eine optimale Parametrisierung ohne die Berechnung des Sollradius und damit unabhängig vom anderen Parameter c_v erfolgen.

Für den Einknickwinkelregler konnte in [9] gezeigt werden, dass bei $\Delta\theta_{12,Soll}$ eine lokale, asymptotisch stabile Ruhelage existiert. Folglich konvergiert der Einknickwinkel gegen den Sollwert, wenn der Anfangsfehler klein genug ist.

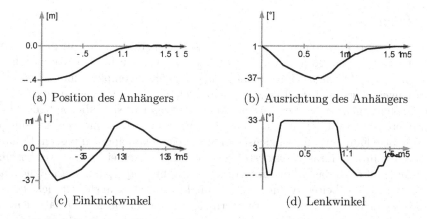

(a) Position des Anhängers   (b) Ausrichtung des Anhängers

(c) Einknickwinkel   (d) Lenkwinkel

Abb. 3. Verlauf der Bewegung des Anhängers sowie des Lenkwinkels und des Einknickwinkels beim Unterfahren einer Wechselbrücke.

5 Evaluierung des Verfahrens

Für die praktische Evaluierung des Pfadverfolgungsverfahrens steht ein Modelfahrzeug im Maßstab 1 : 16 zur Verfügung (siehe Abb. 1). Es verfügt über einen Sensor für die Messung des Einknickwinkels und einen Laserscanner zur Positions- und Ausrichtungsbestimmung. Als Steuergrößen stehen zum einen der Lenkwinkel des Zugfahrzeuges zur Verfügung, der dann mittels eines internen Reglers von einem Servo gesetzt wird und zum anderen die Geschwindigkeit der Hinterachse des Zugfahrzeuges.

Als Fallbeispiel wird hier das Unterfahren einer Wechselbrücke vorgestellt. Dies ist ein Manöver, das in der Praxis sehr häufig vorkommt und dem Fahrer höchste Konzentration abverlangt. Wechselbehälter sind nach DIN 70014 genormt und bieten beim Unterfahren nur eine Toleranz von etwa 150 mm zu beiden Seiten des Fahrzeugs. Im Laborversuch ist der Abstand der Stützen der Wechselbrücke 25 mm breiter als der Modellanhänger. Das Pfadverfolgungsverfahren muss sehr präzise arbeiten, damit die Wechselbrücke tatsächlich unterfahren werden kann, denn Position und Ausrichtung müssen stimmen. Im hier betrachteten Experiment wurde das Fahrzeug etwa eine Gespannlänge vor und zwei Fahrzeugbreiten neben der Wechselbrücke positioniert. Als Sollpfad wurde eine Gerade vorgegeben, die in der Mitte der Wechselbrücke verläuft.

Die Ergebnisse des Versuchs werden in Abb. 3 gezeigt. Nach einer Bewegung von etwa einem Meter ist der Positionsfehler kleiner als ein 1 cm und der Ausrichtungsfehler ist nach etwa 1,5 m kleiner als 1°. Folglich kann die Wechselbrücke erfolgreich unterfahren werden.

Auch für andere Manöver, wie beispielsweise dem rückwärts eine Kurve abfahren oder an eine Rampe andocken, wurden Experimente durchgeführt. Auch dabei zeichnete sich das Verfahren durch ein sehr präzises Verhalten aus.

6   Zusammenfassung

In diesem Beitrag wird ein Verfahren vorgeschlagen, das sich für die präzise Verfolgung von Pfaden sowohl bei der Rückwärts- als auch bei der Vorwärtsfahrt eignet. Es ist effizient zu implementieren, da es ohne komplexe numerische Berechnungen auskommt, und kann deshalb auch in echtzeitkritischen, eingebetteten Umgebungen eingesetzt werden. Außerdem lässt es sich über lediglich zwei Parameter, die mithilfe einer einheitlichen Prozedur bestimmt werden können, an beliebige Fahrzeuge mit einachsigem Starrdeichselanhänger anpassen. Es kann zum einen für Fahrerassistenzsysteme für das Rangieren eingesetzt werden und zum anderen auch das autonome Fahren von Fahrzeuggespannen ermöglichen.

Zukünftige Arbeiten werden sich damit beschäftigen, inwieweit sich die Ergebnisse auch auf Sattelzüge erweitern lassen, die in einigen Situationen ein anderes kinematisches Verhalten zeigen. Außerdem wird untersucht werden, wie die Parameter des Pfadverfolgungsverfahrens quantitativ mit den kinematischen Eigenschaften des Fahrzeuges zusammenhängen, um nicht für jede Kombination von Zugfahrzeug und Anhänger zunächst Experimente durchführen zu müssen und eine Anwendung auf realen Fahrzeugen zu erleichtern.

Literaturverzeichnis

1. C. Altafini. Some properties of the general n-trailer. *International Journal of Control*, 74(4):409–424, 2001.
2. A. Astolfi, P. Bolzern, and A. Locatelli. Path-tracking of a tractor-trailer vehicle along rectilinear and circular paths: a Lyapunov-based approach. *IEEE Transactions on Robotics and Automation*, 20(1):154–160, 2004.
3. P. Bolzern, R. DeSantis, A. Locatelli, and D. Masciocchi. Path-tracking for articulated vehicles with off-axle hitching. *Control Systems Technology, IEEE Transactions on*, 6(4):515–523, 1998.
4. J. Koza. A genetic approach to finding a controller to back up a tractor-trailer truck. In *Proceedings of the 1992 American Control Conference*, volume III, pages 2307–2311, 1992.
5. F. Lamiraux, S. Sekhavat, and J. Laumond. Motion planning and control for Hilare pulling a trailer. *IEEE Transactions on Robotics and Automation*, 15(4):640–652, 1999.
6. S. LaValle. *Planning Algorithms*. Cambridge University Press, Cambridge, Massachusetts, 2006.
7. C. Pradalier and K. Usher. Robust trajectory tracking for a reversing tractor trailer. *Journal of Field Robotics*, 25(6):378–399, 2008.
8. L. Qiu, W.-J. Hsu, S.-Y. Huang, and H. Wang. Scheduling and routing algorithms for agvs: a survey. *International Journal of Production Research*, 40(3):745–760, 2 2002.
9. C. Schwarz. Entwicklung eines Regelungsverfahrens zur Pfadverfolgung für ein Modellfahrzeug mit einachsigem Anhänger, Diplomarbeit, Universität Koblenz-Landau, 2009.
10. D. Zöbel and C. Weyand. On the maneuverability of heavy goods vehicles. In *2008 IEEE International Conference on Systems, Man, and Cynernetics (SMC 2008)*, Singapore, 2008.

Learning New Basic Movements for Robotics

Jens Kober and Jan Peters

Max Planck Institute for Biological Cybernetics, Tübingen, Germany

Abstract. Obtaining novel skills is one of the most important problems in robotics. Machine learning techniques may be a promising approach for automatic and autonomous acquisition of movement policies. However, this requires both an appropriate policy representation and suitable learning algorithms. Employing the most recent form of the dynamical systems motor primitives originally introduced by Ijspeert et al. [1], we show how both discrete and rhythmic tasks can be learned using a concerted approach of both imitation and reinforcement learning, and present our current best performing learning algorithms. Finally, we show that it is possible to include a start-up phase in rhythmic primitives. We apply our approach to two elementary movements, i.e., Ball-in-a-Cup and Ball-Paddling, which can be learned on a real Barrett WAM robot arm at a pace similar to human learning.

1 Introduction

When humans learn new motor skills, e.g., paddling a ball with a table-tennis racket or hitting a tennis ball, it is highly likely that they are represented as elementary or primitive movements and use imitation as well as reinforcement learning [2]. In contrast, most robots are still programmed by a human operator using task and domain knowledge. Such programming is highly efficient but can also become very expensive and is limited to the considered situations. Learning techniques are a plausible alternative for more autonomous skill acquisition and improvement. Inspired by the biological insight, we will discuss the technical counterparts in this paper and show how both single-stroke and rhythmic tasks can be learned efficiently by mimicking the human presenter with subsequent reward-driven self-improvement.

Unfortunately however, off-the-shelf machine learning techniques do not scale into the high-dimensional domains of anthropomorphic robotics. Instead, robot learning requires methods that employ both representations and algorithms appropriate for the domain. If a favorable function approximator is chosen in this context, ideally one that is linear in its parameters, then learning can be sufficiently fast for application in robotics in real-time.

Recently, the idea of using dynamical systems as motor primitives was put forward by Ijspeert et al. [1, 3] as a general approach for representing control policies for basic movements. The resulting movement generation has a variety of favorable properties, i.e., rescalability with respect to both time and amplitude, basic stability properties and the possibility to encode either single-stroke or rhythmic behaviors. Previous applications include a variety of different basic motor skills such as tennis swings [1], T-ball batting [4], planar biped walking [5], constrained reaching tasks [6] and even in tasks with potential industrial application [7]. Nevertheless, most of the previous work in motor primitive learning (with the exceptions of [4] and [6]) has focused on learning by imitation *without* subsequent self-improvement. In real life, a human demonstration is rarely ever perfect nor does it suffice for near-optimal performance. Thus, additional reinforcement learning is essential for both performance-based refinement and continuous adaptation of the presented skill.

In this paper, we present our current best performing setups for motor primitive learning with both the required methods for imitation and reinforcement learning. The appropriate imitation and reinforcement learning methods are given in Section 2. In Section 3, we show how the resulting framework can be applied to both learning *Ball-in-a-Cup* as a discrete task and *Ball-Paddling* as a rhythmic task on a real Barrett WAM[1]. The ball-paddling task is of particular interest as we show how the combination of different motor primitives is possible. It is among the first applications where both rhythmic and discrete dynamical systems motor primitives [1] are used in conjunction to achieve the task.

2   Learning Methods for Motor Primitives

It is likely that humans rely both on imitation and on reinforcement learning for learning new motor skills as both of these approaches have different functions in the learning process. Imitation learning has a given target and, thus, it allows to learn policies from the examples of a teacher. However, imitation learning can only reproduce a policy representing or generalizing an exhibited behavior. Self-improvement by trial-and-error with respect to an external reward signal can be achieved by reinforcement learning. Nevertheless, traditional reinforcement learning algorithms require exhaustive exploration of the state and action space. Given the high-dimensionality of the state-space of anthropomorphic robots (a seven degree of freedom robot defies exhaustive exploration), the "curse of dimensionality" [8] fully applies and we need to rely on local reinforcement learning methods which improve upon the preceding imitation instead of traditional 'brute force' approaches. To some extent, this mimics how children acquire new motor skills with the teacher giving a demonstration while the child subsequently attempts to reproduce and improve the skill by trial-and-error. However, note that not every task requires reinforcement learning and some can be learned purely based on imitations. Nevertheless, few tasks are known which are directly learned by reinforcement learning without preceding mimicking [9]. Thus, we first review how to do imitation learning with dynamical systems motor primitives in Section 2.1 and, subsequently, we show how reinforcement learning can be applied in this context in Section 2.2. The latter section will outline our reinforcement learning algorithm for the application in motor primitive learning.

---

[1] Accompanying video: http://www.youtube.com/watch?v=cNyoMVZQdYM

2.1   Imitation Learning for Dynamical Motor Primitives

In the presented framework, we initialize the motor primitives by imitation learning as in [9]. This step can be performed efficiently in the context of dynamical systems motor primitives as they represent a deterministic policy in the form $\bar{\mathbf{a}} = \boldsymbol{\theta}^{\mathrm{T}}\boldsymbol{\mu}(\mathbf{s})$, where $\boldsymbol{\mu}(\mathbf{s})$ are basis functions [9] depending on the state $\mathbf{s}$ (namely positions, velocities and a phase variable), $\boldsymbol{\theta} \in \mathbb{R}^N$ are policy parameters and $\bar{\mathbf{a}}$ are the actions (namely desired positions, velocities and accelerations). This policy is linear in parameters, thus, we have a standard locally-weighted linear regression problem that can be solved straightforwardly. This general approach has originally been suggested in [1]. Estimating the parameters of the dynamical system is slightly more daunting, i.e., the movement duration of discrete movements is extracted using motion detection and the time-constant is set accordingly. Similarly, the base period for the rhythmic dynamical motor primitives was extracted using first repetitions and, again, the time-constants are set accordingly. As the start-up phase in rhythmic presentations may deviate significantly from the periodic movement, the baseline of the oscillation often needs to be estimated based on the later part of the recorded movement, the amplitude is determined as the mean of the amplitudes of individual oscillations in this part.

2.2   Reinforcement Learning with PoWER

Reinforcement learning [10] of motor primitives is a very specific type of learning problem where it is hard to apply generic reinforcement learning algorithms [4, 11]. For this reason, the focus of this paper is largely on novel domain-appropriate reinforcement learning algorithms which operate on parametrized policies for episodic control problems.

Reinforcement Learning Setup When modeling our problem as a reinforcement learning problem, we always have a high-dimensional state $\mathbf{s}$ and as a result, standard RL methods which discretize the state-space can no longer be applied. The action $\mathbf{a} = \boldsymbol{\theta}^{\mathrm{T}}\boldsymbol{\mu}(\mathbf{s}) + \boldsymbol{\epsilon}$ is the output of our motor primitives augmented by the exploration $\boldsymbol{\epsilon}$. As a result, we have a stochastic policy $\mathbf{a} \sim \pi(\mathbf{s})$ with parameters $\boldsymbol{\theta}$ which can be seen as a distribution over the actions given the states. After a next time-step δt, the actor transfers to a state $\mathbf{s}_{t+1}$ and receives a reward r_t. As we are interested in learning complex motor tasks consisting of a single stroke or a rhythmically repeating movement, we focus on finite horizons of length T with episodic restarts [10]. While the policy representation is substantially different, the rhythmic movement resembles a repeated episodic movement in the reinforcement learning process. The general goal in reinforcement learning is to optimize the *expected return* of the policy with parameters $\boldsymbol{\theta}$ defined by $J(\boldsymbol{\theta}) = \int_{\mathbb{T}} p(\boldsymbol{\tau})R(\boldsymbol{\tau})d\boldsymbol{\tau}$, where $\boldsymbol{\tau} = [\mathbf{s}_{1:T+1}, \mathbf{a}_{1:T}]$ denotes a sequence of states $\mathbf{s}_{1:T+1} = [\mathbf{s}_1, \mathbf{s}_2, \ldots, \mathbf{s}_{T+1}]$ and actions $\mathbf{a}_{1:T} = [\mathbf{a}_1, \mathbf{a}_2, \ldots, \mathbf{a}_T]$, the probability of an episode $\boldsymbol{\tau}$ is denoted by $p(\boldsymbol{\tau})$ and $R(\boldsymbol{\tau})$ refers to the return of an episode $\boldsymbol{\tau}$ and $\mathbb{T}$ is the set of all possible paths. Using the Markov assumption, we can write the path distribution as $p(\boldsymbol{\tau}) = p(\mathbf{s}_1) \prod_{t=1}^{T+1} p(\mathbf{s}_{t+1}|\mathbf{s}_t, \mathbf{a}_t)\pi(\mathbf{a}_t|\mathbf{s}_t, t)$ where $p(\mathbf{s}_1)$ denotes the initial state distribution and $p(\mathbf{s}_{t+1}|\mathbf{s}_t, \mathbf{a}_t)$ is the next state distribution conditioned on last state and action. Similarly, if we assume additive, accumulated rewards, the return of a path is given by $R(\boldsymbol{\tau}) = \frac{1}{T} \sum_{t=1}^{T} r(\mathbf{s}_t, \mathbf{a}_t, \mathbf{s}_{t+1}, t)$, where $r(\mathbf{s}_t, \mathbf{a}_t, \mathbf{s}_{t+1}, t)$ denotes the immediate reward.

While episodic Reinforcement Learning (RL) problems with finite horizons are common in motor control, few methods exist in the RL literature (notable exceptions are model-free method such as Episodic REINFORCE [12] and the Episodic Natural Actor-Critic eNAC [4] as well as model-based methods, e.g., using differential-dynamic programming [13]). In order to avoid learning of complex models, we focus on model-free methods and, to reduce the number of open parameters, we rather use a novel Reinforcement Learning algorithm which is based on expectation-maximization [14]. Our new algorithm is called Policy learning by Weighting Exploration with the Returns (PoWER) and can be derived from the same higher principle as previous policy gradient approaches, see [15] for details.

Policy Learning by Weighting Exploration with the Returns (PoWER)
When learning motor primitives, we intend to learn a deterministic mean policy $\bar{\mathbf{a}} = \boldsymbol{\theta}^{\mathrm{T}}\boldsymbol{\mu}(\mathbf{s})$ which is linear in parameters $\boldsymbol{\theta}$ and augmented by additive exploration $\boldsymbol{\epsilon}(\mathbf{s}, t)$ in order to make model-free reinforcement learning possible. As a result, the explorative policy can be given in the form $\mathbf{a} = \boldsymbol{\theta}^{\mathrm{T}}\boldsymbol{\mu}(\mathbf{s}, t) + \boldsymbol{\epsilon}(\boldsymbol{\mu}(\mathbf{s}, t))$. Previous work in [4, 11], has focused on state-independent, white Gaussian exploration, i.e., $\boldsymbol{\epsilon}(\boldsymbol{\mu}(\mathbf{s}, t)) \sim \mathcal{N}(0, \Sigma)$, and has resulted into applications such as T-Ball batting [4] and constrained movement [6]. Alternatively, as introduced by [16], one could generate a form of structured, state-dependent exploration $\boldsymbol{\epsilon}(\boldsymbol{\mu}(\mathbf{s}, t)) = \boldsymbol{\varepsilon}_t^{\mathrm{T}}\boldsymbol{\mu}(\mathbf{s}, t)$ with $[\boldsymbol{\varepsilon}_t]_{ij} \sim \mathcal{N}(0, \sigma_{ij}^2)$, where σ_{ij}^2 are meta-parameters of the exploration that can be optimized in a similar manner. Each σ_{ij}^2 corresponds to one θ_{ij}. This argument results into the policy $\mathbf{a} \sim \pi(\mathbf{a}_t|\mathbf{s}_t, t) = \mathcal{N}(\mathbf{a}|\boldsymbol{\mu}(\mathbf{s}, \mathbf{t}), \hat{\boldsymbol{\Sigma}}(\mathbf{s}, t))$. This form of policies improves upon shortcomings of directly perturbed policies. Based on the EM updates for Reinforcement Learning as suggested in [11, 15], we can derive the update rule

$$\boldsymbol{\theta}' = \boldsymbol{\theta} + \frac{E_{\boldsymbol{\tau}}\left\{\sum_{t=1}^{T} \boldsymbol{\varepsilon}_t Q^\pi(\mathbf{s}_t, \mathbf{a}_t, t)\right\}}{E_{\boldsymbol{\tau}}\left\{\sum_{t=1}^{T} Q^\pi(\mathbf{s}_t, \mathbf{a}_t, t)\right\}}, \tag{1}$$

where $Q^\pi(\mathbf{s}, \mathbf{a}, t)$ is the state-action value function. Note that this algorithm does not need the learning rate as a meta-parameter. In order to reduce the number of trials in this on-policy scenario, we reuse the trials through importance sampling [10].

3   Robot Evaluation

The methods presented in this paper are evaluated on two learning problems on a real, seven degree of freedom Barrett WAM, i.e., we learn the discrete task of

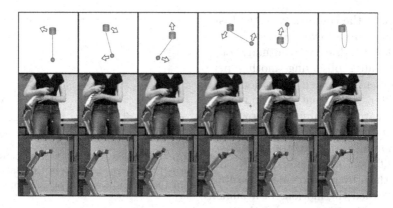

Fig. 1. This figure shows schematic drawings of the *Ball-in-a-Cup* motion, the final learned robot motion as well as a kinesthetic teach-in. The green arrows show the directions of the current movements in that frame. The human cup motion was taught to the robot by imitation learning with 31 parameters per joint for an approximately three seconds long trajectory. The robot manages to reproduce the imitated motion quite accurately, but the ball misses the cup by several centimeters. After roughly 75 rollouts, we have good performance and at the end of the 100 rollouts we have virtually no failures anymore.

Ball-in-a-Cup and the rhythmic task *Ball-Paddling*. The resulting simplicity and speed of the learning process demonstrate the suitability of the motor primitive-based learning framework for practical application.

3.1 Discrete Movement: Ball-in-a-Cup

The children motor game Ball-in-a-Cup, also known as Balero and Bilboquet [17] is challenging even for a grown up. The toy has a small cup which is held in one hand (or, in our case, is attached to the end-effector of the robot) and the cup has a small ball hanging down on a string (the string has a length of 40cm for our toy). Initially, the ball is hanging down vertically in a rest position. The player needs to move fast in order to induce a motion in the ball through the string, toss it up and catch it with the cup, a possible movement is illustrated in Figure 1 in the top row.

The state of the system can be described by joint angles and joint velocities of the robot as well as the the Cartesian coordinates and velocities of the ball. The actions are the joint space accelerations where each of the seven joints is driven by a separate motor primitive with one common canonical system. The movement uses all seven degrees of freedom and is not on a plane. All motor primitives are perturbed separately but employ the same joint final reward. The reward is based on the minimal distance between the center of the ball and the center of the cup.

Due to the complexity of the task, Ball-in-a-Cup is even a hard motor task for children who usually only succeed after observing another person presenting a demonstration first, and after subsequent trial-and-error-based learning. Mimicking how children learn to play Ball-in-a-Cup, we first initialize the motor primitives by imitation and, subsequently, improve them by reinforcement learning. We recorded the motions of a human player by kinesthetic teach-in in order

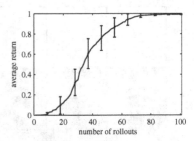

Fig. 2. This figure shows the expected return of the learned policy in the Ball-in-a-Cup evaluation averaged over 20 runs.

to obtain an example for imitation as shown in Figure 1 (middle row). As expected, the robot fails to reproduce the presented behavior even if we use all the recorded details for the imitation. Thus, reinforcement learning is needed for self-improvement. We determined by cross-validation that 31 shape-parameters per motor primitive are needed.

In [15] we benchmarked our novel algorithm and several widely used algorithms on tasks having characteristics similar to this one. As a result we employ our best algorithm, PoWER. Figure 2 shows the expected return over the number of rollouts where convergence to a maximum is clearly recognizable. The robot regularly succeeds at bringing the ball into the cup after approximately 75 rollouts. A nine year old child got the ball in the cup for the first time after 35 trials while the robot got the ball in for the first time after 42 rollouts. However, after 100 trials, the robot exhibits perfect runs in every single trial while, from our experience, the child does not have a comparable success rate. Of course, such a comparison with a child is contrived as a robot can precisely reproduce movements unlike any human being and that children can most likely adapt faster to changes in the setup.

3.2   Rhythmic Movement with Start-up Phase: Ball-Paddling

In Ball-Paddling, we have a table-tennis ball that is attached to a table-tennis paddle by an elastic string. The goal is to have the ball bouncing above the paddle. The string avoids that the ball is falling down but also pulls the ball back towards the center of the paddle if the ball is hit sufficiently hard (i.e., the string is also stretched sufficiently as a consequence). The task is fairly easy to perform open-loop once the player has determined appropriate amplitude and frequency for the motion. Furthermore, the task is robust to small changes of these parameters as well as to small perturbations of the environment. We again recorded the motions of a human player using kinesthetic teach-in in order to obtain a demonstration for imitation learning as shown in Figure 3. From the imitation, it can be determined by cross-validation that 10 shape-parameters per motor primitive are sufficient.

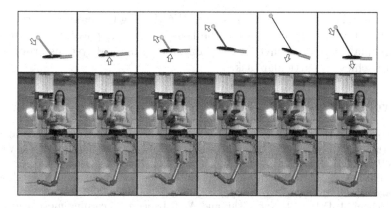

Fig. 3. This figure shows schematic drawings of the *Ball-Paddling* motion, a kinesthetic teach-in as well as the performance of the robot after imitation learning. When the string is stretched it is shown as thinner and darker. The human demonstration was taught to the robot by imitation learning with 10 parameters per joint for the rhythmic motor primitive. An additional discrete motor primitive is used for the start-up phase. Please see Section 3.2 and the accompanying video for details.

However, as we start with a still robot where the ball rests on the paddle, we require a start-up phase in order to perform the task successfully. This initial motion has to induce more energy in order to get the motion started and to extend the string sufficiently. For our setup, the start-up phase consists (as exhibited by the teacher's movements) of moving the paddle slower and further up than during the rhythmic behavior. This kind of movement can easily be achieved in the dynamical systems motor primitives framework by imposing another discrete primitive that gradually adapts the period parameter globally and the amplitude modifier to the ones encountered in the rhythmic behavior. The discrete modifier motor primitive is applied additively to the two parameters. The goal parameter of this modifier primitive is zero and thus, its influence vanishes after the initialization. With this start-up phase, imitation learning from demonstrations suffices to reproduce the motor skill successfully. To our knowledge, this application is probably the first where both rhythmic and discrete dynamical systems primitives are used together to achieve a particular task.

4   Conclusion

In this paper, we present both novel learning algorithms and experiments using the dynamical systems motor primitive [1, 9]. For doing so, we have discussed both appropriate imitation learning methods by locally weighted regression and derived our currently best-suited reinforcement learning algorithm for this framework, i.e., Policy learning by Weighting Exploration with the Returns (PoWER). We show that two complex motor tasks, i.e., *Ball-in-a-Cup* and *Ball-Paddling*, can be learned on a real, physical Barrett WAM using the methods presented in this paper. Of particular interest is the Ball-Paddling application as it requires the combination of both rhythmic and discrete dynamical systems primitives in order to achieve a particular task.

References

1. A. J. Ijspeert, J. Nakanishi, and S. Schaal, "Learning attractor landscapes for learning motor primitives," in *Advances in Neural Information Processing Systems (NIPS)*, 2003.
2. T. Flash and B. Hochner, "Motor primitives in vertebrates and invertebrates," *Current Opinions in Neurobiology*, vol. 15, pp. 660–666, 2005.
3. S. Schaal, J. Peters, J. Nakanishi, and A. J. Ijspeert, "Learning movement primitives," in *International Symposium on Robotics Research 2003 (ISRR)*, ser. Springer Tracts in Advanced Robotics, 2004, pp. 561–572.
4. J. Peters and S. Schaal, "Policy gradient methods for robotics," in *Proceedings of the IEEE/RSJ 2006 International Conference on Intelligent RObots and Systems (IROS)*, 2006, pp. 2219 – 2225.
5. S. Schaal, J. Peters, J. Nakanishi, and A. J. Ijspeert, "Control, planning, learning, and imitation with dynamic movement primitives," in *Proceedings of the Workshop on Bilateral Paradigms on Humans and Humanoids, IEEE 2003 International Conference on Intelligent RObots and Systems (IROS)*, 2003.
6. F. Guenter, M. Hersch, S. Calinon, and A. Billard, "Reinforcement learning for imitating constrained reaching movements," *Advanced Robotics, Special Issue on Imitative Robots*, vol. 21, no. 13, pp. 1521–1544, 2007.
7. H. Urbanek, A. Albu-Schäffer, and P.v.d.Smagt, "Learning from demonstration repetitive movements for autonomous service robotics," in *Proceedings of the IEEE/RSL 2004 International Conference on Intelligent RObots and Systems (IROS)*, 2004, pp. 3495–3500.
8. R. E. Bellman, *Dynamic Programming*. Princeton University Press, 1957.
9. S. Schaal, P. Mohajerian, and A. J. Ijspeert, "Dynamics systems vs. optimal control — a unifying view," *Progress in Brain Research*, vol. 165, no. 1, pp. 425–445, 2007.
10. R. Sutton and A. Barto, *Reinforcement Learning*. MIT PRESS, 1998.
11. J. Peters and S. Schaal, "Reinforcement learning for operational space," in *Proceedings of the International Conference on Robotics and Automation (ICRA)*, 2007.
12. R. J. Williams, "Simple statistical gradient-following algorithms for connectionist reinforcement learning," *Machine Learning*, vol. 8, pp. 229–256, 1992.
13. C. G. Atkeson, "Using local trajectory optimizers to speed up global optimization in dynamic programming," in *Advances in Neural Information Processing Systems 6 (NIPS)*, 1994.
14. P. Dayan and G. E. Hinton, "Using expectation-maximization for reinforcement learning," *Neural Computation*, vol. 9, no. 2, pp. 271–278, 1997.
15. J. Kober and J. Peters, "Policy search for motor primitives in robotics," in *Advances in Neural Information Processing Systems (NIPS)*, 2008.
16. T. Rückstieß, M. Felder, and J. Schmidhuber, "State-dependent exploration for policy gradient methods," in *Proceedings of the European Conference on Machine Learning (ECML)*, 2008, pp. 234–249.
17. Wikipedia, "Ball-in-a-cup," January 2009. [Online]. Available: http://en.wikipedia.org/wiki/Ball_in_a_cup

Nonlinear Landing Control for Quadrotor UAVs

Holger Voos

University of Applied Sciences Ravensburg-Weingarten, Mobile Robotics Lab,
D-88241 Weingarten

Abstract. Quadrotor UAVs are one of the most preferred type of small unmanned aerial vehicles because of the very simple mechanical construction and propulsion principle. However, the nonlinear dynamic behavior requires a more advanced stabilizing control and guidance of these vehicles. In addition, the small payload reduces the amount of batteries that can be carried and thus also limits the operating range of the UAV. One possible solution for a range extension is the application of a mobile base station for recharging purpose even during operation. However, landing on a moving base station requires autonomous tracking and landing control of the UAV. In this paper, a nonlinear autopilot for quadrotor UAVs is extended with a tracking and landing controller to fulfill the required task.

1 Introduction

Unmanned aerial vehicles (UAVs) already have a wide area of possible applications. Recent results in miniaturization, mechatronics and microelectronics also offer an enormous potential for small and inexpensive UAVs for commercial use. One very promising vehicle with respect to size, weight, construction and maneuverability is the so called quadrotor which is a system with four propellers in a cross configuration, see Fig. 1. By varying the speed of the single motors, the lift force can be changed and vertical and/or lateral motion can be generated. However, the quadrotor is a dynamically unstable nonlinear system which requires a suitable vehicle control system. One main drawback of small UAVs in nearly all types of application is the reduced payload and the limited amount of batteries that can be carried. Therefore the UAV has to return to a base station after a comparatively short amount of time for recharging purpose. In addition, in missions where a longer operating range is required such as pipeline, border or coast surveillance, returning to a stationary base station is also not useful. Instead it would be more suitable to operate with an autonomous mobile base station, e.g. a mobile robot or a ship, that is able to carry a higher amount of energy for several recharging cycles. Coordinated parallel operation of the mobile base station and the UAV then leads to an overall system for aerial surveillance with extended range. However, that concept requires basic stabilizing control of the quadrotor, tracking of the mobile base station and finally control of the landing procedure.

Concerning vehicle control design for small quadrotor UAVs, some solutions are already proposed in the literature, see e.g. [1-3] to mention only a few. Many

Fig. 1. A quadrotor in an experimental testbed.

of the proposed control systems are based on a linearized model and conventional PID- or state space control while other approaches apply sliding-mode, H_∞ or SDRE control. Recently, a new nonlinear control algorithm has been proposed by the author which is based upon a decomposition of the overall controller into a nested structure of velocity and attitude control. The controller has the advantage of an easy implementation and proven stability while taking the nonlinearities of the dynamics directly into account, see [4,5] for further details. Here, this controller is used to provide the basis for the development of tracking and landing controller. Tracking and landing control has also been investigated in the literatur, see e.g. [6,7], while this paper proposes a new nonlinear approach which again has the advantage of an easy implementation and proven stability. These control strategies are eplained in some details here, first simulation and experimental results underline the obtained performance.

2   The Vehicle Control System

As previously described, landing control is based upon a vehicle control system which is applied to stabilize any desired velocity vector of the quadrotor. The overall control system as described in [4,5] consist of an inner attitude and an outer velocity control loop. The command to the vehicle control system is a desired velocity vector in an inertial coordinate system given by $\boldsymbol{v}_d^T = (v_{xd}, v_{yd}, v_{zd})$. For the attitude control, feedback linearization is applied that transforms the system into a decoupled linear system in state variable format. This resulting system is controlled via a conventional linear controller, leading to a sufficiently fast and damped closed loop dynamics. The outer control loop applies a nonlinear inversion to compensate a static nonlinearity and a linear control system to control the remaining linear dynamics. The advantage of the derived control system besides the excellent performance is the simple structure and the easy implementation. That leads to a fast computation even on standard embedded micro-controller systems.

In order to evaluate the vehicle control system, an experimental prototype of the quadrotor has been designed (see Fig. 1), the dynamic model has been derived by identification of the system parameters like inertias, dimensions etc., and simulation results of vehicle control system have been obtained, see also [4,5] for a more detailed description. Here, some results of the vehicle controller during experimental test flights are presented. In the experiment the control goal comprises the stabilization of the hovering state, i.e. $v_d = 0$ and $\Omega_d = 0$ (i.e. the Euler angles should be zero), starting from any initial deviations and compensating for any external disturbances. The obtained control result is shown in Fig. 2 as a time plot of all angles of the quadrotor. After a very short transition phase the hovering state is reached and maintained. The small constant deviation of the yaw angle ψ results from a slight misalignment of the inertial measurement unit. It becomes obvious from Fig. 2 that external disturbances at $t = 35$ sec of the roll angle, at $t = 45$ sec of the pitch angle and at $t = 50$ sec at the yaw angle are completely compensated.

The simulation and experimental results underline the performance of the developed vehicle controller, which is now used to stabilize the desired velocity vector commanded by the landing control system. However, the desig of a tracking and landing controller requires a dynamic model of the controlled quadrotor, i.e. the closed loop of quadrotor dynamics and vehicle controller. If we assume that the inner attitude control loops are sufficiently fast as designed in [5], the overall vehicle control system can be decomposed into three independent velocity control loops which can be approximated by linear first-order system, respectively, see e.g. the closed-loop dynamics with respect to v_x:

$$\frac{V_x(s)}{V_{xd}(s)} \approx \frac{1}{T_x \cdot s + 1} \tag{1}$$

with T_x as appropriate time constant. A simulation of the step response also supports this approximation, see Fig. 3. Similar results are obtained for the step response of the two other velocities v_y, v_z. These first-order approximations of

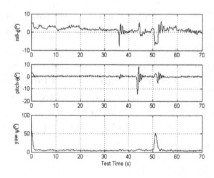

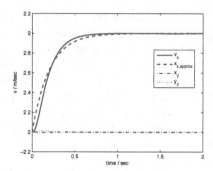

Fig. 2. Experimental results of the vehicle control system.

Fig. 3. Step response with regard to v_x.

the controlled quadrotor UAV are now used for the design of the tracking and landing controllers.

3   Automatic Landing on a Mobile Platform

In the following we consider the problem that a quadrotor UAV stabilized via the previously described vehicle control system should land on a moving platform. The platform is moving on the surface of the underlying terrain at an altitude of $z_s(t)$ with regard to the inertial frame. The overall tracking and landing procedure can be decomposed into two independent control tasks: a tracking procedure in a pure x-y-plane and an altitude control problem in pure z-direction. In the pure x-y-plane, only the planar mappings of the center of mass of the quadrotor and the platform and their respective motions are considered. The 2D-tracking controller has the task to reduce the planar distance between the quadrotor and the platform in this two-dimensional plane to zero and to maintain the zero distance even if disturbances occur. In parallel, an altitude controller has the task to achieve and stabilize required setpoints of the quadrotor's altitude over ground. During a first approaching phase where the planar distance between the quadrotor and the platform is above a threshold, the setpoint of the altitude over ground is set to a safety value, e.g. 5 m. If the planar distance decreases below the defined threshold, e.g. 0.5 m, the final landing procedure starts and the required setpoint of the altitude over ground is set to zero.

The result of the altitude controller is a desired velocity component in z-direction, i.e. v_{zd} for the underlying vehicle controller while the result of the 2D-tracking controller are the two components of the desired velocity vector in x- and y-direction, i.e. v_{xd}, v_{yd}. Finally, the results of these two controllers form the overall desired velocity vector which is commanded to the vehicle controller. In the following, first the altitude controller is derived, then we discuss the developed 2D-tracking controller.

3.1   Altitude Control

The general task of the altitude control system is to achieve and maintain a desired altitude reference which can be either the constant altitude over ground during the approaching phase or a zero altitude over ground during the final landing phase. If z is the altitude of the quadrotor UAV and z_s is the current altitude of the surface (i.e. the platform) in the inertial frame, the difference $\Delta z = z - z_s$ is the relative altitude of the UAV over ground. The current desired altitude over ground commanded by the overall landing control is the value Δz_d. Now we assume that the dynamic behavior of the controlled quadrotor UAV in z-direction can be approximated by a first-order system (1), i.e.

$$F_Q(s) = \frac{V_z(s)}{V_{zd}(s)} \approx \frac{1}{T_z \cdot s + 1} \tag{2}$$

If a linear altitude controller with transfer function $F_{R,z}(s)$ is chosen, the structure of the resulting closed altitude control loop can be depicted as shown in Fig. 4. Herein the altitude of the surface z_s is considered as a non-measurable disturbance, however the quadrotor is able to measure the current altitude over ground Δz with a suitable sensor system. In the literature some solutions based on ultrasonic, optical or laser sensors have already been proposed for this measurement problem, see e.g. [6,7]. It becomes obvious from the structure of the altitude control loop shown in Fig. 4 that a PD-controller can be applied in order to solve the control task:

$$F_{R,z}(s) = K \cdot (1 + T_C \cdot s) \tag{3}$$

The parameters of the controller are adjusted in a way that the closed loop has zero overshoot (in order to avoid collisions with the platform during landing) and is sufficiently fast. The reference altitude Δz_d is set to the desired safety altitude in the approach phase and set to zero in the landing phase.

3.2 Nonlinear 2D-Tracking Controller

The main goal of the tracking controller is to minimize the distance to a moving platform and to track this platform in the pure x-y-plane. For that purpose we consider a platform that is moving with the two velocity components v_{Px} and v_{Py} in x- and y-direction, respectively. The quadrotor is moving with the two velocity components v_{Qx} and v_{Qy}, where the dynamics between the desired velocities v_{Qxd}, v_{Qyd} and the actual velocities is given by a first-order system according to (1). The engagement geometry is depicted in Fig. 5, where σ is the line-of-sight angle and R is the distance or range between the quadrotor and the moving platform. It can be derived from classical missile guidance problems,

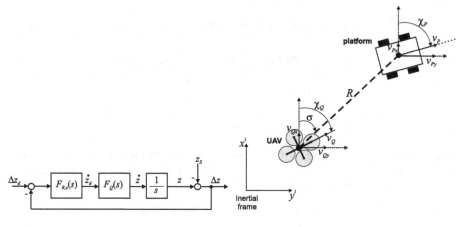

Fig. 4. Altitude control loop.

Fig. 5. Engagement geometry of quadrotor and mobile platform.

see e.g. [8], that the relative kinematics can be described by the two differential equations:

$$\dot{R} = v_{Px} \cos \sigma + v_{Py} \sin \sigma - v_{Qx} \cos \sigma - v_{Qy} \sin \sigma$$

$$\dot{\sigma} = \frac{1}{R} \left(v_{Py} \cos \sigma - v_{Px} \sin \sigma - v_{Qy} \cos \sigma + v_{Qx} \sin \sigma \right) \tag{4}$$

If we now again define a state variable model with the four state variables $x_1 = R, x_2 = \sigma, x_3 = v_{Qx}, x_4 = v_{Qy}$, the input variables $u_1 = v_{Qxd}, u_2 = v_{Qyd}$ and the two measurable disturbance variables $d_1 = v_{Px}, d_2 = v_{Py}$, we finally obtain from (1), (4):

$$\dot{x}_1 = -x_3 \cos x_2 - x_4 \sin x_2 + d_1 \cos x_2 + d_2 \sin x_2$$

$$\dot{x}_2 = \frac{1}{x_1} \left(x_3 \sin x_2 - x_4 \cos x_2 - d_1 \sin x_2 + d_2 \cos x_2 \right)$$

$$\dot{x}_3 = -(1/T_1) \cdot x_3 + (1/T_1) \cdot u_1$$

$$\dot{x}_4 = -(1/T_2) \cdot x_4 + (1/T_2) \cdot u_2 \tag{5}$$

For the design of a suitable controller we first consider a suitable operating point. This is the state where the range and line-of-sight angle are zero and the quadrotor moves in accordance with the platform, i.e. $x_1 = 0, x_2 = 0, x_3 = d_1, x_4 = d_2$. We define the Lyapunov function $V(x_1, x_2, x_3, x_4)$ which is C^1 and positive defined around the operating point:

$$V(x_1, x_2, x_3, x_4) = 0.5 \cdot (x_1^2 + x_2^2 + (x_3 - d_1)^2 + (x_4 - d_2)^2) \tag{6}$$

Now we calculate the first derivative of V using (5) and assume that the platform moves with a constant velocity:

$$\dot{V} = x_1 \dot{x}_1 + x_2 \dot{x}_2 + (x_3 - d_1)\dot{x}_3 + (x_4 - d_2)\dot{x}_4$$

$$= -\frac{x_3^2}{T_1} - \frac{x_4^2}{T_2} + x_3 f_1 + x_4 f_2 + d_1 f_3 + d_2 f_4 \tag{7}$$

with

$$f_1 = -x_1 \cos x_2 + \frac{x_2}{x_1} \sin x_2 + \frac{1}{T_1} u_1 + \frac{1}{T_1} d_1$$

$$f_2 = -x_1 \sin x_2 - \frac{x_2}{x_1} \cos x_2 + \frac{1}{T_2} u_2 + \frac{1}{T_2} d_2$$

$$f_3 = x_1 \cos x_2 - \frac{x_2}{x_1} \sin x_2 - \frac{1}{T_1} u_1$$

$$f_4 = x_1 \sin x_2 + \frac{x_2}{x_1} \cos x_2 - \frac{1}{T_2} u_2 \tag{8}$$

This derivative must be negative defined in order to guarantee that the operating point is asymptotically stable. Using (7),(8) we first set $f_3 = -(1/T_1) \cdot d_1$ and $f_4 = -(1/T_2) \cdot d_2$ which yields

$$u_1 = d_1 + T_1 x_1 \cos x_2 - T_1 \frac{x_2}{x_1} \sin x_2 \tag{9}$$

$$u_2 = d_2 + T_2 x_1 \sin x_2 + T_2 \frac{x_2}{x_1} \cos x_2 \tag{10}$$

Inserting this in f_1, f_2 using (8) leads to $f_1 = (2/T_1) \cdot d_1$ and $f_2 = (2/T_2) \cdot d_2$ which finally results in

$$\dot{V} = -\frac{1}{T_1}(x_3 - d_1)^2 - \frac{1}{T_2}(x_4 - d_2)^2 \tag{11}$$

This proofs that the derivative of V is negative defined and the operating point is asymptotically stable if the tracking control law (9), (10) is applied. However, in order to obtain a limited control input, we set $u_1 = d_1, u_2 = d_2$ if the range x_1 becomes smaller than a defined very small threshold.

In order to apply this 2D-tracking controller, the range $x_1 = R$, the line-of-sight angle $x_2 = \sigma$ as well as the velocity components $d_1 = v_{Px}, d_2 = v_{Py}$ of the platform must be measured. Both R and σ can be easily calculated if the positions of the quadrotor and the platform in the inertial frame are measured. In addition it is assumed that the platform also measures its velocity components. Both position and velocity components of the platform are transmitted via communication to the quadrotor, resulting in a cooperative approach. Regarding the measurements, a DGPS is applied for the determination of the positions, respectively, during the approach phase. However, more accurate measurements are necessary during the landing phase. There are some possible solutions for this problem such as a vision based or ultrasonic based sensor system, see e.g. [6,7]. The velocity components of the platform could be measured with a suitable inertial measurement unit onboard. Since the main focus of this work is on the development of the control system, we do not go into further details of the measurements but describe some first simulation results in the next chapter.

4   Simulation and Experimental Results

The overall landing control system is not yet implemented in the experimental quadrotor prototype and is therefore evaluated in simulations. The simulation consists of a nonlinear dynamic model of the quadrotor of order 12, the vehicle

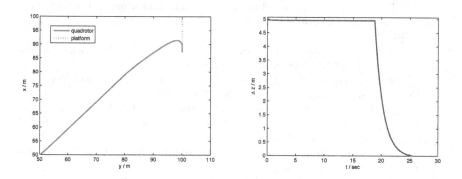

Fig. 6. Simulation of the overall landing control system.

control system as described in [4,5] and the derived landing control system as well as a simulated moving platform. In the simulation, the platform is initially assumed to be located at (x_{P0} = 100 m , y_{P0} = 100 m and moving with a constant speed of V_{Px} = -0.5 m/sec in the x-y-plane. The quadrotor is initially located at (x_{Q0} = 50 m , y_{Q0} = 50 m in the inertial frame at an altitude of Δz_0 = 5 m. The obtained control result of the overall landing control system is depicted in Fig. 6. Diagram (a) shows a top view of the 2D-engagement in which the quadrotor starts from the initial position, tracks the path of the moving platform and finally lands on the platform. Diagram (b) shows the altitude of the quadrotor which descends from the initial altitude over ground until the final landing.

5 Conclusion and Future Works

This paper presents an overall control system for the automatic landing of a quadrotor UAV on a moving platform. Herein, the vehicle control system comprises a nonlinear inner loop attitude control and an outer loop velocity control system based on static inversion. The vehicle control system is finally realized in an experimental prototype and first test flights proof the performance of this novel nonlinear approach. The landing controller consists of a linear altitude controller and a nonlinear 2D-tracking controller. Simulation results finally underline the performance of the landing control system. In our ongoing work we are currently also implementing the landing control system as well as the necessary sensors in the UAV prototype.

6 References

1. Bouabdallah S, Siegwart R: Backstepping and Sliding-mode Techniques Applied to an Indoor Micro Quadrotor. IEEE Int Conf on Robotics and Automation, pp. 2247–2252, 2005.
2. Tayebi A, McGilvray S: Attitude Stabilization of a VTOL Quadrotor Aircraft. IEEE Trans on control systems technology, Vol. 14, pp. 562–571, 2006.
3. Castillo P, et al.: Real-time stabilization and tracking of a four-rotor mini rotor-craft. IEEE Trans on Control Systems Technology, VOL.12, No. 4, July 2004, pp. 510– 516.
4. Voos H: Nonlinear Control of a Quadrotor Micro-UAV using Feedback-Linearization. IEEE Int Conf on Mechatronics, Málaga, Spain, 2009.
5. Voos H: Entwurf eines Flugreglers fuer ein vierrotoriges unbemanntes Fluggeraet (in German). at-Automatisierungstechnik, 57(9), 2009: (to appear)
6. Waslander SL, et al.: Multi-agent quadrotor testbed control design: integral sliding mode vs. reinforcement learning. IEEE/RSJ International Conference on Intelligent Robots and Systems(IROS 2005), 2005.
7. Barber DB, et al.: Autonomous Landing of Miniature Aerial Vehicles. Brigham Young University Press, Provo, UT.
8. Zarchan P: Tactical and Strategic Missile Guidance. AIAA Press, 2007.

Oscillation Analysis in Behavior-Based Robot Architectures

Lisa Wilhelm, Martin Proetzsch and Karsten Berns

Robotics Research Lab, University of Kaiserslautern,
Gottlieb-Daimler-Str., 67663 Kaiserslautern

Abstract. This paper presents a method for detecting oscillations in behavior-based robot control networks. Two aspects are considered. On the one hand, the detection of oscillations inside single behavior modules is based on analyzing the signal in the frequency domain using the Fast Fourier Transformation (FFT). On the other hand, tracing oscillations through the behavior network helps to evaluate its propagation and to find its root cause. Results of the oscillation analysis are presented using appropriate visualization techniques. The suitability of the proposed approach is shown by an indoor application.

1 Introduction

In the domain of robot control architectures, the behavior-based approach is a widely accepted method for building up complex robotic systems. However, an often mentioned criticism is that this methodology is unprincipled and hard to evaluate [1]. Although several implementations [2] have validated the suitability of the approach, the problem of analyzing large scale networks of distributed components with heavy interaction persists.

An aspect with a possibly bad influence on the performance of robotic systems is oscillations occurring inside the control structure. The knowledge about this information may help in diagnosing design errors with negative consequences on the robustness, performance, and reliability of the system. For analyzing these effects, this paper presents techniques for detecting oscillations inside behavior-based networks. The oscillation analysis problem splits up into two aspects. For *oscillation detection*, signals in single behaviors are evaluated concerning the severity using suitable quality criteria. *Oscillation tracing* is used to find the path an oscillation takes through the behavior-based control network.

These problems are also known in mechanical and electrical engineering, where oscillations in control units impair continuous work routines in plants. Therefore, for optimizing processes many techniques for detecting and diagnosing oscillations in plants have been proposed [3]. For software systems, however, it seems that oscillation detection is not sufficiently discussed, although it is a very interesting part of the analysis of robot control systems and can be used to generate quality data for assessing system properties. The algorithm presented here was developed on the basis of the techniques used by electrical engineers and adapted to the behavior-based robot control system iB2C (integrated Behavior-Based Control) [4].

The development of complex robotic systems requires frameworks and tools in order to allow an effective realization in respect to given goals [5]. Three topics have to be addressed: The specification of system properties, the design and implementation of required functionality, and the validation of system characteristics during execution. The work at hand deals with the latter aspect in the sense that desired or unwanted oscillations are tracked and visualized. In this field, several approaches deal with formal verification of systems. Typical examples are proving logical aspects and temporal characteristics of spacecraft applications [6] and real-time systems [7]. However, the complexity of these systems is limited. Furthermore, on-line analysis methods are required to detect effects appearing through the interaction with a dynamic environment. Other approaches (e. g. [8]) analyze systems by determining architectural characteristics under certain hypotheses. However, only quite simple subsystems are evaluated or the possible set of validated properties is limited.

Further analysis techniques involve data visualization tools [9,10]. These approaches have in common that situations have to be evaluated by the developer by looking through the given data, diagrams, or charts. In the field of electrical engineering several oscillation detection approaches are used for optimizing automation processes [3,11]. On account of the applications, the techniques are developed for off-line analysis of logged data and therefore have to be adapted accordingly to be applicable for the on-line analysis of robot control systems.

2   Development Framework

While the chosen approach for oscillation analysis can be applied to applications other than the one presented, the following prerequisites have to be fulfilled:

1. Data acquisition has to be provided with a fixed cycle time due to the FFT.
2. In order to trace oscillations and find the root cause, a modular structure with uniform connection characteristics has to be given.

A framework complying with these demands is the Modular Controller Architecture 2 (MCA2) [12,13] with the iB2C extension made at the Robotics Research Lab at the University of Kaiserslautern (MCA2-KL[1]). It is constructed as a hierarchical control structure composed of components which are connected by edges via standardized interfaces. A *module* is the basic unit of the MCA2 framework providing a special functionality. Furthermore, *groups* can be used to include several modules and therefore add a further level of hierarchical abstraction. Execution of included modules or groups is performed using so-called *parts* which control the internal data flow. iB2C provides a behavior-based extension to the basic MCA2 architecture [4]. Based on the iB2C principles, large scale behavior-based networks for different kinds of robots have been built up. In order to keep track of the system development, several tools are used, e. g. a graph

---

[1] http://rrlib.cs.uni-kl.de/

as presented in Sect. 4. Here, the network is represented as nodes connected by edges transferring data between the behaviors.

3   Oscillation Analysis

The procedure of analyzing oscillations in large scale behavior-based networks is divided into two parts [14]: the detection of oscillations in the signal data of single behaviors and the propagation of oscillations through the behavior network.

Oscillation detection procedure The oscillation detection algorithm is required to find oscillations in a data signal during run time. The method described here is a further development of [11] and analyzes the frequency spectrum of the supervised Fourier transformed signal. Thornhill's method is extended to allow real-time oscillation detection and the calculation of a threshold for the classification of detected oscillations is adapted to the special needs of the behavior system. The algorithm can be used with any data. In our approach, the activity data of the behaviors is used. In order to apply the FFT, the sampled signal data (see Fig. 1 (a)) is stored in a ring buffer. The sampling rate f_s determines the highest detectable frequency f_{max} and the resolution of the frequency spectrum f_{min} depending on the length of the ring buffer $l = 2^n$: $f_{max} = (f_{min} \cdot l)/2 = f_s/2$.

As a first step, the Hann-window is applied to the original signal to avoid leakage effects (see Fig. 1 (b)). Then the signal is transformed to the frequency domain (see Fig. 1 (c)) using the FFTW C subroutine library[2]. The peaks in the power spectrum indicate potential oscillations which need to be further classified in order to neglect false diagnoses, e. g. due to noise. For that purpose two properties – *power* and *regularity* – are introduced. Both are based on a filtered spectrum which contains a certain interval around the related peak (see Fig. 1 (c)). The *power* is calculated by summing up the magnitudes of the filtered spectrum. For calculating the *regularity* – representing the deviation of the distances between zero-crossings of the signal in time domain – the filtered spectra are transformed back to time domain as depicted in Fig. 1 (d). The most powerful and regular oscillations should be further analyzed.

Thresholds for both properties are user defined. Here, the method of [11] is used to indicate a regular oscillation, assuming that the standard deviation of the period is less than one third of the mean value: $r = \overline{T_p}/(3 \cdot \sigma_{T_P})$, with values of $r > 1$ indicating a regular oscillation. The determination of a lower border of the power is derived on the basis of the following consideration. A signal consisting of n oscillations of the same power but different frequencies has a spectrum, where the summed power of all oscillations $\tilde{p} = \sum_{i=0}^{n-1} p_i$ is approximately uniformly distributed between all peaks i with $p_i \approx 1/n$. Therefore, in our approach an oscillation j is said to be relevant if $p_j > \tilde{p}/(n+1)$.

Although the proposed procedure makes use of computationally efficient techniques like the FFT, continuously analyzing all signals in a complex system can

---

[2] http://www.fftw.org/

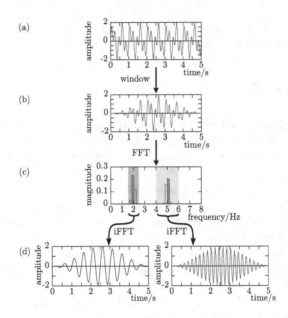

Fig. 1. Three steps of the oscillation detection algorithm

have negative effects on the system's cycle time. To avoid this, only a limited number of modules continuously performs the presented calculations, while the other modules only store relevant data in order to execute the oscillation analysis on demand.

Oscillation tracing In order to facilitate the tracing of oscillations, the behavior network is represented using the Boost Graph Library (BGL)[3]. This way, the tracking of signals is facilitated and a graphical output of the structure with overlaid oscillation information can be automatically generated using Graphviz[4].

The tracing is done recursively starting from the behavior module that first detects an oscillation (see Alg. 1). The algorithm stops if a module has no oscillating neighbors, if its neighbors all have been checked before, or if it has no other in/out edges to behaviors. The course of the oscillation through the networks allows consideration about a possible root cause. In order to reduce the computational complexity, only selected modules continuously execute the oscillation detection algorithm, while all modules buffer the signal data. In the case of an oscillating module, all modules which are connected via activity edges perform the algorithm and report back if they also detect oscillations. In iB2C, activity deals as a measure for the intended impact of a behavior. The results containing the frequency, regularity, and power are temporarily stored.

As an example for the visualization of the oscillation path, Fig. 2 shows the Graphviz representation of the control network of one of our autonomous ro-

---

[3] http://www.boost.org
[4] http://www.graphviz.org

Algorithm 1 Tracing of oscillations

1: start data buffering in every module
2: start oscillation detection in specified module
3: **if** module detects one or more oscillations **then**
4:     save result temporarily
5:     **for all** in/out activity edges **do**
6:         **if** target module has not been checked before **then**
7:             execute line 3 for target module
8:         **end if**
9:     **end for**
10: **end if**

---

bots with overlaid color information depicting the path of a detected oscillation. Furthermore, information about frequency (f), power (p), and regularity (r) are given.

4   Application and Results

The oscillation analysis and tracing algorithm has been applied to some of the robot control systems in our lab to show the different application possibilities mentioned above. Here, the algorithm is used to find modules responsible for jiggling of the indoor robot ARTOS (Autonomous Robot for Transport and Service) during obstacle avoidance maneuvers. ARTOS is a home service robot developed in the Robotic Research Lab for usage in the BelAmI project[5] [13].

The control network of ARTOS consists of over 60 interconnected modules. Fig. 2 shows the group `Behaviors` with all of its nested groups which are responsible for the control of the robot's behavior. The large group `Safety Behaviors` includes components responsible for processing sensor data and for generating motion commands. This data is converted to wheel velocities by the lowest group `Basic Differential Drive Behaviors`.

It is known from former experiments that ARTOS visibly oscillates in certain situations, for example when a small table leg disrupts its path. Therefore, the oscillation tracing method has been used for tracking down involved behaviors. As start modules the four behaviors responsible for forward, backward, turn left, and turn right motion are selected, since these act as an interface for all motion commands. The results of the oscillation tracing algorithm point out that the oscillation begins in different sensor processing modules. Fig. 2 shows one outcome of the oscillation analysis. Here, the path of an oscillation starts in the modules processing the data of the sensors responsible for keeping a certain distance to obstacles by rotating away (`Keep Distance Rot (Front Laser Scanner) (Right)`). The oscillation is further tracked down to the module which is responsible for the control of the actuators. The same oscillation (i. e. same frequency) could be found in the behavior responsible for driving in

---

[5] http://www.belami-project.de

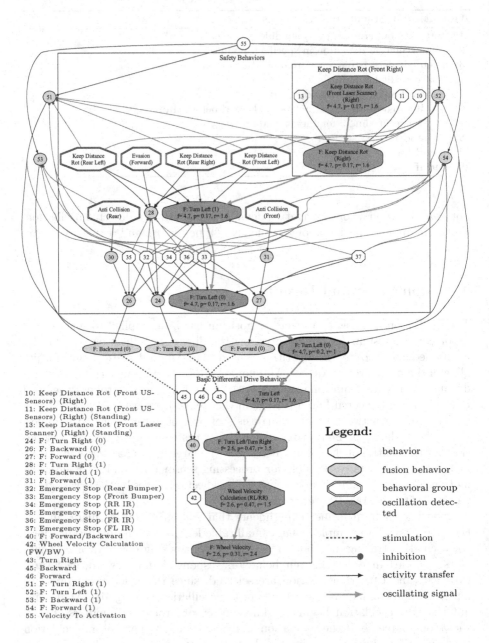

Fig. 2. Boost graph representation of the control network of the mobile robot ARTOS visualized with Graphviz. The course of the oscillation through the network is depicted by marked behaviors and edges, allowing a rapid evaluation of the oscillation tracing result. The module which detected the oscillation first is framed with a thick border.

the opposite direction. The results of the algorithms confirmed the apparently existing oscillation, identified the corresponding frequencies and characteristics and detected the involved behaviors, i. e. the course of the oscillation through the network.

For a further evaluation of the detected oscillation, Fig. 3 (top) shows the activity signal of the Turn Left behavior. The diagram in the middle depicts the frequencies and time intervals of detected oscillations. As can be seen, several different oscillations were found in the signal during the jiggling motion. This test was done with a sampling rate of 100 Hz and a window length of 1024 samples. Fig. 3 (bottom) shows one of the corresponding frequency spectra and the peaks which were classified as oscillation.

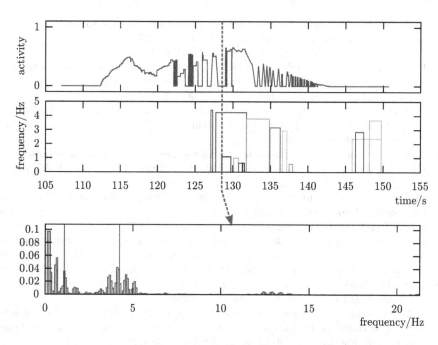

Fig. 3. Activity signal (top) and frequency of detected oscillations (middle) of the module Turn Left. Every detected frequency is shown with a different line type. A peak corresponds to the previous 1024 data values. Bottom: Frequency spectrum of the activity signal after 128 s with markers for the oscillations detected.

5   Conclusion and Future Work

The algorithms presented in this paper introduce methods for on-line oscillation detection and tracing inside behavior-based control networks. It is shown how this procedure deals with the detection of possible malfunctions inside the control structure. This way, the evaluation results can be used as quality data for larger scale system assessments. Furthermore, several visualization techniques facilitate the evaluation of the results.

Future work includes automatic methods for adapting the system behavior in the case of unwanted oscillations in order to improve the system performance.

Acknowledgments

This work was partly funded by the German Federal Ministry of Education and Research (BMBF) in the context of the project ViERforES (No.: 01 IM08003 E).

References

1. R. A. Brooks, "Intelligence without reason," Massachusetts Institute of Technology (MIT), Artificial Intelligence Laboratory," A.I. Memo No. 1293, 1991.
2. R. Arkin, *Behavior-Based Robotics.*   MIT Press, 1998.
3. P. Odgaard and K. Trangbaek, "Comparison of methods for oscillation detection - case study on a coal-fired power plant," in *Proceedings of IFAC Symposium on Power Plants and Power Systems Control 2006*, 2006.
4. M. Proetzsch, T. Luksch, and K. Berns, "Development of complex robotic systems using the behavior-based control architecture iB2C," *Robotics and Autonomous Systems*, vol. 58, no. 1, 2010.
5. E. Coste-Maniere and R. Simmons, "Architecture, the backbone of robotic systems," in *Robotics and Automation, 2000. Proceedings. ICRA 2000. IEEE International Conference on*, vol. 1, 2000.
6. M. Lowry, K. Havelund, and J. Penix, "Verification and validation of AI systems that control deep-space spacecraft," in *Proceedings Tenth International Symposium on Methodologies for Intelligent Systems.*   Springer, 1997.
7. K. Kapellos, D. Simon, M. Jourdan, and B. Espiau, "Task level specification and formal verification of robotics control systems: state of the art and case study," in *Int. Journal of Systems Science*, ser. 11, vol. 35, 1999, pp. 1227–1245.
8. L. Steels, "Mathematical analysis of behavior systems," *From Perception to Action Conference, IEEE Computer Society Press*, 1994.
9. R. Simmons and G. Whelan, "Visualization tools for validating software of autonomous spacecraft," in *In Proc. of the Fourth International Symposium on Artificial Intelligence, Robotics, and Automation for Space (iSAIRAS)*, 1997.
10. Z. Wang, J. Tsai, and C. Zhang, "Fault-toleration by duplication and debugging for distribution real-time systems," *Tamkang Journal of Science and Engineering*, vol. 3, no. 3, pp. 187–194, 2000.
11. N. Thornhill, B. Huang, and H. Zhang, "Detection of multiple oscillations in control loops," *Journal of Process Control*, vol. 13, pp. 91–100, 2003.
12. K. U. Scholl, J. Albiez, and G. Gassmann, "MCA – an expandable modular controller architecture," in *3rd Real-Time Linux Workshop*, Milano, Italy, 2001.
13. J. Koch, M. Anastasopoulos, and K. Berns, "Using the modular controller architecture (MCA) in ambient assisted living," in *3rd IET International Conference on Intelligent Environments (IE07)*, Ulm, Germany, September 24-25 2007, pp. 411–415.
14. L. Wilhelm, "Oscillation detection in behaviour-based robot architectures," Diploma Thesis, University of Kaiserslautern, November 2008, unpublished.

Variable Joint Elasticities in Running

Stephan Peter, Sten Grimmer, Susanne W. Lipfert and Andre Seyfarth

Locomotion Laboratory, University of Jena,
Dornburger Str. 23, D-07743 Jena, Germany
stephan.peter@uni-jena.de,www.lauflabor.uni-jena.de

Abstract. In this paper we investigate how spring-like leg behavior in human running is represented at joint level. We assume linear torsion springs in the joints and between the knee and the ankle joint. Using experimental data of the leg dynamics we compute how the spring parameters (stiffness and rest angles) change during gait cycle. We found that during contact the joints reveal elasticity with strongly changing parameters and compare the changes of different parameters for different spring arrangements. The results may help to design and improve biologically inspired spring mechanisms with adjustable parameters.

1 Introduction

The spring-mass model (Fig. 1, left) introduced by Blickhan [1] and McMahon and Cheng [2] describes the global dynamics of hopping and running gaits. In fact, in fast animal and human locomotion leg behavior is similar to that of a linear spring (e.g. [3,4]). This global spring behavior arises in the segmented leg (Fig. 1, AK & GK). It is not well understood how elastic leg operation is achieved on muscle level.

With a segmented leg the stiffness of the leg can be generated with appropriate combinations of nonlinear torsion springs (with constant spring parameters during contact) in the knee and ankle joint [5,6]. In a two-segmented leg stable running can be achieved even with a linear rotational spring at constant joint stiffness [7,14]. Endo [8] approximated experimental data of human gait dynamics by switchable visco-elastic elements in a segmented leg. A closer look at the experimental torque-angle-characteristics [6] and [9] reveals that adjustable spring parameters of the rotational joint springs are required to mimic the biological leg behavior.

In this paper we present a method to investigate to what extend the spring-like leg behavior in running is represented at joint level. Using stiffness matrices [10] we compute changes in the spring parameters (stiffness, rest angle) of linear rotational springs spanning single joints (knee, ankle) or connecting knee and ankle. We describe the parameter characteristics and evaluate selected spring parameters with respect to the mechanical work required for parameter adjustments during the gait cycle. The results of our work may help to overcome the lack of knowledge and understanding which so far constricts the optimal (biologically inspired) use of adjustable springs (e.g., MACCEPA [11], Jackspring

[12], OLASAT [13]). This knowledge may further facilitate the simulation and construction of legged systems, such as needed for legged robots or for the design of novel prostheses and ortheses.

2   Materials and Methods

2.1   Experimental Data

We analyzed 8 subjects each running on a treadmill at about 75% of its preferred transition speed (approximately $1.65\,m/s$). Ground reaction forces and joint marker positions of the leg were measured. From the marker positions we derived the inner joint angles (Fig. 1). With inverse dynamics [6] we calculated the joint torques acting on knee and ankle joint with extending joint torques were defined to be positive.

We extracted the traces of joint torque and joint angle for a gait cycle (i.e. time between two consecutive touch-downs of one leg). The data for the gait cycle was normalized to 100 equally distributed time steps. Averaging over all gait cycles resulted in angles $\phi_k(i)$, $\phi_a(i)$, $i = 1, \ldots, 100$, and torques $\tau_k(i)$, $\tau_a(i)$, $i = 1, \ldots, 100$, of knee (k) and ankle (a) joint.

2.2   Dynamic Joint Stiffness Analysis

The concept of linear joint stiffness [6] often assumes a constant parameter fit for the complete contact phase. Here, we generalize this concept by allowing for time-variant parameter fits:

$$\begin{pmatrix} \tau_k(i) \\ \tau_a(i) \end{pmatrix} = \begin{pmatrix} c_k(i) & 0 & c_g(i) \\ 0 & c_a(i) & -c_g(i) \end{pmatrix} * \begin{pmatrix} \phi_k^0(i) - \phi_k(i) \\ \phi_a^0(i) - \phi_a(i) \\ \phi_g^0(i) - (\phi_k(i) - \phi_a(i)) \end{pmatrix}, \forall i, \quad (1)$$

where c denotes stiffness, ϕ joint angle, ϕ^0 rest angle and g (or GAS) stands for the gastrocnemius muscle (c_g and ϕ_g^0). To estimate the time depending stiffness and rest angle parameters, we solve Equation (1) by using Matlab's least square method (lsqlin) generally leading to exact solutions.

We apply five adaptation strategies addressing knee (K), ankle (A) and gastrocnemius (G) function:

– *S0-AK:* We assume torsion springs with both variable stiffness and rest angle at knee and ankle but no GAS spring ($c_g(i) = 0\,Nm/deg$, $\forall i$). Thus, for each i there are four unknowns and only two equations. By assuming that stiffness and rest angles are equal for two subsequent times i and $i + 1$ we get 4 equations for 4 unknowns.

– *S1-AK:* We assume torsion springs with variable stiffness and constant rest angles at knee and ankle but no GAS spring. I.e., we have $c_g(i) = 0\,Nm/deg$, $\phi_k^0(i) = 173\,^\circ$, $\phi_a^0(i) = 127\,^\circ$, $\forall i$ and variable stiffness $c_k(t)$ and $c_a(t)$. For each joint, the rest angle is the maximum of all measured angles. Therewith

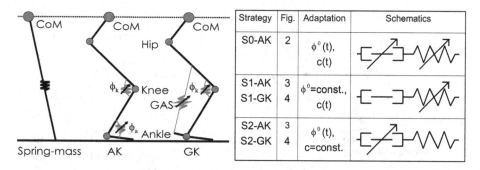

Fig. 1. Schematics of spring-mass model (left), spring arrangements ankle-knee (AK) resp. gastrocnemius-knee (GK) and overview of the spring adaptation strategies (table, right). ϕ^0 refers to the rest angles and c to the stiffness of the springs.

the springs extend the joints if and only if the stiffness is positive. There are two unknowns (c_k and c_a) in the equations which can be resolved for each time step i (that is also the case for the following strategies).

- *S2-AK:* We assume torsion springs with variable rest angles and constant stiffness at knee and ankle but no GAS spring, i.e., $c_g(i) = 0\,Nm/deg$, $c_k(i) = n * c_{ref,k} = n * 5.66\,Nm/deg$, $c_a(i) = n * c_{ref,a} = n * 4.36\,Nm/deg$, $\forall i$, $n = 0.5, 1, 2$. We distinguish three cases, each with a constant stiffness equal a multiple $(0.5, 1, 2)$ times reference stiffness $c_{ref,k}$ resp. $c_{ref,a}$ which are computed as explained in Fig. 2.

- *S1-GK:* We assume a torsion spring at knee (but not at ankle) and GAS spring both with variable stiffness and constant rest angles, i.e., $c_a(i) = 0\,Nm/deg$, $\phi_k^0(i) = 173°$, $\phi_g^0(i) = -19°$, $\forall i$. The rest angle ϕ_g^0 is the minimum of all the measured differences $\phi_k(i) - \phi_a(i)$. Thus, the GAS spring extends the ankle joint and bends the knee joint if and only if its stiffness is positive. Therewith we replace the ankle spring of the previous strategies by a spring, which produces torques dependending on both knee and ankle angle.

- *S2-GK:* We assume a torsion spring at knee (but not at ankle) and GAS spring both with variable rest angle and constant stiffness, i.e., $c_a(i) = 0\,Nm/deg$, $c_k(i) = c_{ref,k} = 10.43\,Nm/deg$, $c_g(i) = c_{ref,g} = 18.90\,Nm/deg$, $\forall i$. For these stiffness values the work required for parameter adaptation is minimized (see below).

To evaluate the different stiffness values in strategy *S2-AK* we calculate the *mechanical work* required for rest angle adaptation during the ground contact. Since the elastic energy of a spring with stiffness c, rest angle ϕ^0 and current angle ϕ equals

$$E(c, \phi^0, \phi) = \frac{1}{2}c(\phi^0 - \phi)^2, \tag{2}$$

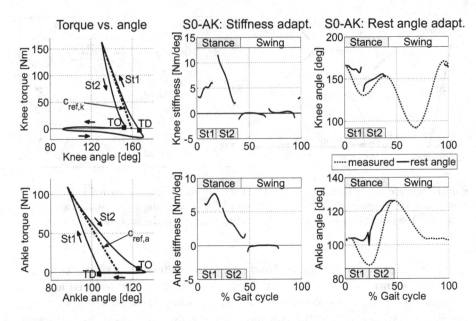

Fig. 2. *Left:* Solid: Measured torque-angle characteristics. TD indicates touch-down, TO take-off. Dotted: Line through the point of maximum torque and the arithmetic mean of the states at touch-down and take-off. The slopes of these lines define the reference stiffness $c_{ref,k} = 5.66\,Nm/deg$ and $c_{ref,a} = 4.36\,Nm/deg$. *Middle:* Stiffness courses. To identify the trends, phases of rapidly changing stiffness (jumps) are cut out. *Right:* Measured joint angles (dotted) and rest angles (solid). Jumps (i.e., rapid changes of the rest angles) as well as points for which the corresponding stiffness is smaller than $1\,Nm/deg$ are removed from the rest angle characteristics.

the work for adapting the rest angle between times i and $i + 1$ is

$$E(c, \phi^0(i + 1), \frac{1}{2}(\phi(i) + \phi(i + 1))) - E(c, \phi^0(i), \frac{1}{2}(\phi(i) + \phi(i + 1))). \quad (3)$$

For strategy *S2-AK* we evaluate the effect of several stiffness by adding up the absolute work required for adjusting the rest angle of knee and ankle joint during the contact phase.

3   Results

The analysis of experimental data of 8 subjects did not reveal any significant differences concerning our interpretation of different subjects. Thus, we state the representative results of one subject (mass $= 62\,kg$, body height $= 1.66\,m$, running speed $= 1.65\,m/s$). For almost all adaptation strategies during swing joint stiffness is much lower than during stance (Fig. 2, middle, Fig. 3, left, Fig. 4, left) and rest angles are similar to measured joint angles (Fig. 2, right, Fig. 3, middle, Fig. 4, right). Only for strategy *S1-AK* there is a negative stiffness

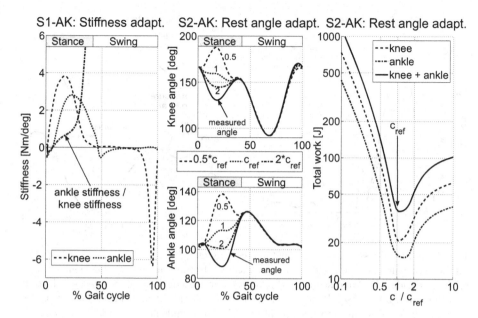

Fig. 3. *Left:* Stiffness courses for constant rest angles (knee joint: 173°, ankle joint: 127°). The dash-dotted line marks the quotient of ankle stiffness divided by knee stiffness. *Upper & lower middle:* Dotted/dashed: Predicted adaptation of rest angle computed assuming a constant stiffness equal to a multiple $(0.5, 1, 2)$ of the reference stiffness $c_{ref,k} = 5.66 Nm/deg$ resp. $c_{ref,a} = 4.36 Nm/deg$ (see Figure 2). Solid: Measured angles. *Right:* For each stiffness the sum of the absolute work performed during contact is plotted. The quotient of stiffness divided by the reference stiffness is assigned to the horizontal axis.

prior to touch-down (Fig. 3, left). For both knee and ankle all strategies reveal joint elasticity during contact. Thereby, the spring parameters change strongly: first, the stiffness increases and then decreases. The same holds true for the difference of the rest angle and the measured angle. For strategy *S0-AK* this even happens simultaneously. There, the extrema of both courses for both knee and ankle all appear at about the same time: 18% of the gait cycle, i.e., when the knee passes from bending to extension (Fig. 2, middle & right). For the strategies with only monoarticular springs with exactly one adjustable parameter (*S1-AK*, *S2-AK*) the extrema are shifted. For the knee they appear at 18% of the gait cycle and for the ankle at 23% of the gait cycle (Fig.3, left & middle). This difference is reduced when the ankle spring is replaced by a gastrocnemius spring (Fig. 4). For strategy *S1-AK* the quotient of ankle and knee stiffness increases during the whole contact (Fig. 3, left) whereas for strategy *S1-GK* it is constant during a major part of the contact (Fig. 4, left). Only strategy *S0-AK* reveals discontinuities in the parameter courses (Fig. 2). Whereas at the transition from joint bending (St1) to joint extension (St2) the knee stiffness increases suddenly and the knee rest angle drops instantaneously, the corresponding courses for the

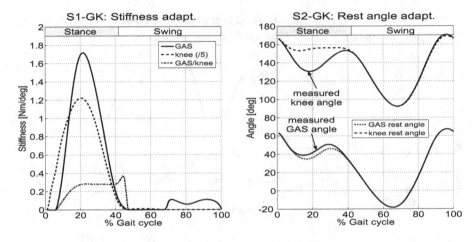

Fig. 4. *Left:* Stiffness courses for constant rest angles: $\phi_k^0 = 173\,°$, $\phi_g^0 = -19\,°$. The knee stiffness is scaled by the factor $1/5$. The dash-dotted line marks the quotient of GAS stiffness divided by knee stiffness. *Right:* Rest angle characteristics (dashed/dotted) and measured angles (solid). Minimizing the total work ($59.25\,J$, knee: $23.68\,J$, GAS: $35.57\,J$) resulted in knee stiffness $10.43\,Nm/deg$ and ankle stiffness $18.90\,Nm/deg$.

ankle continue at about the same values after the transition. Fig. 3, middle, shows that depending on joint stiffness the rest angle courses for strategy *S2-AK* are very different. For about the reference stiffness (see Fig. 2) the mechanical work required for rest angle adaptation is minimal (Fig. 3, right). For lower stiffness the predicted work increases more quickly than for larger joint stiffness. For strategy *S2-GK* there are also stiffness values for which the work is minimal. Thereby the knee rest angle course remains almost constant (Fig. 4, right).

4   Discussion

In this paper different adjustment strategies for joint springs and inter-joint springs are presented. Depending on the arrangement of springs, different energy optimal adjustment protocols could be identified.

All adaptation strategies propose joint elasticities with a parameter adjustment during contact which for both knee and ankle reveals two phases (Fig. 2, middle & right, Fig. 3, left & middle, Fig. 4): first, the stiffness increases and then decreases. The same holds true for the difference of the rest angle and the measured angle. This is a new finding compared to previous works only concerning one or two phases each of constant stiffness for stance [6].

Since for a given joint angle one and the same joint torque can be generated by various combinations of stiffness and rest angles one is confronted with a redundancy when computing strategy *S0-AK*. We solved this problem by using two subsequent times to compute both parameters (stiffness, rest angle). Therewith strategy *S0-AK* is more suitable to reveal local properties of the torque-joint characteristics than the other strategies. Only for strategy *S0-AK* sudden changes (jumps) in the parameter characteristics at the transition from leg bending to extension occur (Fig. 2, middle & right). They could emerge from muscle properties which may be sensitive to the direction of movement like mechanical friction. The Hill curve proposes that the muscle force is very sensitive to the sign of muscle velocity. Since at the point of maximal joint bending this sign changes whereas the joint torques remain constant, the opposing changing rate in the parameters could result in a resetting of the muscles. Thus, the knee joint behavior could be more influenced by friction than the ankle joint.

The bell-shaped stiffness courses of the *S1* strategies (Fig. 3, left and Fig. 4, left) as well as the curvatures of the rest angle courses (Fig. 3, middle and Fig. 4, right) propose nonlinear springs with progressive stiffness. This agrees with modeling outcomes [5]. Since with nonlinear springs parameter adjustment and therewith work can be lowered, we suggest to use nonlinear springs to match the presented parameter courses. Then the maximum velocity of the actuators (e.g., motors), which realize the parameter adjustment could be lowered. However, nonlinear stiffness can be approximated by a combination of linear springs, such as with the OLASAT mechanism [13].

The technical implementation of the adaptation strategy *S0-AK* may be challenging due to the simultaneous change of the stiffness and the rest angle as well as the discontinuities in the knee parameter courses (Fig. 2, upper middle & right).

The asynchronism brought with the single parameter adjustment of the strategies *S1-AK*, *S2-AK* can be resolved by including a biarticular gastrocnemius spring between the knee and the ankle (compare the dash-dotted lines and maxima of the parameter courses of Fig. 3, left and Fig. 4, left). Another advantage of using a gastrocnemius spring in technical systems is that it can prevent the hyperextension of the knee by pulling the heel from the ground instead.

When dealing with adjustable rest angles (strategies *S2-AK*, *S2-GK*) for each strategy there are stiffness values for which the work required for rest angle adaptation is minimized (Fig. 3, right). For strategy *S1-AK* it is approximately the reference stiffness (see Fig. 2, left). It seems that the rest angle courses for minimizing the net mechanical energy are also the most linear ones (Fig. 3, middle, Fig. 4, right), what could be technically beneficial because it may simplify control schemes and actuator requirements.

From a technical point of view it is unsatisfactory that the adaptation strategies *S1-AK*, *S1-GK* reveal big changes of stiffness during contact (Fig. 3, left, Fig. 4, left) and strategy *S1-GK* even reveals negative stiffness (Fig. 3, left). It remains for further work to overcome this by a more sophisticated rest angle choice. E.g., it is reasonable to enforce that the rest angle equals the measured joint angle whenever the torque is zero. This requires non-constant rest angles.

We used the data of one subject to demonstrate a new method. Obviously this method can provide useful informations about how springs with adjustable parameters ([11],[12],[13]) at and between the knee and the ankle joint can be arranged and how their parameters should be adjusted in order to generate human-like leg behavior in mathematical models, robots, prostheses or ortheses.

Acknowledgements

This study is supported by the German Research Foundation (DFG) SE1042/4 and by the EU within the FP7 project Locomorph.

References

1. Blickhan R: The spring-mass model for running and hopping. *J Biomech* 22(11-12):1217–1227, 1989.
2. McMahon TA, Cheng GC: The mechanics of running: how does stiffness couple with speed? *J Biomech* 23(Suppl 1):65–78, 1990.
3. Farley CT, Glasheen J, McMahcon TA: Running springs: speed and animal size. *J Exp Biol* 185:71–86, 1993.
4. Farley CT, Gonzalez, O: Leg stiffness and stride frequency in human running. *J Biomech* 29(2):181–6, 1996.
5. Seyfarth A, Günther M, Blickhan R: Stable operation of an elastic three-segment leg. *Biol Cybern* 84(5):365–382, 2001.
6. Günther M, Blickhan R: Joint stiffness of the ankle and the knee in running. *J Biomech* 35(11):1459–1474, 2002.
7. Rummel J, Seyfarth A: Stable running with segmented legs. *Int J Robot Res* 27(8):919–934, 2008.
8. Endo K, Paluska D, Herr H: A quasi-passive model of human leg function in level-ground walking. *Proc IROS*:4935–4939, 2006.
9. Kuitunen S, Komi PV, Kyrolainen H: Knee and ankle joint stiffness in sprint running. *Med Sci Sports Exercise* 34(1):166–173, 2002.
10. Rozendaal LA: Stabilization of a multi-segment model of bipedal standing by local joint control overestimates the required ankle stiffness. *Gait Posture* 28:525–527, 2008.
11. Vanderborght B, Van Ham R, Lefeber D, Sugar TG Hollander KW: Comparison of mechanical design and energy consumption of adaptable, passive-compliant actuators. *Int J Robot Res* 28(1):90–103, 2009.
12. Hollander KW, Sugar TG, Herring DE: A robotic jack spring for ankle gait assistance. *Proc IDETC/CIE*, 2005.
13. Ghorbani R, Wu Q: Adjustable stiffness artificial tendons: conceptual design and energetics study in bipedal walking robots. *Mechanism and Machine Theory* 44:140–161, 2009.
14. Maykranz D, Grimmer S, Lipfert SW, Seyfarth A: Foot function in spring mass running. *Autonome Mobile Systeme* 2009.
15. Bobbert MF, van Soest AJ: Two-joint muscles offer the solution, but what was the problem? *Motor Control* 4(1):48–52, 2000.

3D-Partikelfilter SLAM

Jochen Welle[1], Dirk Schulz[1] und A.B. Cremers[2]

[1] Fraunhofer FKIE,
Neuenahrer Str. 20, 53343 Wachtberg, Deutschland,
welle@fgan.de, schulz@fgan.de
[2] Institut für Informatik III, Universität Bonn,
Römerstraße 164, 53117 Bonn, Deutschland,
abc@iai.uni-bonn.de

Zusammenfassung. In diesem Artikel wird ein Verfahren zur Erstellung von 3D Punktwolkenkarten der Umgebung vorgestellt, das während der Fahrt aufgenommene Laserentfernungsmessungen verarbeitet. Dabei werden die vollen sechs Freiheitsgrade in der Roboterposition beachtet. Es wird ein partikelfilterbasierter Ansatz verfolgt, der FastSLAM und ähnliche Ansätze aus dem Zweidimensionalen ins Dreidimensionale überträgt. Hierbei werden insbesondere Methoden zur Handhabung der erhöhten Komplexität durch die zusätzlichen Freiheitsgrade und des erhöhten Speicheraufwandes vorgestellt. Des Weiteren kommt das Verfahren mit Odometriebewegungsdaten aus und ist nicht auf zusätzliche Bewegungssensoren angewiesen. Abschließend wird das Verfahren zur Evaluation sowohl auf Simulations- als auch auf Realdaten angewendet.

1 Einleitung

Das Erstellen von Umgebungkarten ist eine grundlegende Aufgabe mobiler Robotersysteme, mit der sich bereits viele Forschungsgruppen beschäftigt haben. Es muss eine Karte aus den Sensordaten erstellt werden (*mapping*), indem von verschiedenen Positionen erfasste Daten korrekt zusammengesetzt werden. Hierzu muss die Position des Roboters bestimmt werden (*localization*). Die Herausforderung liegt darin, dass beide Teilaufgaben, Kartenbau und Lokalisierung, wechselseitig voneinander abhängen und gleichzeitig gelöst werden müssen. In der Literatur ist das für die Erstellung einer Umgebungskarte zu lösende Problem als *Simultaneous Localization And Mapping* (SLAM) bekannt. In diesem Artikel wird ein SLAM-Verfahren zur Erstellung dreidimensionaler Karten aus Laserentfernungsdaten von nicht notwendigerweise ebenen Innen- und Außenumgebungen vorgestellt. Hierzu wird ein partikelfilterbasierten Ansatz verwendet, welcher Teil meiner Diplomarbeit gewesen ist [1].

Partikelfilterbasierte SLAM-Ansätze sind im Zweidimensionalen, das heißt zur Erstellung zweidimensionaler Karten von ebenen Umgebungen, bereits erfolgreich angewendet worden. Nach Vorstellung von Rao-Blackwellized Partikelfiltern zur Lösung des SLAM Problems von Murphy und Doucet [2,3] wurde dieser Ansatz zuerst von Montemerlo et al. im FastSLAM Verfahren [4] für reale Roboter umgesetzt. Dieses landmarkenbasierte Verfahren wurde von Hähnel et al. [5] auf Belegtheitsgitterkarten erweitert und zur Odometrieverbesserung mit Scan-Matching kombiniert. Stachniss et al. [6] verfeinern das Verfahren von Hähnel et al. Sie berechnen statt einer globalen Odometrieverbesserung eine verbesserte Schätzung pro Partikel und führen eine intelligente *Resampling* Technik ein.

Bei der Übertragung dieser Ansätze ins Dreidimensionale ergeben sich insbesondere zwei Probleme. Zum Einen werden mehr Partikel benötigt, weil der Zustandsraum der Roboterpositionen sechs- statt dreidimensional ist. Zum anderen ergibt sich ein erhöhter Speicheraufwand durch die Erstellung dreidimensionaler Karten für jedes Partikel. Fairfield et al. [7] stellen einen 3D Partikelfilter SLAM Ansatz für einen Unterwasserroboter vor. Leider berücksichtigen sie dabei nicht das Speicherplatzproblem, wodurch Ihr Verfahren in dieser Hinsicht nicht gut skaliert.

Im hier vorgestellten Verfahren wird der hohe Speicheraufwand durch eine speicherplatzsparende Organisation der Karten der verschiedenen Partikel reduziert. Hierbei wird das Prinzip der speicherplatzsparenden Kartenrepräsentation aufgegriffen, welches von Eliazar und Parr im zweidimensionalen, partikelfilterbasierten DP-SLAM Verfahren [8] angewendet wurde. Zur weiteren Speicherplatzersparnis haben wir eine Suchstruktur entwickelt, die auf einem Octree [9] basiert und eine spezielle Form von Delta-Kodierung verwendet. Zur Reduzierung der Partikelanzahl und damit zur Laufzeit- und Speicherplatzreduzierung werden die möglichen 6D-Partikelpositionen eingeschränkt. Hierzu wird neben den Odometriedaten zusätzlich die bisher erfasste Karte für die Positionsbestimmung genutzt. Eine Besonderheit des Verfahrens ist, dass Laserentfernungsmessungen während der Fahrt aufgenommen werden. Somit wird ein Anhalten - Aufnehmen - Weiterfahren Zyklus vermieden, wie er in vielen Scan-Matching basierten Ansätzen üblich ist.

Im Folgenden wird zunächst der partikelfilterbasierte Ansatz zur Lösung des SLAM Problems erläutert, gefolgt von der verbesserten Positionsbestimmung, der Partikelgewichtung und der Resamplingstrategie. Anschließend werden in Abschnitt 3 die Verfahren zur Speicherplatzreduzierung erklärt und schließlich die Experimente in Abschnitt 4 diskutiert.

2 Das partikelfilterbasierte SLAM Verfahren

Partikelfilter gehören zur Familie der sequentiellen Monte-Carlo-Methoden. Die Grundidee des Partikelfilters ist es, eine Wahrscheinlichkeitsverteilung durch eine Menge von Stichproben, Partikel genannt, zu approximieren und diese Menge über die Zeit zu aktualisieren.

Um die SLAM-Aufgabe zu lösen, werden die Karte m und die Roboterpositionen $x_{1:t} = x_1, \ldots, x_t$ gesucht, die die aufgenommenen Daten, gegeben durch Odometriemessungen $u_{1:t}$ und Entfernungsmessungen $z_{1:t}$, am besten erklären. Dazu wird die Verteilung $P(x_{1:t}, m | z_{1:t}, u_{1:t})$ bestimmt. Murphy, Doucet et al. nutzen *Rao-Blackwellized* Partikelfilter, um diese Verteilung effizient zu approximieren [2,3]. Die Kernidee ist dabei, die Verteilung zu faktorisieren

$$P(x_{1:t}, m | z_{1:t}, u_{1:t}) = P(m | x_{1:t}, z_{1:t}) \, P(x_{1:t} | z_{1:t}, u_{1:t}) \qquad (1)$$

und nur die Robotertrajektorien $P(x_{1:t} | z_{1:t}, u_{1:t})$ mit einem Partikelfilter zu approximieren. Jedes Partikel repräsentiert eine mögliche zurückgelegte Trajektorie des Roboters. $P(m | x_{1:t}, z_{1:t})$ entspricht dem Kartenbauproblem mit bekannten Positionen, welches für jedes Partikel gelöst wird. Das heißt für jedes Partikel wird eine eigene Karte mitgeführt, die sich aus dem Pfad dieses Partikels und den Sensormessungen ergibt.

Das Partikelfilter verarbeitet inkrementell Paare von Odometrie- und Entfernungsmessungen (u_t, z_t). Sei P die Anzahl der Partikel. Die Aktualisierung der Partikel vom Zeitpunkt $t - 1$ nach t wird in vier Schritten durchgeführt.

(1) Für jedes Partikel wird eine neue Position aus einer Vorschlagsverteilung π gezogen (engl. *proposal distribution*) und dem Partikel hinzugefügt.

(2) Um den Unterschied zwischen der zu approximierenden Verteilung und der Vorschlagsverteilung auszugleichen werden die Partikel gewichtet:

$$w_t = \frac{\text{zu approx. Verteilung}}{\text{Vorschlagsverteilung}} = \frac{P(x_{1:t} | z_{1:t}, u_{1:t})}{\pi(x_{1:t} | z_{1:t}, u_{1:t})} \quad . \qquad (2)$$

(3) Im sogenannten *Resampling*-Schritt werden P Partikel proportional zu ihrer Gewichtung w_t neu gezogen. Ein Partikel kann dabei mehrfach gezogen werden. Die Gewichte der gezogenen Partikel werden zurückgesetzt.

(4) In die Kartenrepräsentation m_t jedes neuen Partikels wird die neue Messung z_t und die aktuelle Roboterposition x_t integriert.

2.1 Ziehen neuer Positionen

Um eine inkrementelle Verarbeitung zu erlauben, muss die Vorschlagsverteilung $\pi(x_{1:t} | z_{1:t}, u_{1:t})$ der rekursiven Formulierung

$$\pi(x_{1:t} | z_{1:t}, u_{1:t}) = \pi(x_t | x_{1:t-1}, z_{1:t}, u_{1:t}) \, \pi(x_{1:t-1} | z_{1:t-1}, u_{1:t-1}) \qquad (3)$$

genügen. Für $\pi(x_t | x_{1:t-1}, z_{1:t}, u_{1:t})$ wird im einfachsten Fall das Bewegungsmodell $P(x_t | x_{t-1}, u_t)$ genutzt. In dreidimensionalen, nicht ebenen Umgebungen kann die Vorschlagsverteilung damit allerdings stark von der Zielverteilung abweichen, da Änderungen der Bodenebene nur durch Odometriedaten nicht erfasst werden. Aus diesem Grund wird die bisher gewonnene Karte m_{t-1} eines Partikels genutzt, um die nächsten Nachbarpunkte an der aktuellen Partikelposition und daraus mittels Singulärwertzerlegung eine Ausgleichsebene zu bestimmen. Der Normalen der Ausgleichsebene wird ein Fehler, abhängig von der Varianz der Ebenenbestimmung, hinzugefügt. Anschließend wird in der durch die Normale definierten Ebene die Roboterbewegung anhand eines Odometriebewegungsmodell wie in [10] durchgeführt. Für künftige Arbeiten ist auch die Einbeziehung der aktuellen Messung z_t zur Verbesserung der Vorschlagsverteilung geplant. Zunächst wurde zur Vereinfachung der Berechnung aber darauf verzichtet. Das Bewegungsmodell ist dann gegeben durch:

$$P(x_t | x_{t-1}, u_t, m_{t-1}) \qquad . \qquad (4)$$

2.2   Gewichtung der Partikel

Im zweiten Schritt des Aktualisierungsvorganges werden die Partikel gewichtet:

$$
\begin{aligned}
w_t &= \frac{\text{Zielverteilung}}{\text{Vorschlagsverteilung}} = \frac{P(x_{1:t}|z_{1:t}, u_{1:t})}{\pi(x_{1:t}|z_{1:t}, u_{1:t})} \\
&= \frac{P(z_t|x_{1:t}, z_{1:t-1}, u_{1:t})\, P(x_t|x_{1:t-1}, z_{1:t-1}, u_{1:t}) P(x_{1:t-1}|z_{1:t-1}, u_{1:t})}{P(z_t|z_{1:t-1}, u_{1:t})\, \pi(x_{1:t}|z_{1:t}, u_{1:t})} \\
&= \eta \frac{P(z_t|x_{1:t}, z_{1:t-1}, u_{1:t})\, P(x_t|x_{1:t-1}, z_{1:t-1}, u_{1:t})}{\pi(x_t|x_{1:t-1}, z_{1:t}, u_{1:t})} \underbrace{\frac{P(x_{1:t-1}|z_{1:t-1}, u_{1:t-1})}{\pi(x_{1:t-1}|z_{1:t-1}, u_{1:t-1})}}_{w_{t-1}} (5)
\end{aligned}
$$

$$
\propto P(z_t|x_t, m_{t-1}) \frac{P(x_t|x_{t-1}, m_{t-1}, u_t)}{\pi(x_t|x_{1:t-1}, z_{1:t}, u_{1:t})} \cdot w_{t-1}   . \tag{6}
$$

Für den Übergang von Gleichung 5 nach Gleichung 6 wird m_{t-1} als hinreichende Statistik für $x_{1:t-1}, z_{1:t-1}$ angenommen. Die im zweidimensionalen Fall übliche Markov-Annahme $P(x_t|x_{1:t-1}, z_{1:t-1}, u_{1:t}) = P(x_t|x_{t-1}, u_t)$ ist hier nicht erfüllt, da u_t nur die gefahrene Strecke auf der Oberfläche misst und nichts über Änderungen der Oberfläche aussagt. Somit hängt x_t auch von $x_{1:t-1}, z_{1:t-1}$ ab, womit die Oberfläche beschrieben werden kann.

Setzt man nun für $\pi(x_t|x_{1:t-1}, z_{1:t}, u_{1:t})$ das zuvor beschriebene Bewegungsmodell aus Gleichung 4, ein, so kürzt sich dieses heraus:

$$
\begin{aligned}
w_t &\propto P(z_t|x_t, m_{t-1}) \frac{P(x_t|x_{t-1}, m_{t-1}, u_t)}{P(x_t|x_{t-1}, m_{t-1}, u_t)} \cdot w_{t-1} \\
&= P(z_t|x_t, m_{t-1}) \cdot w_{t-1}   . \tag{7}
\end{aligned}
$$

Das vorherige Gewicht des Partikels, w_{t-1}, ist gleich eins, wenn in der vorherigen Filteraktualisierung der *Resampling* Schritt durchgeführt wurde. Die Gewichtung wird also anhand des Sensormodells durchgeführt, dazu wird ein Sensormodell ähnlich dem Likelihood-Feld Modell aus [10] verwendet.

2.3   Resampling

Im *Resampling* Schritt werden die neuen Partikel proportional zu ihrem Gewicht aus der bisherigen Partikelmenge gezogen. Das *Resampling* dient dazu wahrscheinlichere Bereiche der Zielverteilung mit mehr Partikeln zu approximieren als unwahrscheinlichere Bereiche. Es birgt allerdings die Gefahr, dass sich die Partikel zu stark auf wenige Positionen konzentrieren und so nur noch die maximum likelihood Trajektorie verfolgt wird. Basierend auf dem Vorschlag von Stachniss et al. [6] wird aus diesem Grund ein *Resampling* Schritt nur dann durchgeführt, wenn

$$
N_{eff} = \frac{1}{\sum_{i=1}^{P} \left(w^{(i)}\right)^2} \tag{8}
$$

unter den Schwellwert von $P/2$ fällt. Wobei P die Anzahl der Partikel ist und $w^{(i)}$ das Gewicht des i-ten Partikels bezeichnet. N_{eff} schätzt wie gut die aktuellen

Partikel die Zielverteilung approximieren. Die Idee dahinter ist, dass die Partikel gleiche Gewichte hätten, wenn sie aus der echten Zielverteilung gezogen würden. Umso schlechter die Approximation der Zielverteilung ist, desto höher ist die Varianz in den Gewichten.

3 Reduktion des Speicherplatzes

Im Zweidimensionalen werden häufig Belegtheitsgitter zur Kartenrepräsentation verwendet. Eine Erweiterung auf drei Dimensionen ist allerdings speicheraufwendig, deshalb werden hier 3D-Punktwolken genutzt. Die Punkte werden hierbei in einer Suchstruktur organisiert, um effiziente Nachbarschaftsanfragen für die Auswertung des Sensormodells zu erlauben. Für die in komplexen Szenarien benötigte Partikelanzahl ist der Speicheraufwand einer kompletten Karte bzw. Suchstruktur pro Partikel immer noch hoch.

Eine Möglichkeit zur Reduktion des Speicheraufwandes bietet das Konzept des Vorfahrenbaumes (engl. *ancestry tree*), welcher von Eliazar und Parr in [8] eingeführt wurde. Durch die *Resampling* Schritte haben einige Partikel eine gemeinsame Vergangenheit und somit gemeinsame Teilkarten, so dass diese in einer Vererbungshierarchie, dem Vorfahrenbaum, gespeichert werden können. Im Gegensatz zu Eliazar und Parr die eine Gitterkarte verwalten, die Änderungsreferenzen aller Partikel enthält, speichern wir in jedem Knoten des Baumes die Kartenänderungen zum Vaterknoten. Die Worst-Case Speicherplatzkomplexität bleibt damit in $O(Pn)$, wobei n die Anzahl der Datenpunkte und P die Anzahl der Partikel ist. Sie tritt aber nur ein, wenn beim *Resampling* keine Partikel wegfallen. In der Praxis können große Teile der Karten gemeinsam genutzt werden.

Auch mit gemeinsamer Nutzung von Karten ist der Speicheraufwand noch hoch. Bei unserem Verfahren wird dieser weiter reduziert, indem die Genauigkeit der 3D-Punkte auf die Anforderungen bzw. die Möglichkeiten des Sensors begrenzt und die Auflösung der Karte beschränkt wird. Auch der Speicherplatzoverhead der Suchstrukturen, der bei den getesteten Kd-Baum Implementierungen [11,12] bei einem Faktor von 3 bis 6 gegenüber den reinen Datenpunkten liegt, wird reduziert. Zum Erreichen dieser Ziele wurde eine auf dem Octree [9] basierende, Suchstruktur entworfen, welche wir DeltaOctree nennen.

Im DeltaOctree werden die Datenpunkte relativ zum Zentrum ihres Oktanten abgespeichert. Die Vorgehensweise beruht auf dem Verfahren der Delta-Kodierung zur Datenkompression, bei dem nur die Änderungen von einem Datensatz zum anderen gespeichert werden. Mit dieser Technik ist es möglich einen Punkt, je nachdem wie tief er im Baum eingeordnet wird und welche Genauigkeit gewünscht wird, mit einem oder zwei Bytes pro Koordinate zu speichern. Damit ergeben sich Punktgrößen von drei bis sechs Bytes im Gegensatz zu zwölf Bytes (float 32-bit pro Koordinate) ohne Deltakodierung. Die Zentren der Oktanten müssen auch nicht explizit gespeichert werden, da sie sich eindeutig während der Traversierung des Baumes berechnen lassen. Die Begrenzung der Auflösung wird durch Festlegung einer minimalen Kantenlänge realisiert, Oktanten mit dieser Kantenlänge werden nicht weiter unterteilt.

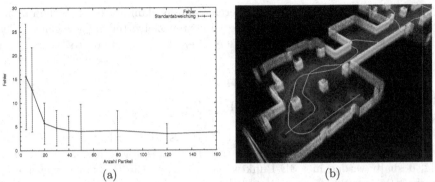

(a)   (b)

Abb. 1. (a) Mittelwert und Standardabweichung des Fehlers e_{mse} in Exp1 mit unterschiedlicher Partikelanzahl (b) 3D-Ansicht auf die berechnete Karte in Exp1.

Die Suchgeschwindigkeit im DeltaOctree ist im experimentellen Vergleich etwa halb so hoch wie in den zuvor genannten Kd-Bäumen. Dies kommt durch die Umrechnungen zwischen relativen und absoluten Punkten zustande. Der Speicherplatzverbrauch liegt dafür aber unter dem Platzverbrauch der reinen Punkte ohne Suchstruktur.

4   Experimentelle Ergebnisse und Evaluation

Die Experimente wurden sowohl in einer realen Umgebung als auch in der Simulation mit der mobilen Roboterplattform Pioneer P3-AT durchgeführt. Die Umgebungen wurden mit einem vertikal auf einem Drehteller montierten Sick LMS Laserentfernungsmesser erfasst. Für die Simulationen wurde der Simulator Gazebo verwendet. Insgesamt konnte das Verfahren in unterschiedlichen Szenarien erfolgreich eingesetzt werden. Davon werden im Folgenden eine Simulation einer einfachen Innenumgebung (Exp1), gefolgt von einem Experiment in realer Außenumgebung (Exp2), beschrieben. Tabelle 1 listet einige Details zu diesen Experimenten auf.

Für die Simulation steht die tatsächlich gefahrene Trajektorie des Roboters zur Verfügung. Damit kann der Positionsfehler $e_{\mathrm{mse}} = \frac{1}{T}\sum_{t=1}^{T}|p_t - \bar{p}_t|^2$ in den vom Verfahren berechneten Trajektorien bestimmt werden. T ist hierbei die Anzahl der Positionen, $p_t = (x, y, z)^T$ die berechneten Roboterkoordinaten der Trajektorie und $\bar{p}_t = (\bar{x}, \bar{y}, \bar{z})^T$ die korrespondierenden tatsächlichen Koordinaten. Bereits mit niedriger Partikelanzahl unterschreitet das bestbewertete Partikel den Fehler der Odometrietrajektorie, der bei 53,7 liegt. Der Fehler sinkt erwartungskonform kontinuierlich bis zu einer Anzahl von 50 Partikeln und stagniert danach auf ungefähr gleichem Level, siehe Abb. 1(a). Der verbleibende Fehler resultiert meist aus kleinen Rotationsfehlern auf der Hinfahrt und der sich daraus ergebenden Abweichung von der Referenztrajektorie im weiteren Verlauf. Bei visueller Bewertung der resultierenden 3D-Karten zeigt sich, dass das Verfahren ab 40 Partikeln konsistente Karten produziert und der Kreisschluß gelingt, sie-

Tabelle 1. Daten zum Simulationsexperiment (1) und Realexperiment (2). Die Rechenzeit wurde auf einem 2Ghz Dual Core Laptop gemessen.

Exp.	Fläche	Strecke	Laserscans	Partikel	Aufnahmezeit	Rechenzeit	Speicher
1	79m x 34m	181m	≈ 20000	40	5 min	2:40 min	131 mb
2	105m x 100m	385m	≈ 69000	1000	26 min	255 min	784 mb

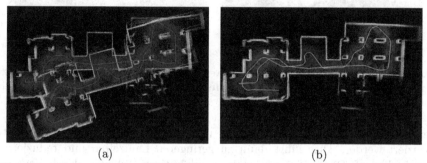

(a)   (b)

Abb. 2. Ansicht von oben auf Exp1. (a) Odometrietrajektorie und resultierende Karte. (b) Karte des am Ende bestbewerteten Partikels.

he Abb. 2(b). Zum Vergleich zeigt Abb. 2(a) die aus der Odometrietrajektorie resultierende Karte. Abb. 1(b) zeigt eine 3D-Ansicht auf die Karte.

Beim Experiment in realer Umgebung wurde die Mensa des Instituts für Informatik der Uni Bonn umrundet. Auch hier gelingt die Korrektur der Odometrietrajektorie und der Kreisschluß. Allerdings sind für die zuverlässige Korrektur 1.000 Partikel nötig, womit das Verfahren nicht mehr echtzeitfähig ist. Desweiteren haben sich Fehler im Höhenverlauf der berechneten Trajektorie ergeben. Die Trajektorie steigt an und fällt wieder ab, obwohl die reale Umgebung relativ eben ist. Die Fehler entstehen, weil sich lokale Fehler in der Bodenebenenschätzung fortpflanzen und erst beim Kreisschluß wieder korrigiert werden können. Abb. 3(a) zeigt die aus der Odometrietrajektorie resultierende Karte und Abb. 3(b) die korrigierte Karte.

5   Schlussfolgerung und Ausblick

In diesem Artikel wurde ein partikelfilterbasiertes SLAM-Verfahren vorgestellt, welches erfolgreich dreidimensionale Karten von nicht ebenen Umgebungen erstellt, die mit einer mobilen Roboterplattform während der Fahrt erfasst werden. Zur Reduktion des Speicherplatzes wurden die Partikel im Vorfahrenbaum organisiert um Karten zwischen Partikeln gemeinsam zu nutzen. Zusätzlich wurde mit dem DeltaOctree eine speicherplatzsparende Suchstruktur eingeführt.

Verbesserungen am Verfahren können durch eine komplexere Bodenebenenbestimmung erzielt werden, welche nicht nur das lokale Umfeld zum aktuellen Zeitpunkt berücksichtigt. Ergänzend kann durch weitere Sensorinformationen, wie z.B. Beschleunigungssensoren zur dreidimensionalen Lageerfassung, die

(a)   (b)

Abb. 3. Exp2: (a) Odometrie-Karte. Die weiß markierten Wände sollten übereinander liegen. (b) Karte des am Ende bestbewerteten Partikels, berechnet mit 1.000 Partikeln.

Bewegung des Roboters besser erfasst und dadurch die Partikelanzahl weiter reduziert werden. Dies führt dann zu geringeren Laufzeiten und reduziertem Speicherbedarf. Dieses Ziel soll auch in zukünftigen Arbeiten durch Verbesserung der Vorschlagsverteilung verfolgt werden. Die Scan-Matching-Ansätze von [5] oder [6] sind hier allerdings nicht direkt umsetzbar, da durch die Datenaufnahme während der Fahrt lokale Teilkarten schon in sich fehlerhaft sind.

Literaturverzeichnis

1. Welle, J.: FastSLAM basierte Erstellung eines 3D-Umgebungsmodells während der Fahrt. Master's thesis, Rheinische Friedrich-Wilhelms-Universität Bonn, 2009.
2. Doucet, A., de Freitas, N., Murphy, K., Russell, S.: Rao-blackwellised particle filtering for dynamic bayesian networks. In UAI '00, pages 176 – 183, 2000.
3. Murphy, K.: Bayesian map learning in dynamic environments. In NIPS, pages 1015–1021. MIT Press, 1999.
4. Montemerlo, M., Thrun, S., Koller, D., Wegbreit B.: FastSLAM: A factored solution to the simultaneous localization and mapping problem. In Proceedings of the AAAI Nat. Conf. on AI, Edmonton, Canada, 2002.
5. Hähnel, D., Fox, D., Burgard, W., Thrun, S.: A highly efficient FastSLAM algorithm for generating cyclic maps of large-scale environments from raw laser range measurements. In IROS, 2003.
6. Stachniss, C., Grisetti, G., Hähnel, D., Burgard, W.: Improved rao-blackwellized mapping by adaptive sampling and active loop-closure. In SOAVE, Germany, 2004
7. Fairfield, N., Kantor, G., Wettergreen, D.: Towards particle filter slam with three dimensional evidence grids in a flooded subterranean environment. In ICRA, Orlando Florida USA, May 2006.
8. Eliazar, A., Parr R.: DP-SLAM: Fast, robust simultaneous localization and mapping without predetermined landmarks. In IJCAI-03, pages 1135–1142. 2003.
9. Samet, H.: Spatial data structures. Addison-Wesley, 1995.
10. Thrun, S., Burgard, W., Fox, D.: Probabilistic Robotics. MIT Press, 2005.
11. Mount, D., Arya S.: ANN. http://www.cs.umd.edu/ mount/ANN/, August 2006.
12. Kennel, M. B.: Kdtree 2. http://arxiv.org/abs/physics/0408067v2, 2004.

Absolute High-Precision Localisation of an Unmanned Ground Vehicle by Using Real-Time Aerial Video Imagery for Geo-referenced Orthophoto Registration

Lars Kuhnert, Markus Ax, Matthias Langer, Duong Nguyen Van and Klaus-Dieter Kuhnert

University of Siegen, FB 12 - Electrical Engineering and Computer Science, Institute for Real-Time Learning Systems, Hölderlinstr. 3, 57068 Siegen

Abstract. This paper describes an absolute localisation method for an unmanned ground vehicle (UGV) if GPS is unavailable for the vehicle. The basic idea is to combine an unmanned aerial vehicle (UAV) to the ground vehicle and use it as an external sensor platform to achieve an absolute localisation of the robotic team. Beside the discussion of the rather naive method directly using the GPS position of the aerial robot to deduce the ground robot's position the main focus of this paper lies on the indirect usage of the telemetry data of the aerial robot combined with live video images of an onboard camera to realise a registration of local video images with apriori registered orthophotos. This yields to a precise driftless absolute localisation of the unmanned ground vehicle. Experiments with our robotic team (AMOR and PSYCHE) successfully verify this approach.

1 Introduction

Cooperation among robotic teams has become a vibrant field of research in the recent past [1]. While many research projects in this special context focus on homogenous swarms of ground robots [2] the emphasis of this work lies on the cooperation between land-based and aerial vehicles. The complementary characteristics and features of these two types of robots suggest a combined usage in order to solve complex tasks in the field of outdoor robotics. The following explanations give a short overview of current research developments in the special context of (absolute) localisation and target detection with cooperative air/ground robot teams.

In [3] an extensive report on an adaptive system of heterogenous robots for urban surveillance using several aerial as well as land-based robots is presented. Beside performing mapping tasks the system is able to search and locate ground targets cooperatively. Cooperative ground target localisation has also been tackled in [4]. In [5] a method to realise an aerial image-to-GPS mapping is introduced which is used to generate a position measurement of a micro-UAV while the position of the accompanying ground vehicle is assumed to be known.

This renders absolute localisation hardware unnecessary for the aerial robot. In [6] a vision-based target geo-location is achieved by using the position of the target in images taken from a UAV and the UAV's position, attitude and camera parameters to calculate the target's world coordinates. Furthermore extensive thoughts are spent on error reducing optimizations like RLS filtering or bias estimation. A method for self-localisation of an UGV by fusing high-resolution aerial LADAR data and local geometrical information of the environment recorded by the UGV is described in [7]. The structure of this approach is similar to our approach in this paper though the great difference of viewing points while recording the data to be matched induces problems that we overcame by using an additional UAV as external sensor platform. The registration of on-line aerial video images to prior geo-referenced imagery has been reviewed and successfully implemented in [8]. In this spirit our approach is similar to [8] but differs in several details. In [8] a feature based matching algorithm is proposed while we are using a template-based matching method. Furthermore we present a practical use case in the form of an GPS-less absolute localisation technique for an UGV which is described in detail in section 3.3.

2   Robotic Platforms

Our cooperative robotic team consists of the unmanned ground vehicle AMOR and the unmanned aerial vehicle PSYCHE.

(a)   (b)

Fig. 1. Cooperative robotic team: Autonomous Mobile Outdoor Robot AMOR (a) and Unmanned Aerial Vehicle PSYCHE (b)

AMOR (Fig. 1(a)) is built upon a commercial ATV (All Terrain Vehicle) platform by Yamaha. The mechanical platform allows a wide area of operational scenarios as it is robust and has notable cross-country capabilities on the one hand and is able to drive at high speeds while having a big operating range on the other hand. The sensor equipment of AMOR comprises various internal and external sensors enabling the robot to solve different autonomous tasks like obstacle detection/avoidance, vehicle/person following and textured 3D-map creation to mention only a few. Additional detailed information on AMOR and its system architecture can be found in [9,10].

The mechanical basis of the aerial robot PSYCHE (Fig. 1(b)) is a md4-200 quadrocopter by Microdrones. The basic platform which is already stabilized by inertial sensors and capable of holding the current GPS position, was extended at our institute by an additional ARM-microcontroller board, a 5,4 GHz wireless link and a self-constructed low-cost camera board to allow the real-time transmission of in-flight sensor and status information, video imagery and control commands using a standard PC equipped with a wireless link.

3   Cooperative UGV/UAV Localisation

The precise self-localisation of a robotic system is an integral feature for a robust behaviour in an outdoor environment. Especially the absolute localisation of current state-of-the-art robotic systems is heavily dependent on a reliable signal by a GPS sensor. This signal is obviously determined by various uncontrollable external factors (e.g. vegetation, building density, satellite positions, ...) which forbid the assumption that a global position measurement of a robot can always be guaranteed by exclusive usage of GPS. Several ways of GPS-loss coverage have been investigated. These concepts - if depending on a GPS signal - always assume that there has been a valid GPS measurement in the past. At least for the problem of finding an initial GPS position at a mission starting point of a robotic system this assumption is not applicable. Beside this fact our system aims at a higher precision and sensor drift avoidance concerning the global position measurement of a robot while a GPS signal is unavailable.

Therefore we took a different approach to this problem by combining an unmanned aerial vehicle to the unmanned ground vehicle as we found that the negative factors influencing the GPS signal only apply to land-based vehicles in the majority of cases. Assuming that an aerial vehicle operating at a certain height always has a valid GPS signal (neglecting any weather-originating effects) we deduce the GPS position of the ground vehicle by the position of aerial vehicle using different techniques which will be presented in the following subsections.

3.1   Video Tracking of UGV

At the beginning the most straight-forward solution for the task described in the previous section should be mentioned here shortly. To realize a very rough estimation of where the ground robot is located it is sufficient to enable the aerial vehicle to track the ground robot and while doing that submitting its current GPS position to the ground robot. The detection and tracking is realized solely by the application of digital image processing methods using data from the onboard camera of the UAV. Our implementation is able to detect our ground robot AMOR by applying a color segmentation technique which is detecting the prominent color of the back section of AMOR. Using this data it is possible to track our ground vehicle. Obviously the quality of the tracking is highly dependent on the quality of the detection of the UGV via color segmentation. Due to the fact that no further model-like information on our UGV is used the maximal error of the detection is approximately 50 centimeters while the typical detection error is approximately 25 centimeters with our implementation.

Clearly this method is only suited to generate a very rough global position estimation as it does not take parameters like the camera model or the aerial vehicle's pose into account and it cannot be assumed that the aerial robot is always located directly above the ground vehicle. These considerations will be discussed in the next subsection.

3.2   Pitch and Roll Compensation

To enhance the method described in the previous subsection an integration of aerial robot's pose and the camera model of the camera attached to it is of big importance. The pitch, roll and yaw angles of the aerial robot are used to realise a transformation into a fixed coordinate system originating from the center of gravity of the UAV. The x-axis of this coordinate system is pointing north while the y-axis is pointing west and the z-axis is parallel to the gravity vector. As the ground is assumed to be flat within our considerations the projection of the center of gravity of the UAV along the z-axis onto the ground plane can be calculated in the following using the height over ground of the UAV. Now the position of the ground vehicle has to be determined relating to the fixed coordinate system of the UAV. The previously measured position of the ground vehicle in camera coordinates (see 3.1) is subsequently transformed using the pose and the height over ground of the UAV. The result is the position of the UGV on the flat ground plane in the fixed coordinate system of the UAV. With that the position of the UGV and the projected position of the UAV on the ground plane are known in the same coordinate system and can therefore be used to deduce the UGV's absolute position in world coordinates from the UAV's absolute position.

This method appears to yield to an acceptable solution to our problem of localising a GPS-less UGV with a cooperating UAV. The inspection of the UGV positioning error introduced by even small errors in the relevant parameters unfortunately leads to a somewhat different assessment. Although the effect of erronous angle or altitude measurements is linear it is big enough to compromise the precision of the results severly. When flying at a height of 20 meters an error of 1 degree in either the pitch or roll angle of the UAV results in a positioning error of approximately 0.35 meters if the UGV is located directly in center of the camera image. If the UGV is located in the peripheral region of the aerial image the error even increases. Altitude measurement errors increases the positioning error further. With an average positioning error of 0.26 meters per erronous altitudal meter the effect is not as severe compared to the angular errors. These facts demand a high-precision measurement of pose and height of the UAV to realise an acceptable position measurement of the observed UGV which is not available due to limited hardware capabilities of small UAVs like our robot PSYCHE. This lead us to developing a fundamentally different concept which is presented in the following.

3.3   Orthophoto Registration

As pitch and roll compensation suffer from a high dependency on the measurement quality of the pose of the aerial vehicle an alternative cooperative localisation method is presented here that takes advantage of the broad availability of high-quality geo-referenced aerial photos recorded by specially equipped airplanes or satellites. The root idea of this approach is to find the position of the image taken by the aerial robot in a global database of orthophotos to realize a global registration of a real-time locally recorded aerial photo.

To ease this process and to narrow down the set of orthophotos which come into consideration the GPS position, heading and height of the aerial robot are used to choose the right map section and to rotate and scale the current image from the aerial robot as a pre-processing step for the following registration procedure. To realize a rotational correction of the aerial image in the way that the y-axis of the image is pointing into a northern direction the heading of the UAV is directly used as the heading angle describes the angular difference between current attitude of the UAV and the vector pointing north in our case. The scaling of the aerial image is a bit more complicated as it depends on the altitude of the aerial vehicle and the parameters of the onboard camera. Thus we first had to determine the horizontal camera opening angle using a calibration procedure. After that the width w_{pixel} of the area that one camera pixel covers in real world coordinates is (h_{og} denotes the height over ground and α_h the horizontal opening angle of the recording camera)

$$w_{pixel} = 2h_{og} \tan \frac{\alpha_h}{2}. \tag{1}$$

The pixel width ratio $r = \frac{w_{uav}}{w_{map}}$ of the UAV's image and the geo-referenced images can now be used to scale the image of the UAV to have the same per-pixel-width so that a direct template matching is possible. After obtaining all needed parameters the rotation and scaling is realized by an affine transformation. In our experiments the scaling procedure of the images leads to bilinear interpolated geo-referenced images with a grid width of 0.06 meters. The physical resolution of the geo-referenced imagery is approximately 0.30 meters. The images recorded with our aerial robot PSYCHE have a grid width of 0.052 meters when taken at an altitude of 20 meters.

After the pre-processing of both images a template matching is performed to uncover the exact location of the local aerial photo in the global aerial photo. This of course implies that the global aerial photo is covering a bigger map section than the local aerial photo. Our experiments show that combining global aerial photos taken at a virtual height of 100 meters and local aerial photos taken at a height of 20 meters yield to good matching results. This finding has several reasons. The altitude at which an aerial photo is recorded has a direct effect on the area in the world that one pixel of the image covers. Therefore, it is on the one hand advisable to choose an image recording altitude which is low enough to preserve as much details as possible in the image and on the other hand high enough to have sufficient visual context information to allow a unambigous matching result.

The matching algorithm itself is implemented with the Fast Template Matching method proposed in [11] which is based on the template matching functionality that is provided by the well-known open-source image processing library OpenCV. The implemented template matching method uses an image pyramid to speed up the actual matching process. The bigger the images and/or templates are the more image pyramid levels should be used. Our experiments show that this decreases the runtime of the algorithm by the factor 2 per pyramid level without sacrificing much of the matching result's quality when using a small number (≤ 3) of pyramid levels. After generating the image pyramids the template matching is executed on the down sampled images with the lowest resolution. The result R of this step is a normed cross-correlation image obtained by the application of the following equation. I denotes the source image in which the template T is to be found.

$$R(x, y) = \frac{\sum\limits_{x'y'} T(x', y') I(x + x', y + y')}{\sqrt{\sum\limits_{x'y'} T(x', y')^2 \sum\limits_{x'y'} I(x + x', y + y')^2}} \tag{2}$$

A search for the maximal value in the normed cross-correlation image uncovers the template location with the highest confidence in the next step. To optimize the template's position an additional search in a small area around the previously found location of the template is performed as a fine-tuning postprocessing step. If the confidence increases by this step the position of the template is corrected. As we are only looking for a single object in the aerial image all matching results with a lower confidence are discarded. In summary our approach realises a real-time subpixel cross-correlation method depending on the above mentioned accuracy of the geo-referenced imagery.

4   Results

Figure 2 demonstrates the capability of our registration method to successfully match aerial imagery from an UAV to previously taken orthophotos from a global database of geo-referenced aerial images. As the global aerial images are already geo-referenced the absolute position of the unmanned ground vehicle can easily be deduced by using the previously determined width-per-pixel measure w_{pixel}. The processing is all done on the UGV as the UAV's processing capabilities are limited and would not yield to a desirable runtime of the algorithm at the moment.

The precision of our implementation can be quantified as follows. Due to our sub-pixel cross-correlation approach we realised a maximal registration precision of approximately 0.06 meters (see Section 3.3). Additionally the precision

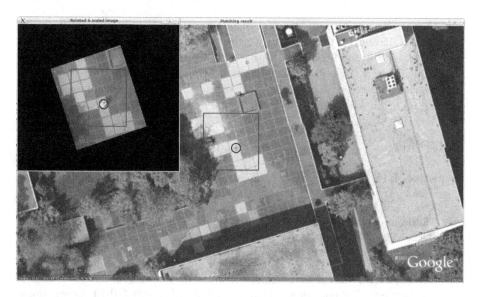

Fig. 2. Template matching results with localised UGV. The UAV's photo after rotation and scaling is shown in the top left corner. The red rectangle marks the area which is used for template matching. The blue circle marks the UGV.

of our UGV segmentation is approximately 0.25 meters (see Section 3.1). These facts produce an overall precision of approximately 0.30 meters of our system. Certainly the applied segmentation technique is very simple and has a big potential of improvement which lets us hope to achieve a registration precision of approximately 10-15 centimeters in the future. Nevertheless the precision of our implementation at present is already comparable to a DGPS sensor system which is definitely a satisfactory performance.

Concerning the runtime of our system it can be stated that our implementation achieves an average runtime of 76 ms per processed video frame on a *Intel Core2Duo L7100@1.20GHz* when using a 3-level image pyramid and thus the system is perfectly suited for real-time application.

5   Conclusion

In this paper we presented an alternative approach to the absolute localisation problem of an unmanned ground vehicle by considering different cooperative behaviours involving an additional unmanned aerial vehicle. The direct usage of the UAV's GPS position to deduce the UGV's absolute position turns out to be very error-prone. Therefore we implemented a registration method to match real-time imagery from an UAV to geo-referenced images from a global database. By doing that the absolute position of the UGV can be calculated from its position in the onboard camera image. Our absolute localisation method has a localisation precision of approximately 0.30 meters and is able to perform in real-time which is both remarkable. Finally the system has been successfully verified with our robots AMOR and PSYCHE to prove the practical usability of our method in the context of outdoor robotics. Future developments of the system will focus on an optimised UGV video image segmentation technique as this component induces the biggest error in our system. Besides geo-referenced images with a higher resolution will be used to increase the accuracy of the system.

References

[1]   Parker L.E.: Current research in multirobot systems. 7th International Symposium on Artificial Life and Robotics, Oita, Japan, January 16-18, 2002.

[2]   Madhavan R., Fregene K. and Parker L.E.: Distributed Cooperative Outdoor Multirobot Localization and Mapping. Autonomous Robots 17(1):23-39, 2004.

[3]   Hsieh M.A., Cowley A., Keller J.F., et al.: Adaptive teams of autonomous aerial and ground robots for situational awareness. Journal of Field Robotics 24:991-1014, 2007.

[4]   Grocholsky B., Swaminathan R., Keller J., et al.: Information Driven Coordinated Air-Ground Proactive Sensing. Proceedings of the 2005 IEEE International Conference on Robotics and Automation, 2211-2216, 18-22 April, 2005.

[5]   Vaughan R.T., Sukhatme G.S., Mesa-Martinez F.J., et al.: Fly Spy: Lightweight Localization and Target Tracking for Cooperating Air and Ground Robots. In Proc. Int. Symp. Distributed Autonomous Robot Systems, 315-324, 2000.

[6]   Barber D.B., Redding J.D., McLain T.W., et al.: Vision-based Target Geolocation using a Fixed-wing Miniature Air Vehicle. J. Intell. Robotics Syst. 47(4):361-382, 2006.

[7]   Vandapel N., Donamukkala R.R. and Hebert M.: Unmanned Ground Vehicle Navigation Using Aerial Ladar Data. Intl. Journal of Robotics Research 25(1):31-51, 2006.

[8]   Kumar R., Sawhney H.S., Asmuth, J.C., et al.: Registration of video to georeferenced imagery, Proceedings of the 14th International Conference on Pattern Recognition 2:(1393-1400), 1998.

[9]   W. Seemann and K.-D. Kuhnert: Design and realisation of the highly modular and robust autonomous mobile outdoor robot AMOR. 13th IASTED International Conference on Robotics and Applications, Würzburg, Germany, August 29-31, 2007.

[10]   Kuhnert, K.-D.: Software architecture of the Autonomous Mobile Outdoor Robot AMOR. IEEE Intelligent Vehicles Symposium 2008, Eindhoven, 4-6 June, 2008.

[11]   Fast Match Template, Weblink: http://opencv.willowgarage.com/wiki/FastMatch Template, last visited 20.06.2009.

An Improved Sensor Model on Appearance Based SLAM

Jens Keßler, Alexander König and Horst-Michael Gross

Neuroinformatics and Cognitive Robotics Lab, Ilmenau University of Technology,
98693 Ilmenau, Germany

Abstract. In our previous work on visual, appearance-based localization and mapping, we presented in [14] a novel SLAM approach to build visually labeled topological maps. The essential contribution of this work was an adaptive sensor model, which is estimated online, and a graph matching scheme to evaluate the likelihood of a given topological map. Both methods enable the combination of an appearance-based, visual localization and mapping concept with a Rao-Blackwellized Particle Filter (RBPF) as state estimator to a real-world suitable, online SLAM approach. In this paper we improve our algorithm by using a novel probability driven approximation of the local similarity function (the sensor model) to deal with dynamic changes of the appearance in the operation area.[1]

1 Introduction

Using mobile robots in everyday life, robust map building and self localization plays a central role while navigating the robot in its environment. In the realm of visual SLAM two types of methods are typically used: landmark-based methods and appearance- or view-based approaches. While landmark-based methods require the extraction and reassignment of distinct visual landmarks, appearance-based methods use an description of the view at a certain point, leading to a more global impression of a scene. Appearance-based approaches compare the appearance of the current view with those of the reference images to estimate the robot's pose ([16],[19]).

Feature/Landmark-based approaches: In many SLAM approaches, the map representation is assumed to be a vector of point-like feature positions (landmarks) [18]. The advantage of feature/landmark-based representations for SLAM lies in their compactness. However, they rely on *a priori* knowledge about the structure of the environment to identify and distinguish potential features or landmarks. Furthermore, a data association problem arises from the need to recognize the landmarks robustly not only in local vicinities, but also when returning to

---

[1] The research leading to these results has received funding from the European Community's Seventh Framework Programme ([FP7/2007-2013] [FP7/2007-2011]) under grant agreement n° 216487 (CompanionAble: http://www.companionable.net/)

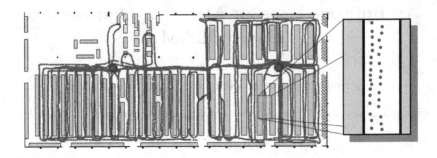

Fig. 1. A manually built map of the operation area, a regularly structured, maze-like home improvement store with a size of $100x50m^2$ (taken from [13]). The dots (nodes of the map) show the positions of stored observations.

a position from an extended round-trip. In the field of visual landmark-based SLAM algorithms, Lowe's SIFT-approach [15],[10] has often been used so far. Further important feature/landmark-based approaches are those proposed by Davison using stereo vision [5] or monocular vision [4]. To estimate the landmark positions, popular methods like the Extended Kalmanfilter (EKF) [4] or Rao-Blackwellized Particle Filters (RBPF), [6] like FastSLAM [3], are applied.

Appearance-based SLAM/CML approaches: The Concurrent Map-building and Localization (CML) approach of Porta and Kroese proposed in [17] was one of the first techniques to simultaneously build an appearance-map of the environment and to use this map, still under construction, to improve the localization of the robot. Another way to solve the SLAM-problem was proposed by Andreasson et. al. [1]. Here, a topological map stores nodes with appearance-based features and edges, containing relations between observations and their poses. An essential drawback of this approach is the required offline relaxation phase to correct the nodes' spatial positions by using the found observation matches. The method to estimate the pose difference between images applying the image similarity introduced by Andreasson [1] has been picked up and extended in our SLAM approach. Further approaches that use a topological map representation are described in [2], where a Bayesian inference scheme is used for map building, and in [7], where a fast image collection database is combined with topological maps allowing an online mapping, too.

Contribution of this paper: In our previous approaches ([12],[13]), dealing with an appearance-based Monte Carlo Localization, a static topological model of the environment was developed (see Fig. 1). The nodes of this environment model were labeled with appearance features extracted from an omni directional image. The essential contribution of our approach presented in [14] was the combination of the appearance-based, visual localization concept with a RBPF as state estimator to a visual SLAM approach, to estimate a topological map of the environment. Instead of a single observation, typically used in the field of appearance-based localization and mapping, another key idea of our approach

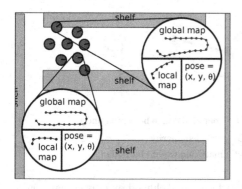

Fig. 2. The map representation of the particles in our approach: Each particle models its current pose estimation, an estimation of the complete global map, and a local map. Some maps are more likely to be correct than others.

was to utilize local graphs to perform the evaluation step. These graphs containing the last n observations in n nodes, representing a kind of short-term memory of the very latest observations and pose estimations (see Fig. 2). Another novel idea consisted in online estimating an environment-depending sensor model to evaluate the likelihood of each map. In continuation of this work, we developed a method to further reduce the demand on memory of the environment model and prevent the algorithm from collecting new observations infinitely. Furthermore, we are introducing a method to deal with dynamical changing environments to improve the reliability of the sensor model.

2   Appearance-Based SLAM Approach with RBPF

In this section the basic idea of our algorithm presented in [14] is explained briefly. Particularly, the graph matching process to determine the likelihood of the map to be correct will be described more precisely. Furthermore, the adaptive sensor model is discussed.

2.1   RBPF with Local and Global Graph Models

Our appearance-based SLAM approach utilizes the standard Rao-Blackwellized Particle Filter approach to solve the SLAM problem, where each particle contains a pose estimate x_i (position x, y and heading direction φ) as well as a map estimate (see Fig. 2). The environment model (map) used in our appearance-based approach is a topological graph representation, where each node i, representing a place x_i in the environment, is labeled with appearance-based features z_i of one or more omni directional impressions at that node. To solve the SLAM problem, the RBPF has to determine the likelihood of the graph-based maps in the particles to be correct. Therefore, our approach uses two different types of maps: a global map $m^G = \langle x_{1:(l-1)}, z_{1:(l-1)} \rangle$, which represents the already known environment model learned so far and a local map $m^L = \langle x_{l:t}, z_{l:t} \rangle$ representing the n latest observations and the local path between them (e.g. the last two meters of the robot's trajectory). To prevent the filter from under-/oversampling of the estimated probability distribution we use the KLD sampling technique (see [11]) to adjust the particle count as needed.

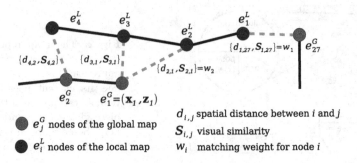

Fig. 3. Basic idea of our map matching algorithm: the likelihood of a given map configuration is determined by using the spatial distances d_{ij} and visual similarities S_{ij} for comparison between each pair of nodes i (in the local graph) and j (in the global graph).

2.2   Graph Matching

In the context of RBPF, the probability distribution of the sensor model is determined directly by comparing the local and global map, giving the importance weight $w \approx p(\boldsymbol{z}|\boldsymbol{x}, \boldsymbol{m})$ of a particle. For this purpose, corresponding pairs of nodes $\langle e_i^L, e_j^G \rangle$ in both maps are selected by a simple nearest neighbor search in the position space, where each node e_i^L of the local map is related to the nearest neighbor node e_j^G of the global map. To keep the computational complexity for the nearest neighbor search as small as possible, we use a quad-tree-like structure for indexing the nodes, so the search does not depend on the total count of nodes. The relation between each selected pair of corresponding nodes $\langle e_i^L, e_j^G \rangle$ provides two pieces of information, a geometric one, the spatial distance d_{ij}, and a visual one, the visual similarity S_{ij} (see Fig. 3). Both aspects are used to determine a matching weight w_i for the respective node e_i^L of the local map. Assuming an independence between the node weights of the local map, the total matching weight $w^{[k]}$ for a particle k is simply calculated as follows:

$$w^{[k]} = \prod_{i=1}^{n} w_i^{[k]} \tag{1}$$

with n describing the number of nodes in the local map. To evaluate the matching weight w_i we have to compute the probability that two observations i and j got a similarity S_{ij} by a given distance d_{ij}.

2.3   Adaptive Sensor Model

To compute the matching weights between corresponding nodes, an adaptive sensor model had been developed. In the context of appearance-based observations, the visual similarity between observations is not only depending on the difference in the positions but also on the environment itself. If the robot moves, for example over a wide plane, the appearance will not change at all when moving a short distance. While moving along narrow hallways the appearance of the scene will change more significant.

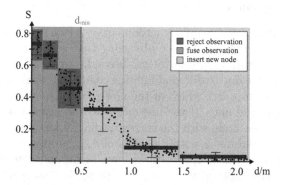

Fig. 4. The histogram model with mean value and σ per bin. The bins are not equally spaced. Points in the light green area ($d_{ij} > d_{min}$) are always included as new nodes. If points in the dark green area ($d_{ij} \leq d_{min}$) are within the model expectation (red area) they need not be included, otherwise they extend the local model by adding a new appearance variant to the node.

Hence, our sensor model estimates online the dependency between environment specific visual similarities $\hat{S}_{ij}$ of the observations z_i and z_j and their spatial distance $\hat{d}_{ij}$. Fig. 4 shows an example of such a function. Again the use of a local map is of help here. The samples to built such a model are taken from the nodes of the *local map* where each node is compared the others. We assume here that the resulting statistic represents $S(d)$ in the local map as well as in the global map. In [14] different approaches to approximate the model were investigated, e.g. the Gaussian Process Regression (GPR) of Rasmussen [9], while we used a parametric polynomial description of the sensor model and its variance. In this paper, we use an non-parametric histogram-based sensor model to create a more general model. For that purpose the distance d is divided in bins of different size, and for each bin the mean similarity and its variance are computed (see Fig. 4). The non-linear size of the bins is required to get a higher resolution for small distances, resulting in a higher accuracy of the matching process. The bin index idx is computed by a parametric exponential function $idx(d) = \alpha \cdot (d + \beta)^\gamma - 1$. The likelihood that two nodes i and j of particle k are matching the sensor model $S(d)$ is computed as follows, where $\hat{S}$ and $\hat{\sigma}$ are derived from the sensor model:

$$w_i^{[k]} = p\left(S_{ij}|d_{ij}\right) \approx \exp -\frac{\left(S_{ij} - \hat{S}\left(d_{ij}\right)\right)^2}{2 \cdot \hat{\sigma}(d_{ij})^2} \tag{2}$$

For our experiments we decided to use SIFT feature sets as appearance-based image description and similarity measure, because of their ability to re-detect the position of observation with good selectivity. For this specific image description we set the parameters of the bin indexing function to $\alpha = 8.0, \beta = 0.05, \gamma = 0.7$. These parameters are derived empirical.

2.4   Dynamic Changes

To meet the challenges of dynamic environments, we face two main problems. At first, the map grows unlimited while observing the environment and including every estimated position and observation. Second, the visual impression at the same place can change due to different lighting conditions, occlusions and moving objects. So we have to select which of the new positions and observations need to be included into the map. If the distance d to the nearest neighbor exceeds a distance d_{min} a new node with the corresponding observation is added to the map. So we do not add nodes within a circle of d_{min} around existing nodes. We just have to consider which observations have to be added to existing nodes. Hence we extend the nodes of the global map to collect observations of different appearance states by using the similarity model $\hat{S}(d_{ij}), \hat{\sigma}(d_{ij})$ (see Fig. 4) to decide whether new observations have to be included into an existing node or not. For each node of the local map e_i^L we assume to be in a certain position x_i with a global map m. We choose the highest similarity S_{ij} between all observations stored in the nearest node e_j^G in the global map m and the observation stored into node e_i^L to evaluate the existing sensor model $(S_{max} = max_k(S_{ij}(k)))$. According to equation 2, we can calculate the probability $p(S_{max}|d)$. If this probability is above a certain threshold ξ, the observation matches the expected similarity (as we have seen this particular scene in a similar configuration before) and can be ignored. If the observation does not match the model, it is associated to the current node e_j^G in the global map.

3   Experiments and Results

To evaluate the extensions of our approach, we used two alternative test environments with specific characteristics, the home improvement store shown in Fig. 1 with large straight hallways, and a small home-like section of our lab with narrow rooms with little space to navigate. All data for the analysis were recorded under realistic conditions, i.e. people walking through the operation area, shelves were rearranged, and other dynamic changes (e.g. illumination, occlusion) happened. In addition, laser data were captured to generate a reference map to evaluate the results of our approach.

The resulting graph of the store (Fig. 5, left) covers an area of 120 x 50 meters and was generated by a mean value of 250 particles (max. 2000 particles) in the RBPF. Figure 5 only shows the most likely final trajectory and a superimposed occupancy map for visualization. The home like area (see Fig. 5, right) was much smaller (10 m x 10 m). To evaluate the visual estimated path shown as trajectories in Fig. 5 a ground truth path and map built by means of a Laser-SLAM algorithm were calculated (GMapping of G. Grisetti [8] taken from www.openslam.org). The Laser-SLAM estimated reference path was used to determine the mean and the variance of the position error of our approach, shown in table 1. These experimental results demonstrate, that our approach is able to create a consistent trajectory and based on this, a consistent graph representation, too. Furthermore, in contrast to grid map approaches (up to 4GB

Fig. 5. In the home store: The red path shows the robot's movement trajectory only estimated by our appearance-based SLAM approach. In the home lab: additionally the nodes of the resulting graph are shown. For visualization of the localization accuracy, a laser-based occupancy map was built in parallel and superimposed to the estimated movement trajectory (visual SLAM).

Table 1. Overview of the achieved results in all environments.

Experiment	Home store	Home lab
Size of area	50x120m	10x10m
Total path length	2400m	20m
# of particles	250 (mean) *2000* (max)	50 (mean) *150* (max)
Error Mean/Var/Max	**0.53**/0.21/1.76 m	**0.21**/0.14/0.42 m
Time per cycle	0.250 s	0.250 s

for our home store environment), topological maps require less memory (up to 1.5GB for 4800 observations) because of the efficient observation storage. The observation's features are stored in a central data set and are only linked to the nodes in all maps and only the positions have to be stored in each node. So the memory requirements are nearly independent from the used number of particles. The results show that in small environments, like the home-like lab, where the robot is able to move along smaller loops, the visual SLAM approach achieved a higher accuracy than in large loops. We are able to demonstrate that our approach not only works in large scale environments but also in narrow home environments.

4   Conclusion and Future Work

In this paper we presented extensions of our appearance-based SLAM approach to limit the memory consumption and to deal with dynamic changes that occur in common real-world environments. These improvements allow an appearance-based on-line SLAM in dynamic real-world environments at long term time windows. For the near future we plan to implement a visual scan-matching technique to limit the number of required particles to close loops correctly and to further increase the accuracy of estimated maps. Furthermore, we want to study the influence of dynamic changes in the home environment in more detail.

References

1. H. Andreasson, T. Duckett, and A. Lilienthal. Mini-slam: Minimalistic visual slam in large-scale environments based on a new interpretation of image similarity. In *Proc. IEEE Int. Conf. on Robotics and Automation*, pages 4096–4101, 2007.
2. A.Ranganathan, E. Menegatti, and F. Dellaert. Bayesian inference in the space of topological maps. In *IEEE Trans. on Robotics, vol.22, no.1*, pages 92–107, 2006.
3. T D. Barfoot. Online visual motion estimation using fastslam with sift features. In *Proc. of 2005 IEEE/RSJ IROS*, pages 579–585, 2005.
4. A. Davison. Real-time simultaneous localisation and mapping with a single camera. In *Proc. Int. Conf. on Computer Vision(ICCV'03)*, pages 1403–1410, 2003.
5. A. Davison and D. Murray. Simultaneous localization and map-building using active vision. *IEEE Trans. on PAMI*, 24(7):865–880, 2002.
6. P. Elinas, R. Sim, and J. J. Little. σSLAM: Stereo vision SLAM using the Rao-Blackwellised particle filter and a novel mixture proposal distribution. In *Proc. of the IEEE Int. Conf. on Robotics and Automation*, pages 1564–1570, 2006.
7. F. Fraundorfer et al. Topological mapping, localization and navigation using image collections. In *Proc. IEEE/RSJ IROS*, pages 3872–3877, 2007.
8. G. Grisetti et al. Improved techniques for grid mapping with rao-blackwellized particle filters. In *IEEE Transactions on Robotics*, pages 34–46, 2006.
9. Rasmussen et al. *Gaussian Processes for Machine Learning*. MIT Press, 2006.
10. S. Se et al. Mobile robot localization and mapping with uncertainty using scale-invariant visual landmarks. *Int.Journal of Robotics Research*, 21(8):735–758, 2002.
11. D. Fox. Kld-sampling: Adaptive particle filters. In *Advances in Neural Information Processing Systems 14*. MIT Press, 2001.
12. H.-M. Gross, A. Koenig, H.-J. Boehme, and Chr. Schroeter. Vision-based monte carlo self-localization for a mobile service robot acting as shopping assistant in a home store. In *Proc. IEEE/RSJ IROS*, pages 256–262, 2002.
13. H.-M. Gross, A. Koenig, Chr. Schroeter, and H.-J. Boehme. Omnivision-based probabilistic self-localization for a mobile shopping assistant continued. In *Proc. IEEE/RSJ IROS*, pages 1505–1511, 2003.
14. A. Koenig, J. Kessler, and H.-M. Gross. A graph matching technique for an appearance-based, visual slam-approach using rao-blackwellized particle filters. In *IEEE/RSJ Int. Conf. on Intelligent Robots and Systems*, pages 1576–1581, 2008.
15. D.G. Lowe. Object recognition from local scale-invariant features. In *Proc. Int. Conf. on Computer Vision ICCV'99*, pages 1150–1157, 1999.
16. E. Menegatti, M. Zoccarato, E. Pagello, and H. Ishiguro. Hierarchical Image-based Localisation for Mobile Robots with Monte-Carlo Localisation. In *Proc. 1st European Conf. on Mobile Robots (ECMR'03)*, pages 13–20, 2003.
17. J. M. Porta and B. J.A. Kroese. Appearance-based Concurrent Map Building and Localization using a Multi-Hypotheses Tracker. In *Proc. IEEE/RSJ Int. Conf. on Intelligent Robots and Systems (IROS'04)*, pages 3424–3429, 2004.
18. R. Smith, M. Self, , and P. Cheeseman. A stochastic map for uncertain spatial relationships. In *Robotics Research, 4th Int. Symposium*, pages 467–474, 1988.
19. I. Ulrich and I. Nourbakhsh. Appearance-based place recognition for topological localization. In *Proc. IEEE ICRA*, pages 1023–1029, 2000.

Monte Carlo Lokalisierung Fahrerloser Transportfahrzeuge mit drahtlosen Sensornetzwerken

Christof Röhrig[1], Hubert Büchter[2] und Christopher Kirsch[1]

[1] Fachhochschule Dortmund, Fachbereich Informatik,
Emil-Figge-Str. 42, 44227 Dortmund
[2] Fraunhofer-Institut für Materialfluss und Logistik IML
Joseph-von-Fraunhofer-Str. 2-4, 44227 Dortmund

Zusammenfassung. Ein drahtloses Sensornetzwerk ist ein Funknetz aus Kleinstrechnern, das aus vielen kleinen, dicht verteilten Sensorknoten besteht. Neben den klassischen Anwendungen wie z.B. dem Umweltmonitoring kann es auch zur Lokalisierung von Objekten verwendet werden. Der Beitrag beschreibt die Lokalisierung von Fahrerlosen Transportfahrzeugen mit dem drahtlosen Sensornetzwerk nanoLOC des Herstellers Nanotron Technologies. Aufbauend auf einem angepassten Monte Carlo Algorithmus wird ein Sensormodell entwickelt, welches eine Lokalisierung durch Entfernungsmessung zu ortsfesten Sensorknoten ermöglicht. Es werden experimentelle Ergebnisse präsentiert, die zeigen, dass mit dem nanoLOC-System eine Positionsbestimmung eines Fahrerlosen Transportfahrzeugs mit einem Fehler kleiner als 0,5 m erreichbar ist.

1 Einführung

Fahrerlose Transportfahrzeuge (FTF) gelten in der Automatisierung des innerbetrieblichen Materialflusses als die Technologie, die dem Anwender/Betreiber ein Höchstmaß an Flexibilität bietet. FTF können sich unabhängig von einem physischen Transportnetz bewegen und Güter transportieren. Sie bieten die Möglichkeit, Systeme mit geringem Aufwand an neue, veränderte oder erweiterte Aufgabenstellungen oder veränderte Umgebungsbedingungen anzupassen. Ziel aktueller Forschungsarbeiten ist es, herkömmliche Stetigfördertechnik durch eine Gruppe kompakter und kostengünstiger FTF – quasi ein Schwarm von FTF – zu ersetzen [1]. Das von Kivasystems[1] entwickelte und bereits eingesetzte „KIVA Mobile Fulfillment System" (Kiva MFS) zeigt, dass der Einsatz von kleinen kostengünstigen Fahrzeugen in der Intralogistik ein hohes kommerzielles Potenzial besitzt. Beim Kiva MFS transportieren mobile Roboter innerhalb eines Kommissionierssystems Regale zum manuellen Kommissionierer. Es wurden von Kivasystems bereits mehrere Systeme, darunter ein Distributionszentrum von Staples in Chambersburg, Pennsylvania mit 500 mobilen Robotern, realisiert [2].

Derzeit bekannte und eingesetzte Lokalisierungsverfahren für FTF sind für einen FTF-Schwarm nicht geeignet, da diese Verfahren entweder zu unflexibel (Leitdraht) oder zu teuer (Lasernavigation) sind. Beim Kiva MFS wird eine Kombination aus Odometrie und optischen Bodenmarken eingesetzt. Als optische Bodenmarken werden 2D-Barcodes eingesetzt, die mit preisgünstigen Kameras von den mobilen Robotern aus

---

[1] http://www.kivasystems.com

gelesen werden können. Die optische Erkennung ermöglicht so eine globale Positionsbestimmung der Roboter, solange sich diese genau über einer Bodenmarke befinden.
Für die relative Lokalisierung zwischen den Bodenmarken werden die Radencoder der
Roboter genutzt. Um den Lokalisierungsfehler gering zu halten, bewegen sich die mobilen Roboter auf einem festen Raster, welches durch die Bodenmarken vorgegeben wird.
Die Verwendung von optischen Bodenmarken hat den Nachteil, dass diese manuell
auf den Boden angebracht werden müssen und sie gegenüber Verschmutzung anfällig
sind. Durch die Verwendung eines festen Rasters geht auch ein Teil der Flexibilität
der mobilen Roboter verloren. Aus diesen Gründen werden alternative kostengünstige
Lokalisierungsverfahren untersucht.

2 Funklokalisierung

Ein mögliches kostengünstiges Lokalisierungsverfahren ist die Funklokalisierung mit
einem drahtlosen Sensornetzwerk, bei dem die für die Datenübertragung notwendige Funkkommunikation gleichzeitig zur Positionsbestimmung genutzt wird. Drahtlose
Sensornetzwerke bieten neben den typischen Anwendungen wie z.B. dem Umweltmonitoring auch das Potential zu Lokalisierung mobiler Roboter [3]. Funklokalisierungsver-
fahren haben sich jedoch bisher noch nicht bei der Lokalisierung von FTF durchgesetzt.
Dies liegt einerseits in der noch relativ kurzen Zeit, in der derartige Systeme verfügbar
sind, und andererseits in der im Vergleich zur Lasernavigation geringeren Genauigkeit.

2.1 Stand der Technik

Es sind mehrere Verfahren zur Funklokalisierung bekannt, wobei die empfange Signalstärke, die Signallaufzeit oder der Einfallswinkel eines Signals als Information für
die Positionsbestimmung genutzt werden kann. Die empfangene Signalstärke ist in den
meisten Funktechnologien als Informationsquelle verfügbar und kann dazu genutzt werden, die Entfernung zu einem Sender zu bestimmen. Im Innenbereich ist diese Distanz-
bestimmung durch Störungen wie Reflektionen und Dämpfungen jedoch sehr ungenau,
so dass meist die genaueren Radio-Map-basierten Methoden Anwendung finden [4].
Allerdings ist hierbei der manuelle Aufwand für die Generierung der Radio-Map recht
hoch, außerdem liegt die Genauigkeit von Radio-Map-basierten Verfahren bestenfalls
im Bereich weniger Meter und ist damit für die Lokalisierung von FTF zu ungenau. Modellbasierte Ansätze, die die empfangene Signalstärke nutzen, sind deshalb auf den Au-
ßenbereich beschränkt [3]. Durch Winkelmessung empfangener Signale kann wie bei
der Laser-Triangulation die Position und Orientierung bestimmt werden, wobei auch
hier der technische Aufwand und somit die Investitionskosten sehr hoch sind. Laufzeitbasierte Verfahren bieten die höchste Genauigkeit bei relativ geringem technischem
Aufwand. Hierbei wird durch Laufzeitmessung die Distanz zu stationären Referenz-
knoten bestimmt und mittels Trilateration die Position des mobilen Knotens berechnet.
Diese Technik findet mittlerweile auch Einzug in drahtlose Sensornetzwerke. Aufbauend auf dem Funkstandard IEEE 802.15.4 wurden die neuen Physical Layer Ultra Wide
Band (UWB) und Chirp Spread Spectrum (CSS) in IEEE 802.15.4a definiert, um eine
Entfernungsbstimmung zu anderen Knoten besser 1 m zu ermöglichen [5]. CSS wird

von der Firma Nanotron Technologies[2] im nanoLOC-System zur Distanzmessung und Kommunikation eingesetzt. Das nanoLOC-System ermöglicht als preiswerte Technologie neben der Lokalisierung einzelner Knoten die Funkkommunikation mittels eines einzigen Bausteins [6].

Laufzeitbasierte Distanzmessungen unterliegen bei Innenraumanwendungen Messfehlern, die durch Reflektionen und Mehrwegeausbreitung verursacht werden. Die von Nanotron angegebene Lokalisierungsgenauigkeit des nanoLOC-Systems liegt im Innenbereich bei 2 m, was für Applikationen in der Intralogistik nicht ausreichend ist. Eigene Untersuchungen haben gezeigt, dass sich diese Fehler durch Einsatz eines Erweiterten Kalman Filters reduzieren lassen [7]. Da die auftretenden Messfehler jedoch nicht normalverteilt sind, bietet ein Monte Carlo Partikelfilter bessere Möglichkeiten, ein angepasstes Sensormodell zu integrieren.

2.2 Funklokalisierung mit dem nanoLOC System

Das nanoLOC-System ermöglicht gleichzeitig eine drahtlose Kommunikation und Echtzeit-Lokalisierung. Das dabei verwendete Ranging-Verfahren „Symmetrical Double-Sided Two Way Ranging" (SDS-TWR) gestattet eine funkbasierte Distanzmessung anhand der Signallaufzeiten und bietet die Grundlage für eine metergenaue Positionsbestimmung eines mobilen Objektes. Die drahtlose Kommunikation sowie das Ranging-Verfahren sind in einem einzigen Chip, dem Transceiver nanoLOC TRX integriert. Dieses Hochfrequenz-Funkmodul arbeitet in dem weltweit verfügbaren ISM-Band von 2,4 GHz. Die drahtlose Kommunikation basiert auf der von Nanotron patentierten Chirp-Modulationstechnik Chirp Spread Spectrum (CSS).

Der Vorteil von SDS-TWR liegt darin, dass keine zeitliche Synchronisierung zwischen den Knoten erforderlich ist und dadurch bekannte Probleme anderer zeitbasierter Lokalisierungsverfahren behoben werden. Das Verfahren basiert auf „Roundtrip Time of Flight" (RToF), wobei dieses symmetrisch und doppelseitig ausgeführt wird. Bei SDS-TWR wird die Signalübertragungszeit in zwei Richtungen gemessen (Two-Way Ranging). Dabei entstehen zwei Zeitspannen: Die Signallaufzeit (Signal Propagation Delay) die benötigt wird, um ein Frame von Knoten A zu B zu übermitteln und eine Bestätigung zurückzusenden, wird von Knoten A gemessen. Die Zeit um das eintreffende Datenpaket zu verarbeiten, die Bestätigung zu generieren und um das Versenden vorzubereiten, wird als Verzögerungszeit (Processing Delay) bezeichnet und von Knoten B gemessen. Die Differenz der beiden Zeitangaben (Signallaufzeit - Verzögerungszeit) beschreibt somit die zweifache Signalübertragungszeit. Zudem wird eine doppelseitige Messung (Symmetrical Double-Sided) durchgeführt, um den Fehler der Uhrenabweichungen (Clock Drift) zu eliminieren. Dazu wird das gleiche Verfahren in umgekehrter Laufrichtung durchgeführt, also von Knoten B zu A und zurück zu B.

3 Monte Carlo Funklokalisierung

Die verwendete Monte Carlo Methode ist ein Partikelfilter und kann zur Positionsbestimmung von mobilen Robotern genutzt werden. Für die Positionsbestimmung durch

---

[2] http://www.nanotron.de

den Monte Carlo Algorithmus werden über den Zustandsraum, in welchem sich der Roboter aufhalten kann, eine endliche Menge von Partikeln verstreut. Diesen Partikeln wird innerhalb des Algorithmus mit Bezug auf die Position und auf Sensormessungen eine Wahrscheinlichkeit zugeordnet. Diese Wahrscheinlichkeit spiegelt die Aufenhaltswahrscheinlichkeit des Roboters für genau diesen Punkt wieder. Diese Wahrscheinlichkeit wird auch als Bewertung bezeichnet und mit den Sensormessungen basierend auf einem Sensormodell durchgeführt. Nach jeder Bewertung findet eine Neuverteilung der Partikel statt und nach jeder Bewegung findet eine Verschiebung mit dem Bewegungsmodell des Roboters statt [8].

Die Monte Carlo Lokalisierung wurde an die Anforderungen der Funklokalisierung mit dem nanoLOC-System angepasst. Es wurde ein Sensormodell entwickelt, welches die Wahrscheinlichkeit $p_d(d_k \mid x_t)$ angibt. Dies ist die Wahrscheinlichkeit der Distanzmessung d_k von dem zu lokalisierenden FTF an der Position x_t zu einem Anker k. Die Position x_t wird dabei durch einen Partikel repräsentiert.

3.1 Anfangsverteilung der Partikel

Vor der ersten Bewegung des FTF müssen Partikel im Zustandsraum des FTF platziert werden. Um den Bereich einzugrenzen, in welchem die Partikel verstreut werden, wird am Anfang eine Ankerbox erstellt. Die Ankerbox grenzt den Bereich ein, indem sich das Fahrzeug befinden kann. Die Ankerbox bildet ein Rechteck um die Schnittfläche der Kreise, die durch die gemessenen Distanzen zu den Ankerknoten gebildet werden. Die Berechnung der Ankerbox lehnt sich an ein Verfahren an, das in [9] vorgestellt wird. Dabei werden die Eckpunkte der Ankerbox wie folgt berechnet:

$$x_{\min} = \max_{k=1}^{K}(x_k - d_k), \quad x_{\max} = \min_{k=1}^{K}(x_k + d_k),$$

$$y_{\min} = \max_{k=1}^{K}(y_k - d_k), \quad y_{\max} = \min_{k=1}^{K}(y_k + d_k), \tag{1}$$

dabei stehen x_k und y_k für die Position des Ankers k und d_k für die Distanzmessung zum Anker k, K ist die Anzahl der Ankerknoten.

3.2 Sensormodell der Distanzmessung

Eigene Untersuchungen haben gezeigt, dass das nanoLOC-System in Innenraumanwendungen infolge der Mehrwegeausbreitung der Funksignale in der Regel zu große Entfernungen liefert [7]. Die Messfehler hängen dabei von der Umgebung und der Anordnung der Sensorknoten ab. Wird für die Lokalisierung ein Kalman Filter eingesetzt, führt dies zu Fehlern in der Positionsschätzung. Eine Möglichkeit den Positionsfehler durch Mehrwegeausbreitung zu reduzieren, bietet das Biased Kalman Filter [10]. Ein Monte Carlo Partikelfilter bietet allerdings noch bessere Möglichkeiten, das Sensormodell an die Verteilung der Messfehler anzupassen.

Zur heuristischen Bestimmung des Sensormodells wurde eine Messfahrt mit einem FTF in der Demonstrationshalle des Fraunhofer IML durchgeführt. Es wurden die Messfehler der Distanzmessungen zu sechs fest installierten Ankerknoten aufgenommen.

Abb. 1 zeigt die Häufigkeit der Messfehler exemplarisch für vier Ankerknoten. Daraus ist ersichtlich, dass die größte Häufigkeit bei einem Messfehler von 1,5 - 2 m liegt, wobei auch noch deutlich größere Messfehler auftreten.

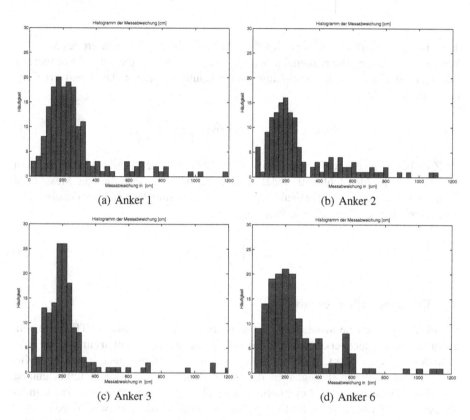

(a) Anker 1

(b) Anker 2

(c) Anker 3

(d) Anker 6

Abb. 1. Fehlerhäufigkeit bei verschiedenen Sensorknoten

Aufbauend auf den Messungen wurde ein Sensormodell entwickelt, welches über die Wahrscheinlichkeit $p_d(d_k \mid x_t)$ die gemessene Häufigkeitsverteilung approximiert. $p_d(d_k \mid x_t)$ ist die Wahrscheinlichkeit der Distanzmessung d_k von dem zu lokalisierenden FTF an der Position x_t zum Anker k. Um $p_d(d_k \mid x_t)$ im Monte Carlo Algorithmus zu berechnen, wird der Euklidische Abstand d_t^{k*} zwischen dem Partikel an der Position x_t und dem Anker k mit der gemessenen Distanz d_k verglichen. Der Euklidische Abstand d_t^{k*} wird nach Gl. 2 berechnet:

$$d_t^{k*} = \sqrt{(x_k - p_x)^2 + (y_k - p_y)^2}, \tag{2}$$

dabei sind x_k und y_k die kartesischen Koordinaten des Ankers k und p_x und p_y die kartesischen Koordinaten des Partikels x_t. Die Wahrscheinlichkeit $p_d(d_k \mid x_t)$ wird als unsymmetrisch Gaußverteilung modelliert:

$$p_d(d_k \mid x_t) = \begin{cases} c_s \mathcal{N}(d_k, d_t^{k*} + d_c^k, \sigma_s) & \text{falls} \quad 0 \le d_k < d_t^{k*} + d_c^k \\ c_l \mathcal{N}(d_k, d_t^{k*} + d_c^k, \sigma_l) & \text{falls} \quad d_t^{k*} + d_c^k \le d_k \le d_{\max} \\ 0 & \text{sonst} \end{cases} \tag{3}$$

dabei ist d_c^k eine ankerspezifische Rangingkonstante, die den Zentralwert des Messfehlers darstellt, $d_{\max}$ ist die maximal mögliche Distanz, c_s und c_l dienen zur Normierung und σ_s, σ_l sind die Standardabweichungen der Gaußverteilungen. Die Gaußverteilung ist gegeben durch:

$$\mathcal{N}(x, \mu, \sigma) = \frac{1}{\sigma \sqrt{2\pi}} \exp\left(-\frac{1}{2}\left(\frac{x - \mu}{\sigma}\right)^2\right) \tag{4}$$

Zur oben angegebenen Wahrscheinlichkeit wird noch eine Grundwahrscheinlichkeit p_{rand} addiert, um Messfehler zu modellieren. Unter der Annahme, dass die Messungen zu den einzelnen Ankerknoten unabhängig voneinander sind, lässt sich die Gesamtwahrscheinlichkeit eines Partikels wie folgt angeben:

$$p_g = \prod_{k=1}^{K} p_d(d_k \mid x_t) \tag{5}$$

3.3   Experimentelle Ergebnisse

Die oben beschriebene Monte Carlo Lokalisierung wurde mit einem FTF und einem nanoLOC Sensornetzwerk getestet. Dabei wurden sechs Ankerknoten entlang der Fahrbahn des FTFs installiert. Das FTF bewegt sich dabei entlang einer 10 m langen Geraden. Es wurde davon ausgegangen, dass die Anfangsposition des FTF unbekannt ist. Da mittels Trilateration die Orientierung des FTF nicht bestimmt werden kann, muss die Anfangsorientierung der Partikel anders ermittelt werden. Es wird davon ausgegangen, dass die Orientierung mittels Sensorik bestimmt werden kann, so dass allen Partikeln die richtige Orientierung vorgegeben wurde. Die Orientierung lässt sich z.B. mittels Magnetfeldsensoren oder in einem Funknetz auch mittels Richtantenne und Signalstärkemessung bestimmen [4].

Grundsätzlich ist durch Bewegung des FTF und Positionsbestimmung auch eine Bestimmung der Orientierung des FTF möglich. Experimente haben gezeigt, dass dazu mehrere Meter Fahrstrecke notwendig sind. Da die Bewegung des FTF in eine noch unbekannte Richtung erfolgt, ist dieses Verfahren für viele industrielle Applikationen ungeeignet. Als Bewegungsmodell für das mit einem Differentialantrieb ausgestattete FTF wurde das Odometriemodell aus [8] entnommen, welches sowohl die Unsicherheit in der Position als auch in der Orientierung berücksichtigt.

Abb. 2 zeigt die Ergebnisse der Lokalisierung. In Abb. 2(a) wird die Anfangsverteilung der Partikel durch die Ankerbox mit schwarzen Punkten dargestellt. Dabei ist zu erkennen, dass sich der Startpunkt der Bahn (rote Gerade) innerhalb der Ankerbox befindet. Abb. 2(a) zeigt weiterhin sechs Partikelwolken (in blau) während der Bewegung. Es ist deutlich zu erkennen, dass sich die Partikelwolken mit der zurückgelegten

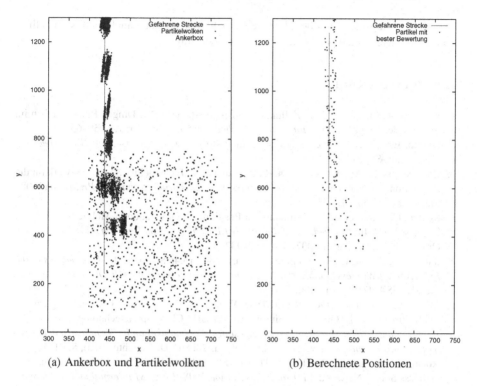

(a) Ankerbox und Partikelwolken   (b) Berechnete Positionen

Abb. 2. Ergebnisse einer Fahrt entlang einer Geraden von 10 m Länge

Stecke weiter konzentrieren. Abb. 2(b) zeigt die geschätzte Position des FTF, die durch den am besten bewerteten Partikel angegeben wird. Anfangs weicht die geschätzte Position noch deutlich von der realen Position auf der Bahn ab, nach etwa der Hälfte der Bewegung pendelt sich der Fehler auf weniger als 0,3 m ein.

4 Zusammenfassung

Für die Positionsbestimmung von FTF wurde ein Monte Carlo Partikelfilter verwendet, das aus den Distanzdaten zu festen Ankerknoten die Position des FTF ermittelt. Dazu wurde ein Sensormodell der nanoLOC-Distanzmessung entwickelt, das die Wahrscheinlichkeit einer Distanzmessung bei vorgegebener Position ermittelt. Die experimentelle Ergebnisse zeigen, dass eine Positionsbestimmung mit einem Fehler kleiner als 0,5 m möglich ist. Diese Genauigkeit ist für die Bewegung der FTF auf einer freien Fläche ausreichend, aber für Andockvorgänge zur Lastübergabe muss eine höhere Genauigkeit im Bereich von wenigen cm erreicht werden. Mit einem Funklokalisierungssystem ist derzeit diese Genauigkeit wohl nicht erreichbar. In aktuellen Untersuchungen werden die Distanzmessungen deshalb mit weiteren Messdaten, wie z.B. einem Laserabstandssensor fusioniert um die Genauigkeit zu erhöhen. Die zusätzliche Sensorik muss sich dabei nicht zwangsläufig auf dem FTF selbst befinden, sie kann auch ortsfest installiert sein und ihre Messdaten per Funk an das FTF übermitteln.

Literaturverzeichnis

1. TEN HOMPEL, M. ; NAGEL, L.: Zellulare Transportsysteme – Den Dingen Beine machen im „Internet der Dinge". In: *it – Information Technology* 50 (2008), Nr. 1, S. 59–65
2. GUIZZO, E.: Three Engineers, Hundreds of Robots, One Warehouse. In: *IEEE Spectrum* (2008), Juli, S. 26–34
3. GRÄFENSTEIN, J. ; ALBERT, A. ; BIBER, P. ; BOUZOURAA, M.E.: Verteiltes Sensornetzwerk für die Navigation eines mobilen Roboters. In: *atp - Automatisierungstechnische Praxis* 50 (2008), März, Nr. 3, S. 56–61
4. RÖHRIG, C. ; KÜNEMUND, F.: Estimation of Position and Orientation of Mobile Systems in a Wireless LAN. In: *Proceedings of the 46th IEEE Conference on Decision and Control.* New Orleans, USA, Dezember 2007, S. 4932–4937
5. SAHINOGLU, Z. ; GEZICI, S.: Ranging in the IEEE 802.15.4a Standard. In: *Proceedings of the IEEE Annual Wireless and Microwave Technology Conference, WAMICON '06.* Clearwater, Florida, USA, Dezember 2006, S. 1–5
6. SCHLICHTING, F.: nanoLOC TRX: Präzise Abstandsbestimmung und Lokalisierung mittels Laufzeitmessung (RTOF) durch Einsatz der 2,4 GHz Chirp Spreiztechnologie (CSS). In: *Tagungsband Wireless Automation: Funkgestützte Kommunikation in der industriellen Automatisierungstechnik,* VDI Verlag GmbH, Februar 2008 (VDI-Berichte 2010), S. 61–70
7. RÖHRIG, C. ; SPIEKER, S.: Tracking of Transport Vehicles for Warehouse Management using a Wireless Sensor Network. In: *Proceedings of the 2008 IEEE/RSJ International Conference on Intelligent Robots and Systems (IROS 2008).* Nice, France, September 2008, S. 3260–3265
8. THRUN, S. ; BURGARD, W. ; FOX, D.: *Probabilistic Robotics (Intelligent Robotics and Autonomous Agents).* MIT Press, 2005
9. BAGGIO, A. ; LANGENDOENA, K.: Monte Carlo localization for mobile wireless sensor networks. In: *Ad Hoc Networks* 6 (2008), Juli, Nr. 5, S. 718–733
10. RÖHRIG, C. ; MÜLLER, M.: Indoor Location Tracking in Non-line-of-Sight Environments Using a IEEE 802.15.4a Wireless Network. In: *Proceedings of the 2009 IEEE/RSJ International Conference on Intelligent Robots and Systems (IROS 2009).* St. Lous, USA, Oktober 2009

Using a Physics Engine to Improve Probabilistic Object Localization

Thilo Grundmann

Siemens AG Corporate Technology, Information and Communications
Intelligent Autonomous Systems, Otto-Hahn-Ring 6, Munich, Germany

Abstract. Each robot that is meant to handle objects must identify and localize
the designated objects prior to any manipulation attempt. Commonly the locations of the objects are estimated separately, assuming full mutual probabilistic
independence between all of them.

Hereby information is lost in constellations where objects are probabilistically
dependent in their state. A full state estimation could cope with this problem,
although it seems infeasible due to the enormous computational demands.

In this paper we present an approach that models such local dependencies and
utilizes a physic engine to exploit those within a probabilistic particle filter multi
object localization system, in order to improve the accuracy of the estimation
results.

1   Introduction

Common solutions for multiple object localization or tracking tasks rely on the assumption that the objects are mutually independent in their states, as well as in the motion
and measurement models. In other words, it is assumed that the information about one
object never carries any information about another object. This assumption is not abso-
lutely correct as for instance, if you know the whereabout of one cube in the world you
gain the information that any other cube can not be in the same place. Dependency in the
state in this context means probabilistic dependency, not rigid connections or "on top"
relations where the joint state of two objects can be reduced by dimension reduction.

In this paper we present an extension to a multiple object localization system which
makes explicit use of dependencies in the state that originate from 3D object shapes and
the physical fact that rigid objects cannot intersect to increase the estimation precision.
Another interpretation of our approach would be to use localized objects as sensors for
other objects. The approach is in particular valuable in situations where different objects
are localized with a broad range of precision. This can happen due to the fact that some
objects have been measured repeatedly or with better sensors. Furthermore in the case
that the acquisition of suitable additional measurements for a precision improvement is
impossible or too expensive, the above named approach is advantageous.

The method is to be integrated in the mobile service robot of the Desire project. This
robot is a two armed service device, mounted on an omni directional drive, that is hea-
ded for household tasks like cleaning up or sorting objects into shelves. It is equipped
with two four-fingered hands that allow for highly articulated object manipulation.

2 State of the Art

Robot systems that compare to the Desire Robot are most often equipped with a one-shot type of recognition system, so they do not keep track of their objects over time. Note, that in many common situations and depending on the accuracy of the recognition system and the tasks such an approach can be sufficient [1].

There has been work on the handling of dependencies between objects in the measurement model, and in that field mainly handling of occlusions. Rasmussen and Hager have proposed a multiple target tracking system, called Joint Likelihood Filter [2] that explicitly reasons about occlusion. Since their system estimates a 2D position the depth information of the targets is not included in the state, it is estimated separately.

The topic of scene analysis is closely related to multiple target tracking, which has been studied for a long time, starting with military applications based on radar measurements [3].

Kreucher et al. propose a multi target tracking system [4], that estimates the joint multi target probability density using a particle filter approach, leaving data association obsolete. They propose a measurement likelihood that considers the full state space and is able to handle occlusions. They do not reason about dependencies in the state, assuming that two targets can hold the same state.

A lot of tracking algorithms track multiple instances of the same class as in the field of people or car or face tracking. There has been a lot of work to tackle the problem of data association that occurs when multiple objects are tracked individually instead of jointly [5] [6]. Up to now, no other approaches to exploit dependencies in the states of multiple objects are known to the authors.

3 Theoretical Concept

To estimate the state of n entities $X^n = (x^1, x^2, ...x^n)$ which are assumed to be mutually independent in their states, one single implementation of the Bayesian filtering scheme can be applied for each object. We will make use of the common abbreviation $bel(x_t)$ that stands for $p(x|z_{0..t})$ [6]. When the state of a single entity is x^i and $x^{i,j}$ denotes the joint state space of two entities, the assumption of full probabilistic independence can be described as follows:

$$bel(x^i{}_t) = bel(x^i{}_t | x^j{}_t) \tag{1}$$
$$p(z^i_t | x^i{}_t) = p(z^i_t | x^{i,j}{}_t) \tag{2}$$
$$p(x^i{}_t | u^i_{t-1}, x^i{}_{t-1}) = p(x^i{}_t | u^{i,j}_{t-1}, x^{i,j}{}_{t-1}) \tag{3}$$

As long as these independence assumptions are valid and data association has been solved, separate Bayesian filters can be used. However in most real world applications and also in our service robot scenario these assumptions are violated often and whenever one of these assumptions is violated, the result of an independent estimation will be erroneous.

In this paper we focus on the implementation of an extension to a standard multiple object localization system, the rule set joint state update (RSJSU) which tackles violations of equation (1) and has been proposed in [7].

3.1 Rule Set Joint State Update

The concept of this method is to switch to a joint state representation of two objects, then to update the joint state under the consideration of a set of rules (f.i. physical laws) and to switch back to the independent state representation by a marginalization of the joint state. As this method is only advantageous when objects are dependent in their states, a dependency estimator can be used as trigger for it.

For a better illustration we consider two objects with states x^1 and x^2, which are dependent in their states (f.i.: both touching the other). Furthermore, let us assume that there is a function $F()$, which is able to detect such state dependencies and a set of physical models and laws r. The dependency detection function $F()$ works as trigger for the rule set joint state update during the normal independent object filtering process.

The algorithm performing the proposed method is composed of the following steps:

1. If state dependency is detected e.g. $F(x_1, x_2) = 1$ after a normal update the states x^1 and x^2 are joined according to (4).

$$bel(x^{i,j}) = bel(x^i)bel(x^j) \qquad (4)$$

2. Update the joint state with help of the dependency model according to (5).

$$bel^s(x^{i,j}) = \alpha p(x^{i,j}|r)bel(x^{i,j}) \qquad (5)$$

3. Finally the joint space is marginalized back into the individual state spaces (6).

$$bel(x^i) = \int bel^s(x^{i,j})dx^j \qquad (6)$$

4 Implementation of the Proposed System

To implement a system with rule set joint state update we decided to use a multiple object bootstrap particle filter [8][9] with maximum likelihood data association as base system. We will describe our implementation of the RSJSU which uses a fourteen dimensional particle filter and an open source physic simulator.

4.1 Probabilistic Models

The state In our framework, the state of a single static object consists of the objects class c and its pose ψ with reference to a world frame. This seven dimensional state is called a hypothesis h consisting of one discrete and six continuous dimensions. $h = (c, \psi)$. For the pose we use a Rodriguez representation, which means that the first three entries of a pose vector describe its translational part and the last three entries form the rotation axis (e^1, e^2, e^3). Its length determines the rotation angle α.

$$\psi = (x, y, z, \alpha e^1, \alpha e^2, \alpha e^3)$$

To describe a probability density over a hypothesis we decompose the state in two parts, class and pose, and we describe the distribution over the class with a histogram as it is a discrete value. $p(h) = p(c) \cdot p(\psi|c)$.

The distribution over poses is represented by a set of m particles $\psi_t^{[1..m]}$ with corresponding weights $w_t^{[1..m]}$. One particle represents one hypothetical pose of an object, described with a Rodriguez axis as mentioned before.

Herewith a distribution over a hypothesis consists of a classification probability for each class and attached to each of those a probability distribution over the pose given the class.

The prior $p(h_0)$ in our system is assumed to be equally distributed over classes and poses. As we consider only static objects in our scenario, the system model consists of a static state transition plus additional white gaussian noise to account for the un-modeled errors in the system. The correct parameters of that distribution have been determined by experiment.

The measurement model Probabilistically we describe our sift based localization method with the conditional probability $p(z|h, \psi_c)$, h being a seven dimensional object hypothesis, w_c being the camera position and z being the measurement hypothesis as the underlying detection system delivers a full hypothesis. The evaluation of the measurement model $p(z|h, \psi_c)$ for specified z, h and ψ_c consists of two steps:

1. Check visibility:
    a) object is visible in the camera cone.
    b) distance between camera and object is small enough to detect sift features on the object.
2. Evaluate the likelihood for the measurement, given a hypothesis.

We will not go into detail at this point since this model is not the focus of this article. Nevertheless this model can be applied for a wide range of different camera based localization methods.

4.2   The Trigger Function

For all objects we have 3D models describing the object's shape. In our case of a monte carlo probability distribution, we define the full particle set convex hull as the convex hull over all vertices of those 3D models taken from all particles.

The evaluation whether the convex hulls of two objects intersect can be used as an estimate of dependency between the objects. In our setup we use a 10% overlap as threshold to trigger the RSJSU, this value has to be carefully chosen as it is highly related to the underlying scenario. Also other factors as the estimated dependency like the actual computational load of the robot or demands of the current task can influence the decision to trigger the method.

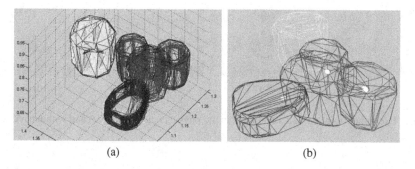

| (a) | (b) |

Fig. 1. (a) Full particle set convex hulls for a scene. (b) Points of maximal penetration depth between the objects in the scene.

4.3 Implementation of the Rule Set Joint State Update

Our rule set joint state update works as follows: Establish a joint particle set by com-

Rule set joint state update:
$\bar{\chi}_{12} = \chi_{12} = \emptyset$
for $n = 1$ *to* N **do**
    sample $x_1^{[n]} \sim bel(x_1)$
    sample $x_2^{[n]} \sim bel(x_2)$
    $x_{12}^{[n]} = \left\{ x_1^{[n]}, x_2^{[n]} \right\}$
    $w_{12}^{[n]} = p(x_{12}^{[n]}|r)$
    $\bar{\chi}_{12} = \bar{\chi}_{12} + \left\langle x_{12}^{[n]}, w_{12}^{[n]} \right\rangle$
end for
for $n = 1$ *to* N **do**
    draw i *with probability* $\propto w_{12}^{[i]}$
    $\chi_{12} = \left\{ \chi_{12}, x_{12}^{[n]} \right\}$
end for
marginalizeχ_{12} *into* χ_1 *and* χ_2

bining drawings from the sole particle sets. Weight the joint particles according to the rule set joint prior $p(x_{12}^{[n]}|r)$. Resample from the weighted set and marginalize the joint distribution back into the sole particle sets.

4.4 The Physical Model: Bullet Physic Engine

The rule set joint prior in this setup is defined binary and so constellations with colliding objects as regarded to be impossible (likelihood value equals zero). The collision detection is done with PAL [10], using the Bullet Engine. To account for errors in the

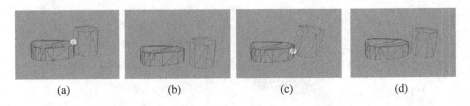

(a)	(b)	(c)	(d)

Fig. 2. Exemplary joint particles evaluated in the physic engine with (a/c) and without(b/d) collision.

3D models of the objects and the imperfect representation of the probability distribution that occurs due to the limited number of particles a threshold is defined. Only if the collision has a penetration depth that is higher than the threshold, a collision is detected.

5   Experimental Results

Fig. 3. Initial Test setup (1st). Particle sets of localized objects after five measurement updates (2nd). Scene with added can object (3rd).

Test setup As test situation we consider a complex scene: some objects of different classes, including one instance of an unknown class that can not be detected, are located on a table (Fig.3a). The robot takes measurements of this setup from five different locations and updates its estimated scene model accordingly (Fig. 3b). Then another can is added to the scene and the robot takes another measurement (Fig.3c).

Rule set joint state update applied The estimated scene as depicted in Figure 3c and Figures 4a-c serves as entry point for this test. Figures 4d-f show the particle representation of the scene after the incorporation of the new measurement that includes the new can. It is clearly visible, that after one measurement the localization accuracy of the new found object is much lower than the accuracy of the established ones. Note that their accuracy has not changed significantly as they are already at the system noise level. Since the full bounding volume of the new object intersects with the full bounding volumes of the three adjacent objects, the rule set joint state update is executed for all three objects.

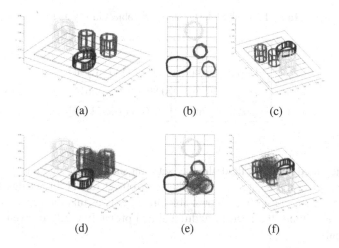

(a)   (b)   (c)

(d)   (e)   (f)

Fig. 4. ParticleSet before (a/b/c), directly after the introduction of the additional can (d/e/f)

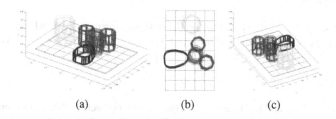

(a)   (b)   (c)

Fig. 5. Particle set after the application of the rule set joint state update (a/b/c)

After the application of the physical constraints, the particle sets of all involved objects have changed. The distribution of the particle sets of the established objects is only slightly changed, whereas the set representing the new object is reduced strongly in its variance (Tab. 1). The runtime for a rule set joint state update with our implementation with 10.000 joint particles is approximately 3 sec. on a 1.5 GHz laptop.

This example shows, that instead of using another probably expensive measurement (an appropriate view point might even be unreachable for a robot) the method of rule set joint state update is able to increase the localization accuracy purely by applying world knowledge (in this implementation a basic physical law).

Note that the general concept is not restricted to physical models as in our example, since $p(x^{12}|r)$ could model any dependency between x^1 and x^2.

6   Conclusions and Future Works

In this article we proposed a system that is able to identify and to localize multiple objects of multiple classes over time. It applies one single Bayesian filter for each object, which is implemented using a bootstrap particle filter. To counteract the errors that are introduced to the system due to the un-modeled physical dependences between the ob-

Table 1. Standard deviation of new object in x, y and z

	x	y	z
stddev/cm Fig.4(d-f)	1.327	0.857	1.130
stddev/cm Fig.5(a-c)	0.808	0.758	1.017
relative gain	38.5%	11.6%	21.7%

jects we integrated a new method, the rule set joint state update into the system, which is able to improve the estimates on the basis of object model knowledge and physical laws. That way, the service robot is able increase its estimation accuracy in certain constellations without the need of additional and probably costly or even impossible measurements.

Acknowledgment

This work was partly funded as part of the research project DESIRE by the German Federal Ministry of Education and Research (BMBF) under grant no. 01IME01D.

References

1. P. Azad, T. Asfour, and R. Dillmann, "Stereo-based 6d object localization for grasping with humanoid robot systems," in *Proc. of the IEEE/RSJ Int. Conf. on Intelligent Robots and Systems (IROS)*, San Diego, CA, USA, 2007.
2. C. Rasmussen and G. D. Hager, "Probabilistic data association methods for tracking complex visual objects," *IEEE Transactions on Pattern Analysis and Machine Intelligence*, vol. 23, no. 6, pp. 560–576, 2001.
3. Y. Bar-Shalom and L. Xiao-Rong, *Estimation and Tracking: Principles, Techniques and Software*. London: Artech House Publishers, 1993.
4. C. Kreucher, K. Kastella, and A. Hero, "Multitarget tracking using the joint multitarget probability density," *IEEE Transactions on Aerospace and Electronic Systems*, vol. 41, pp. 1396–1414, 2005.
5. R. Karlsson and F. Gustafsson, "Monte carlo data association for multiple target tracking," 2001.
6. S. Thrun, W. Burgard, and D. Fox, *Probabilistic Robotics*. MIT Press, Cambridge, MA, 2005.
7. T. Grundmann, R. Eidenberger, and R. Zoellner, "Local dependency analysis in probabilistic scene estimation," in *ISMA 2008. 5th International Symposium on Mechatronics and Its Applications*, Amman, Jordan, 2008, pp. 1–6.
8. A. Doucet, N. de Freitas, and N. Gordon, *Sequential Monte Carlo Methods in Praktice*. Springer, New York, 2001.
9. K. Gadeyne, "BFL: Bayesian Filtering Library," http://www.orocos.org/bfl, 2001.
10. A. Boeing and T. Bräunl, "Evaluation of real-time physics simulation systems," in *GRAPHITE '07: Proceedings of the 5th international conference on Computer graphics and interactive techniques in Australia and Southeast Asia*. New York, NY, USA: ACM, 2007, pp. 281–288.

Visual Self-Localization with Tiny Images

Marius Hofmeister, Sara Erhard and Andreas Zell

University of Tübingen, Department of Computer Science, Sand 1, 72076 Tübingen

Abstract. Self-localization of mobile robots is often performed visually, whereby the resolution of the images influences a lot the computation time. In this paper, we examine how a reduction of the image resolution affects localization accuracy. We downscale the images, preserving their aspect ratio, up to a tiny resolution of 15×11 and 20×15 pixels. Our results are based on extensive tests on different datasets that have been recorded indoors by a small differential drive robot and outdoors by a flying quadrocopter. Four well-known global image features and a pixel-wise image comparison method are compared under realistic conditions such as illumination changes and translations. Our results show that even when reducing the image resolution down to the tiny resolutions above, accurate localization is achievable. In this way, we can speed up the localization process considerably.

1 Introduction

Mobile robots need to localize themselves in an environment to solve complex tasks. Positioning is often done visually, since cameras are inexpensive and flexible sensors and nowadays provide high resolutions. But even if computational power has increased significantly during the past decade, there are still fields in which it keeps restricted. For example, swarm robotics requires a large number of relatively simple agents that have to be reasonably priced at a small size. And even in case of unmanned aerial vehicles, processing power is often restricted due to the limited weight and battery power that the robots can carry.

Visual self-localization is often performed using image retrieval techniques that store images in a database. For localization, a new image is taken and compared to all or a subset of previously recorded images. The computed similarity leads then to an estimation of the robot's position. Mostly, this task is performed by extracting features from the images. Such features often promise to be robust to changes in the environment and the viewpoint of the observer. The extraction time of those features depends mainly on the image resolution and thus could be decreased. However, by reducing the resolution of images we lose information that might be helpful for the localization task. Thus, the focus of this paper lies in the investigation to what extent a reduction of image data affects localization accuracy and computation time. We therefore examine the localization process on two different platforms: a small two-wheeled mobile robot indoors and a flying quadrocopter outdoors.

Fig. 1. Employed robots and example images at highest and lowest resolutions.

2   Related Work

Approaches to the visual self-localization problem mainly differ in the type of image features that are extracted from the images. We distinguish two kinds of image features: local and global ones. While local features, like the *Scale-Invariant Feature Transform* (SIFT) by Lowe [1], describe only patches around interest points in an image, global features describe the whole image as one single fixed-length vector.

Many local features are invariant to scale and rotation and robust to illumination changes [1]. As the number of local features in an image can be high, however, it may take a long time to find, match, and store them. Global image features have also shown a good localization accuracy [2,3,4], that is, however, lower. Their main advantage is their short computation time. As our applications require onboard image processing on microcontrollers with limited computation power, we decided to employ global image features in this work.

Ulrich and Nourbakhsh [5] established self-localization for place recognition using color histograms. They applied a nearest-neighbor algorithm to all color bands and combined it with a simple voting scheme based on the topological map of the environment. Zhou et al. [6] extended this approach to the use of multidimensional histograms, taking into concern features like edges and texturedness. Wolf et al. [7] performed visual localization by combining an image retrieval system with Monte Carlo localization. They used local image features that are invariant to image rotations and limited scale [8] and that are also the basis for the global *Weighted Grid Integral Invariants*, which are employed in this paper.

Our approach to use tiny images was also inspired by Torralba et al. [9] who stored millions of images from the internet in a size of 32×32 pixels and performed object and scene recognition on this dataset. Self-localization with small images was earlier performed by Argamon-Engelson [10]. He used images with a resolution of 64×48 pixels using measurement functions based on edges, gradients, and texturedness, but did not compare the localization rate and computation time to other image resolutions.

3   Robots

We conducted our experiments on two different robots: a small, two-wheeled *c't-Bot* (http://www.ct-bot.de), which was developed by the German computer magazine *c't*, and a quadrocopter *X3D-BL Hummingbird* distributed by *Ascending Technologies* [11] (see Fig. 1). The image processing is performed on separate modules: in case of the *c't-Bot* on a *POB-Eye* camera module equipped with a 60 MHz ARM7 microcontroller and in case of the quadrocopter on a *Nokia N95* mobile phone with a 332 MHz ARM11 processor. On the *c't-Bot*, feature vectors are saved on a SD card that is connected via I^2C, while on the quadrocopter feature vectors can be stored directly in the internal memory. On both systems, computation power is restricted and thus is a valuable resource.

4   Global Image Features

The selection of image features results from the limited processing power of our robots. Color and grayscale histograms are simple and fast methods for computing the feature vectors. More complex methods are *Weighted Gradient Orientation Histograms (WGOH)* and *Weighted Grid Integral Invariants (WGII)*, which yielded good results in earlier research, especially under illumination changes [2,3,4].

All features are investigated for different resolutions. Therefore, we downscale the images preserving their aspect ratio up to a tiny resolution of 15×11 and 20×15 pixels by interpolating the pixel intensities in a bilinear fashion. This downscaling also permits a pixelwise image comparison in a reasonable computation time. All selected features, except the pixelwise image comparison, are based on a grid which divides the image into a number of subimages. This makes the features more distinctive through adding local information. Changes within one subimage only influence a small part of the feature vector. We tested the methods at different grid sizes and image resolutions and discovered that a 4×4 grid leads to the best results.

4.1   Weighted Gradient Orientation Histograms

Weighted Gradient Orientation Histograms (WGOH) were presented by Bradley et al. [2] and were intended for outdoor environments because of their robustness to illumination changes. Their design was inspired by SIFT features [1]. Bradley et al. first split the image into a 4×4 grid of subimages. On each subimage, they calculated an 8-bin histogram of gradient orientations, weighted by the magnitude of the gradient at each point and by the distance to the center of the subimage. In our implementation of WGOH, we use a 2D Gaussian for weighting, where the mean corresponds to the center of the subimage and the standard deviations correspond to half the width and the height of the subimage, respectively [3]. This choice is similar to SIFT, where a Gaussian with half the width of the descriptor window is used for weighting. The 16 histograms are concatenated to a 1×128 feature vector, which is normalized subsequently. To reduce the dependency on particular regions or some strong gradients, the elements of the feature vector are limited to 0.2, and the feature vector is normalized again.

4.2   Weighted Grid Integral Invariants

The key idea of integral invariants was to design features which are invariant to Euclidean motion, i.e., rotation and translation [7,8]. In order to achieve that, all possible rotations and translations are applied to the image. In our case, two relational kernel functions are applied to each pixel. These functions compute the difference between the intensities of two pixels p_1 and p_2 lying on different radii and phases around the center pixel. The described procedure is repeated several times, where p_1 and p_2 are rotated around the center up to a full rotation while the phase shift is preserved. By averaging the resulting differences, we get one value for each pixel and kernel. We experimentally found out that the following radii for p_1 and p_2 lead to the best results: radii 2 and 3 for kernel one and radii 5 and 10 for kernel two, each with a phase shift of $90°$. One rotation is performed in ten $36°$ steps. Weiss et al. [4] extended the basic algorithm by dividing the image into a set of subimages to add local information. Each pixel is then weighted by a Gaussian as with WGOH (see Sect. 4.1) to make the vector more robust to translations. The output is a 2×8 histogram for each subimage and a 1×1024 histogram for the entire image.

4.3   Color/Grayscale Grid Histograms

For the color and grayscale histograms, we use eight bins for each subimage. Through concatenation we get a 1×128 feature vector of the 16 subimages. In case of the color histogram we process the hue value of the HSV color space. This choice of space promises to be more robust to illumination changes. As stated above, we weight each pixel by a Gaussian to make the vector more robust to translations and normalize it afterwards.

4.4   Pixelwise Image Comparison

The reduction of the image resolution permits also to compare the image data in a pixelwise fashion rather than extracting first the features. In this way, computation time may be saved. Therefore, the image data is treated as a vector. To keep the data small, we only compare the normalized grayscale image and discard color information.

5   Localization Process

Our localization process consists of two steps, the mapping phase and the localization phase. In the mapping phase, *training images* are recorded and feature vectors are extracted. These vectors are saved together with their current global position coordinates. In the localization phase, *test images* are recorded and features are again extracted. These features are subsequently compared to all other previously saved feature vectors. The mapped position of the vector with the highest similarity is then chosen to become the current position estimate of the robot.

To perform the image comparison, we calculate the similarity $sim(Q, D)$ of two images Q and D from their corresponding normalized feature histograms q and d through the *normalized histogram intersection* $\bigcap_{norm}(q, d)$:

$$sim(Q, D) = \bigcap_{norm}(q, d) = \sum_{k=0}^{m-1} \min(q_k, d_k). \tag{1}$$

Here, m is the number of histogram bins and q_k denotes bin k of histogram q. In [4], this method showed good results. For the pixelwise image comparison, the normalized histogram intersection did not yield satisfactory results. In this case, we use the L_1-norm with the normalized images Q^* and D^*:

$$L_1(Q^*, D^*) = \sum_{k=0}^{r-1} |Q_k^* - D_k^*|, \tag{2}$$

where r is the number of pixels and Q_k^* denotes pixel k of image Q^*. The similarity $sim(Q, D)$ of two images can now be computed as:

$$sim(Q, D) = 1 - min(1, L_1(Q^*, D^*)). \tag{3}$$

Note that in general $0 \leq L_1(Q^*, D^*) \leq 2$ (although $L_1(Q^*, D^*) > 1$ rarely happens for images).

6   Experimental Results

We conducted our experiments with the *c't-Bot* in an office environment. Since the robot does not have the ability to determine its ground truth position through GPS or other accurate sensors like laser scanners, we grabbed images every 0.5 m in an area of appr. 75 m^2. To limit possible viewpoints and thus faciliate the localization, we employed a compass. Our dataset consists of 190 training images, that were grabbed facing west (determined by the compass) with a manually oriented robot. Due to magnetic deflections of furniture etc., the direction indicated by the compass was not always true but repeatable, thus it can be seen as a function of the position. The test data were grabbed at randomly chosen positions. 100 images, in the following called *test data A*, were grabbed at stable illumination. Another 100 images, *test data B*, were grabbed at different lighting conditions with and without ceiling lights, at shining sun or dull daylight. In both datasets, the robot rotated autonomously towards west by means of the compass. Because of weak odometry and compass errors, the robot's rotation is affected by errors which appear approximately as translations in the images.

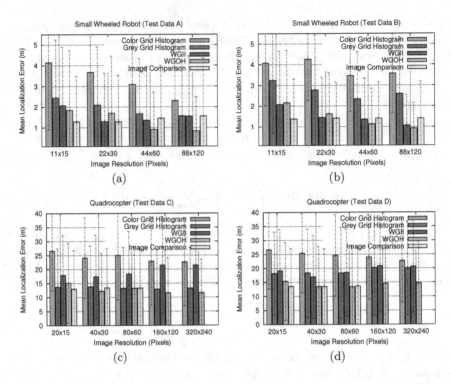

Fig. 2. Localization results in case of the *c't-Bot* (a,b) and quadrocopter (c,d). Shown are mean localization errors of the image features at different image resolutions. The pixelwise image comparison is referred to as image comparison. No measurements were taken for the pixelwise image comparison under high resolutions because of database restrictions.

To perform the experiments with the quadrocopter, we steered it at altitudes around eight meters, flying rounds of appr. 180 m in a courtyard. The view of the camera pointed in course direction. In total, we grabbed 1275 images in several rounds at a frequency of appr. one image per second. Each round consisted of a different number of images due to the different velocity of the quadrocopter. In the mapping phase we grabbed 348 images at dull daylight. For the localization phase we used two different datasets: *Test data C* consists of 588 images (four rounds) at similar lighting conditions, *test data D* of 369 images (three rounds) at sunny daylight.

Figure 2 shows the localization accuracies of the examined methods. The mean localization error is measured in 2D only; in case of the quadrocopter we tried to keep the flying altitude constant. The smallest mean localization error we obtain is in case of the *c't-Bot* 0.84 m and in case of the quadrocopter 11.55 m, using WGOH. Further experiments showed that by using a particle filter to compute a probabilistic position estimate, the localization errors can be reduced to about 0.50 m on the *c't-Bot* and about 6 m on the quadrocopter. However, in this paper we focus on feature extraction techniques.

Looking at the different methods in detail, we find out that in most cases WGOH lead to best results. The results of WGII are worse, even if it also computes differences of pixel intensities. It provides rotation invariance, but that comes with the cost of losing orientation information. The straightforward pixelwise image comparison yielded surprisingly high accuracies. This may be because the normalization helps to cope with illumination changes and the use of wide-angle lenses limits the influence of translations. A localization was not possible with the color grid histograms. The reason for this may be the poor color quality of our cameras and the lack of meaningful color information in the environments. As it could be expected, the overall accuracy on *test data B* and *test data D* was worse, due to the different lighting conditions. The grayscale grid histograms did not perform well here. Generally, despite the reduction of the image resolution we achieved a reasonable localization accuracy. While WGOH and WGII may have suffered from averaging over the subimages at small image resolutions, the pixelwise image comparison provided constant localization rates at all resolutions.

We also examined the computation times of the whole localization process on the training data (see Table 1). We chose WGOH since it revealed a good accuracy at a reasonable feature extraction time and the pixelwise image comparison on the small size images since it is the fastest method of all with respect to feature extraction time.

Table 1. Computation times of the localization process at different resolutions using WGOH and the pixelwise image comparison (referred to as Img. Comp.).

	WGOH (full res.)	WGOH (smallest res.)	Img. Comp. (smallest res.)
c't-Bot	4.812 s	3.841 s	4.002 s
Quad.	0.639 s	0.267 s	0.397 s

By the use of tiny images, we achieve a speed up of 20.2 % in case of the *c't-Bot* and in case of the quadrocopter of 58.2 %, comparing WGOH at the highest and the smallest resolution. The localization process can roughly be divided into feature extraction and feature matching. The pixelwise image comparison is not the fastest method since the corresponding vector has a higher dimensionality than the WGOH vector and thus requires more time to be compared. On the *c't-Bot*, the localization time is highly affected by the matching step and needs 3.841 s, which is quite long, but we should also keep in mind the computational limitations of small mobile robots. To further speed up the feature matching, different approaches could be employed in the future, e.g. a kd-tree for a more efficient search or a particle filter to limit the number of feature comparisons.

7 Conclusion

In this paper, we examined to what extent a reduction of the image resolution affects accuracy and computation time in the visual self-localization process. Therefore, we compared four well-known global image features in an indoor and outdoor scenario where computation power is restricted. The reduction of the image resolution made it also possible to apply a straightforward pixelwise image comparison. Generally, WGOH provided good performance with relatively low computation times.

We state that in our medium-sized indoor and outdoor test beds, tiny grayscale images of 15×11 and 20×15 pixels contained enough information to establish efficient self-localization at satisfactory accuracy. In this way, we could speed up the localization process considerably. These results are especially interesting for researchers working on systems with restricted computation power to achieve visual self-localization in similar environments in a fast and efficient way.

References

1. Lowe D.: Distinctive Image Features from Scale-Invariant Keypoints. Int. Journal of Computer Vision 60(2), pp. 91–110, 2004.
2. Bradley D. M., Patel R., Vandapel N., Thayer S. M.: Real-Time Image-Based Topological Localization in Large Outdoor Environments. Proc. of the IEEE/RSJ Int. Conf. on Intelligent Robots and Systems (IROS), Edmonton, Canada, pp. 3670–3677, 2005.
3. Weiss C., Masselli A., Zell A.: Fast Vision-based Localization for Outdoor Robots Using a Combination of Global Image Features. Proc. of the 6th Symposium on Intelligent Autonomous Vehicles (IAV), Toulouse, France, 2007.
4. Weiss C., Masselli A., Tamimi H., Zell A.: Fast Outdoor Robot Localization Using Integral Invariants. Proc. of the 5th Int. Conf. on Computer Vision Systems (ICVS), Bielefeld, Germany, 2007.
5. Ulrich I., Nourbakhsh I.: Appearance-Based Place Recognition for Topological Localization. Proc. of the IEEE Int. Conf. on Robotics and Automation (ICRA), San Francisco, CA, USA, pp. 1023–1029, 2000.
6. Zhou C., Wei Y., Tan T.: Mobile Robot Self-Localization Based on Global Visual Appearance Features. Proc. of the IEEE Int. Conf. on Robotics and Automation (ICRA), Taipei, Taiwan, pp. 1271–1276, 2003.
7. Wolf J., Burgard W., Burkhardt H.: Robust Vision-based Localization by Combining an Image Retrieval System with Monte Carlo Localization. IEEE Transactions on Robotics, 21(2), pp. 208–216, 2005.
8. Siggelkow S.: Feature Histograms for Content-Based Image Retrieval. Ph.D. dissertation, Institute for Computer Science, University of Freiburg, Germany, 2002.
9. Torralba A., Fergus R., Freeman W. T.: 80 million tiny images: A large dataset for non-parametric object and scene recognition. IEEE Transactions on Pattern Analysis and Machine Intelligence, 30(11), pp. 1958–1970, 2008.
10. Argamon-Engelson S.: Using Image Signatures for Place Recognition. Pattern Recognition Letters, 19(10), pp. 941–951, 1998.
11. Gurdan D., Stumpf J., Achtelik M., Doth K.-M., Hirzinger G., Rus D.: Energy-efficient Autonomous Four-rotor Flying Robot Controlled at 1 kHz. Proc. of the Int. Conf. on Robotics and Automation (ICRA), Rome, Italy, pp. 361–366, 2007.

Coordinated Path Following for Mobile Robots

Kiattisin Kanjanawanishkul, Marius Hofmeister and Andreas Zell

University of Tübingen, Department of Computer Science, Sand 1, 72076 Tübingen

Abstract. A control strategy for coordinated path following of multiple mobile robots is presented in this paper. A virtual vehicle concept is combined with a path following approach to achieve formation tasks. Our formation controller is proposed for the kinematic model of unicycle-type mobile robots. It is designed in such a way that the path derivative is employed as an additional control input to synchronize the robot's motion with neighboring robots. A second-order consensus algorithm under undirected information exchange is introduced to derive the control law for synchronization. Our controller was validated by simulations and experiments with three unicycle-type mobile robots.

1 Introduction

Compared with a single mobile robot, multi-robot systems (MRS) offer many advantages, such as flexibility of operating the group of robots and failure tolerance due to redundancy. Coordination and formation control has been a popular topic of study in multi-robot systems [1]. The problem is defined as the coordination of multiple mobile robots to follow given references and to maintain a desired spatial formation. In the literature, there have been roughly three strategies to formation control of multiple robots: leader-following [2], virtual structure [3], and behavior-based [4]. Each approach has its own advantages and disadvantages. In this paper, we develop a control law based on a virtual vehicle approach for coordinated path following of a group of N mobile robots. The controller is designed in such a way that the derivative of the path parameter is used as an additional control input to synchronize the formation motion. This coordinated path-following problem can be divided into two subproblems, i.e., the path following control problem and the coordination problem. In the first subproblem, a desired geometric path is parameterized by the curvilinear abscissa $s(t) \in \mathbb{R}$ and a path following controller should look at (i) the distance from the robot to the path and (ii) the angle between the robot's velocity vector and the tangent to the path, and then reduce both to zero, without any consideration in temporal specifications. Pioneering work in this area can be found in [5] and references therein. In contrast to trajectory tracking, we have the freedom to select a temporal specification for $s(t)$ in path following. The reference point on the path is the location of a so-called virtual vehicle. The path derivative can be considered as an additional control input, as seen in [6,7].

In the second subproblem, the robot's motion has to be synchronized with its neighbors in order to achieve a desired formation configuration. In [8], synchronized path following is solved by using passivity-based designs and is validated by simulation with marine surface vessels. Ghabcheloo, et al. [9] derive the control law for autonomous underwater vehicles (AUVs). Some approaches for coordinated path following control of multiple wheeled mobile robots are proposed in [10,11]. In this work, we derive our control law based on a Lyapunov function candidate and a consensus algorithm for a simplified kinematic model of mobile robots. Both path errors and coordination errors are considered in the Lyapunov function and the path parameter is used to synchronize coordination motions via a second-order consensus protocol with a reference velocity.

2   Problem Statement

We consider a group of N mobile robots, each of which has the following kinematic equations

$$\begin{bmatrix} \dot{x}_i \\ \dot{y}_i \\ \dot{\theta}_i \end{bmatrix} = \begin{bmatrix} v_i \cos \theta_i \\ v_i \sin \theta_i \\ \omega_i \end{bmatrix}, \tag{1}$$

where $\mathbf{x}_i(t) = [x_i, y_i, \theta_i]^T$ denotes the state vector in the world frame of the i-th robot. v_i and ω_i are the linear and angular velocities, respectively.

We first consider path following for each mobile robot in the formation, i.e., we wish to find control law v_i and ω_i such that the robot follows a virtual vehicle with position $\mathbf{x}_{di} = [x_{di}, y_{di}, \theta_{di}]^T$ and inputs v_{di} and ω_{di}. A unicycle-type mobile robot is depicted in Fig. 1, together with a spatial path Γ_i to be followed. The path error with respect to a robot frame is given by

$$\begin{bmatrix} x_{ei} \\ y_{ei} \\ \theta_{ei} \end{bmatrix} = \begin{bmatrix} \cos \theta_i & \sin \theta_i & 0 \\ -\sin \theta_i & \cos \theta_i & 0 \\ 0 & 0 & 1 \end{bmatrix} \begin{bmatrix} x_{di} - x_i \\ y_{di} - y_i \\ \theta_{di} - \theta_i \end{bmatrix}. \tag{2}$$

Then, the error dynamics are

$$\begin{aligned} \dot{x}_{ei} &= y_{ei}\omega_i - v_i + \dot{s}_i \cos \theta_{ei} \\ \dot{y}_{ei} &= -x_{ei}\omega_i + \dot{s}_i \sin \theta_{ei} \\ \dot{\theta}_{ei} &= \kappa_i \dot{s}_i - \omega_i \end{aligned} \tag{3}$$

where κ_i is the path curvature and $\dot{s}_i$ is the velocity of a virtual vehicle. It is bounded by $0 \le \dot{s}_i \le \dot{s}_{\max,i}$.

Next, we consider the coordination problem. To maintain the motion coordination of the whole group, each robot requires an individual parameterized path so that when all path's parameters are synchronized, all robots will be in formation. The velocities at which the mobile robots are required to travel can be handled in many ways. In this paper, there are three velocities to be synchronized, i.e., the velocity v_0 (or v_{di} in the robot frame) specifying how fast the whole group of robots should move, the velocity $\dot{s}_i$ denoting how fast an individual virtual vehicle moves along the path, and the velocity v_i determining how fast an individual real mobile robot travels (see Fig. 2).

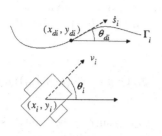
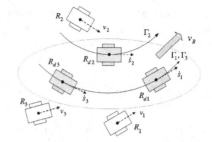

Fig. 1. A graphical representation of a mobile robot and a path.

Fig. 2. A graphical representation of coordinated path following.

As well known, the formation graph can be used to describe the relationship among members in the group. It is defined as $\mathcal{G} = (\mathcal{V}, \mathcal{E})$, where $\mathcal{V} = 1, ..., N$ is the set of robots and $\mathcal{E} \subset \mathcal{V} \mathrm{x} \mathcal{V}$ is the set of relative vectors between robots. Two robots i and j are called neighbors if $(i, j) \in \mathcal{E}$, and the set of neighbors of robot i is denoted by $N_i \in \mathcal{V}$. All graphs considered in this paper are undirected and we assume that the undirected $\mathcal{G}$ is connected. In this case, the *Laplacian* matrix L, constructed from $L = D - A$, where the adjacency matrix $A = (a_{ij})$ and the diagonal degree matrix D, is symmetric positive semi-definite. It has a simple zero eigenvalue and all the other eigenvalues are positive if and only if the graph is connected [12]. This matrix forms the basis for distributed consensus dynamics and captures many properties of the graph (see [12]).

3 Controller Design

Define the following variable

$$\dot{\tilde{s}}_i = \dot{s}_i - v_{di},$$ (4)

where $\dot{\tilde{s}}_i$ represents the formation speed tracking error of robot i. Let us choose

$$V = \frac{1}{2} \sum_{i=1}^{N} \left(x_{ei}^2 + y_{ei}^2 + \frac{1}{k_4} (\theta_{ei} - \delta_i(y_{ei}, v))^2 + k_5 \dot{\tilde{s}}_i^2 + k_6 \bar{s}_i^2 \right)$$ (5)

as a candidate Lyapunov function, where k_4, k_5, and k_6 are positive gains. $\bar{s}_i = s_i - s_j - s_{dij}, j \in N_i$ is the coordination error of robot i and s_{dij} is the desired distance between two neighbors i and j. The function δ_i can be interpreted as the desired value for the orientation θ_{ei} during transients [5]. It is assumed that $\lim_{t \to \infty} v(t) \neq 0$, $\delta_i(0, v) = 0$, and $y_{ei} v \sin(y_{ei}) \leq 0, \forall y_{ei} \forall v$. The function $\delta_i(y_{ei}, v)$ taken from [6] is $\delta_i(y_{ei}, v) = -\mathrm{sign}(v_{di})\theta_a \tanh y_{ei}$ with $\theta_a = \frac{\pi}{4}$.

The derivative of V can be computed to give

$$\dot{V} = \sum_{i=1}^{N} \left[x_{ei} \dot{x}_{ei} + y_{ei} \dot{y}_{ei} + \frac{1}{k_4} (\theta_{ei} - \delta_i) \left(\dot{\theta}_{ei} - \dot{\delta}_i \right) + k_5 \dot{\tilde{s}}_i \ddot{\tilde{s}}_i + k_6 \bar{s}_i \dot{\bar{s}}_i \right].$$ (6)

We first design a controller to stabilize the x_{ei}, y_{ei}, and θ_{ei} dynamics. Substituting (4) into (3), adding $y_{ei}v_{di}\sin\delta_i - y_{ei}v_{di}\sin\delta_i$ to (6), the time derivative along the solutions of (3) yields

$$\dot{V} = \sum_{i=1}^{N}\Bigl[x_{ei}\left(y_{ei}\omega_i - v_i + (\dot{s}_i + v_{di})\cos\theta_{ei}\right) + y_{ei}\left(-x_{ei}\omega_i + (\dot{s}_i + v_{di})\sin\theta_{ei}\right)$$
$$+ \frac{1}{k_4}(\theta_{ei} - \delta_i)\left(\dot{\theta}_{ei} - \dot{\delta}_i\right) + y_{ei}v_{di}\sin\delta_i - y_{ei}v_{di}\sin\delta_i + k_5\dot{s}_i\ddot{s}_i + k_6\bar{s}_i\dot{\bar{s}}_i \Bigr]. \tag{7}$$

Let the control laws for v_i and ω_i be defined as

$$v_i = k_1 x_{ei} + v_{di}\cos\theta_{ei} \tag{8}$$

$$\omega_i = k_2(\theta_{ei} - \delta_i) + \omega_{di} - \dot{\delta}_i + k_4 y_{ei}v_{di}\left[\frac{\sin\theta_{ei} - \sin\delta_i}{\theta_{ei} - \delta_i}\right], \tag{9}$$

where k_1 and k_2 are positive gains, and $\omega_{di} = \kappa_i v_{di}$. Then

$$\dot{V} = \sum_{i=1}^{N}\Bigl[-k_1 x_{ei}^2 - \frac{k_2}{k_4}(\theta_{ei} - \delta_i)^2 + x_{ei}\dot{s}_i\cos\theta_{ei} + y_{ei}\dot{s}_i\sin\theta_{ei}$$
$$+ \frac{1}{k_4}(\theta_{ei} - \delta_i)\kappa_i\dot{s}_i + y_{ei}v_{di}\sin\delta_i + k_5\dot{s}_i\ddot{s}_i + k_6\bar{s}_i\dot{\bar{s}}_i \Bigr]. \tag{10}$$

To make the derivative of the Lyapunov function V negative, we choose the following consensus controller with a reference velocity

$$\ddot{s}_i = \dot{v}_{di} - k_3(\dot{s}_i - v_{di}) - x_{ei}\cos\theta_{ei} - y_{ei}\sin\theta_{ei} - \frac{1}{k_4}(\theta_{ei} - \delta_i)\kappa_i$$
$$- 2k_5\sum_{j\in N_i}(s_i - s_j - s_{dij}) - k_6\sum_{j\in N_i}(\dot{s}_i - \dot{s}_j), \tag{11}$$

where $k_3 > 0$. Then we can achieve

$$\dot{V} = \sum_{i=1}^{N}\left(-k_1 x_{ei}^2 - k_2(\theta_{ei} - \delta_i)^2 - k_3(\dot{s}_i - v_{di})^2\right) - k_6\dot{s}^T L\dot{s} \leq 0, \tag{12}$$

where $\dot{s}\in\mathbb{R}^N$ is the stack vector of the robots' path derivative. We now state the main result of the coordinated path-following control for the mobile robots.

Theorem 1. *Assume that the undirected formation graph is connected. The control inputs v_i, ω_i, and $\ddot{s}_i$ given in (8), (9), and (11), respectively, for robot i solve the coordinated path-following objective.*

Proof. From (12), we have that $\dot{V} \leq 0$, which means that

$$V \leq V(t_0), \quad \forall t \geq t_0. \tag{13}$$

From the definition of V, the right hand side of (13) is bounded by a positive constant depending on the initial conditions. Since the left hand side of (13) is bounded, it implies the boundedness of x_{ei}, y_{ei}, $(\theta_{ei} - \delta_i)$, $\dot{\bar{s}}_i$ and $\bar{s}_i$ for all $t \geq t_0 \geq 0$. We also assume boundedness of $\dot{s}_i$ and v_{di}, implying the boundedness of the the overall closed-loop coordination system on the maximal interval of definition $[0, T)$. This rules out finite escape time so that $T = +\infty$.

From the above argument on the boundedness of x_{ei}, y_{ei}, $(\theta_{ei} - \delta_i)$, $\dot{\bar{s}}_i$ and $\bar{s}_i$, applying Barbalat's lemma [13] to (12) results in

$$\lim_{t \to \infty} (x_{ei}, \theta_{ei} - \delta_i, \dot{\bar{s}}_i, \dot{\bar{s}}_i) = 0. \tag{14}$$

To satisfy path-following tasks, we have to show that y_{ei} converges to zero as $t \to \infty$. In the closed loop of the θ_{ei} dynamics

$$\dot{\theta}_{ei} = \kappa_i \dot{\bar{s}}_i - k_2(\theta_{ei} - \delta_i) - y_{ei} v_{di} \left[\frac{\sin \theta_{ei} - \sin \delta_i}{\theta_{ei} - \delta_i} \right],$$

we can conclude that $\lim_{t \to \infty}(y_{ei}) = 0$ since $\lim_{t \to \infty}(\theta_{ei} - \delta_i, \dot{\bar{s}}_i) = 0$ and v_{di} does not converge to zero.

Since L is positive semidefinite, it follows that $L\dot{s} = 0$. L has a single zero eigenvalue with corresponding eigenvector $\overrightarrow{1}$. It follows that $\dot{s}$ belongs to span$\{\overrightarrow{1}\}$. Hence $\dot{s}_i = \dot{s}_j, \forall i, j \in N$, and $\dot{s}_i$ converges to v_{di}, which in turn, implies that $\ddot{s}_i = \dot{v}_{di}$. From this fact, we can get

$$\lim_{t \to \infty} (s_i - s_j - s_{dij}) = 0. \tag{15}$$

Define $s_{dij} = s_{di} - s_{dj}$, where s_{di} and s_{dj} are the path's desired parameters of robot i and robot j, respectively. We then have $s_i - s_j - s_{dij} = s_i - s_j - (s_{di} - s_{dj}) = (s_i - s_{di}) - (s_j - s_{dj}) = \hat{s}_i - \hat{s}_j$. Then we obtain $Ls + s_d = 0 \Rightarrow L\hat{s} = 0$. Thus, all $\hat{s}_i$ are equal to a common value, i.e., $s_i - s_j = s_{dij}, j \in N_i, \forall i, j$. We conclude that the robots converge to the desired configuration.   □

4   Results

Simulations and real-world experiments of the control system as established in the previous section were carried out to evaluate the performance of our control law. Regarding more realistic situations in robot motions, we took into account the maximum velocities: $|v_i| \leq 0.5$ m/s, $|\omega_i| \leq 1.0$ rad/s. We performed a velocity scaling given in [14] so as to preserve the curvature radius corresponding to the nominal velocities. The control gains were set to $k_1 = 0.25$, $k_2 = 1.0$, $k_3 = 0.2$, $k_4 = 5.0$, $k_5 = 0.5$, $k_6 = 0.2$ and the desired speed for the whole group of robots was $v_0 = 0.2$ m/s.

4.1   Simulations

Six mobile robots were required to follow a lemniscate curve given by

$$x_d(t) = \frac{2.3 \cos \theta_d(t)}{1 + \sin^2 \theta_d(t)}, \quad y_d(t) = \frac{2.3 \sin \theta_d(t) \cos \theta_d(t)}{1 + \sin^2 \theta_d(t)},$$

and to maintain a desired formation described by the following elements of the adjacency matrix: $a_{14} = a_{13} = a_{36} = a_{56} = a_{25} = 1$. The superimposed snapshots are shown in Fig. 3 and the coordination errors converging to zero are seen in Fig. 4. The velocity tracking errors and the path errors of each robot also converge to zero, satisfying the path-following objective. Due to lack of space, those errors are not shown in this paper.

4.2 Real-World Experiments

The mobile robots, shown in Fig. 5, were used in real-world experiments in this paper. The robot controller is an ATMEGA644 microprocessor with 64 KB flash program memory, 16MHz clock frequency and 4 KB SRAM. The robot orientation was measured by a Devantech CMPS03 compass. The localization was given by a camera looking down upon the robot's workplace and a PC was used to compute the control inputs and then sent these inputs to the robot via WLAN. The lemniscate curve similar to the path in the simulation was employed in the first experiment. Each robot was required to maintain a column formation described by $s_{d12} = s_{d23} = 75$ cm. The elements $a_{12} = a_{21} = 1$, $a_{23} = a_{32} = 1$ in the adjacency matrix represented the information exchange in the formation graph. The experimental results are plotted in Fig. 6. As seen in Fig. 7, the coordination tasks are satisfied. The coordination errors are less than 10 cm and the virtual vehicle of each robot can travel at the desired speed $v_0 = 0.2$ m/s. Likewise, the path-following tasks are attained as seen in Fig. 8. In the second experiment, each robot followed its own path, i.e., a sinusoidal curve for robot 1 and robot 3, and a straight line for robot 2. s_{dij} was set to 0 and the elements of the adjacency matrix were set to $a_{12} = a_{21} = 1$, $a_{23} = a_{32} = 1$. The results are depicted in Fig. 9. The coordination errors and the velocity of each virtual vehicle are seen in Fig. 10. The experimental results show the effectiveness of our proposed control law: the group of robots can travel at the desired speed v_0 while keeping a desired formation. The main sources of disturbances during

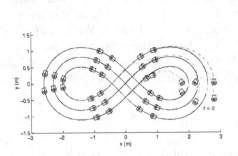

Fig. 3. Simulation: the superimposed snapshots.

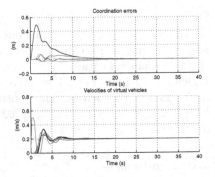

Fig. 4. Simulation: the coordination errors and the velocities of virtual vehicles.

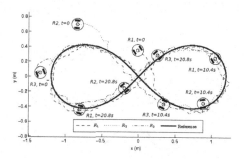

Fig. 5. The mobile robots (12 cm diameter) used in experiments.

Fig. 6. Exp. 1: the superimposed snapshots at t = 0 s, t = 10.4 s, and t = 20.8 s.

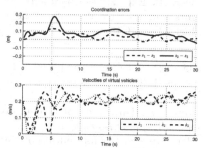

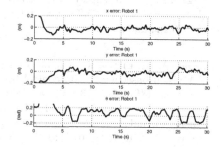

Fig. 7. Exp. 1: the coordination errors and the velocities of virtual vehicles.

Fig. 8. Exp. 1: the position errors of robot 1.

experiments include sensor distortion, vision-system delays, and communication delays.

5   Conclusions and Future Work

In this paper, we developed a new control law for coordinated path following of mobile robots. Each mobile robot can be steered along a set of given spatial paths, while it can keep a desired inter-vehicle coordination pattern. The solution adopted for coordinated path following built on Lyapunov function techniques and consensus algorithms. The desired formation pattern was achieved by controlling the path derivative such that the coordination error converges to zero.

Future research includes the extension of our results to robots in more complex environments. For example, communication can introduce time-delays in signal propagation among members, the information exchange topology is not necessarily fixed, and obstacles may appear in the robot's path.

References

1. Murray, R. M.: Recent research in cooperative-control of multivehicle systems. Journal of Dynamics, Systems, Measurement and Control, 129(5), pp. 571-583, 2007

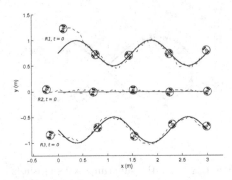
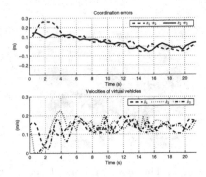

Fig. 9. Exp. 2: the superimposed snapshots at t = 0 s, t = 5.2 s, t = 10.6 s, t = 16.2 s, and t = 21.6 s.

Fig. 10. Exp. 2: the coordination errors and the velocities of virtual vehicles ($v_0 = 0.15$ m/s).

2. Das, A. K., Fierro, R., Kumar, V., Ostrowski, J. P., Spletzer, J., and Taylor, C. J.: A vision-based formation control framework. IEEE Trans. on Robotics and Automation, 18(5), pp. 813-825, Oct. 2002

3. Lewis, M. A. and Tan, K. -H.: High precision formation control of mobile robots using virtual structures. Autonomous Robots, 4(4), pp. 387-403, 1997

4. Balch, T. and Arkin, R. C.: Behavior-based formation control for multirobot teams. IEEE Trans. on Robotics and Automation, 14(6), pp. 1-15, 1998

5. Micaelli, A. and Samson, C.: Trajectory-tracking for unicycle-type and two-steering-wheels mobile robots. Technical Report No. 2097, INRIA, Sophia-Antipolis, 1993

6. Soeanto, D., Lapierre, L. and Pascoal, A.: Adaptive non-singular path-following, control of dynamic wheeled robots. Proc. of Int. Conf. on Advanced Robotics, Coimbra, Portugal, pp. 1387-1392, 2003

7. Egerstedt, M., Hu, X., and Stotsky, A.: Control of mobile platforms using a virtual vehicle approach. IEEE Trans. on Automatic Control, 46(11), pp. 1777-1782, 2001

8. Ihle, I. A. F., Arcak, M., and Fossen, T. I.: Passivity-based designs for synchronized path-following. Automatica, 43(9), pp. 1508-1518, 2007

9. Ghabcheloo, R., Aguiar, A., Pascoal, A., Silvestre, C., Kaminer, I., and Hespanha, J.: Coordinated path-following in the presence of communication losses and time delays. SIAM - Journal on Control and Optimization, 48(1), pp. 234-265, 2009

10. Ghabcheloo, R., Pascoal, A., Silvestre, C., and Kaminer, I.: Nonlinear coordinated path following control of multiple wheeled robots with bidirectional communication constraints. Int. Journal of Adaptive Control and Signal Processing, 20, pp. 133-157, 2007

11. Ghomman, J., Saad, M., and Mnif, F.: Formation path following control of unicycle-type mobile robots. Proc. of IEEE Conf. on Robotics and Automation, Pasadena, CA, pp. 1966-1972, 2008

12. Fax, J. A. and Murray, R. M.: Graph laplacians and vehicle formation stabilization. Proc. of the 15th IFAC World Congress, Barcelona, Spain, 2002

13. Khalil, H. K.: Nonlinear Systems. Prentice Hall, 2002

14. Oriolo, G., De Luca, A., and Vendittelli, M.: WMR control via dynamic feedback linearization: design, implementation and experimental validation. IEEE Trans. on Control Systems Technology, 10(6), pp. 835-852, 2002

Kooperative Bewegungsplanung zur Unfallvermeidung im Straßenverkehr mit der Methode der elastischen Bänder

Christian Frese[1], Thomas Batz[2] und Jürgen Beyerer[2,1]

[1] Lehrstuhl für Interaktive Echtzeitsysteme, Institut für Anthropomatik, Universität Karlsruhe (TH), frese@ies.uni-karlsruhe.de
[2] Fraunhofer Institut für Informations- und Datenverarbeitung IITB, Karlsruhe, {Thomas.Batz,Juergen.Beyerer}@iitb.fraunhofer.de

Zusammenfassung. Die Fortschritte der Kommunikationstechnologie ermöglichen neuartige kooperative Sicherheitssysteme, die deutlich über heutige Fahrerassistenzfunktionen hinausgehen. Mit abgestimmten Fahrmanövern mehrerer Fahrzeuge lassen sich Unfälle vermeiden, die ein einzelnes Fahrzeug nicht mehr verhindern könnte. Eine wichtige Komponente eines solchen Systems ist ein Verfahren zur kooperativen Bewegungsplanung. Dieser Beitrag stellt die Methode der elastischen Bänder vor, die bei der Simulation kooperativer Fahrmanöver vielversprechende Ergebnisse liefert.

1 Einleitung

Die Zahl der Verkehrstoten in Europa ist in den letzten Jahren deutlich zurückgegangen, was auch auf die zunehmende Ausrüstung der Fahrzeuge mit passiven und aktiven Sicherheitssystemen zurückgeführt wird. Die Technologie der Funkkommunikation eröffnet Möglichkeiten für neuartige aktive Assistenzsysteme, die den Verkehr noch sicherer machen könnten. Bisher werden auf dieser Basis vor allem Warnsysteme untersucht [1]. Darüber hinaus sind aber auch kooperative Fahrmanöver denkbar, die über Fahrzeug-Fahrzeug-Kommunikation abgestimmt werden. Damit ließen sich durch vollautomatisches kooperatives Ausweichen an einem unerwarteten Hindernis oder durch kooperatives Einscheren nach einem Überholmanöver bei Gegenverkehr Unfälle verhindern (Abb. 1). Ein solches System kann als Erweiterung der heute in der Markteinführung befindlichen Notbremsassistenten auf Ausweichmanöver und kooperative Manöver aufgefasst werden.

In Abschnitt 2 wird das Anwendungsszenario der kooperativen Unfallvermeidung genauer vorgestellt. Dieser Beitrag fokussiert anschließend auf den Teilaspekt der kooperativen Fahrmanöverplanung: Abschnitt 3 enthält allgemeine Überlegungen zur kooperativen Bewegungsplanung. In Abschnitt 4 wird die Methode der elastischen Bänder als ein möglicher Lösungsansatz präsentiert. Simulationsergebnisse werden in Abschnitt 5 dargestellt. Der Beitrag schließt mit einem Fazit und einem Ausblick in Abschnitt 6.

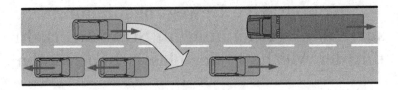

Abb. 1. Beispielszenario Überholen: Um dem überholenden Fahrzeug ein rechtzeitiges Einscheren zu ermöglichen, müssen die Fahrzeuge auf der rechten Spur durch Beschleunigen bzw. Verzögern (Pfeile) eine Lücke schaffen.

2 Anwendungsszenario

In komplexen Verkehrssituationen sind menschliche Fahrer häufig nicht in der Lage, optimale Entscheidungen zu treffen. Insbesondere in Gefahrensituationen mit mehreren beteiligten Fahrzeugen können die Fahrer nicht schnell genug reagieren und sich abstimmen, um ein gemeinsames unfallvermeidendes Manöver einzuleiten. Zukünftige Assistenzsysteme könnten an dieser Stelle eingreifen und kooperativ abgestimmte Handlungen vollautomatisch durchführen.

Um kooperative Manöver in Echtzeit berechnen zu können, muss zunächst eine sinnvolle Teilmenge der Fahrzeuge ausgewählt werden. Dazu dient das Konzept der kooperativen Gruppe, in der diejenigen Fahrzeuge zusammengefasst werden, die möglicherweise ein gemeinsames Manöver ausführen müssen [2]. Die Notwendigkeit eines automatischen Eingriffs ist dann gegeben, wenn die Fahrer aufgrund ihrer Reaktionszeiten einen Unfall voraussichtlich nicht mehr verhindern können. Eine auf diesem Kriterium beruhende Erkennung von Gefahrensituationen wurde in [3] beschrieben. Die dann erforderliche Planung eines kooperativen Fahrmanövers zur Unfallvermeidung bildet den Schwerpunkt dieses Beitrags. Der resultierende Plan wird auf Korrektheit und verbleibende Freiräume geprüft. Wenn im Einzelfall kein kollisionsfreier Plan gefunden werden kann, muss das Assistenzsystem auf eine andere Lösung wie etwa eine Notbremsung zur Reduzierung der Kollisionsschwere zurückgreifen oder ganz auf einen Eingriff verzichten. Ein korrekter Plan wird über Funkkommunikation an die Mitglieder der kooperativen Gruppe verteilt, die eine Feinplanung innerhalb der berechneten Toleranzen vornehmen und das Manöver ausführen.

3 Kooperative Bewegungsplanung

3.1 Problemstellung

Im Kontext mehrerer, sich mit hoher Geschwindigkeit bewegender Fahrzeuge ist eine Bewegungsplanung erforderlich, die den zeitlichen Ablauf explizit mitberücksichtigt. Eine Bahnplanung, die nur den örtlichen Verlauf betrachtet, genügt offensichtlich nicht. Die resultierende Konfigurationsraumzeit hat für m Fahrzeuge die Dimension $m \cdot d_0 + 1$, wenn d_0 die Anzahl der Freiheitsgrade eines einzelnen Fahrzeugs bezeichnet. Berücksichtigt man Position und Orientierung

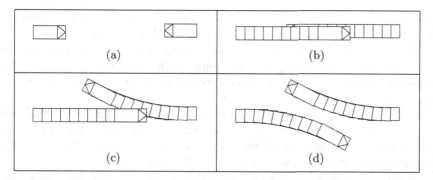

Abb. 2. Vergleich verschiedener Ansätze zur Bewegungsplanung. (a) Ausgangsszenario: zwei Fahrzeuge auf Kollisionskurs, (b) Entkopplung von Bahn- und Geschwindigkeitsplanung, (c) prioritätsbasierte Planung, (d) kooperative Bewegungsplanung.

des Fahrzeugs in der Ebene, so ist $d_0 = 3$, wobei zusätzlich die Nichtholonomie der Kinematik zu beachten ist. Im Straßenverkehr ist eine aktive Vorausplanung der Bewegungen erforderlich, da rein reaktive Mechanismen nicht die Sicherheit der Verhaltensentscheidung garantieren können. Zusätzlicher Planungsspielraum ergibt sich dadurch, dass die Zielpositionen der Fahrzeuge nicht fest vorgegeben sind, sondern vom Bewegungsplanungsverfahren so bestimmt werden können, dass ein kollisionsfreies kooperatives Fahrmanöver ermöglicht wird.

3.2 Ansätze aus der Robotik

Während im Automobilbereich kooperatives Fahren bisher vorwiegend im Hinblick auf Verkehrsflussoptimierung in speziellen Szenarien wie Kreuzungen [4] untersucht wurde, gibt es in der Robotik zahlreiche Arbeiten zur kooperativen Bewegungsplanung. Dort werden häufig vereinfachende Annahmen getroffen, um in niedrigdimensionalen Räumen planen zu können. Zwei verbreitete Vereinfachungen werden im Folgenden kurz vorgestellt.

Die Entkopplung von Bahn- und Geschwindigkeitsplanung geht auf [5] zurück und wurde in zahlreichen weiteren Arbeiten verwendet [6]. Bei diesem Verfahren plant jeder Roboter seine Bahn im d_0-dimensionalen Konfigurationsraum und ignoriert dabei zunächst die anderen Roboter. Anschließend werden die Geschwindigkeiten der Roboter entlang der geplanten Bahnen so koordiniert, dass keine Kollisionen auftreten. In der Robotik ist dieses Vorgehen häufig praktikabel, weil Geschwindigkeiten und Trägheitsmomente der Roboter vergleichsweise gering sind. Bei der Unfallvermeidung im Straßenverkehr ist jedoch eine gegenseitige Berücksichtigung der Fahrzeugdynamiken bei der Bewegungsplanung erforderlich. Durch eine nachgelagerte Geschwindigkeitskoordination kann dies nicht erreicht werden, wie schon das einfache Beispiel in Abb. 2(b) zeigt.

Der zweite verbreitete Ansatz nimmt die Bewegungsplanung für die einzelnen Roboter in einer vorgegebenen Prioritätsreihenfolge vor [7]. Dabei berücksichtigt jeder Roboter die bereits geplanten Bewegungen der höher priorisierten Roboter als dynamische Hindernisse in der $(d_0 + 1)$-dimensionalen Raumzeit. Die niederprioren Roboter werden hingegen ignoriert. Für die Unfallvermeidung im Straßenverkehr hat dies in vielen Situationen eine zu starke Einschränkung der möglichen Manöverkombinationen zur Folge. Auch eine optimale Wahl der Prioritätsordnung wie in [8] kann dieses Problem nicht prinzipiell lösen, wie das symmetrische Beispiel in Abb. 2(c) zeigt.

Eine kooperative Bewegungsplanung in der $(m \cdot d_0 + 1)$-dimensionalen Raumzeit eröffnet einen deutlich größeren Lösungsraum, sodass kritischere Situationen noch bewältigt werden können bzw. ein Unfall auch zu einem späteren Eingriffszeitpunkt noch verhindert werden kann (Abb. 2(d)).

Bereits das einfachste denkbare Szenario von Abb. 2 zeigt den deutlich größeren Handlungsspielraum der kooperativen Bewegungsplanung gegenüber den Entkopplungs- und Priorisierungsansätzen. Ähnliches gilt auch für komplexere Situationen wie in Abb. 1. Das in diesem Beitrag beschriebene Verfahren zur kooperativen Unfallvermeidung im Straßenverkehr basiert daher auf einer kooperativen Bewegungsplanung ohne entkoppelnde Annahmen.

4   Die Methode der elastischen Bänder

Bei den meisten Bewegungsplanungsalgorithmen wächst der Aufwand exponentiell mit der Dimension des Konfigurationsraums, d. h. in der vorliegenden Anwendung mit der Anzahl der Fahrzeuge. Die Methode der elastischen Bänder ist hingegen eines der wenigen Verfahren, das die beschriebenen Anforderungen unter Echtzeitbedingungen erfüllen kann. Sie wurde bisher zur Bahnplanung für Roboter [9] und für Einzelfahrzeuge [10] eingesetzt. Die Übertragung auf die kooperative Bewegungsplanung wurde in [11] vorgeschlagen und wird im Folgenden detaillierter ausgearbeitet und weiterentwickelt.

4.1   Grundlagen

Die geplante Bewegung des i-ten Fahrzeugs wird durch ein elastisches Band modelliert, das aus Knoten $\mathbf{x}_{i,j}$, $j = 0, \ldots, T$ besteht. Dabei repräsentiert $\mathbf{x}_{i,j} = (x_{i,j}, y_{i,j})^T$ die Position des Fahrzeugs in der Straßenebene zu einem festgelegten Zeitpunkt $t(j) := j \cdot \Delta t$ (siehe Abb. 3(a)). Diese äquidistante Zeitdiskretisierung ist für alle Fahrzeuge identisch gewählt. Der rotatorische Freiheitsgrad wird implizit durch die relative Lage aufeinanderfolgender Knoten repräsentiert.

Die Anforderungen an eine kollisionsfreie, ausführbare Fahrzeugbewegung werden durch virtuelle Kräfte $\mathbf{f}_{i,j}$ beschrieben, die auf die Knoten $\mathbf{x}_{i,j}$ der elastischen Bänder einwirken. Im Kräftegleichgewicht liegt dann eine bezüglich der modellierten Kriterien lokal optimale kooperative Bewegung vor.

4.2   Modellierung der Kräfte

Innere Kräfte: Die inneren Kräfte wirken antisymmetrisch zwischen zwei aufeinanderfolgenden Knoten eines elastischen Bands. Sie modellieren die Einschränkungen der Fahrzeugbewegung, die durch die Kinematik und Dynamik

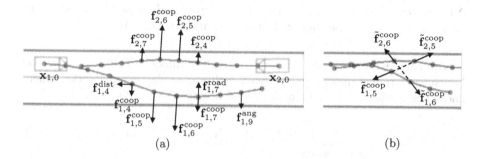

(a)   (b)

Abb. 3. (a) Visualisierung elastischer Bänder und ausgewählter Einzelkräfte. (b) „Verklemmung" zweier elastischer Bänder, die in (a) durch die Mittelung der Richtungsvektoren verhindert wird (vgl. Erläuterungen in Abschnitt 4.2).

bedingt sind:

$$\mathbf{f}_{i,j}^{\text{dist}} := \tilde{\mathbf{f}}_{i,j}^{\text{dist}} - \tilde{\mathbf{f}}_{i,j+1}^{\text{dist}} \tag{1}$$

$$\tilde{\mathbf{f}}_{i,j}^{\text{dist}} := w^{\text{dist}}(i,j,a_{\text{lon,min}},a_{\text{lon,max}})(\mathbf{x}_{i,j} - \mathbf{x}_{i,j-1}) \tag{2}$$

$$\mathbf{f}_{i,j}^{\text{ang}} := \tilde{\mathbf{f}}_{i,j}^{\text{ang}} - \tilde{\mathbf{f}}_{i,j+1}^{\text{ang}} \tag{3}$$

$$\tilde{\mathbf{f}}_{i,j}^{\text{ang}} := w^{\text{ang}}(i,j,a_{\text{lat,max}}) \left(\mathbf{x}_{i,j-1} + \frac{\|\mathbf{x}_{i,j} - \mathbf{x}_{i,j-1}\|}{\|\mathbf{x}_{i,j-1} - \mathbf{x}_{i,j-2}\|}(\mathbf{x}_{i,j-1} - \mathbf{x}_{i,j-2}) - \mathbf{x}_{i,j} \right)$$

Die Kraft $\mathbf{f}_{i,j}^{\text{dist}}$ wirkt auf den Abstand der Knoten und beschränkt somit die zulässige Verzögerung bzw. Beschleunigung. Die Kraft $\mathbf{f}_{i,j}^{\text{ang}}$ begrenzt die Querbeschleunigung, indem sie ihr Minimum für die Geradeausfahrt annimmt. Die nichtlinearen Gewichtungsfunktionen w^{dist} und w^{ang} steigen stark an, sobald die auftretenden Längs- und Querbeschleunigungen ihre zulässigen Bereiche $[a_{\text{lon,min}}, a_{\text{lon,max}}]$ bzw. $[-a_{\text{lat,max}}, a_{\text{lat,max}}]$ verlassen. Diese Einschränkungen sind physikalisch gesehen v. a. durch die notwendige Haftreibung zwischen Straße und Reifen bedingt und dominieren bei den hier betrachteten Geschwindigkeiten die Begrenzungen aus der nichtholonomen Kinematik. Um die Einhaltung der Beschränkungen zu erzwingen, werden die Gewichte bei Bedarf während des Minimierungsprozesses erhöht.

Äußere Kräfte: Die äußeren Kräfte stoßen das elastische Band vom Straßenrand und von Hindernissen ab:

$$\mathbf{f}_{i,j}^{\text{road}} := w^{\text{road}}(\mathbf{x}_{i,j})\mathbf{n}(\mathbf{x}_{i,j}) \tag{4}$$

$$\mathbf{f}_{i,j}^{\text{obst}} := \sum_k \left(e^{-\|\mathbf{x}_{i,j} - \mathbf{p}_{k,j}\| + r_k} \sum_{l=0}^{T} e^{-\|\mathbf{x}_{i,l} - \mathbf{p}_{k,l}\| + r_k}(\mathbf{x}_{i,l} - \mathbf{p}_{k,l}) \right) \tag{5}$$

Darin ist $\mathbf{n}(\mathbf{x})$ die Normalenrichtung des Straßenverlaufs am Punkt $\mathbf{x}$, $w^{\text{road}}(\mathbf{x}_{i,j})$ eine Funktion des Abstands vom Straßenrand, $\mathbf{p}_{k,j}$ die Position des k-ten Hindernisses zum Zeitpunkt $t(j)$ und r_k sein Radius. Hindernisse können als Überdeckung mehrerer kreisförmiger Objekte beschrieben werden [10].

Kooperative Kräfte: Die kooperative Kraft verhindert Kollisionen zwischen Fahrzeugen, indem diejenigen Knoten verschiedener elastischer Bänder voneinander abgestoßen werden, die demselben Zeitschritt zugeordnet sind:

$$\mathbf{f}_{i,j}^{\text{coop}} := \sum_{k=1,\ldots,m,\ k\neq i} e^{-\|\mathbf{x}_{i,j}-\mathbf{x}_{k,j}\|} \sum_{l=0}^{T} e^{-\|\mathbf{x}_{i,l}-\mathbf{x}_{k,l}\|}(\mathbf{x}_{i,l}-\mathbf{x}_{k,l}) \tag{6}$$

Die Mittelung der Richtungsvektoren für die abstoßenden Kräfte $\mathbf{f}_{i,j}^{\text{obst}}$ und $\mathbf{f}_{i,j}^{\text{coop}}$ (Summe über l in (5), (6)) bewirkt, dass sich mehrere benachbarte Knoten in einer gemeinsamen Ausweichbewegung vom anderen Band bzw. vom Hindernis entfernen. Sie verhindert eine „Verklemmung" wie in Abb. 3(b), bei der sich die nicht gemittelten abstoßenden Kräfte $\tilde{\mathbf{f}}_{i,j}^{\text{coop}}$ gegenseitig kompensieren und somit keine ausreichende Separierung der Bänder erreichen können.

Die inneren Kräfte verteilen die äußeren und kooperativen Kräfte auf die Nachbarknoten des elastischen Bands, sodass sich eine glatte Bewegung ergibt. Diese implizite Vorausschau unterscheidet das Verfahren von einfachen Potenzialfeldansätzen, die nur eine instantane Entscheidung treffen.

4.3   Numerische Kräfteminimierung

Die Anfangspositionen der Knoten werden momentan so initialisiert, dass die Fahrzeuge mit konstanter Geschwindigkeit ihrer Spur folgen. Auf jeden Knoten $\mathbf{x}_{i,j}$ wirkt nun die resultierende Kraft $\mathbf{f}_{i,j}$, die als gewichtete Summe der vorgestellten Einzelkräfte definiert ist. Iterativ werden die Knoten so lange bewegt, bis sich ein Kräftegleichgewicht einstellt: $\forall i, j : \mathbf{f}_{i,j} = 0$. Eine Ausnahme bilden die Startpositionen der Fahrzeuge $\mathbf{x}_{i,0}$, die unverändert bleiben.

4.4   Interpolation der Bewegung

Um eine kontinuierliche Fahrtrajektorie zu erhalten, werden die diskreten Knoten des elastischen Bands durch kubische Splines interpoliert [10]. Man erhält dadurch eine parametrische Kurve der Fahrzeugposition über der Zeit.

5   Simulationsergebnisse

Das beschriebene Verfahren wurde mit Hilfe des im SFB/Transregio 28 „Kognitive Automobile" entwickelten Verkehrssimulators [12] getestet. Der Simulator macht die Fahrzeugdaten über gemeinsamen Speicher zugänglich und erlaubt die Steuerung der Fahrzeuge durch externe Prozesse. Die Straßeninformation wird aus einer XML-Konfigurationsdatei gelesen.

Mit vorgeschlagenen Verfahren wurden verschiedene Ausweich-, Einscher-, Überhol- und Kreuzungsszenarien erfolgreich simuliert. Bei den im Folgenden

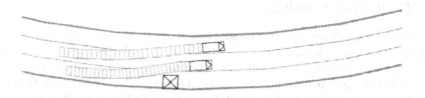

Abb. 4. Kooperatives Ausweichmanöver bei einem statischen Hindernis.

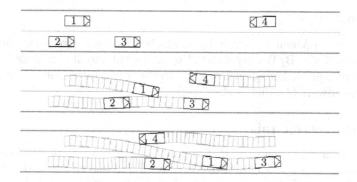

Abb. 5. Kooperative Unfallvermeidung in einer Überholsituation. Zur besseren Veranschaulichung ist die Situation zu drei verschiedenen Zeitpunkten dargestellt.

dargestellten Beispielen hatten die elastischen Bänder 10 bis 20 Knoten in einem äquidistanten Zeitabstand von $\Delta t \in [0.15\,\text{s}, 0.2\,\text{s}]$. Damit ergibt sich ein Planungshorizont von 2 bis 3 Sekunden. Die Anfangsgeschwindigkeiten der Fahrzeuge lagen bei 15 bis 20 m/s.

In Abb. 4 und Abb. 5 sind die geplanten Fahrzeugbewegungen dargestellt. Zur Visualisierung wurden die Fahrzeugpositionen im Zeittakt von 50 ms eingezeichnet. Abb. 4 zeigt ein kooperatives Ausweichmanöver bei einem Hindernis in einer Kurve. Abb. 5 zeigt den Abbruch eines Überholmanövers, um eine Kollision mit dem Gegenverkehr zu vermeiden. Wie in Abb. 1 angedeutet, bremst Fahrzeug 2, um eine Lücke für das Spurwechselmanöver von Fahrzeug 1 zu schaffen. Die gewählten Dynamikbeschränkungen $a_{\text{lon,min}} = -8\,\text{m/s}^2$, $a_{\text{lon,max}} = 3\,\text{m/s}^2$ und $a_{\text{lat,max}} = 6\,\text{m/s}^2$ werden eingehalten. Die individuellen Zahlenwerte[1] für jedes Fahrzeug können den aktuellen Fähigkeitsbeschreibungen im gemeinsamen Lagebild der kooperativen Gruppe entnommen werden [11].

Die dargestellten Szenarien lassen sich auf einem gewöhnlichen Arbeitsplatzrechner in Rechenzeiten von etwa 0.5 s bzw. 0.9 s lösen. Somit hat die Methode der elastischen Bänder zweifellos das Potenzial zu einem echtzeitfähigen Verfahren, zumal die derzeitige Implementierung noch einige Optimierungsmöglichkeiten bietet.

---

[1] bzw. bei genauerer Modellierung funktionale Abhängigkeiten der Beschleunigungsgrenzen untereinander und von der Geschwindigkeit etc.

6   Fazit und Ausblick

Mit der Methode der elastischen Bänder lassen sich kooperative Fahrmanöver für zukünftige kommunikationsbasierte Assistenzsysteme planen, die die Verkehrssicherheit weiter erhöhen können. Der nächste wichtige Schritt ist die Anpassung des Verfahrens auf unsicherheitsbehaftete Wahrnehmungsdaten, die z. B. durch Einführung entsprechender Sicherheitsreserven in der Kräftemodellierung erfolgen kann.

Danksagung

Die vorliegende Arbeit wird von der Deutschen Forschungsgemeinschaft (DFG) im Rahmen des SFB/Transregio 28 „Kognitive Automobile" gefördert.

Die Autoren danken allen Projektpartnern, die an der Entwicklung der Simulationssoftware beteiligt sind.

Literaturverzeichnis

1. G. Toulminet, J. Boussuge, C. Laurgeau. Comparative synthesis of the 3 main European projects dealing with Cooperative Systems (CVIS, SAFESPOT and COOPERS) and description of COOPERS Demonstration Site 4. In *Proc. IEEE Intelligent Transportation Systems Conf.*, Beijing, China, Okt. 2008.
2. C. Frese, J. Beyerer. Bildung kooperativer Gruppen kognitiver Automobile. In *Autonome Mobile Systeme*, S. 177–183. Springer, 2007.
3. T. Batz, K. Watson, J. Beyerer. Recognition of dangerous situations within a cooperative group of vehicles. In *Proc. IEEE Intelligent Vehicles Symposium*, S. 907–912, Xi'an, China, Juni 2009.
4. T. Bruns, A. Trächtler. Kreuzungsmanagement: Trajektorienplanung mittels Dynamischer Programmierung. *at – Automatisierungstechnik*, 57(5), S. 253–261, 2009.
5. K. Kant, S. Zucker. Toward Efficient Trajectory Planning: The Path-Velocity Decomposition. *Int. J. Robotics Research*, 5(3), S. 72–89, 1986.
6. P. Švestka, M. Overmars. Coordinated path planning for multiple robots. *Robotics and Autonomous Systems*, 23, S. 125–152, 1998.
7. M. Erdmann, T. Lozano-Pérez. On Multiple Moving Objects. *Algorithmica*, 2, S. 477–521, 1987.
8. M. Bennewitz, W. Burgard, S. Thrun. Optimizing Schedules for Prioritized Path Planning of Multi-Robot Systems. In *Proc. IEEE Conf. on Robotics and Automation*, Seoul, Mai 2001.
9. S. Quinlan, O. Khatib. Elastic Bands: Connecting Path Planning and Control. In *Proc. IEEE Conf. on Robotics and Automation*, 1993.
10. J. Hilgert, K. Hirsch, T. Bertram, M. Hiller. Emergency Path Planning for Autonomous Vehicles Using Elastic Band Theory. In *Proc. IEEE/ASME Conf. on Advanced Intelligent Mechatronics*, 2003.
11. C. Frese, T. Batz, J. Beyerer. Kooperative Verhaltensentscheidung für Gruppen kognitiver Automobile auf Grundlage des gemeinsamen Lagebilds. *at – Automatisierungstechnik*, 56(12), S. 644–652, Dez. 2008.
12. S. Vacek, R. Nagel, T. Batz, F. Moosmann, R. Dillmann. An Integrated Simulation Framework for Cognitive Automobiles. In *Proc. IEEE Intelligent Vehicles Symposium*, S. 221–226, Istanbul, Türkei, Juni 2007.

Perception of Environment Properties Relevant for Off-road Navigation

Alexander Renner, Tobias Föhst and Karsten Berns

Robotics Research Lab, Department of Computer Sciences, University of
Kaiserslautern, PO Box 3049, 67653 Kaiserslautern, Germany
E-mail: {renner,foehst,berns}@cs.uni-kl.de
http://rrlab.cs.uni-kl.de

Abstract. In this paper a set of physical properties is presented that
can be utilized for save and efficient navigation in unstructured terrain.
This set contains properties of positive obstacles, i.e. flexibility, shape,
dimensions, etc. as well as properties of negative obstacles and ground,
i.e. slope, carrying capacity, slippage, etc. By means of these properties a
classifier is developed that supports the discrimination from traversable
to non-traversable areas. Furthermore, an overview of different sensor
systems, that can be employed to determine some these properties, is
given.

1 Introduction

Unmanned autonomous off-road vehicles offer a great chance to reduce the risk
of human lives during search and rescue tasks in case of disasters or accidents.
Furthermore, industries like agriculture and forestry benefit from efficient, robust
and highly maneuverable platforms that find their way through their working
environment and perform their tasks unsupervised.

But navigation in unknown, unstructured and thus also dangerous environment is a very difficult task. Besides an agile and robust hardware, maneuvering
in the variety of terrains that can be found in forests requires a sophisticated control software that performs obstacle detection/avoidance and navigation
tasks. This needs a sufficient representation of the environment considering physical properties of the found material and object formations to classify areas that
can be used to securely drive to a given target.

In the following a set of properties is presented which are essential for an
efficient navigation in rough terrain and how these properties can be measured.
Moreover, it is presented how these can describe the local environment of a land
robot in terms of traversability and how this environment can be represented in a
map. Furthermore, the methods already implemented on the Robotics Research
Lab's[1] off-road vehicle RAVON[2] are presented. Finally, an overview based on the
experiences gained with RAVON is given and possible techniques for achieving
still missing aspects are discussed.

---

[1] http://rrlab.cs.uni-kl.de/
[2] Robust Autonomous Vehicle for Off-road Navigation [2]

2   Controlling Properties of the Environment

Driving in unknown environment implies that the robot has to detect traversable regions. Whether an area is traversable or not depends on several properties as depicted in Fig. 1. In order to navigate more sophisticated all mentioned properties have to be taken into account. Tab. 1 gives a short overview of the properties and the according sensors for measurement.

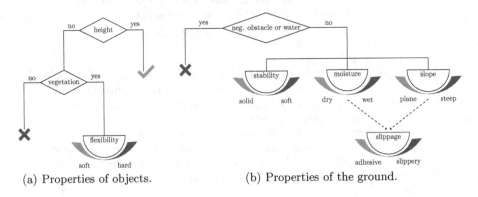

(a) Properties of objects.   (b) Properties of the ground.

Fig. 1. Property based traversability classification.

2.1   Positve Obstacles

The most important properties of objects for traversability classification are flexibility, height and shape. Whether the robot can pass over an object or not depends on its height and shape with respect to the ground clearance of the vehicle. The solidness of recognized objects gives a hint whether the potential obstacle is classified as highly flexible and consequently traversable (e.g. herbage), limited flexible (e.g. bushes) or solid (e.g. stones). The latter indicates that it is untraversable. Very flexible objects such as herbage usually allow to push through without getting damaged. In situations where a passage between two bushes is just a little bit too narrow, it might be possible to drive through by pushing the branches away (Fig. 2.1). In case of two trees this is obviously impossible.

Fig. 2. Overhanging branches the robot can push away.

Height and Shape A rough resolution can be achieved by stereo camera systems or 3D laser range finders. The 3D point cloud of a PMD sensor can also be employed to extract polygons and hence the shape of detected objects as presented in [19]. The major drawback of this approach is the runtime of the algorithm, which prevents an online analysis.

(a) Color and depth image of a stereo camera system.

(b) Distance image delivered by a PMD sensor.

Fig. 3. Examples of several sensors system for height and shape extraction.

Flexibility Determination is possible by trying to push away assumed obstacles. This can be realized using a spring mounted bumper (Fig. 4). Pushing against a flexible object, will result in low resistance and the robot can drive ahead. In case of a solid obstacle the bumper will be deflected. The simplicity and robustness of this mechanism indicate the feasibility of this solution. However, as the bumper has to touch the object a foresighted navigation is impossible. An alternative approach draws conclusion about the flexibility of an object from its material. The special kind of material can be identified using a spectroscope. A spectroscope with the needed measurement range and optics is certainly no off-the-shelf

Fig. 4. RAVON's spring mounted bumper.

component. Instead, a differentiation between vegetation and other materials should be a sufficient first approach. As described in [4] a NIR-Camera is one sensor that can solve this problem.

2.2 Negative Obstacles, Water and Ground

While driving in outdoor environments, several types of ground can be found. Some have critical properties, which affect the robot's safety. Fig. 5 shows an exemplary situation in the Palatine Forest. Being an obstacle itself the creek increases the moisture of the surrounding soil. Thus, the area nearby the creek should be avoided but remains an option while driving through the narrow passage between the tree and the creek. The following presents the most important properties as well as sensor systems that allow their measurement.

Fig. 5. Typical scene that can be found in the Palatine Forest.

Slope Laser range finders, PMD or stereo cameras are suited for measuring slopes relative to the robot's pose as presented in [9]. Therefore, the trend of the assumed ground is supervised. Roll and pitch of the robot's pose are determined by an IMU[3]. Fusing the information of the pose and the identified terrain allows to avoid too steep areas.

Slippage is detectable by corellating the odometry with the acceleration measured using an IMU. Again, this method detects slippage not before the robot drives on slippery ground. A provident slippage detection is presented in [1].

Degree of Moisture and Water A spectroscope seems to be the only way to determine the degree of moisture without physical contact. The detection of puddles and other water hazards allows the usage of several sensor systems. The camera-based water detection presented in [17] uses color, texture and stereo range data. A polarization-based approach is described in [20]. The infrared spectrum offers two more methods for water detection, as described in [15]. Finally, [10] recognizes water hazards even in the dark using 3D laser range finders. As this approach usually utilizes a panning laser range finder it takes some time to scan the whole area in front of the robot.

Carrying Capacity Roads almost inherently guarantee a safe driving environment. An overview about several techniques can be found in [7]. In [8] a technique is introduced that combines the edge detection-based approach with color segmentation to find areas probably containing pavement. Requiring a very good match of the real situation to the pre-defined expectations these methods are limited to urban terrains with clean road boundaries and visible road markings. The method proposed in [11] therefore tries to cope with less well-maintained or unstructured non-asphalt roads without markings and not following smooth curves.

Property	Sensors
height	laser, pmd, stereo camera system
vegetation	infrared camera, spectroscope
flexibility	bumper, infrared, spectroscope
slope	laser, pmd, stereo camera system, IMU
slippage	RGB camera, spectroscope, IMU, wheel encoder
moisture	spectroscope
water	several camera systems, laser, spectroscope
carrying capacity	RGB camera, spectroscope

Table 1. List of properties and according sensors.

---

[3] Internal Measuring Unit

3   Representation and Navigation Strategy

A grid map is a suitable data structure to store every property and its position. In this approach a scrollable grid map is applied as displayed in Fig. 6(a). The middle element represents the origin of the map. As soon as the robot position P_{robot} differs more than one element size from the map origin the grid map scrolls one element row or column. The orientation of the map does not change as its movement is aligned to the x- and y-axes, to avoid resampling issues. In this way the map can be interpreted as local extract of a global map.

Many of the mentioned properties cannot be measured in terms of "*yes*" or "*no*". Instead, just a probability is available or in case of vegetation a degree of flexibility. Moreover, some properties depend on others such as slippage is influenced by slope and moisture. These values must be fused to the required *traversability*.

As every sensor and its interpretations have dedicated update frequencies each pair needs one instance of the grid map. Finally, the information of all grid maps is fused into one (Fig. 6(b)). Based on this map the traversability of each element can be calculated. In order to determine an appropriate path a potential field represents one suitable method.

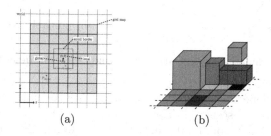

(a)   (b)

Fig. 6. Property and fusion grid map. (a) Structure of the used grid map; (b) Resulting grid map of the fusion algorithm

4   Classification Methods Realized on RAVON

The authors use the experimental platform RAVON (Fig. 4) at the Robotics Research Lab (University of Kaiserslautern) to implement and test different approaches to solve the problem of traversability classification. Besides the below presented classification methods it features a gridmap framework for sensor data fusion that is connected to a behavior-based control system.

Fig. 7. RAVON and its sensor tower

In [18] a method is proposed, that uses a 2D laser range finder rotated around a vertical axis to create a 3D view of the environment. As this is done during movements through rough terrain, a proper point cloud cannot be reconstructed. Instead, each slice is analyzed for different kinds of obstacle types (Fig. 8) and allows to discriminate vegetation from solid obstacle using a heuristic classifier for the density of scanned objects (Fig. 9). At the moment the panned 2D laser range finder is the primary sensor used for obstacle detection in the RAVON project.

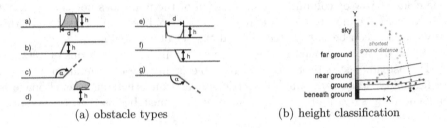

(a) obstacle types   (b) height classification

Fig. 8. Obstacle detection using a panned laser scanner as described in [18].

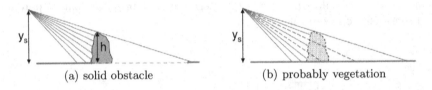

(a) solid obstacle   (b) probably vegetation

Fig. 9. Discrimination of vegetation from solid objects as described in [18].

In terms of slope the RAVON project uses a stereo camera system and fits small planes into the scene [5]. The normal gives a hint for the slope at the plane's position. The absolute value of that slope as well as the transition between adjacent planes are used as traversability classifier. Additionally, the color images are segmented and analyzed w.r.t. to texture (LBP), color (HSV) and variance (i.e. contrast) [6]. The resulting descriptors are classified using the knn algorithm and the knowledge gained from observing the obstacle avoidance. RAVON uses this classification on a higher navigation level to plan a path through free space (Fig. 10).

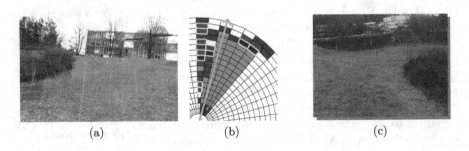

(a)   (b)   (c)

Fig. 10. Terrain classification as described in [5] and [6]. (a) planes fitted into the scene; (b) traversability map; (c) learned descriptors

A laser range finder-based water detection is also implemented. A statistical analysis of void readings from the panning laser range finder recognizes water hazards (Fig. 11). As these void readings only sporadically appear a grid map is utilized for short-term memory. Using neighborhood correlations of the grid map cells allows an estimation of the size of the water hazards. Small puddles are ignored and bigger ones are taken into account by the obstacle avoidance. One drawback of this approach is the dead-time caused by the pan frequency of the 3D laser range finder. The main advantage in contrast to camera-based methods is the ability to work in the dark.

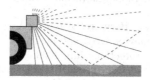

Fig. 11. Principle of laser-based water detection as implemented in RAVON's sensor processing system. The statistical analysis is able to identify water-caused void readings.

5   Conclusion and Future Work

In this paper the basic idea for a traversability classifier for off-road terrain was presented. The combination of various properties allows a modular creation of a map to navigate on. Some of the presented properties are popular and successfully used during the last years. Other properties such as the degree of moisture remain rather unconsidered.

Furthermore, an overview of the already available classifiers of the RAVON project was presented. The panning laser range finder is used for the detection of positive obstacles and water as well as for a heuristic vegetation discrimination. A color, texture and variance-based traversability prediction based upon self-supervised learning is also integrated.

The extension of RAVON's sensor systems by a spectral imaging sensor is planed. This sensor is supposed to improve the vegetation discrimination and to facilitate flexibility analysis and moisture measurement. The expected information considering the present materials in the robot's environment in conjunction with the already available sensor system will significantly increase RAVON's ability to recognize traversable terrain. This clarifies some currently doubtful situations that would stop the robot for safety reasons.

Acknowledgements

Team RAVON thanks the following companies for their technical and financial support: IK elektronik, Mayser, Hankook, MiniTec, SICK, DSM Computer, Johannes Hübner Giessen, John Deere, Optima, ITT Cannon, MOBOTIX, Unitek Industrie Elektronik, and Werkzeug Schmidt GmbH.

References

1. Angelova A., Matthies L., Helmick D. et al.: Learning to predict slip for ground robots. IEEE ICRA, pp.3324–3331, May 15-19 2006.
2. Armbrust C., Braun T., Föhst T. et al.: RAVON — The Robust Autonomous Vehicle for Off-road Navigation. RISE, January 12–14 2009.
3. Bergquist U.: Colour Vision and Hue for Autonomous Vehicle Guidance. Master Thesis, University of Linköping, December 1999.
4. Bradley D. M., Unnikrishnan R., Bagnell J.: Vegetation Detection for Driving in Complex Environments. IEEE ICRA, Roma, Italy, April 10–14 2007.
5. Braun T., Bitsch H., Berns K.: Visual Terrain Traversability Estimation using a Combined Slope/Elevation Model. KI Conference, pp. 177–184, 2008.
6. Braun T., Seidler B., Berns K.: Adaptive Visual Terrain Traversability Estimation using Behavior Observation. IARP Workshop on Environmental Maintenance and Protection, July 2008.
7. Broggi A., Bertè S.: Vision-Based Road Detection in Automotive Systems: A Real-Time Expectation-Driven Approach. Journal of Artificial Intelligence Research, Vol. 3, pp. 325–348, 1995.
8. He Y., Wang H., Zhang B.: Color-based road detection in urban traffic scenes. IEEE ITSS, Vol. 5, pp. 309–318, 2004.
9. Hong T., Abrams M., Chang T. et al.: An Intelligent World Model for Autonomous Off-Road Driving. Computer Vision and Image Understanding, Hook, S. ASTER Spectral Library, 2000.
10. Hong T., Rasmussen C., Chang T. et al.: Fusing Ladar and Color Image Information for Mobile Robot Feature Detection and Tracking. IAS, 2002.
11. Hu M., Yang W., Ren M., Yang J.: A Vision Based Road Detection Algorithm. IEEE RAM, pp. 846–850, December 2004.
12. Kim D., Sun J., Oh S.M. et al.: Traversability Classification using Unsupervised On-line Visual Learning for Outdoor Robot Navigation. IEEE ICRA, pp. 518–525, May 15-19 2006.
13. Kuhnert K.-D., Stommel M.: Fusion of Stereo-Camera and PMD-Camera Data for Real-Time Suited Precise 3D Environment Reconstruction, IEEE IROS, pp. 4780–4785, 2006.
14. Manduchi R., Castano A., Talukder A. et al.: Obstacle Detection and Terrain Classification for Autonomous Off-Road Navigation. Journal of Autonomous Robots, vol. 18, pp. 81–102, 2005.
15. Matthies L., Bellutta P., McHenry M.: Detecting water hazards for autonomous off-road navigation. IEEE IROS, October 27, 2003.
16. May S., Werner B., Surmann H., Pervölz K.: 3D time-of-flight cameras for mobile robotics. IEEE IROS, pp. 790–795, 2006.
17. Rankin A., Matthies L., Huertas A.: Daytime Water Detection by Fusing Multiple Cues for Autonomous Off-Road Navigation. 24th Army Science Conference, Orlando, Florida, USA, November 29 - December 2 2004.
18. Schäfer H., Hach A., Proetzsch M., Berns K.: 3D Obstacle Detection and Avoidance in Vegetated Off-road Terrain. IEEE ICRA, pp. 923–928, Pasadena, USA, May 2008.
19. Vaskevicius N., Birk A., Pathak K. et al.: Fast Detection of Polygons in 3D Point Clouds from Noise-Prone Range Sensors. IEEE SSRR, 2007.
20. Xie B., Pan H., Xiang Z. et al.: Polarization-Based Water Hazards Detection for Autonomous Off-road Navigation.IEEE ICMA, pp. 1666–1670, 2007.

Aufbau des humanoiden Roboters BART III

Dimitri Resetov, Björn Pietsch und Wilfried Gerth

Institut für Regelungstechnik, Leibniz Universität Hannover
Appelstr. 11, 30167 Hannover
{resetov,pietsch,gerth}@irt.uni-hannover.de

Zusammenfassung. Der vorliegende Beitrag präsentiert den humanoiden Roboter BART III, der am Institut für Regelungstechnik als eine robuste und erweiterbare Plattform für weiterführende Grundlagenforschung zur zweibeinigen Fortbewegung entwickelt wurde. Im Gegensatz zu den bisher am IRT genutzten Robotern BARt-UH und LISA besitzt der neue Roboter einen beweglichen Oberkörper mit einem Bauchgelenk und Armen. BART III besitzt insgesamt 19 aktive Freiheitsgrade, 12 davon im Unterkörper. Ein weiteres Merkmal des Roboters ist die im gesamten Körper verteilte Ansteuerelektronik, die neben der lokalen Motorregelung diverse sicherheitsrelevante Funktionen übernimmt.

1 Einleitung

Serviceroboter, die in der menschlichen Umgebung zum Einsatz kommen, sollen eine große Flexibilität bei der Fortbewegung aufweisen. Die menschenähnliche Bewegung auf zwei Beinen ist hierfür eine geeignete Strategie.

BART III ist der erste am Institut für Regelungstechnik entwickelte zweibeinige Roboter mit einem aktiven Oberkörper. Bei den bislang am Institut für Regelungstechnik für Untersuchungen der zweibeinigen Fortbewegung genutzten Robotern BARt-UH [1] und LISA [2] ist nur der Unterkörper beweglich, der Torso hingegen ein starrer Körper. Ein Oberkörper mit angetriebenen Armen eröffnet weitere Möglichkeiten, die ein Roboter mit einem starren Oberkörper nur schwer bzw. gar nicht realisieren kann. Beispiele sind stabilisierende Eingriffe ohne eine Änderung der zur Fortbewegung genutzten Beintrajektorien oder das Aufrichten des Roboters nach einem Sturz [3]. Außerdem erhöht ein Oberkörper mit Armen die Akzeptanz eines zweibeinigen Serviceroboters.

Es existieren weltweit mehrere Projekte, die humanoide Roboter entwickeln und die Fortbewegung auf zwei Beinen erforschen. Die zurzeit wohl bekanntesten humanoiden Roboter in menschenähnlicher Größe sind ASIMO [5], die HRP-Serie[6], JOHNNIE und LOLA[7]. ASIMO kann in der aktuellen Version mit bis zu 6 km/h „rennen". Mit den HRP Robotern wird der Einsatz der Zweibeiner in einer Industrieumgebung untersucht. Die Roboter von TU München versuchen dem menschlichen Gangbild möglichst nah zu kommen.

Das Ziel des BART-Projekts ist die Entwicklung und der Aufbau eines robusten, zuverlässigen und kostengünstigen humanoiden Roboters zur Erforschung verschiedener Algorithmen der zweibeinigen Fortbewegung. Um die Erweiterbarkeit des Roboters für zukünftige Forschungsprojekte zu gewährleisten, wurde bei der Entwicklung des Roboters besonderer Wert auf einen modularen Aufbau gelegt. Dieser wurde sowohl bei der mechanischen Konstruktion als auch bei den elektrischen Komponenten zur Ansteuerung der Aktoren umgesetzt. Durch die relativ einfache Roboterkonstruktion und die Verwendung sich wiederholender Komponenten wurden der Aufbau beschleunigt und die Kosten reduziert.

Der Roboter wurde vollständig aufgebaut und getestet und hat erste Versuche mit statisch stabilem Gang absolviert (siehe Abschnitt 4).

2 Mechanischer Aufbau

2.1 Übersicht

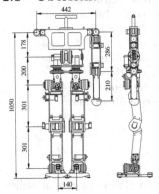
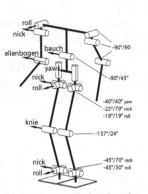
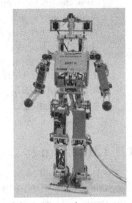

(a) Abmaße des Roboters   (b) Kinematische Struktur   (c) Aufbau (mit einem
                            und Gelenkarbeitsbereiche   Kamerakopf-Prototyp)

Abb. 1. BART III

Der in diesem Artikel beschriebene Roboter BART III besitzt eine Schulterhöhe von 1,05 m und eine Masse von 34,5 kg. Die Abmessungen des Roboters sind an die Proportionen eines 10 jährigen Kindes angelehnt (s. Bild 1(a)). Der Roboter besitzt insgesamt 19 angetriebene Freiheitsgrade (DOF).

Das Bild 1(b) zeigt einen Überblick über die kinematische Struktur des Roboters. Die orthogonale Anordnung der Gelenke und deren Reihenfolge reduziert die Komplexität des kinematischen und kinetischen Modells.

Die kinematische Struktur des Unterkörpers ermöglicht mit 6 DOF pro Bein eine freie Positionierung und Orientierung der Füße im Raum. Die Hüftgelenke vom BART III sind im Gegensatz zum parallelkinematischen Gelenk von LISA [2] als eine serielle Kinematik realisiert, die eine einfachere Ansteuerung zulässt. Die Nachteile höherer beschleunigter Massen werden durch eine steifere Konstruktion aufgewogen, die aus der Trennung der Antriebe und der tragenden Konstruktion resultiert.

Die Kinematik des Oberkörpers ermöglicht die Verlagerung des Schwerpunktes des Roboters und das Applizieren stabilisierender, kompensierender Momente. Die laterale Orientierung des Bauchgelenks ermöglicht die Verbiegung des

Oberkörpers nach vorne bzw. hinten, was zum Beispiel für das Aufrichten des Roboters nach einem Sturz erforderlich ist [3].

2.2 Konstruktion der Gelenke

Alle aktiven Freiheitsgrade des Roboters sind als Drehgelenke ausgeführt. Die Gelenke werden mit einem Elektromotor mit einem Harmonic Drive Untersetzungsgetriebe angetrieben. Einzelne Gelenke bilden weitgehend geschlossene Module, die mit Aluminiumplatten miteinander verbunden sind, so dass sich das gewünschte modulare Konzept ergibt.

Bei dem Bauch- und dem Kniegelenk ist der Antriebsmotor koaxial mit dem Harmonic Drive Getriebe angeordnet und direkt mit der Antriebsseite des Letzteren verbunden. Bei allen anderen Gelenken ist zusätzlich eine Zahnriemen-Übertragung zwischen dem Motor und der Antriebsachse des Harmonic Drive Getriebes eingebaut. Somit kann der Motor außerhalb der Gelenkachse, z. B. in den Robotergliedern, platziert werden, was zu einer kompakteren Gelenkkonstruktion führt. Zusätzlich kann die Untersetzung nachträglich mit den Zahnriemenscheiben angepasst werden.

Knöchel- und Hüftgelenk sind als Kreuzgelenke mit orthogonalen Achsen ausgeführt. Die tragende Konstruktion besteht im Wesentlichen aus einem mittleren Kreuz und den zwei mit ihm verbundenen Gabeln. Die Gabeln stützen sich auf zwei Lager, was im Vergleich zu einer Cantilever-Konstruktion eine steifere Struktur ermöglicht. Um die Steifigkeit der Struktur weiter zu erhöhen, wurden die wichtigsten tragenden Elemente aus vollem Aluminium gefräst.

Um dem Hüftgelenk einen zusätzlichen Freiheitsgrad zu geben, wurde die Gabel der Rollachse drehbar um die senkrechte Achse gelagert. Als Lager dient dabei ein Kreuzrollenlager mit einem großen Durchmesser, das sowohl axiale als auch radiale Kräfte und Kippmomente aufnehmen kann. Die Konstruktion des Hüftgelenks ermöglicht eine dichte Platzierung der Gelenke im Becken, was die Belastung der Rollachse des Hüftgelenks beim Einbeinstand verringert.

Die Arme des Roboters bestehen je aus drei identischen Gelenkmodulen mit jeweils einer Drehachse. Die Module sind zu einer kinematischen Kette gekoppelt, dabei liegen zwei Gelenke sehr dicht beieinander und bilden ein Schultergelenk mit zwei Freiheitsgraden nach. Die Konstruktion der Arm-Gelenkmodule integriert neben dem Getriebe auch den Motor und bildet mit der kompakten Leistungselektronik eine universell einsetzbare Servo-Einheit.

2.3 Komponenten

Die Auswahl des Getriebes spielt bei dem Aufbau eines laufenden Roboters eine sehr wichtige Rolle. Das Getriebe soll leistungsfähig, präzise und gleichzeitig leicht sein. Die Präzision der Getriebe ist erforderlich, da eine genaue und wiederholbare Positionierung der Gelenke die Stabilisierung des Roboters vereinfacht.

Die Untersetzung in allen Gelenken von BART III wurden durch Harmonic Drive Getriebe realisiert. Im Vergleich mit anderen Getriebetypen besitzt diese

Art des Getriebes ein sehr günstiges Masse/Leistungs-Verhältnis und einen relativ hohen Wirkungsgrad. Außerdem besitzen die Harmonic Drive Getriebe ein geringes Spiel auf der Abtriebsseite, was eine präzise Bewegung ermöglicht. Die Untersetzung und die Leistungsdaten der Getriebe wurden unter der Berücksichtigung der Untersuchungen an den Robotern BARt-UH und LISA ausgewählt.

Bei vielen Gelenken ist eine zusätzliche Getriebevorstufe mit einem Zahnriemen eingebaut. Die resultierenden Untersetzungen sind in der Tabelle 1 aufgelistet. Um die Präzision der Harmonic Drive Getriebe zu unterstützen, wurde ein spielfreies HTD-Zahnriemenprofil in den Bein-gelenken verwendet, das zudem eine geringe Geräuschentwicklung aufweist. Auf den Einsatz gefederter Riemenspanner wurde zwecks Gewichtsersparung verzichtet. Die Zahnriemenspannung wird durch die Änderung der Motorbefestigungsposition oder durch das Verstellen einer exzentrischen Umlenkrolle eingestellt.

Tabelle 1. Getriebedaten

Untersetzung	Gelenk
1:101	Knie, Bauch
1:125	Armgelenke
1:220	Hüfte (roll)
1:137	alle anderen

3 Elektrischer Aufbau

Die elektrischen Systeme des Roboters bestehen aus den Antrieben mit Leistungselektronik, den Sensoren und dem Leitrechner. In BART III kommt ein – mit Ausnahme des Leitrechners – dezentrales Konzept zum Einsatz. Zu jedem Gelenk gehört ein Mikrocontroller, der den Antrieb über eine Leistungselektronik ansteuert und die Sensorsignale des Gelenks verarbeitet; Kraft- und Beschleunigungssensoren, die keinem Gelenk zugeordnet sind, verfügen ebenfalls über eigene Controller. Alle Mikrocontroller sind über CAN-Busse mit dem Leitrechner verbunden.

Die dezentrale Datenverarbeitung erhöht die Modularität des Systems, weil die Controller mit dem Leitrechner Daten austauschen, die von der physikalischen Realisierung abstrahiert sind. Gelenkspezifische Parameter wie Getriebeübersetzungen oder Sensorbauweisen stören daher nicht die einheitliche Modellierung der Gelenke in den höheren Schichten. Zugleich entlasten die Controller den Leitrechner durch die lokale Ausführung von Regelungen und ermöglichen eine Isolation von Fehlern.

Konstruktiv ermöglichen die dezentralen Elektroniken eine kompaktere Bauweise des Roboters, weil sie über den gesamten Körper verteilt werden können, und reduzieren Aufwand und Gewicht der Verkabelung. Erweiterungen können ohne zusätzliche Leitungen einfach an den Bus angeschlossen werden.

3.1 Antriebe

Als Antriebe werden Gleichstrommotoren mit Bürsten verwendet (Daten siehe Tabelle 2). Sie besitzen ein höheres Anhalte- und Dauerdrehmoment als bürstenlose Motoren derselben Gewichts- und Preisklasse. Durch die einfachere Ansteuerung wird zudem die Leistungselektronik kleiner und leichter. Diese Vorteile wiegen das schlechtere thermische Verhalten sowie die durch das Bürstenfeuer bedingten elektromagnetischen Störungen auf.

Für die Antriebe wird wie bei den übrigen Robotern des Instituts eine Betriebsspannung von 30 V verwendet. Dies stellt einen Kompromiss zwischen dem erforderlichen Sicherheits- und Isolationsaufwand bei hohen Spannungen einerseits und den hohen Strömen und Leitungsverlusten bei niedrigen Spannungen andererseits dar.

Tabelle 2. Motordaten

P [W]	M_{max} [Nm]	n_{max} [U/s]	Gelenk
150	2,29	126	Knie, Bauch
90	1,25	112	Hüfte (nick, roll)
60	1,02	147	alle anderen

3.2 Sensoren

Die Kontaktkräfte zwischen dem Roboter und dem Boden werden über vier Kraftsensoren pro Fuß erfasst. Die Sensorsignale erlauben Messungen der Normalkraft und den beiden Kippmomenten. Die Signale werden von einem im Fuß integrierten Prozessor lokal verarbeitet und per CAN an den Leitrechner geleitet.

Als Gleichgewichtssensor dient eine im Torso des Roboters montierte inertiale Messeinheit (μIMU). Die μIMU wurde am Institut entwickelt und erlaubt die Messung von Beschleunigungen und Drehraten um die drei Achsen [4].

Die in den Gelenken verbauten Sensoren erlauben die Messung des Motorstroms und der Winkelposition. Zusätzlich ist der Arbeitsraum mit Endschaltern abgesichert. Es ist außerdem ein Anschluss für die externen Temperatursensoren zur Überwachung der Leistungselektronik und des Motors vorgesehen.

Zur Messung der Winkelpositionen des Gelenkes stehen antriebsseitig ein Inkremental-Impulsgeber und abtriebsseitig ein selbst entwickelter Absolutwertgeber zur Verfügung. Durch die zwei Winkelgeber ist es möglich, den Roboter in kurzer Zeit aus einer beliebigen Position zu initialisieren und die durch die Elastizität des Harmonic Drive Getriebes verursachte unerwünschte Verdrehung des Gelenkes zu erfassen und zu kompensieren.

Der im Roboter verbaute Absolutwertgeber basiert auf einem optischen Zeilensensor, der einen Code-Streifen abtastet. Der Code-Streifen mit einem aufgedruckten Muster ist an dem dem Sensor gegenüber liegenden, drehbaren Gelenkteil angeklebt. Das Auslesen des Zeilensensors und die Auswertung des aufgenommenen Bildes übernimmt der Prozessor des entsprechenden SmartPower-

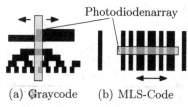

(a) Graycode   (b) MLS-Code

Abb. 2. Anordnung des Sensors

Moduls (s. Abschnitt 3.3). Die erreichbare Abtastrate liegt bei etwa 1 kHz. Die Verunschärfung wegen der Bildverschiebung während der Abtastung kann bei der eingestellten Belichtungszeit von ca. 200 μs vernachlässigt werden.

Die Sensoren in den Armgelenken basieren auf dem Graycode. Hier ist ein Photodiodenarray quer zu der Verschieberichtung installiert (s. Bild 2). Die Winkelauflösung ist in diesem Fall durch die Montageungenauigkeiten und die Linsenqualität beeinflusst und beträgt in den Armgelenken 0.86°.

Die neuen Sensoren in den Beingelenken basieren auf dem sogenannten „Maximum Length Sequence"-Code (MLS). Der MLS-Code ist so ausgewählt, dass der vom Sensor abgetastete Code-Ausschnitt im Arbeitsbereich des Gelenkes stets eindeutig ist. Das Photodiodenarray in diesen Sensoren ist parallel zu der Verschieberichtung orientiert (s. Bild 2(b)). Diese Anordnung ist tolerant gegenüber Montagefehlern und einer leichten Unschärfe des Bildes. Die Winkelauflösung des Sensors ist in diesem Fall durch die Auflösung des Photodiodenarrays (300 dpi) begrenzt und beträgt je nach Gelenk zwischen 0.236° und 0.11° (abhängig von dem Abstand des Drehpunktes von der Bildebene).

3.3 SmartPower-Module

Als Steuereinheit für die Gelenke wurden die sogenannten SmartPower-Module entwickelt. Sie verarbeiten die Signale aller zu einem Gelenk gehörigen Sensoren und steuern mit ihrer Leistungselektronik den Motor an. Ein SmartPower-Modul besteht aus einer Prozessor- und einer Leistungseinheit (Bild 3). Die Trennung ermöglicht einen kompakten Einbau und ermöglicht die Wiederverwendung der Teileinheiten in anderen Projekten.

Als Prozessor kommt ein Mikrocontroller 56F805 von Motorola zum Einsatz. Er kommuniziert über einen CAN-Kanal mit dem Leitrechner, verarbeitet die Daten der beiden Positionssensoren und steuert die Leistungselektronik über eine Datenverbindung und pulsweitenmodulierte Signale (PWM). In der Leistungselektronik übernimmt ein programmierbarer Logikbaustein (CPLD) die Erzeugung der Steuermuster für die MOSFETs der H-Brücke sowie Sicherheitsfunktionen. Dazu gehören die Überwachung der Endschalter und des Motorstroms sowie die Gültigkeitsprüfung der PWM-Signale.

Die Reaktionen auf Fehler sind im CPLD und im Mikrocontroller jeweils parametrierbar. Die Fehlerbehandlung ist aber nicht auf die jeweils höheren Schichten angewiesen und arbeitet auch bei deren Ausfall. Dies erhöht die Systemsicherheit und entlastet die höheren Schichten von hohen Anforderungen an die Reaktionszeit.

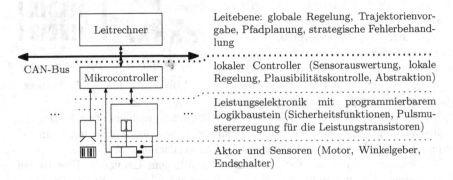

Abb. 3. Schichtenmodell der Ansteuerung; der Controller und die darunter liegenden Einheiten wiederholen sich in jedem Gelenk

3.4 Leitrechner

Als Leitrechner wird eine 1GHz-CPU MPC7447 von Motorola verwendet, die als PMC-Modul auf einer im Institut entwickelten CompactPCI-Trägerkarte installiert ist. Das System verfügt über 512 MiB RAM, zwei Ethernetanschlüsse und vier CAN-Kanäle. Es kann wegen seiner niedrigen Leistungsaufnahme von 10-20 W und der geringen Größe für den autonomen Betrieb in den Roboter eingebaut werden. Der Betrieb erfolgt mit dem Echtzeitbetriebssystem RTOS-UH.

Der Leitrechner übernimmt die Aufgaben der globalen ZMP-Regelung[1] , der Bahnplanung und der Trajektorienverwaltung. Die implementierten Bahnplanungsalgorithmen generieren alle 10 ms Sollwerte, die dann an die Gelenkcontroller gesendet werden.

4 Erste Gehversuche

Zwecks Inbetriebnahme und Validierung des aufgebauten Roboters wurde neben diversen Testbewegungen ein statisch stabiler Gang implementiert. Der Gang wird als eine Folge von Fußabdrücken und Torsopositionen in einem Textfile beschrieben. Die Trajektorien der Roboterteilkörper zwischen den Stützpunkten werden abschnittsweise mit Hilfe von Sinus-Funktionen interpoliert.

Das Bild 4 zeigt die Messergebnisse des implementierten Gang-Algorithmus. Die Teilbilder 4(a) und 4(c) zeigen die Winkelverläufe und die Regelabweichungen ausgewählter Gelenke. Die maximale Regelabweichung tritt erwartungsgemäß im Knie auf und beträgt ca. 1°. Als Gelenkregler kam dabei ein einfacher

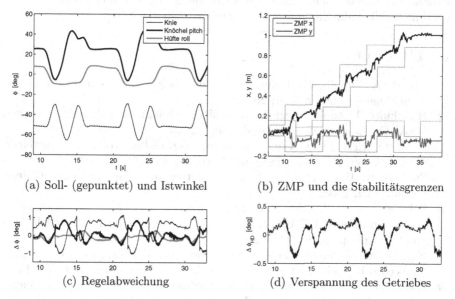

(a) Soll- (gepunktet) und Istwinkel

(b) ZMP und die Stabilitätsgrenzen

(c) Regelabweichung

(d) Verspannung des Getriebes

Abb. 4. Statisch stabiler Gang von BART III

---

[1] Der **Z**ero **M**oment **P**oint wird oft als Stabilitätskriterium verwendet (z.B. [1]-[3])

P-Regler zum Einsatz. Der ZMP-Verlauf (Bild 4(b)) liegt stets innerhalb des Stabilitätsgebiets, weist jedoch zum Teil starke Schwankungen auf, die durch das Beschleunigen der Teilmassen hervorgerufen sind. Der implementierte Gang ist also streng genommen nicht mehr statisch stabil, ist aber gut dafür geeignet, den Roboter zu testen.

Das Bild 4(d) zeigt die Differenz zwischen dem antriebs- und abtriebsseitig gemessenen Winkel im Kniegelenk; diese lässt auf die Verspannung des Getriebes schließen und kann zur Verbesserung der Regelung dienen, die sich bislang nur auf die antriebsseitige Messung stützt.

Untersuchungen mit dem montierten Prototyp eines Kamerakopfes (Bild 1(c) auf der Seite 210) zeigten, dass der Roboter imstande ist, eine Last von etwa 3, 5 kg zusätzlich zum eigenen Gewicht zu tragen. Diese Reserve ermöglicht den Einsatz eines Akkupacks, was, neben der in Abschnitt 3.4 erläuterten Integration des Leitrechners in den Roboter, eine vollständig autonome Arbeitsweise erlaubt. Der gemessene mittlere Energiebedarf des Roboters beim Gehen beträgt max. 200 W, was eine Betriebsdauer von ca. 1 Stunde in diesem Modus ermöglicht.

5   Zusammenfassung

Der vorgestellte Artikel beschreibt den am IRT entwickelten humanoiden Roboter BART III. Neben den Besonderheiten der mechanischen Konstruktion wurde das universal einsetzbare „SmartPower" Modul und der optische Absolutwertgeber vorgestellt. Anschließend wurden erste Gehversuche, mit denen die Funktionalität des Roboters validiert wurde, präsentiert. Die Implementierung des dynamisch stabilen Gehens sowie die Erhöhung der Autonomie des Roboters sind die für die nahe Zukunft vorgesehenen nächsten Schritte.

6   Literatur

1. Albert, A.: Intelligente Bahnplanung und Regelung für einen autonomen, zweibeinigen Roboter. VDI, 2002
2. Hofschulte, J.: Zweibeiniger Roboter mit parallelkinematischen Hüftgelenken. Books On Demand GmbH, Norderstedt, 2006
3. Höhn, O.: Erkennung, Klassifikation und Vermeidung von Stürzen zweibeiniger Roboter. Books On Demand, Norderstedt, 2008.
4. Strasser, R.: Untersuchung von Beobachterverfahren für eine inertiale Messeinheit. VDI, 2005.
5. Sakagami, Y.; Watanabe, R. et al: The intelligent ASIMO: system overview and integration. IEEE/RSJ International Conference on Intelligent Robots and System, pp. 2478 - 2483, 2002.
6. Kaneko, K.; Kanehiro, F. et al: Humanoid robot HRP-2. International Conference on Robotics and Automation IEEE 2004, pp. 1083 - 1090 Vol.2
7. Lohmeier, S.; Buschmann, T. et al.: Modular joint design for performance enhanced humanoid robot LOLA. International Conference on Robotics and Automation IEEE 2006, pp. 88-93

Development of Micro UAV Swarms

Axel Bürkle and Sandro Leuchter

Fraunhofer Institut für Informations- und Datenverarbeitung,
Fraunhoferstraße 1, 76131 Karlsruhe

Abstract. Some complex application scenarios for micro UAVs (Unmanned Aerial Vehicles) call for the formation of swarms of multiple drones. In this paper a platform for the creation of such swarms is presented. It consists of modified commercial quadrocopters and a self-made ground control station software architecture. Autonomy of individual drones is generated through a micro controller equipped video camera. Currently it is possible to fly basic maneuvers autonomously, such as take-off, fly to position, and landing. In the future the camera's image processing capabilities will be used to generate additional control information. Different co-operation strategies for teams of UAVs are currently evaluated with an agent based simulation tool. Finally complex application scenarios for multiple micro UAVs are presented.

1 Introduction

Groups of flying platforms are necessary to implement some complex monitoring and surveillance applications. While the control of a single UAV is already well understood and a wide range of commercial products is available the use of multiple platforms still needs investigation. This paper presents ongoing work on the development and simulation of devices and strategies for the formation of swarms of micro UAVs.

After a short survey of related work the apparatus used for this work is presented. It consists of a modified commercial flight platform and a self-made ground control station. Coordination and control of the micro UAVs is realized by a micro controller equipped „smart" video camera mounted on the drones. Different strategies for the coordination of individual UAVs are currently evaluated by using agent-based simulation tools. This report closes with a presentation of different applications for groups of micro UAVs.

2 Related Work

The cooperative control of groups or swarms of UAVs makes high demands on the flight platform and requires new control strategies. With an increasing number of team members manual control becomes more and more impractical. A general approach is to equip the UAVs with a certain amount of autonomy. This requires capabilities such communication between drones, autonomous real-time navigation, sensing, and collision avoidance. With recent advances in corresponding areas, those capabilities can be integrated into micro UAVs. The following section gives an overview of research efforts in building collaborative micro UAVs.

The projects Flying Gridswarms and UltraSwarm [1,2], both carried out at the University of Essex, investigated the flocking of a group of MAVs (Micro or Miniature Aerial Vehicles) for the purpose of solving tasks by making use of the unique advantages of swarms. While Flying Gridswarms used a fixed wing platform, UltraSwarm aimed at building an indoor flocking system using small co-axial rotor helicopters. The key idea is using biologically inspired rules of group behaviour (flocking) to enable a group of UAVs to control its own motion. The swarm members wirelessly network to form a single powerful computing resource.

The chosen aerial platform for the UltraSwarm project was an off-the-shelf model helicopter. Due to their low costs swarms can be built at reasonable costs. The platform was fitted with an onboard computer and a miniature wireless video camera. To compensate for the additional weight it was necessary to upgrade the motors and batteries.

The ongoing μDRONES (Micro Drone autonomous navigation for environment sensing) project [3], funded by the European Commission under the 6th Framework Programme, aims at developing a small size UAV designed for autonomous inspection and survey tasks in urban area. The core of the project is focused on the development of software and hardware modules providing autonomy to a small size drone in terms of navigation, localization and robustness to unexpected events. Key research areas are the development of a mission control system with an intuitive human-machine interface, the development of perception and command algorithms allowing the more efficient flight autonomy and development of a micro UAV prototype.

SUAAVE (Sensing, Unmanned, Autonomous Aerial VEhicles) [4] focus on the creation and control of swarms of helicopter UAVs that are individually autonomous but collaboratively self-organising. The project investigates the principles underlying the control of clouds of networked resource-limited UAVs that are targeted towards achieving a global objective in an efficient manner.

limited by tghe platforms insufficiencies (weakness)

While Flying Gridswarms and UltraSwarm are limited by the insufficiencies of the chosen aerial platform, our approach is based on highly reliable and expandable UAVs. Whereas μDRONES focuses on the platform and autonomous navigation of a single UAV, we look at the operation and collaboration of a group of UAVs. SUAAVE follows an approach similar to ours. However, their project is still at an early stage.

3   Platform

The development for swarm UAVs is based on a modified commercial flight platform that can be controlled by a ground control station. In the following section these two elements of the platform are described.

3.1 Flight Platform

A lot of effort has been put into the selection of the flight platform. A platform that already comes with a range of sensors, an advanced control system and autonomous flight features significantly reduces the effort necessary to realize a co-operative swarm of micro drones. Furthermore, when it comes to flying autonomously, the system has to be highly reliable and possess sophisticated safety features in case of malfunction or unexpected events.

Other essential prerequisites are the possibility to add new sensors and payloads and the ability to interface with the UAV's control system in order to allow autonomous flight. A platform that fulfils these requirements is the quadrocopter AR100-B by AirRobot (s. Fig. 1). It can be either controlled from the ground station through a command uplink or by its payload through a serial interface. The latter feature was used to realize autonomous navigation (s. Section 4).

Fig. 1. A quadrocopter serves as flight platform

3.2 Ground Control Station

The ground control station is an adaptable prototype system for managing sensor data acquisition with stationary sensors, mobile ad-hoc networks, and mobile sensor platforms. The main task of the ground control station is to work as an ergonomic user interface and a data integration hub between multiple sensors possibly mounted on moving platforms such as micro UAVs (but also ground vehicles or underwater vessels) and a super-ordinated control centre. The system is able to control different mobile platforms (among them the AirRobot quadrocopter) and direct them to potentially interesting locations in order to cope with large or not beforehand sensor equipped areas.

The actual prototype demonstrator (s. Fig. 2) is mobile and portable, allowing it to be conveniently taken to any location and put into operation there.

The sensor carriers of this multi-sensor system can be combined in a number of different configurations to meet a variety of specific requirements. The functions of the ground control station include: task management, mission planning, control of mobile platform (without line of sight through a virtual cockpit), sensor control, dynamic situation display/situation awareness, fusion of sensor data, sensor data exploitation, reporting, generation of alarms, and archiving.

A GIS (Geographic Information System) based landscape model is used as the basis for visualization and data integration. The software architecture is component oriented. It uses the .NET 3.0 framework. The system offers support for information perception and management. This is achieved by optimized information visualization and information fusion e.g. in the situation display.

Besides this, there are active facilities to support the coordination tasks of the sensor data exploitation. Such a support system for the automatic combination and selection of sensor data sources in a surveillance task was implemented using a production system with the Drools rule engine. It repeatedly assesses the current situation and selects the most appropriate rules to execute. The Drools engine can be packaged as a .NET component.

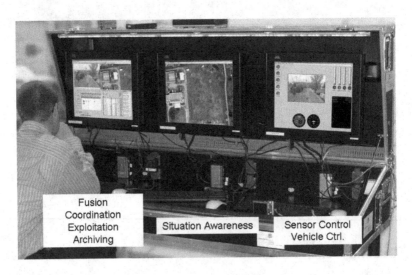

Fig. 2. Ground control station

The ground control station is realized as a modular framework allowing the adaptation to different operational needs. The platform has the function to process the data streams gathered from a range of sensors. It is also used to control the different platforms. The underlying software architecture has a generic connector for interfacing the ground control station with different sensor types and other streaming data sources. This connector has to be adapted to the specific protocol used by every sensor. It produces a unified data model from proprietary device specific formats.

4 Towards Autonomy

To allow the highest degree of autonomy possible, the quadrocopter should be controlled by a micro computer that it carries as a payload. Due to space, weight and power constraints of the payload, this computer module has to be small, lightweight and energy-efficient. Furthermore, a camera as sensor system should not be left out. A perfect solution is the use of a „smart" camera, i.e. a camera that not only captures images but also processes them. Processing power and functionalities of modern smart cameras are comparable to PCs. Even though smart cameras became more compact in recent years, they usually still are too heavy to be carried by a quadrocopter. In most applications, smart cameras are used stationary where their weight is of minor importance. However, a few models are available as board cameras, i.e. without casing and the usual plugs and sockets (s. Fig. 3, left). Thus, their size and weight is reduced to a minimum. The camera we chose has a freely programmable DSP (400MHz, 3200MIPS), a Linux-based real-time operating system and several interfaces (Ethernet, I^2C, RS232). With its weight of only 60g (without lens), its compact size and a power consumption of 2.4W it is suitable to replace the standard video camera payload.

Fig. 3. A „smart" camera (left) controls the UAV and is carried as a payload (right)

The camera can directly communicate with the drone's controller though a serial interface. The camera receives and processes status information from the UAV such as position, altitude or battery power, and is able to control it by sending basic control commands or GPS-based waypoints.

A drawback of the board camera is its lack of an analogue video output thus preventing the use of the quadrocopter's built-in video downlink. Image data is only available through the camera's Ethernet interface. Communication between the smart camera and the ground control station was enabled by integrating a tiny WiFi module into the payload. The WiFi communication link is used to stream live video images and status information from the UAV to the ground control station. Furthermore, new programs can be uploaded to the camera on the fly.

Currently, we are able to perform basic maneuvers autonomously, such as take-off, fly to position, and landing. In the future we will also use the camera's image processing capabilities to generate control information. As a safety feature, it is always possible to override the autonomous control and take over control manually.

5   Simulation and Evaluation

In order to assess different co-operation strategies for teams of UAVs, a simulation tool has been realized. Modeling and visualization of scenarios is done using a computer game engine with corresponding editing tools. An interface to the engine has been implemented. It allows full control of the implemented entities as well as feedback from the virtual world.

An example scenario that simulates an intrusion has been implemented (s. Fig. 4). Besides the UAVs and the actors in the scenario, also sensors have been modeled. Different kinds of sensors such as motion detectors, cameras, ultra sonic or LIDAR (light detection and ranging) sensors can be modeled with their specific characteristics. The simulation tool can decide if an object lies within the range of a sensor. This helps to evaluate and optimize the use of different sensing techniques.

Fig. 4. Simulation of an intrusion scenario

The intelligence of team members is implemented in software agents. They interface with the simulation engine using the same syntax as the actual quadrocopters. That way, the simulation environment can be exchanged with the real world without having to modify the agents.

6 Application Scenarios

In a recent Frost & Sulivan report [5] application scenarios for general UAV platforms are divided into military and civil applications. According to this report micro UAVs are already used in vast and diverse civil applications. Some of the tasks that can be supported with UAVs in general are in agriculture, police surveillance, pollution control, environment monitoring, fighting fires, inspecting dams, pipelines or electric lines, video surveillance, motion picture film work, cross border and harbor patrol, light cargo transportation, natural disaster inspection, search and rescue, and mine detection. Obviously some of these tasks cannot be supported by micro UAVs due to their limited operating range and payload. But many surveillance and monitoring scenarios can be implemented using micro UAVs. With groups or swarms of micro UAVs it is even possible to monitor larger areas and with more diverse sensory than with a single drone.

Military users such as tactical units on patrol missions can apply micro UAVs for intelligence, surveillance and reconnaissance tasks. Swarms would additionally bring the capability of coordinated area surveillance. Also the application of micro UAVs in „military operations in urban terrain" (MOUT) is publically discussed. Especially the capability to safely look into buildings is something that is asked for today. Such a feature is not yet ready available but is actively investigated e.g. in the DARPA program VisiBuilding. The use of micro UAVs acting as relay node into buildings is also discussed.

Many needed features of micro UAV swarms can be investigated using the scenario of protecting a safety critical infrastructure site such as a military camp or a large industrial installation. In such an application the perimeter or outer fence could be monitored by movement detection sensors (e.g. visual or passive infrared). In case of a perimeter violation a quadrocopter could be directed to the place of the event in order to follow and monitor a potential intruder. Several cases could rise the demand for a swarm of quadrocopters in such a situation.

- The distance is too far for transmission of signals to a ground control station. A relay station is needed. A line of quadrocopters can act as network. All start together. If the swarm reaches a predefined distance from the ground control station one drone from the group is „parked" and takes over relay function between the rest of the swarm and the ground control station.
- A group of intruders enters the site, later divides, and individual intruders take different directions. Then every single intruder has to be followed by its own. This can be achieved by smart functionality of tracking targets and following them. But initially a swarm of drones has to go to the group of intruders in order to build up stocks of later needed single UAVs.
- The duration of surveillance is too long for one battery charge. Single quadrocopters have to call for substitution. When the replacement quadrocopter is arriving on site it has to take over and the first one can go back to the base for recharge.
- A thread has to be monitored with different sensor types. For example an intruder who is best visually controlled suddenly places an object. Besides

the visual sensor some CBRNE (chemical, biological, radiological, nuclear, and explosive) detection devices are needed. Since the payload of every one quadrocopter is limited a swarm could carry different sensors.
- Multi-sensor capability could also be needed to visually control the action of different drones. For example an infrared sensor equipped quadrocopter could be used by the operator located in the ground control station to navigate a chemical sensor equipped micro UAV through a dark building.

These cases illustrate that there is a need of different swarm and coordination based capabilities for micro UAVs.

7   Conclusions

Forming teams of micro UAVs opens new application fields. However, the coordination of teams requires advanced control strategies and an extended degree of autonomy of the individual drones. Our approach is to equip commercial micro drones with „smart" cameras that control the UAVs. The drones are integrated into a modular sensor network whose central part is an adaptable ground control station.

Currently, we use a simulation tool to test and evaluate different team collaboration strategies, sensor techniques, as well as collision avoidance and path planning algorithms.

In the future, we will raise the level of autonomy by implementing vision algorithms on the camera. Possible capabilities range from tracking of objects to the detection of suspicious behavior.

8   References

1. Holland O, Woods J, De Nardi R, Clark A: Beyond swarm intelligence: The Ultraswarm, Proceedings of the IEEE Swarm Intelligence Symposium (SIS2005), June 2005.
2. De Nardi R, Holland O, Woods J, Clark A: Swarmav: A swarm of miniature aerial vehicles. Proceedings of the 21st Bristol International UAV Systems Conference, April 2006.
3. The μDRONES Project: http://www.ist-microdrones.org.
4. Teacy W T L, Nie J, McClean S, Parr G, Hailes S, Julier S, Trigoni N, Cameron S: Collaborative Sensing by Unmanned Aerial Vehicles, Proceedings of the 3rd International Workshop on Agent Technology for Sensor Networks, May 2009, Budapest, Hungary.
5. Frost & Sullivan: Advances in platform technologies for unmanned aerial vehicles, Technical Insights Report D1B0, San Antonio, TX, 2009.

Die sechsbeinige Laufmaschine LAURON IVc

M. Ziegenmeyer, A. Rönnau, T. Kerscher, J.M. Zöllner und R. Dillmann

FZI Forschungszentrum Informatik, Intelligent Systems and Production Engineering (ISPE), Haid-und-Neu-Str. 10–14, 76131 Karlsruhe
{ziegenmeyer, roennau, kerscher, zoellner, dillmann}@fzi.de

Zusammenfassung. Die biologisch motivierte sechsbeinige Laufmaschine LAURON wurde entwickelt um in Szenarien eingesetzt zu werden, die für den Menschen zu gefährlich und für rad- oder kettengetriebene Systeme nur schwer passierbar sind. LAURON IVc ist mittlerweile die vierte Generation aus der LAURON-Laufmaschinen-Reihe. In diesem Beitrag wird ein aktueller Überblick über Hard- und Softwaresysteme der Laufmaschine LAURON IVc gegeben. Abschließend wird auf die Frage eingegangen, wie weit LAURON noch vom realen Einsatz in teileingestürzten Häusern oder dem Auffinden von Abfall in unstrukturiertem Gelände entfernt ist.

1 Einleitung

Im Gegensatz zu rad- oder kettengetriebenen Fahrzeugen, können sich Laufmaschinen in unstrukturiertem, schwierigem Gelände bewegen und komplexe Hindernisse überwinden ohne Schäden an diesen zu verursachen. Solche Maschinen eignen sich daher hervorragend für den Einsatz in Gebieten, die für rad- oder kettengetriebene Fahrzeuge schwer zugänglich und gefährlich sind oder in denen ein möglichst schonender Umgang mit der Umgebung im Vordergrund steht. Die Suche nach Verschütteten in teileingestürzten Gebäuden, die Erkundung von Vulkanen, das Räumen von Minenfeldern oder die Suche nach Abfall in ökologisch sensiblen Bereichen sind beispielhafte Szenarien, in denen zukünftig Laufmaschinen eingesetzt werden sollen.

Da es sich beim Laufen um einen natürlichen Vorgang handelt, ist es naheliegend, dass sich die Konstruktionen und Steuerungskonzepte vieler Laufmaschinen an biologischen Vorbildern orientieren. So orientiert sich zum Beispiel die sechsbeinige Laufmaschine ANTON [7] am Vorbild der Ameise. Andere Robotersysteme wie AMOS-WD06 [8], Ajax [5] und RHex [9] basieren auf Studien der amerikanischen Kakerlake. Auch die Stabheuschrecke dient für einige Systeme, wie z.B. Tarry [13] und LAURON, als Vorbild.

Die an der Stabheuschrecke orientierte sechsbeinige Laufmaschine LAURON wurde am Forschungszentrum Informatik (FZI) entwickelt um statisch stabiles Laufen in unstrukturiertem Gelände zu untersuchen. Anfang der 90er Jahre wurden in der Abteilung Interaktive Diagnose- und Servicesysteme (IDS) am FZI erste grundlegende theoretische und modellbildende Untersuchungen zum sechsbeinigen Laufen durchgeführt. Im Jahr 1994 wurde dann der erste lauffähige

Roboter LAURON (LAUfender ROboter Neuronal gesteuert) als Ergebnis dieser Untersuchungen auf der CeBIT in Hannover der Öffentlichkeit vorgestellt. Die Forschung konzentrierte sich in den ersten Jahren primär auf das Laufen in unwegsamen und schwierigen Umgebungen. Über die Jahre und Robotergenerationen hinweg wurden neben der eigentlichen Robotersteuerungssoftware auch die Mechanik und Sensorik stetig weiterentwickelt. Die aktuellste Laufmaschine, LAURON IVc, wurde im Jahr 2005 fertiggestellt (siehe Abb. 1).

Abb. 1. Die sechsbeinige Laufmaschine LAURON IVc.

In dieser Arbeit wird zunächst ein kurzer Überblick über die Hardware des aktuellen LAURON IVc-Systems gegeben. Dies umfasst den mechanischen Aufbau des Systems, die verwendete Sensorik sowie die Hardwarearchitektur. Anschließend werden wesentliche Komponenten der Steuerungssoftware vorgestellt. Hierbei wird auf die verhaltensbasierte Steuerung, die Lokalisation und Umweltmodellierung, die Navigation sowie die semantischen Missionssteuerung näher eingegangen.

2   Systemüberblick

Die Konstruktion der Laufmaschine LAURON orientiert sich am biologischen Vorbild der Stabheuschrecke. Wie dieses Vorbild besitzt sie sechs Beine an einem länglichen Zentralkörper, in dem die notwendige Steuerungselektronik untergebracht ist. Jedes der sechs identischen Beine besitzt einen federgedämpften Fuß und kann mit Hilfe von drei Gelenken bewegt werden. Zusätzlich kann die Blickrichtung des Kopfes durch zwei unabhängige Achsen (Schwenken und Neigen) verändert werden, so dass LAURON insgesamt über 20 Freiheitsgrade verfügt.

LAURON wurde mit zahlreichen Sensorsystemen ausgestattet. In jedem Fuß befinden sich 3D-Kraftsensoren und Federkraft-Messsysteme, die zusammen mit einer Motorstrommessung genutzt werden um Kollisionen und den Kontakt mit dem Boden zu erkennen. Zur Bestimmung der Orientierung und der Position verfügt LAURON über eine Inertiales Navigationssystem (INS) und einen GPS-Sensor. Zwei Kamerasysteme, ein Stereokamerasystem auf dem Kopf und eine 360°-Kamera auf dem Rücken, liefern Informationen über die Umgebung des Roboters. Eine kleine und leichte Time-of-Flight Kamera (SwissRanger SR-3000), die sich auf dem Kopf befindet, ergänzt diese Informationen um detaillierte Tiefendaten. Die Gelenkwinkel der Beine werden durch hochpräzise, optische Encoder erfasst. Zudem verfügt jeder Motor über einen hochauflösenden Encoder, der zusätzliche Informationen über die Gelenkwinkel liefert.

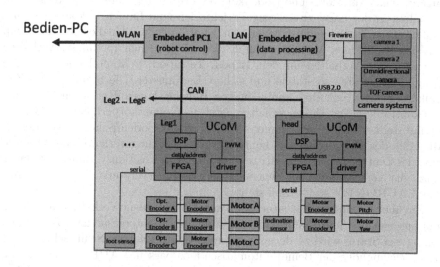

Abb. 2. Die Hardwarearchitektur von LAURON IVc.

Die Bewegungen der sechs Beine und des Kopfes werden mit Hilfe von so genannten UCoMs (Universal Controller Module) geregelt [11]. Jedes dieser sieben UCoMs verfügt unter anderem über einen eigenen DSP und FPGA. Alle UCoMs sind über einen CAN-Bus miteinander und mit dem Steuer-Rechner (PC-104 System) verbunden. Neben der PWM-basierten Motoransteuerung werden die UCoMs eingesetzt um zahlreiche Sensoren (z.B. 3D-Kraftsensoren, optische Gelenkencoder) auszulesen. Auf den UCoMs sorgt ein Geschwindigkeits-Kaskaden-Regler dafür, dass die von der verhaltensbasierten Steuerung erzeugten Beintrajektorien auch korrekt abgefahren werden. Ein Überblick über die gesamte Hardwarearchitektur kann Abb. 2 entnommen werden. Alle im Folgenden vorgestellten Komponenten der Steuerungssoftware wurden mit Hilfe des Softwarerahmenwerks MCA2 [14] realisiert.

3   Verhaltensbasierte Steuerung

Die auf LAURON IVc eingesetzte verhaltensbasierte Steuerung erzeugt und überwacht sämtliche Bewegungstrajektorien der Laufmaschine. Diese verhaltensbasierte Steuerung setzt sich aus einer großen Anzahl einfacher so genannter Basisverhalten zusammen [4], die durch Interaktion und Fusion in der Lage sind auch äußerst komplexe Aufgaben, wie das Überwinden von Hindernissen, zu bewältigen.

Die grundlegenden Schwing-Stemm-Trajektorien der Beine werden von zwei beinlokalen Verhalten, dem Schwing- und Stemmverhalten generiert. Jedes Bein verfügt über eigene beinlokale Verhalten. Zu diesen beinlokalen Verhalten gehören außerdem ein Kollisions- und Bodenkontaktverhalten. Zusammen sind diese vier Verhalten in der Lage, zuverlässig Trajektorien zum Laufen in komplexen und unstrukturierten Gebieten zu generieren. Koordiniert werden die einzelnen Gruppen der beinlokalen Verhalten durch die verschiedenen Laufmusterverhalten. Eigenständige Verhalten für den Tripod, Tetrapod, Pentapod und den freien Gang gewährleisten so stabile und sichere Laufmuster. Die Stabilität des Zentralkörpers wird von drei unabhängigen Haltungskontrollverhalten überwacht und kontrolliert. Das Höhenverhalten passt die Gesamtkörperhöhe dem Gelände an und stellt so sicher, dass immer ausreichend viel Bodenfreiheit vorhanden ist. Mit Hilfe des Neigungssensors kontrolliert das Neigungsverhalten die Orientierung des Zentralkörpers. Das dritte Verhalten, das Positionsverhalten, verlagert durch die Verschiebung des Zentralkörpers den Schwerpunkt des Roboters so, dass LAURON IVc stets stabil steht.

Ein übergeordnetes Statusverhalten nutzt verschiedene Verhaltensaktivitäten und ausgewählte Sensorinformationen um einen Robotergesamtstatus zu erzeugen. Dieser Status wird wiederum verwendet um verschieden Schlüsselparameter (z.B. Schwinghöhe der Beine) automatisch anzupassen. LAURON IVc ist so in der Lage sich auch schwierigen Situationen autonom anzupassen. Weitere Details zur verhaltensbasierten Steuerung finden sich in [4].

4   Lokalisation und Umweltmodellierung

Die Lokalisation einer Laufmaschine ist eine sehr anspruchsvolle Aufgabe. Eine rein gelenkwinkelbasierte Odometrie ist aufgrund der hohen Anzahl an Freiheitsgraden und den stets vorhandenen mechanischen Ungenauigkeiten eine sehr fehleranfällige Lokalisationsmethode. Deshalb wird auf LAURON eine Kombination aus verschiedenen Lokalisationsmethoden eingesetzt. Zum einen werden die Informationen der Odometrie mit den Daten des GPS-Sensors und des Inertialen Navigationssystems fusioniert [3]. Zum anderen werden die Tiefendaten der Time-of-Flight-Kamera dazu verwendet, zusätzlich die Position des Roboters zu bestimmen [12]. Durch diese Kombination ist es möglich, die Laufmaschine LAURON ausreichend genau zu lokalisieren.

Das eingesetzte Umweltmodell basiert auf den Daten der Tiefenbildkamera. Diese zeichnet sich besonders durch ihre kleine und leichte Bauform, ihre hohen

Datenraten und ihren verhältnismäßig niedrigen Stromverbrauch aus. Zudem liegen die erreichbaren Genauigkeiten im Bereich von einigen wenigen Millimetern. Allerdings erzeugen diese Kameras in gewissen Situationen fehlerhafte Daten, so dass vor einer weiteren Verwendung der Daten zusätzliche Vorverarbeitungsschritte notwendig sind.

Abb. 3. Nach der Filterung (z.B. Intensitätsfilter) werden die Tiefendaten in das richtige Koordinatensystem transformiert. Anschließend können sie in das Umweltmodell übernommen werden. Bei diesem Modell handelt es sich um eine gridbasierte 2,5D-Höhenkarte, welche neben der Höhe für jede Zelle auch einen Zuverlässigkeitswert speichert.

Das Umweltmodell (siehe Abbildung 3) wurde so konzipiert, dass es in der Lage ist, die großen Datenmengen (380.000 Messpunkte/Sekunde) des SwissRangers in Echtzeit in das Modell einzutragen. Weitere Informationen zum entwickelten Umweltmodell werden in [12] beschrieben.

5   Navigation

Die Navigation unterteilt sich in eine globale und eine lokale Planung. Die Aufgabe der globalen Navigationsplanung [10] besteht darin, anhand einer grobaufgelösten Umgebungskarte Pfade zum Erreichen von Zielpunkten und zum systematischen Absuchen von Regionen zu planen. Als probabilistisches Bahnplanungsverfahren werden hierfür so genannte *Rapidly Exploring Random Trees* (RRTs) verwendet. Mit Hilfe der RRTs ist es möglich, Pfade zu mehreren Zielen gleichzeitig zu berechnen sowie zusätzliche Parameter, wie z.B. den Energieverbrauch, bei der Planung zu berücksichtigen. Zum systematischen Absuchen von Regionen wird ein auf einem numerischen Potentialfeldverfahren basierender Ansatz verwendet.

Die von der globalen Navigationsplanung erzeugten Pfade berücksichtigen keine dynamischen Hindernisse und dienen daher lediglich zur Generierung von Zwischenpunkten. Die Navigation zwischen diesen Zwischenpunkten wird von der lokalen Navigationsplanung übernommen, welche mit Hilfe des lokalen, hochaufgelösten Umweltmodells und einer Potentialfeldmethode [2] geeignete Pfade bestimmt.

Mit Hilfe der Kombination aus globaler und lokaler Navigationsplanung kann sich LAURON IVc auch in unbekannten oder nur teilweise bekannten Gebieten sicherer bewegen und dabei sowohl im Voraus bekannte als auch dynamische Hindernisse berücksichtigen.

6   Semantische Missionssteuerung

Ziel der semantischen Missionssteuerung [16] ist die autonome Durchführung von Inspektionsmissionen mit LAURON IVc. Wesentliche Idee hierbei ist, dem System menschliches Expertenwissen in Form eines semantischen Inspektionsmodells zur Verfügung zu stellen. Als konkretes Inspektionsszenario wird die Detektion und Klassifikation von Abfall in unstrukturiertem Gelände, wie z.B. Wiesen, Wäldern und Böschungen von vielbefahrenen Straßen, Flüssen und Kanälen untersucht.

Die Architektur der semantischen Missionssteuerung wurde bereits in [15] vorgestellt. Zentrales Element der Missionssteuerung ist die Wissensbasis, welche das für die Durchführung von autonomen Inspektionsmissionen benötigte Wissen enthält. Die Wissensbasis besteht aus mehreren Ontologien und ist in drei Abstraktionsebenen unterteilt: eine Basisontologie, eine Kernontologie und eine Domänenontologie (siehe Abb. 4).

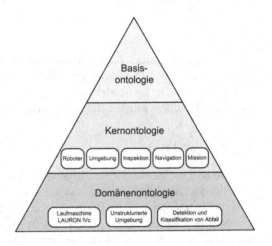

Abb. 4. Die Struktur der Wissensbasis. Die Basisontologie umfasst grundlegende Konzepte wie Parameter, Zeitstempel, Bedingung und Datentyp. Die Kernontologie enthält die Unterontologien *Roboter, Umgebung, Inspektion, Navigation* und *Mission,* welche die zentralen Konzepte und Relationen des jeweiligen Themenfelds modellieren. Die Domänenontologie enthält die applikationsspezifischen Unterontologien *LAURON IVc, Unstrukturierte Umgebung* und *Detektion und Klassifikation von Abfall.*

Die Inspektion von komplexen Umgebungen erfolgt in Zyklen von Inspektionsplanung, Planausführung, Bewertung der Datenauswertungsergebnisse, Entscheidungsfindung und Neuplanung. Für die Repräsentation von Inspektionsplänen werden so genannte *Flexible Programme* (FPs) [6] verwendet, welche an Hierarchische Aufgabennetzwerke angelehnt sind. Ein Inspektionsplan besteht somit aus einem Baum von Knoten.

Zur Inspektionsplanung wird ein hierarchischer Ansatz verwendet, der komplexe Inspektionsaufgaben rekursiv in einfachere Unteraufgaben zerlegt, bis diese mit Elementaraktionen gelöst werden können. Das für die Zerlegung notwendige Wissen ist in Form der verfügbaren FP Knoten in der Wissensbasis gespeichert. Für jede Aufgabe wird ein entsprechender Wurzelknoten ausgewählt und in Abhängigkeit von der aktuellen Situation rekursiv in ein ausführbares Flexibles Programm zerlegt. Während der Ausführung wird das Flexible Programm gemäß einer Tiefensuchstrategie abgearbeitet.

Für die Bewertung der Datenauswertungsergebnisse und die Entscheidungs-findung werden Bayes'sche Entscheidungsnetzwerke verwendet. Die verfügbaren Entscheidungsoptionen korrespondieren hierbei mit in der Wissensbasis gespeicherten Inspektionsaufgaben. Die ausgewählten Inspektionsaufgaben werden entsprechend ihrer Prioritäten und Ressourcenanforderungen in den Gesamtinspektionsplan integriert, indem der Planungsprozess für diese erneut aufgerufen wird.

Die bildbasierte Erkennung von Abfall in unstrukturiertem Gelände wird mit Hilfe eines aufmerksamkeitsbasierten Ansatzes [1] realisiert. Zur Berechnung von so genannten Auffälligkeitskarten (engl. *saliency maps*) wird die iNVT Bibliothek[1] eingesetzt. Die so gewonnenen Aufmerksamkeitsbereiche werden anschließend mittels eines merkmalsbasierten Klassifikationsansatzes auf das Vorhandensein von Abfallobjekten überprüft. Als Merkmale werden Farbverbundhistogramme (engl. *color-co-occurence histogram*, CCH), Lokale Binäre Muster (engl. *local binary patterns*, LBP) sowie lokal invariante SURF-Deskriptoren (engl. *speeded up robust features*, SURF) verwendet. Die Klassifikation erfolgt mittels Support Vektor Maschinen (SVMs).

Die semantische Missionssteuerung ist ein wichtiger Schritt auf dem Weg zur Anwendung für die sechsbeinige Laufmaschine LAURON. Mit ihrer Hilfe können erste autonome Inspektionsmissionen, wie das Auffinden von Abfall in unstrukturiertem Gelände, untersucht und prototypisch umgesetzt werden. Weitere Informationen zur semantischen Missionssteuerung finden sich in [16].

7   Zusammenfassung und Ausblick

Die robustere Mechanik und die verhaltensbasierte Steuerung ermöglichen es LAURON IVc sich flexibel an unbekannte Situationen anzupassen und sich in unebenem und unstrukturiertem Gelände zu bewegen. Mit Hilfe der beschriebenen Verfahren zur Lokalisation, Umweltmodellierung und Navigation ist es LAURON IVc zudem prinzipiell möglich, autonom vorgegebene Zielpunkte zu erreichen und vorgegebene Regionen systematisch abzusuchen und dabei sowohl im Voraus bekannte als auch dynamische Hindernisse zu berücksichtigten. Die semantische Missionssteuerung ermöglicht es darüber hinaus, erste autonome Inspektionsmissionen, wie zum Beispiel das Auffinden von Abfall in unstrukturiertem Gelände, zu untersuchen und prototypisch umzusetzen. Somit ist die aktuelle Generation der LAURON-Laufmaschinen-Reihe dem realen Einsatz in schwierigen Szenarien ein gutes Stück näher gekommen.

Basierend auf den mit LAURON IVc gesammelten Erfahrungen, befindet sich die nächste Generation der erfolgreichen Laufmaschinen-Reihe bereits in der Planung und Entwicklung. Diese nächste Generation soll über eine noch robustere Mechanik, zusätzliche Sensorik, sowie weitere Freiheitsgrade verfügen. Dadurch wird diese zukünftige Laufmaschine noch vielseitiger einsetzbar sein und die biologisch motivierten Laufmaschinen im Allgemeinen einen weiteren Schritt in Richtung realer Anwendungen bringen.

---

[1] iLab Neuromorphic Vision C++ Toolkit, http://ilab.usc.edu/toolkit/

Literaturverzeichnis

1. B. Bertram. *Bildbasierte Methoden zur Erkennung von Abfall in unstrukturiertem Gelände.* Diplomarbeit, FZI Forschungszentrum Informatik an der Universität Karlsruhe (TH), 2009.
2. B. Gaßmann. *Modellbasierte, sensorgestützte Navigation von Laufmaschinen im Gelände.* Dissertation, Fakultät für Informatik, FZI Forschungszentrum Informatik an der Universität Karlsruhe (TH), 2007.
3. B. Gaßmann, F. Zacharias, J. M. Zöllner, and R. Dillmann. Localization of walking robots. In *Proceedings of the IEEE International Conference on Robotics and Automation*, 2005.
4. T. Kerscher, A. Rönnau, M. Ziegenmeyer, B. Gaßmann, and et al. Behaviour-based control of a six-legged walking machine LAURON IVc. In *Proceedings of CLAWAR2008, 11th International Conference on Climbing and Walking Robots*, 2008.
5. D. A. Kingsley, R. D. Quinn, and R. E. Ritzmann. Cockroach inspired robot with artificial muscles. In *Proceedings International Symposium on Adaptive Motion of Animals and Machines (AMAM2003)*, 2003.
6. S. Knoop. *Interaktive Erstellung und Ausführung von Handlungswissen für einen Serviceroboter.* Dissertation, Fakultät für Informatik, Institut für Technische Informatik (ITEC), Universität Karlsruhe (TH), 2007.
7. M. Konyev, F. Palis, Y. Zavgorodniy, A. Melnikov, A. Rudskiy, and A. Telesh. Walking robot ANTON: Design, simulation, experiments. In *Proceedings of CLAWAR 2008, 11th International Conference on Climbing and Walking Robots*, 2008.
8. P. Manoonpong and F. Woergoetter. Neural control for locomotion of walking machines. In *Proceedings of 4th International Symposium on Adaptive Motion of Animals and Machines (AMAM2008)*, 2008.
9. E. Z. Moore and M. Buehler. Stable stair climbing in a simple hexapod robot. In *Proceedings of CLAWAR 2001, International Conference on Climbing and Walking Robots*, 2001.
10. L. Pfotzer. *Entwicklung einer Navigationsplanung zur Inspektion von komplexen Umgebungen mit einem sechsbeinigen Laufroboter.* Diplomarbeit, FZI Forschungszentrum Informatik an der Universität Karlsruhe (TH), 2009.
11. K. Regenstein, T. Kerscher, and C. Birkenhofer et al. Universal controller module (ucom) - component of a modular concept in robotic systems. In *Proceedings of 2007 IEEE International Symposium on Industrial Electronics*, 2007.
12. A. Rönnau, T. Kerscher, M. Ziegenmeyer, and et al. Adaptation of a six-legged walking robot to its local environment. In *Seventh International Workshop on Robot Motion and Control, RoMoCo'09*, 2009.
13. J. Schmitz, A. Schneider, M. Schilling, and H. Cruse. No need for a body model: Positive velocity feedback for the control of an 18-dof robot walker. *Applied Bionics and Biomechanics*, 2008.
14. K. Uhl and M. Ziegenmeyer. MCA2 - an extensible modular framework for robot control applications. In *Proceedings of CLAWAR, 10th International Conference on Climbing and Walking Robots*, 2007.
15. K. Uhl, M. Ziegenmeyer, B. Gaßmann, J. M. Zöllner, and R. Dillmann. Entwurf einer semantischen Missionssteuerung für autonome Serviceroboter. In *Fachgespräche Autonome Mobile Systeme*, 2007.
16. M. Ziegenmeyer, K. Uhl, J. M. Zöllner, and R. Dillmann. Autonomous Inspection of Complex Environments by Means of Semantic Techniques. In *Workshop on Artificial Intelligence Applications in Environmental Protection (AIAEP)*, 2009.

Dynamic Bayesian Network Library
Ein C++ Framework für Berechnungen auf dynamischen Bayes'schen Netzen

Ralf Kohlhaas, Ferdinand Szekeresch, Tobias Gindele und Rüdiger Dillmann

Institut für Anthropomatik, Universität Karlsruhe (TH), 76128 Karlsruhe
{ralf.kohlhaas, ferdinand.szekeresch}@student.kit.edu
{gindele, dillmann}@ira.uka.de

Zusammenfassung. Anwendungen, wie sie beispielsweise bei autonomen, mobilen Systemen vorkommen, erfordern die Bearbeitung und Auswertung von heterogenen, unsicheren Messwerten. Probabilistische Ansätze bieten die Möglichkeit, derartige Probleme zu lösen. Präsentiert wird die DBNL, eine C++ Bibliothek, welche die Repräsentation und Inferenz von dynamischen, hybriden Bayes'schen Netzen in komfortabler Weise ermöglicht. Zu den Stärken der DBNL zählen ihre modulare Architektur, die flexible Formulierung von Anfragen, die Unterstützung von beliebigen, benutzerdefinierten Übergangsfunktionen sowie die einfache Erweiterbarkeit um neue Inferenzalgorithmen und Wahrscheinlichkeitsverteilungen.

1 Stand der Technik

1.1 Bayes'sche Netze

Um Vorgänge, die sich in der Natur abspielen, modellieren zu können, bedarf es stets einer geeigneten Repräsentation. Hinter jeder dieser Repräsentationen steht die Zielsetzung, komplexe Vorgänge derart zu abstrahieren, dass mathematische Berechnungen auf dem zugrunde liegenden Zustandsraum möglich werden. Eine mögliche Repräsentation dieser Art ist das Bayes'sche Netz (BN):

Ein BN [1] ist ein gerichteter, azyklischer Graph, dessen Knoten einzelne Variablen darstellen, während die Kanten die bedingten Abhängigkeiten der Knoten untereinander repräsentieren. Es ist somit eine faktorisierte Darstellung der Verbundwahrscheinlichkeit der dargestellten Variablen. Besitzen zwei Knoten keine direkte Verbindung im Netz, so hängen sie nicht direkt voneinander ab.

Ein dynamisches Bayes'sches Netz (DBN) [2] ist ein rekursives BN (Abbildung 4). Es wird also auch die zeitliche Entwicklung der Zufallsvariablen modelliert. Dynamisch bedeutet in diesem Zusammenhang i. A. nicht, dass die Topologie des Netzes sich über die Zeit ändert, sondern nur die Verteilungen der jeweiligen Zufallsvariablen. Dennoch kann es von Nutzen sein, auch solche Veränderungen zu erlauben.

Die Hauptaufgaben bei der Inferenz auf DBNs sind folgende [2]: das Inferieren von Verteilungen von Zeitpunkten, die in der Vergangenheit liegen, unter

Zuhilfenahme neuerer Messwerte (Glätten), das Inferieren von Verteilungen zum aktuellen Zeitpunkt (Filtern) sowie das Inferieren von Verteilungen in der Zukunft, für die noch keine Messwerte vorliegen (Prädizieren).

Einige Spezialfälle des DBN sind das Hidden Markov Model (HMM) [2] und das Kalman Filter Model (KFM) [2]. In einem HMM werden die nicht messbaren Knoten nicht als individuelle Objekte betrachtet, sondern als eine einzige Zufallsvariable. In einem KFM wird angenommen, dass die bedingten Wahrscheinlichkeitsdichtefunktionen lineare Funktionen mit additivem Rauschen sind und die Verteilungen sich durch die ersten beiden stochastischen Momente beschreiben lassen.

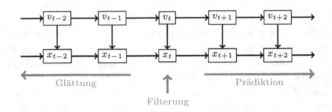

Abb. 1. Die Inferenzaufgaben - Glättung, Filterung, Prädiktion

1.2   Andere C++ Bibliotheken zur probabilistischen Inferenz

Die BAT Bibliothek [3] bietet Werkzeuge zur Modellierung und Inferenz von BNs an. BAT unterstützt benutzerdefinierte Funktionen, welche die Bibliothek sehr flexibel machen. Eine weitere, angenehme Fähigkeit ist die Unterstützung verschiedener Modelle für eine Problemstellung sowie die anschließende Bewertung dieser.

Auch SMILE [4] ist eine Bibliothek, die Inferenz auf BNs ermöglicht. Allerdings beschränkt sich SMILE auf statische Netze sowie diskrete Wertebereiche.

Die frühere Intel PNL Bibliothek [5], die unter dem Namen openpnl eine Zeit lang weitergeführt wurde, unterstützte sowohl kontinuierliche Wertebereiche als auch dynamische Netze. Sie schöpfte jedoch die Möglichkeiten, die durch C++ geboten werden, nicht aus. Leider wird die openpnl nicht mehr weiter entwickelt.

Die dLib C++ Bibliothek [6] realisiert exakte Inferenz und Gibbs Sampling auf BNs mit diskreten Knoten.

Die ProBT C++ Bibliothek [7] bietet Werkzeuge zur probabilistischen Inferenz auf statischen und dynamischen BNs an, es werden diskrete und kontinuierliche Wertebereiche unterstützt. Leider ist ProBT nicht frei erhältlich.

Generell schränken viele erhältliche Bibliotheken die Wertebereiche der Zufallsvariablen ein und bieten wenig Unterstützung für die Modellierung dynamischer Netze. Dadurch sind sie oftmals nur für spezielle Anwendungsbereiche geeignet. Die Modellierung von Übergangsfunktionen auf kontinuierlichen Wertebereichen wird oftmals nicht realisiert, besonders hybride Netze werden selten unterstützt.

2 Konzept

Die Dynamic Bayesian Network Library (DBNL) ist eine umfangreiche C++ Bibliothek zur Generierung von DBNs und zur Inferenz auf diesen. Sie verzichtet auf häufig anzutreffende Limitierungen, wie Vorgaben über die verwendeten Verteilungsfunktionen oder Beschränkungen der Zufallsvariablen auf diskrete Werte. Durch die Unterstützung benutzerdefinierter Funktionen zur Abbildung der lokalen bedingten Wahrscheinlichkeiten werden diskrete, kontinuierliche und hybride Netze unterstützt. Das verwendete Konzept ermöglicht das Fortschreiben des Netzes über beliebig viele Zeitschritte hinweg. Auch eine Modifikation der Netztopologie zwischen zwei Zeitschritten ist möglich. In der aktuellen Version ist ein partikelbasierter Inferenzalgorithmus mit Likelihood Weighting [8] implementiert. Durch die klare Modularisierung ist eine Erweiterung um andere Inferenzalgorithmen leicht möglich.

Abgerundet wird die DBNL durch eine graphische Benutzeroberfläche, die mit Hilfe des Qt Frameworks [9] realisiert wurde. Sie erlaubt das Visualisieren der Netze sowie der inferierten Verteilungen. Neben dem C++ Interface wird auch ein XML-Parser angeboten, der das Laden von Modellen aus XML-Dateien erlaubt. Hierfür wurden schon zahlreiche Übergangsfunktionen implementiert. Des Weiteren steht die Möglichkeit zur Verfügung, verschiedene Funktionen zu einer Übergangsfunktion zu kombinieren.

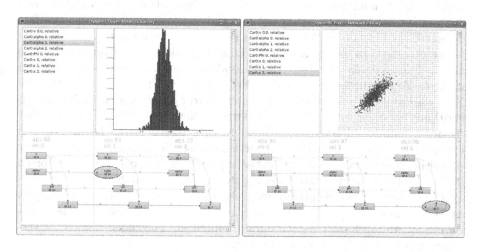

Abb. 2. Die graphische Benutzeroberfläche der DBNL

2.1 Struktur der DBNL

Die DBNL ist hierarchisch aufgebaut. Die untere Ebene bildet das BN, repräsentiert durch einen Graph und lokale (bedingte) Wahrscheinlichkeitsverteilungen. Auf diesem arbeitet ein Inferenzalgorithmus. An ein Netz können verschiedene Anfragen gestellt werden, die Gruppen von zu observierenden Knoten sowie Informationen über priore Verteilungen und Evidenzen enthalten. Durch alle Hierarchieebenen hindurch ist die Bibliothek zusätzlich in einen statischen und einen dynamischen Teil untergliedert. Die grobe Struktur und Kommunikationswege sind in Abbildung 3 dargestellt.

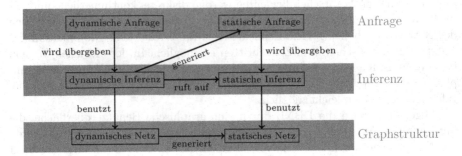

Abb. 3. Die Struktur der DBNL

Die einzelnen Komponenten arbeiten auf unterschiedliche Weise zusammen. Die dynamischen Komponenten wie Anfrage, Inferenzalgorithmus und Netz werden von der Benutzerapplikation angelegt und angesteuert. Dabei wird aus dem dynamischen Netz durch Ausrollen ein statisches Netz für den aktuellen Zeitpunkt generiert. In jedem Zeitschritt können Modifikationen an der Anfrage durchgeführt werden. So können z. B. Evidenzen hinzugefügt werden. Danach kann ein Zeitschritt im dynamischen Netz durchgeführt werden. Das statische Netz wird automatisch aktualisiert. Durch Aufruf des dynamischen Inferenzalgorithmus wird die Anfrage auf dem aktuellen Netz bearbeitet. Hierzu wandelt sie der dynamische Inferenzalgorithmus in eine aktuelle statische Anfrage um und übergibt diese zur Bearbeitung an den statischen Inferenzalgorithmus. Der Algorithmus arbeitet sie auf dem statischen Netz ab. Die generierten Antworten laufen in die entgegengesetzte Richtung zurück zur dynamischen Anfrage.

Diese Modularisierung erlaubt es, einzelne Komponenten auszutauschen. So ist es z. B. möglich, verschiedene Inferenzalgorithmen einzusetzen, ohne Änderungen an Anfragen oder Netzen durchzuführen. Im Folgenden werden die verschiedenen Komponenten der DBNL vorgestellt.

2.2 Statische Netze

In einem statischen BN wird die zeitliche Entwicklung der einzelnen Knoten nicht berücksichtigt. Es ist gewissermaßen eine Momentaufnahme der Situation. Für die Modellierung eines solchen Netzes stützt sich die DBNL auf die Boost Graph Library (BGL) [10]. Merkmale, wie z. B. bedingte Wahrscheinlichkeitsverteilungen wurden ergänzt.

Die bedingten Wahrscheinlichkeiten werden durch lokale Übergangsfunktionen modelliert. Diese weisen dem zugehörigen Knoten für jede Belegung der Elternknoten eine Wahrscheinlichkeitsverteilung zu. So kann z. B. eine Übergangsfunktion erstellt werden, die dem Knoten eine Normalverteilung zuweist, deren Mittelwert und Varianz auf Basis der Zustände der Elternknoten berechnet wird. Übergangsfunktionen können vom Benutzer selbst erstellt werden und sind in ihrer Mächtigkeit nicht durch die DBNL beschränkt.

2.3 Dynamische Netze

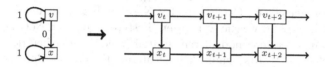

Abb. 4. Einfache Positionsschätzung - Dynamisches Bayes'sches Netz und Ausschnitt des ausgerollten Dynamischen Bayes'schen Netzes

Die Hauptaufgabe der DBNL ist die Modellierung und Inferenz auf DBNs. Der übliche Ansatz bei einer solchen Modellierung ist es, ein prototypisches Netz anzugeben, das die Länge der längsten zeitlichen Abhängigkeiten haben muss. Dafür werden mehrere Instanzen jeder Zufallsvariablen benötigt. Bei dieser Art der Modellierung wird viel Flexibilität eingebüßt.

In der DBNL wird eine zeitlich veränderliche Zufallsvariable als ein einziges Objekt interpretiert. Die lokalen Abhängigkeiten werden auf diesen Objekten definiert. Dabei wird immer auch der zeitliche Versatz der Abhängigkeit angegeben. Sowohl für Zufallsvariablen als auch für Abhängigkeiten können Gültigkeitsintervalle definiert werden. Dies ermöglicht sowohl das einfache Konstruieren des Netzes als auch das Ändern der Netztopologie zur Laufzeit und bietet ein großes Maß an Flexibilität. Bei der Beobachtung von Situationen im Straßenverkehr wird es hierdurch möglich, die Anzahl der Knoten je nach Anzahl der erfassten Verkehrsteilnehmer zu variieren. Insbesondere ist die zeitliche Ausdehnung des Netzes nicht festgelegt, was u. A. zur Folge hat, dass auch Markov-Annahmen höherer Ordnung unterstützt werden.

2.4 Anfragen

An ein statisches BN können verschiedene Anfragen gestellt werden. Eine Anfrage beinhaltet die prioren Verteilungen der Knoten, Evidenzen für einzelne Knoten sowie Gruppen von Knoten, deren Verteilung inferiert werden soll. Für jede Knotengruppe aus der Anfrage wird während des Inferenzvorgangs eine Verbundwahrscheinlichkeitsverteilung ermittelt und als Antwort zur Verfügung gestellt.

Im Allgemeinen müssen für alle Knoten, die keine Elternknoten besitzen, priore Wahrscheinlichkeitsdichtefunktionen angegeben werden. Für statische Netze ist es in der DBNL nicht unbedingt nötig, priore Verteilungen in der Anfrage anzugeben, da diese auch als argumentlose Übergangsfunktionen bei der Generierung des Netzes definiert werden können. Es ist jedoch trotzdem möglich, für beliebige Knoten priore Übergangsfunktionen zu definieren. In diesem Fall wird bei der Inferenz die Übergangsfunktion eines Knotens ignoriert und an ihrer Stelle die priore Übergangsfunktion verwendet. In der Regel sind solche Übergangsfunktionen argumentlos. Für spezielle Anwendungen sind aber auch Funktionen denkbar, die Elternknoten voraussetzen.

Evidenzen ordnen ebenfalls einem Knoten eine Übergangsfunktion zu. Diese darf jedoch nicht von Elternknoten abhängen. Evidenzen werden eingesetzt, um Wissen über gemessene Größen in das Netz einfließen zu lassen. Die DBNL unterstützt harte und weiche Evidenzen. Erstere fügen dem Netz einen exakten Messwert hinzu, letztere modellieren zusätzlich die Unsicherheit des Messwertes. Es sind beliebige Wahrscheinlichkeitsdichtefunktionen zur Repräsentation der Unsicherheit verwendbar.

Bei der Betrachtung eines dynamisch fortschreitenden Netzes werden umfangreiche Anfragemöglichkeiten benötigt. Diese werden in einer dynamischen Anfrage zusammengefasst. Hier werden Knoten nicht mehr als absolute Objekte eines statischen Netzes adressiert. Ein Knoten wird über den ihm zugrunde liegenenden dynamischen Knoten und eine absolute oder relative Zeitangabe festgelegt. Dieses Konzept wird auf priore Verteilungen, Evidenzen und zu inferierende Knoten angewendet. Bei Evidenzen und prioren Verteilungen ist es häufig sinnvoll, diese für einen absoluten Zeitpunkt zu definieren. Für die Observation von Knoten sind jedoch beide Möglichkeiten von praktischer Relevanz.

2.5 Inferenz

Für die Inferenz auf DBNs wird durch den dynamischen Inferenzalgorithmus ein statisches BN generiert („ausgerollt"), auf welchem die statische Inferenz stattfindet. Dabei wird für jeden dynamischen Knoten für den betrachteten Zeitraum eine Serie von statischen Knoten generiert. Die Kanten des BN werden entsprechend der dynamischen Abhängigkeiten gesetzt. Durch die Rückführung des DBN auf ein BN wird für verschiedene Inferenzverfahren nur jeweils ein Algorithmus zur Inferenz statischer Netze benötigt. Abbildung 4 zeigt ein dynamisches Netz und einen Ausschnitt des zugehörigen statischen Netzes.

Beim Fortschreiben des Netzes zum nächsten Zeitpunkt wird das statische BN nicht neu generiert. Es fallen lediglich alte Knoten weg und es werden neue für den nächsten zu betrachtenden Zeitschritt hinzugefügt. Hierbei können Inkonsistenzen am Ende des Netzes auftreten, wenn sich Abhängigkeiten zu Elternknoten über mehrere Zeitschritte verteilen und Inferenzergebnisse des letzten Zeitschrittes verloren gehen. Dies wird durch temporäres Speichern der wegfallenden Knoten sowie Hinzufügen spezieller priorer Übergangsfunktionen zur statischen Anfrage aufgelöst.

Im Hinblick auf heterogene Daten und nicht-lineare Übergänge wurde ein statischer Inferenzalgorithmus implementiert, der auf einer Monte-Carlo Methode basiert und Likelihood Weighting verwendet. Likelihood Weighting ist eine Form von Importance Sampling, bei der als Importance Funktion evtl. vorhandene Evidenzen oder priore Verteilungen bzw. bedingte Wahrscheinlichkeitsverteilungen verwendet werden. Dieses Verfahren bietet bei vielen praktischen Anwendungen eine schnelles Konvergenzverhalten.

Der verwendete Algorithmus lässt sich gut parallelisieren. Es ist mit einer annähernd linearen Skalierung mit der Anzahl der Prozessoren zu rechnen. Vor allem bei großen Netzen konnte auf Mehrkernsystemen bereits eine vielversprechende Geschwindigkeitssteigerung verzeichnet werden. Weitere Inferenzalgorithmen sind bis dato noch nicht implementiert, allerdings stellt die DBNL ein komfortables, benutzerfreundliches Interface für weitere Algorithmen zur Verfügung.

3 Evaluation

Die DBNL wurde bereits im Bereich der Positionsschätzung und -prädiktion von (beobachteten) Verkehrsteilnehmern mit Erfolg eingesetzt. In der Anwendung wurde Lage, Geschwindigkeit und Lenkwinkel eines simulierten Fahrzeuges gefiltert und in die Zukunft prädiziert. Abbildung 5a zeigt die Prädiktion einer nicht-linearen Trajektorie. Unsicherheiten werden durch Varianz-Ellipsen dargestellt. Das Laufzeitverhalten der zugehörigen partikelbasierten Inferenz wurde gemessen und beschreibt einen linearen Anstieg mit der Anzahl der Knoten im Netz (siehe Abbildung 5b). Erste Tests mit parallelisierten Inferenzalgorithmen zeigen vielversprechende Resultate.

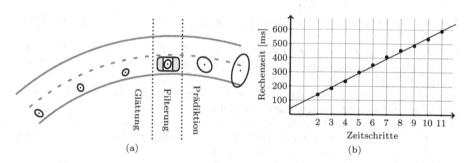

Abb. 5. Filterung der Position eines Fahrzeugs mit dynamischem Netz aus 4 Knoten pro Zeitschritt und 1000 Samples pro Verteilung

4 Ausblick

Die DBNL ist ein umfangreiches Werkzeug zur Modellierung und Inferenz auf DBNs. Sie ist modular und sehr flexibel in der Anwendung gestaltet. Es ste-

240 R. Kohlhaas et al.

hen mehrere Verteilungstypen und kombinierbare Übergangsfunktionen sowie
ein partikelbasierter Inferenzalgorithmus zur Verfügung. Für die Zukunft ist
die Optimierung des bestehenden Algorithmus sowie Implementierung weiterer Inferenzalgorithmen geplant. Darunter fallen sowohl exakte Verfahren, als
auch gemischte (Rao Blackwellisierte [2]) Algorithmen. Mit der Parallelisierung
der eingesetzten Algorithmen wurde bereits begonnen. Im Hinblick auf aktuelle
Mehrkernprozessoren ist hier großes Potential vorhanden. Durch den Einsatz in
unterschiedlichen Gebieten werden mehr vorgefertigte Übergangsfunktionen und
Wahrscheinlichkeitsverteilungen implementiert werden. Ein weiteres interessantes Gebiet, das bisher noch nicht abgedeckt wird, ist das Lernen von Parametern
der Übergangsfunktionen und Netztopologien.

Danksagung

Diese Arbeit wurde von der Deutschen Forschungsgemeinschaft (DFG) im Rahmen des Sonderforschungsbereiches "SFB/TR-28 Kognitive Automobile" gefördert.

Literaturverzeichnis

1. Judea Pearl: *Probabilistic Reasoning in Intelligent Systems*, 1988, Revised second printing, Morgan Kauffmann Publishers Inc.
2. Kevin P. Murphy: *Dynamic Bayesian Networks: Representation, Inference and Learning*, 2002, University of California, Berkeley.
3. http://www.mppmu.mpg.de/bat/, Internetseite der BAT Bibliothek, 07.07.2009
4. http://genie.sis.pitt.edu/wiki/SMILE_Documentation, Dokumentation der SMILE Bibliothek, 07.07.2009
5. http://sourceforge.net/projects/openpnl/, Internetseite der openpnl Bibliothek 07.07.2009
6. http://dclib.sourceforge.net/, Internetseite der dLib Bibliothek, 07.07.2009
7. http://emotion.inrialpes.fr/BP/spip.php?rubrique6, Internetseite der ProBT Bibliothek, 07.07.2009
8. Haipeng Guo and William Hsu: *A survey of algorithms for real-time bayesian network inference*, 2002, Kansas State University.
9. http://www.qtsoftware.com/ Internetseite von Qt-Software, 08.07.2009
10. http://www.boost.org/doc/libs/1_39_0/libs/graph/doc/index.html, Internetseite der Boost Graph Library, 08.07.2009

Modellgetriebene Softwareentwicklung für Robotiksysteme

Andreas Steck, Dennis Stampfer und Christian Schlegel

Hochschule Ulm
Fakultät Informatik*, Prittwitzstr. 10, 89075 Ulm
{steck,stampfer,schlegel}@hs-ulm.de

Zusammenfassung. Die Erschließung breiter Anwendungspotenziale für Serviceroboter erfordert den Schritt weg von manuell erstellten Einzelentwürfen hin zu baukastenartig zusammengesetzten Systemen. Grundlegend hierfür ist der Schritt weg von codezentrierten hin zu modellgetriebenen Systemen. In modellgetriebenen Ansätzen wird langlebiges Lösungswissen von kurzlebigen Implementierungstechnologien entkoppelt. Durch das Explizieren von Eigenschaften wie Ressourcenbedarf und Kommunikationsverhalten wird die Systemebene adressiert, so dass Zusammensetzbarkeit von ausgereiften Komponenten ebenso unterstützt werden kann wie der Nachweis von Systemeigenschaften. Die so möglichen ressourcenadäquaten Lösungen mit zugesicherten Eigenschaften und der Wiederverwendung ausgereifter Lösungen wird als grundlegend für die effiziente Umsetzung der geforderten Qualitätsmaßstäbe vieler zukünftiger Servicerobotikapplikationen gesehen. Diese Arbeit beschreibt die Umsetzung eines modellgetriebenen Softwareentwicklungsprozesses in OpenArchitectureWare auf der Basis eines Komponentenansatzes und eines Ausführungscontainers, der beispielsweise völlig unabhängig von der Middleware ist.

1 Einleitung

Obwohl Software einen großen Einfluss auf die Entwicklung von Robotiksystemen hat, werden die meisten Systeme dennoch von Hand programmiert. Dabei hat sich in anderen Domänen, wie der Automobilindustrie und der Avionik, längst gezeigt, dass der modellgetriebene Ansatz einen vielversprechenden Weg bietet, um die stetig steigende Komplexität beherrschen zu können. Entscheidend für diesen modellgetriebenen Ansatz ist die Verwendung eines komponentenbasierten Frameworks. Es bildet den Schlüssel zum Erfolg, um Systeme aus mehreren wiederverwendbaren Bausteinen zusammenzusetzen. In diesem Artikel wird der Weg zur modellgetriebenen Softwareentwicklung für die Robotik vorgestellt. Es werden die Schritte von der abstrakten Repräsentation zum ausführbaren Code dargestellt und anhand eines Beispiels verdeutlicht.

---

* Zentrum für angewandte Forschung an Fachhochschulen Servicerobotik (ZAFH Servicerobotik) http://www.zafh-servicerobotik.de/

2   Motivation und Stand der Technik

Durch grundsätzliche Mängel in der Softwareentwicklung von Robotersystemen werden die vorhandenen Fähigkeiten der Community nicht ausreichend genutzt. So ist die Wiederverwendung von Software meist nur auf der Ebene von Bibliotheken möglich. Die Möglichkeit, Software als Komponenten-Bausteine mit garantierten Services und Funktionalitäten zu nutzen, findet dabei bisher keine ausreichende Verbreitung. Um die zunehmende Komplexität zu beherrschen, ist daher ein hoher Grad an Wiederverwendbarkeit durch ein solches Baukastensystem anzustreben. Bei der Integration der einzelnen Bestandteile zu einem Gesamtsystem wird häufig auf einer unzureichenden oder keiner Basis aufgebaut. Der Aufwand und die Qualität der Integration hängt dann von den Möglichkeiten der Middleware ab. Dieses Vorgehen ist teuer und kostet den Entwickler unnötig viel Zeit, die an anderer Stelle sinnvoller investiert wäre.

Der Schritt von der codegetriebenen zur modellgetriebenen Softwareentwicklung ist entscheidend, um die genannten Schwierigkeiten zu lösen. Zusätzlich können auf der Modellebene komfortabel komponentenbasierte Systeme entworfen werden. Die Services können mit Contracts versehen und später mit geeigneter Toolunterstützung verifiziert werden. Bereits während der Entwicklung wird so verifiziert, ob das Zielsystem beispielsweise garantierte Antwortzeiten oder Ressourcenbeschränkungen (*Resource-Awareness*) einhalten kann. Es können Sicherheitsaspekte einbezogen und *Quality of Service (QoS)*-Parameter expliziert werden.

Im Bereich *distributed real-time und embedded (DRE)* gibt es Anforderungen aus der Automobilindustrie und Avionik, die vergleichbar komplex zur Robotik sind. Dort werden ähnliche Fragestellungen beispielsweise vom *Artist2 Network of Excellence on Embedded Systems Design* [1] bezüglich Echtzeitkomponenten und Echtzeit-Ausführungsumgebungen behandelt. Durch die *OMG MARTE* [2] Initiative wird ein standardisiertes UML Profil zur Entwicklung von *DRE* Systemen zur Verfügung gestellt. Die Komponenteninteraktionen sind sehr generisch beschrieben. Die Granularität, wie ein komplexes System aus seinen Bestandteilen zusammengesetzt wird, ist nicht eindeutig festgelegt und lässt sehr viel Spielraum. Unsere Konzepte dagegen leiten den Entwickler durch den vorgegebenen Rahmen an, ohne dabei die Freiheiten einzuschränken.

Die Automobilindustrie ist dabei, den *AUTOSAR* Standard [3] für Softwarekomponenten und den modellgetriebenen Entwurf zu etablieren. Dort werden Fragestellungen behandelt, die auch in der Servicerobotik in ähnlicher Form relevant sein können.

Die *OMG Robotics Domain Task Force* [4] arbeitet an einem modellgetriebenen Standard zur Integration von Robotiksystemen aus modularen Komponenten. Die Komponenten verfügen wie in unserem Komponentenmodell über einen internen Zustandsautomaten und interagieren über Serviceports. Diese Ports sind jedoch nicht genau spezifiziert. Die Referenzimplementierung ist stark von *CORBA* getrieben. In dieser Arbeit wird eine von der Middlewarestruktur unabhängige Abstraktionsebene vogestellt.

OROCOS [5] adressiert die Entwicklung von Echtzeit-Regelungssystemen, bei denen der Komponentenentwickler sogenannte Hotspots ausfüllt. Die Interaktionen im *Real-Time Toolkit* basieren im Kern auf einer Dataflow Architektur, während unser Fokus darauf liegt ein breites Spektrum an Interaktionsschemata zu unterstützen.

Das V^3 Studio [6] befindet sich noch in der Entwicklung und ist bisher nicht öffentlich verfügbar. Beispielsweise sind die Transformationen aus einem V^3 Studio Modell in ein Robotik Framework nicht implementiert. Wir teilen die grundlegenden Sichtweisen von Iborra et al.

Das *Eclipse* Projekt [7] entwickelt sich zum De-facto-Standard und bietet eine Vielzahl an Plugins für den modellgetriebenen Ansatz. So ist sowohl *open-ArchitectureWare (oAW)* [8] als auch *Papyrus UML* [9] vollständig in *Eclipse* integriert.

3   SmartSoft

Um die Komplexität der Robotik beherrschen zu können, ist ein komponentenbasierter Ansatz nötig. Das Gesamtsystem wird aus mehreren Komponenten zusammengesetzt, die über vorgegebene Interaktionsmuster mit festgelegter Semantik miteinander kommunizieren [10]. Dieser Ansatz wird bei SMARTSOFT verfolgt und bildet die Grundlage für unsere Arbeit. Die Auswahl der Muster ist ausreichend, da sie sowohl Request/Response Interaktionen als auch asynchrone Mitteilungen und Push Services zur Verfügung stellen. Daraus ergeben sich lose gekoppelte Komponenten, die über Services kommunizieren und einen Contract erfüllen (Abb. 1). Demnach kann SMARTSOFT unter zwei verschiede-

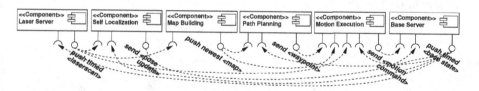

Abb. 1. Typische Komponenten einer Navigationsanwendung, die über standardisierte Interaktionsmuster miteinander interagieren.

nen Gesichtspunkten betrachtet werden. Zum einen handelt es sich um ein abstraktes, komponentenbasiertes Konzept, welches völlig unabhängig von jeglicher Implementierungstechnologie und Middlewarestruktur ist. Zum anderen existieren spezifische Implementierungen wie beispielsweise CORBASMARTSOFT [11], das auf *ACE/TAO* [12] basiert. Bei den spezifischen Implementierungen sind die Ideen, die durch SMARTSOFT beschrieben sind, mit den jeweiligen Technologien und Middlewarestrukturen umgesetzt. Die Mechanismen skalieren vom 8 Bit Mikrocontroller bis zum hochperformanten Standardsystem [13].

4   Der modellgetriebene Ansatz

Grundlegend für den modellgetriebenen Ansatz ist die Differenzierung zwischen dem plattformunabhängigen Modell (PIM), dem plattformspezifischen Modell (PSM) und der plattformspezifischen Implementierung (PSI). Im ersten Schritt modelliert der Komponentenentwickler eine Komponentenhülle mit definierten Serviceports unabhängig von der Zielplattform (Abb. 2). Er bedient sich dabei aus einer Menge vorgegebener Elemente (Tasks, Ports, Handler, ...). Durch

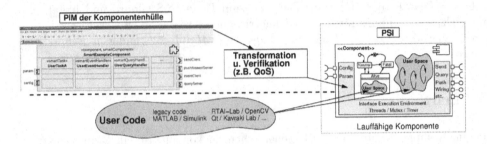

Abb. 2. Die Komponentenhülle wird durch Transformationen in ein PSI überführt. Der Komponentenentwickler fügt beliebige Implementierungen hinzu.

Knopfdruck wird der Code für die Hülle erzeugt und Parameter des Modells werden verifiziert. Es wird ausschließlich die Hülle generiert und eigener Code sowie externe Bibliotheken können integriert werden. Die im Hintergrund ablaufenden Schritte werden im Folgenden beschrieben. Die Abbildung 3 gibt den Gesamtüberblick über den Workflow.

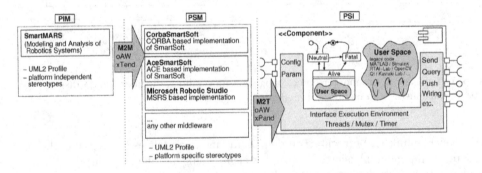

Abb. 3. Der Workflow zeigt die Übergänge vom plattformunabhängigen Modell (PIM) hin zu einem der plattformspezifischen Modelle (PSM) und von dort zur jeweiligen plattformspezifischen Implementierung (PSI).

4.1 Platform Independent Model (PIM)

Das plattformunabhängige Modell (PIM) ist frei von jeglichen Technologie- und Middlewarestrukturen. Nachdem die SMARTSOFT Konzepte seit Jahrzehnten erfolgreich in verschiedenen Robotiksystemen eingesetzt werden, bieten sie eine vielversprechende Ausgangssituation auf dem Weg zur modellgetriebenen Softwareentwicklung solcher Systeme. Diese allgemeinen Konzepte bilden die Grundlage für das plattformunabhängige Modell SMARTMARS: *Modeling and Analysis of Robotics Systems* (Abb. 4). Eine Komponente stellt verbindliche interne Struk-

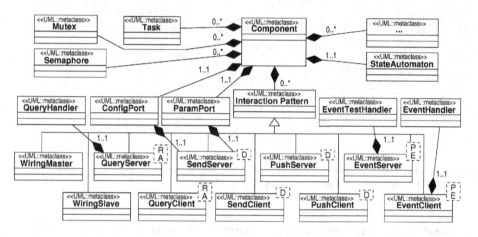

Abb. 4. Ein Ausschnitt des SMARTMARS UML Profils

turen zur Verfügung [13], wie spezielle standardisierte Ports zur Parametrierung und Konfiguration des internen Komponentenverhaltens. Ein interner Zustandsautomat setzt sich aus Zuständen wie beispielsweise neutral, alive und fatal zusammen. Die Ports einer Komponente werden aus den vorgegebenen Interaktionsmustern zusammengestellt. Durch Kommunikationsobjekte ist der Austausch beliebiger Datenstrukturen möglich. Dies stellt sicher, dass sich interne Verhaltensweisen nicht über Komponentengrenzen ausweiten können. Durch die an die Stereotypen angehängten *Tagged Values* können die Metaelemente parametriert werden.

Die Elemente im Modell erlauben eine Zuweisung von *QoS* Parametern. Dies bietet die Möglichkeit, externe Tools zur Verifikation der Parameter in den Entwicklungsprozess einzubinden. So können beispielsweise Ressourcen- und zeitliche Anforderungen gegenüber den Möglichkeiten der Zielplattform überprüft werden. Um Verhalten abbilden zu können, wird ein Statechart modelliert, der sich in den alive Zustand des internen Zustandsautomaten einbindet. An den Statechart angehängte Annotationen vereinheitlichen die Komponentenzugriffe, um das Verhalten der Komponenten des Gesamtsystems zu instrumentieren. Damit kann beispielsweise durch externe Events der Datenfluss zwischen den Komponenten zur Laufzeit geändert werden.

4.2   Platform Specific Model (PSM)

Je nach Implementierungstechnologie und Middlewarestruktur kann es beliebig viele plattformspezifische Modelle geben. Diese PSMs werden durch Model-
Model Transformation (M2M / oAW xTend) aus dem PIM erzeugt. Das PSM bildet die Zwischenebene zwischen dem PIM und der plattformspezifischen Implementierung (PSI). Es abstrahiert die Konzepte und Eigenheiten des Frameworks,
gegen das bei der späteren Codegenerierung generiert wird (Abb. 5 *links*). Diese

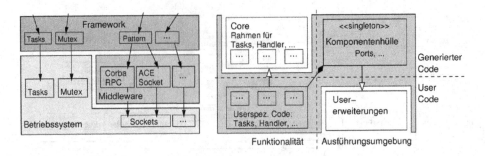

Abb. 5. *Links:* Die Schnittstelle des Frameworks, gegen die der Generator generiert;
Rechts: Die Struktur der Komponente auf Quellcodeebene.

Zwischenebene muss für jede Middleware nur einmal implementiert werden. Der
Aufwand ist abhängig davon, wie leicht sich die Konzepte aus SMARTSOFT dort
umsetzen lassen. Werden von der Ziel-Middleware nur wenige der geforderten
Konzepte unterstützt, müssen diese durch das Framework mit den vorhandenen Mechanismen realisiert werden. Die PSMs werden ebenfalls als UML Profile
realisiert, wie beispielsweise das CORBASMARTSOFT UML Profil. Unsere Arbeit
konzentriert sich derzeit hauptsächlich auf dieses PSM, obwohl auch PSMs für
andere Robotik-Frameworks integriert werden können (z.B. Microsoft Robotics
Studio [14]).

4.3   Codegenerierung aus dem PSM in die PSI

Aus dem PSM wird der Quellcode für die Komponentenhülle durch Model-Text
Transformation (M2T / oAW xPand) generiert. Der Entwickler integriert seine
Algorithmen und kann sich dabei frei innerhalb der Hülle bewegen. Es können
sowohl Quellen aus anderen Tools (MATLAB Simulink, RTAI Lab, ...) als auch
beliebige Libraries (OpenCV, Qt, Kavraki Lab, ...) eingebunden werden.
    Um die Wiederverwendbarkeit unabhängig vom PSM und die Einbindung
von Bibliotheken sicherzustellen, ist es notwendig, bei der Codegenerierung strikt
zwischen generierten Code und userspezifischen Code zu trennen (Abb. 5 *rechts*).
    Die Trennung basiert auf dem Generation Gap Pattern [15]. Durch Ableiten
von den entsprechenden Core-Klassen (Tasks, Handler, ...) kann der Entwickler

eigenen Quellcode integrieren. Um auf alle Elemente (Serviceports, Tasks, Mutex, ...) der Komponente zugreifen zu können, ist die Klasse, welche die Komponente selbst repräsentiert, als Singleton realisiert. Die Verwendung des Singleton hat keinen Einfluss auf die Außensicht der Komponente, da Komponenten in der verwendeten Implementierung von SMARTSOFT (CORBASMARTSOFT) als Prozess abgebildet sind.

Beim Wechsel des PSM von CORBASMARTSOFT auf eine andere SMART-SOFT Implementierung erfolgt die Generierung der PSI transparent. Gleiches gilt beispielsweise für Anpassungen an den Serviceports, wenn diese im PIM von aktiver auf passive Behandlung der Anfragen umgeschaltet werden. Es sind in beiden Fällen keine Anpassungen am Usercode notwendig.

5 Beispiel

Abbildung 6 zeigt einen möglichen Workflow am Beispiel einer Mapper Komponente (SmartMapperGridMap). Unter Verwendung des SMARTMARS Profils wird die Komponente mit ihren Serviceports, Tasks und Handlern mit *Papyrus UML* modelliert. In dieser Ebene legt der Entwickler die gesamte Struktur seiner Komponente fest. Durch die Model-Model Transformation (M2M) wird das

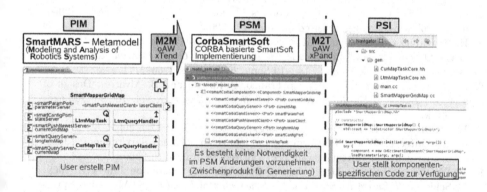

Abb. 6. Der Workflow anhand eines praktischen Beispiels. *Links:* PIM der Mapper-Komponente; *Mitte:* UML Modell des PSM; *Rechts:* Ausschnitt zeigt generierten Code.

PSM erzeugt. Das Beispiel verwendet das CORBASMARTSOFT Profil als Metamodell für das PSM. Diese Ebene bleibt jedoch vor dem Komponentenentwickler verborgen. Schließlich wird aus dem PSM durch Model-Text Transformation (M2T) der Quellcode generiert. Der Entwickler fügt nun die für den Mapper spezifischen Algorithmen hinzu und erhält so eine lauffähige Komponente. Im PIM können Änderungen, wie beispielsweise das Setzen des *Tagged Values* isActive eines Handlers von passiver auf aktive Behandlung, vorgenommen werden. Durch Knopfdruck wird die PSI neu generiert. Die veränderten Serviceeigenschaften sind nun ohne Quellcodeänderungen verfügbar.

6   Zusammenfassung und Ausblick

Der vorgestellte Ansatz zeigt die maßgeblichen Schritte, die auf dem Weg zur modellgetriebenen Softwareentwicklung in der Robotik nötig sind. Basierend auf einem komponentenbasierten Konzept wird die middlewarespezifische Komponentenhülle von der eigentlichen Userimplementierung getrennt. Dadurch, dass nur die Komponentenhülle genertiert wird und der Entwickler seine spezifischen Implementierungen und Bibliotheken selbst einbindet, ist dieser Ansatz der Schlüssel zum Erfolg. Das vorgestellte Beispiel zeigt anhand einer einfachen Komponente die Toolchain im praktischen Einsatz [11]. Einer der nächsten Schritte ist es, das Deployment der einzelnen Komponenten auf die Zielsysteme und eine darauf basierende Verifikation der *Quality of Service* Parameter zu realisieren.

Literaturverzeichnis

1. ARTIST, "Network of excellence on embedded system design," 2009, http://www.artist-embedded.org/, visited on June 17th 2009.
2. OMG MARTE, "Modeling and analysis of real-time and embedded systems," 2009, http://www.omgmarte.org/, visited on June 17th 2009.
3. AUTOSAR, "Automotive open system architecture," 2009, http://www.autosar.org/, visited on June 17th 2009.
4. OMG Robotics, "OMG Robotics Domain Task Force," 2009, http://robotics.omg.org/, visited on June 17th 2009.
5. H. Bruyninckx, P. Soetens, and B. Koninckx, "The real-time motion control core of the Orocos project," in *Proc. IEEE International Conference on Robotics and Automation ICRA '03*, vol. 2, 14 - 19 Sept. 2003, pages 2766–2771.
6. A. Iborra, D. Caceres, F. Ortiz, J. Franco, P. Palma, and B. Alvarez, "Design of service robots," *IEEE Robotics and Automation Magazine*, vol. 16, no. 1, pages 24–33, March 2009.
7. ECLIPSE, 2009, http://www.eclipse.org/, visited on June 17th 2009.
8. openArchitectureWare, "Platform for model-driven software development," 2009, http://www.openarchitectureware.org/, visited on June 17th 2009.
9. PAPYRUS UML, 2009, http://www.papyrusuml.org/, visited on June 17th 2009.
10. C. Schlegel, *Software Engineering for Experimental Robotics*, STAR series. Springer, 2007, vol. 30, ch. Communication Patterns as Key Towards Component Interoperability, pages 183–210.
11. SmartSoft, 2009, http://smart-robotics.sourceforge.net, visited on June 17th 2009.
12. D. Schmidt, "Adaptive Communication Environment, The ACE ORB", 2009, http://www.cs.wustl.edu/schmidt/ACE.html, visited on June 17th 2009.
13. C. Schlegel, T. Haßler, A. Lotz and A. Steck, "Robotic Software Systems: From Code-Driven to Model-Driven Designs" In *Proc. 14th Int. Conf. on Advanced Robotics (ICAR)*, Munich, 2009.
14. Microsoft, "Microsoft robotics developer studio," 2009, http://msdn.microsoft.com/en-us/robotics/default.aspx, visited on June 17th 2009.
15. John Vlissides, "Pattern Hatching - Generation Gap Pattern," 2009, http://researchweb.watson.ibm.com/designpatterns/pubs/gg.html, visited on June 17th 2009.

Situation Analysis and Adaptive Risk Assessment for Intersection Safety Systems in Advanced Assisted Driving

Prof. Dr. Jianwei Zhang[1] and Bernd Roessler[2]

1: University of Hamburg, Faculty of Mathematics, Informatics and Natural Sciences, Department Informatics, Group TAMS, Vogt-Kölln-Straße 30, D - 22527 Hamburg, 2: Ibeo Automobile Sensor GmbH, Merkurring 20, 22143 Hamburg

Abstract. Intersection Safety Systems (ISS) are a relative new but an important research topic in the field of Advanced Driver Assistance Systems as accident statistics show. Unfortunately, intersections are one of the most complex scenarios out of all traffic related scenarios which complicates the development of such ISS. This paper presents situation analysis and risk assessment algorithms for Intersection Safety Systems which are suitable for online implementation. The demonstrator system is able to observe the intersection environment with several onboard sensors and to build an appropriate scene model including behaviors, intentions and interrelations of all vehicles in the scene. The subsequent risk assessment judges possible individual risks for the vehicle that is equipped with the safety system.

1 Introduction

Detailed personal car accident analysis shows that there is an urgent need to assist drivers at intersections. From [ROS+05] three main scenarios can be extracted which cover a crucial number of intersection accidents. They define the basis for the ISS and the pertinent interpretations which are required in this paper. These scenarios are the "left turn across path scenario", the "turn into/straight crossing path scenario" and the "red light crossing scenario". Each situation is covered by a separate assistance function in this work. At first the scenario is analyzed by a behavior modeling and prediction with a Dynamic Bayesian Network approach. In a next step, the risk of the current situation is computed by an adaptive fuzzy logic based approach. Finally, the risk is presented to the driver of the equipped vehicle through an appropriate HMI.

The demonstrator vehicle used for this work has two laser scanners integrated in its two front corners. An additional video camera is mounted inside of the vehicle behind the windscreen (see Fig. 1). The specifications of the sensors can be found in [HST+05]. The laser scanners are used for host vehicle landmark localization, object detection classification and tracking [RF06]. The video camera is used for lane detection. A time stamp based data fusion combines both localization outputs in order to gain a precise position and orientation of the vehicle within the intersection. Fig. 1 shows the test vehicle with the mounting positions of each sensor.

Fig. 1. Sensor integration in the test vehicle

2   Intersection Modeling

Intersections can include different lanes for different tasks (e.g. turning lanes), boundaries (e.g. curbstones, refuges, lane-markings) and last but not least complex right of way regulations (e.g. traffic-signs, traffic lights). Therefore, intersections are very complex since all traffic participants can move in nearly arbitrary directions and with different aims. This is the reason why intersections were neglected in the past and many situation analysis tasks for driver assistance applications were built upon freeway scenarios. In this work, this complex structure of intersections is reduced to a model that allows the formulation of many assistance functions for intersection scenarios with only few restrictions. The modeling developed in this work is a modification of the GDF (Geographic Data Files) description [fS02] and is named Lane Model Description (LMD). The idea is to introduce a lane as the most basic feature of its description. A road element of GDF turns into a lane in LMD and a junction into a lane link respectively. The road of GDF is interpreted as a road element in LMD. Fig. 2(a) shows the LMD in a GDF like format in order to express the different approach. For an advanced driver assistance system like the one developed in this work, it is crucial to have exact information on the driving lanes of a road. The developed ISS uses lane information amongst others in order to recognize possible conflicts and to identify the road users aims. In addition to *real* lanes with markings at each side, lanes of the LMD can also express *virtual* lanes that describe the possible paths a vehicle can take within the intersection. They provide an abstraction of the complex structure of an intersection by reducing it to the minimum required information. We will see later that this is highly suitable for high level assistance functions at intersections.

3   Behavior Modeling

The driving behavior in this work is represented in terms of a few geometric entities which facilitates the calculation of possible trajectories and therefore the determination of possible conflicts within an intersection. This drastically reduces the computational complexity of the whole system and makes it suitable for online analysis tasks. The entities for the behavior modeling are the driving lanes (real and virtual lanes) of the intersection. The idea is that each traffic participant only drives in predefined areas within the intersection, i.e. the lanes. This form of modeling can be interpreted as the definition of one common trajectory with a tolerance area on both sides which corresponds to the width of a lane. Accident analysis [ROS+05] shows that accidents resulting from wrong lane changes are of no relevance in intersection accidents. Thus, the proposed behavior modeling is suitable for the proposed ISS.

In order to represent the behavior of all traffic participants, a common structure is needed. For this representation the LMD (see Section 2) is transferred into a probabilistic graph model for each object.

A **directed** graph is a tuple $G = (V, E)$ where $V(G)$ is the set of vertices and $E(G) \subseteq V(G) \times V(G)$ the set of edges in the graph G, respectively. The graph G is called **undirected** if $E(G) = E(G)^{-1}$ with $E(G)^{-1} = \{(u, v) | (v, u) \in E(G)\}$.

The k-th path $pa(v_s, v_e)$ of a directed graph G from vertex v_s to vertex v_e is a tuple $(v_1, \ldots, v_{n_k})$ where $v_1 = v_s, v_{n_k} = v_e$ and $(v_i, v_{i+1}) \in E(G) \forall i \in (1, \ldots, n_k - 1)$.

The so-called Microscopic Behavior (MiB) of a driver forms a probabilistic behavior network which is a directed graph with lanes as vertices and transition probabilities at the edges. Those transition probabilities from vertex v_1 to vertex v_2 are denoted by $prob(v_1, v_2)$. The MiB is build out of the LMD starting at the initial position of the appropriate traffic participant. The possible next lanes from the driving lane at initialization time are traversed and inserted into the graph. The possible next lanes are *the lanes connected to the same link as the considered lane* and *the neighboring lanes at the left and right side of the considered lane*. The transition probabilities describe the likelihood of a traffic participant moving from one lane to another. Normally, the likelihoods at the edges of the MiB are uniformly distributed over the number of outgoing edges for each vertex but they can also express terms like the most probable path at an intersection by assigning different probabilities to the outgoing edges. Nevertheless, the probabilities at the outgoing edges of one node must add up to 1.

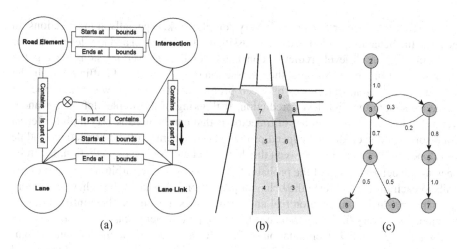

(a)   (b)   (c)

Fig. 2. LMD and Microscopic Behavior

Fig. 2 shows a sample intersection and the corresponding MiB for one approaching direction. In Fig. 2(b) the lanes which are used in the MiB of Fig. 2(c) are shaded and numbered in order to state the relationship. Nevertheless, the shown MiB has additional nodes whose lanes are not shown in the intersection figure. A new lane, i.e. a new node, is used if there are changes in the attributes of the corresponding lane. The shown MiB also uses the mentioned deflection from the uniformly distributed probabilities at the edges, i.e. here it is more likely for a traffic participant to be going straight ahead than to be turning left. The initial global probabilities for a maneuver at an intersection (e.g. straight, left, right) can be computed from the MiB by summing the multiplied probabilities of all possible paths that lead to the destination starting from a specific vertex. Therefore the following has to be calculated: $p(v_s \overset{*}{\rightarrow} v_e) = \Sigma_{k=0}^{n} p(v_s \overset{k}{\rightarrow} v_e)$, where n is the number of possible paths from v_s to v_e and $p(v_s \overset{k}{\rightarrow} v_e)$ is the probability for reaching v_e beginning at v_s in the k-th path $pa_k(v_1 = v_s, v_{n_k} = v_e)$ which is computed by $p(v_s \overset{k}{\rightarrow} v_e) = \Pi_{i=1,...,n_k-1} prob(v_i, v_{i+1})$.

In this example, the initial global probability for a left turn is the limit of a geometric series $p(v_s = 2 \overset{*}{\rightarrow} v_e = 7) = \lim_{n \to \infty} \Sigma_{k=0}^{n} (0.3 \cdot 0.8) \cdot (0.3 \cdot 0.2)^k \approx 0.255$. Initially, the probabilities at the edges are uniformly distributed or assigned due to statistical background knowledge on the driving behavior at the intersection. Nevertheless, they can be modified by the application if the distribution changes due to some reason. Each MiB covers a specific maximum distance which can be seen as the range of vision for the appropriate traffic participant. Within this distance the behavior of the vehicle is described. It is mainly driven by the field of view of the sensors. The wider the field of view, the more extensive the maneuver decision as well as the behavior prediction can become.

4   Behavior Prediction

The prediction of human behavior is a very complex task, especially at intersections. In general, the behavior prediction can be classified into high-level and low-level behavior prediction. The high-level prediction considers global maneuver decisions like e.g. the intention to turn left or to stop at the intersection (e.g. due to a red traffic light). In the low-level prediction, trajectories or speed profiles are considered which describe the maneuvers from the high-level prediction. If thinking of a "simple" left turn maneuver at the low-level, the number of trajectories that can be used is very high (different trajectories and even different speed profiles). The accuracy of the prediction module developed in this work lies between this high-level and low-level prediction. It can be seen as the determination of the probability $P(v_1 \overset{*}{\rightarrow} v_2)$ of two arbitrary vertices of the MiB in each time step. Since the behavior prediction is based on the behavior network description which is defined on real and virtual lanes, the current lane information of a vehicle is of very high importance. The developed model is capable of solving two problems in parallel: 1) Computation of $P(x_t)$ for all lanes of the model (lane assignment for the current time step) and 2) Computation of $P(x_{t+\delta})$ for all lanes of the model (maneuver prediction for a vehicle).

For the realization of the behavior prediction, the theory of Dynamic Bayesian Networks (DBN) was used. Generally, the used network can be interpreted as an estimator for the lane a vehicle is driving on. Due to the description of the vehicle's behavior

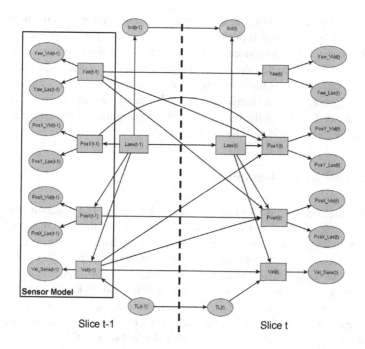

Fig. 3. 2 TBN Dynamic Bayesian Network for Behavior Prediction

solely by lanes, the intention of a driver can be inferred from the model. Fig. 3 shows the DBN that is used for current lane estimation as well as the behavior prediction. The observed states, i.e. the evidences in each slice, are the position of the vehicle, the indicator state (especially important for the approaching phase to an intersection and intersections with no separate turning lanes), the velocity and the status of the traffic light. The hidden state is the current lane. Through a filtering process the actual lane can be estimated for the current time t.

If the behavior of all traffic participants is analyzed, it has to be evaluated if the predicted plans are at odds with each other. In a first step, the possible conflicts that arise because of the construction of the intersection have to be identified and expressed by a so-called Conflict Graph (CG). In a second step, the conflicts that could arise because of the current combination of the objects and their predicted plans have to be analyzed. At the end a comprehensive view on the scene emerges.

The CG is a graph that results from an interconnection of the different MiBs of each traffic participant currently in the scene. An interconnection between two vertices of two MiBs exists if there is a potential conflict with the lanes belonging to these vertices. A potential conflict exists if two lanes have an overlapping area called conflict zone. The conflict zone can be reduced to the Conflict Point (CP) which is the intersection of the middle line of both lanes. The edges that represent a conflict are undirected edges in order to differentiate them from the transition edges of the initial MiBs. The initial CG does not take the traffic control at the intersection into account, i.e. it cannot be seen which lane of the connection is preferred in terms of right-of-way regulations.

If the computed CG is reduced to the conflicts where the host vehicle has to give right-of-way to other vehicles, the Right-of-Way Graph (RoWG) is obtained. Therefore, the RoWG is only valid for the host vehicle. While the CG is a *static* graph, the RoWG is a *dynamic* graph that can change continuously during system operation. Every time a new vehicle is detected at the intersection or the categories of the lanes change (e.g. due to a traffic light), the RoWG has to be updated.

5   Adaptive Risk Assessment

Calculating the risk for a driver is a complex task as well. The situation analysis provides all possible conflicts and the assigned probabilities of the driving behavior of the vehicles. With an analytical approach it would be very hard to try to compute the occurrence of the conflicts, to cope with the fact of imperfect sensor data and to include aspects like the subjective assessment of the current risk for a specific driver. Here, a fuzzy rule-base is built to reproduce "human thinking" for risk assessment so that an adequate strategy can be formulated. Input variables are speed, acceleration and distance to the conflict. In addition, inputs such as the type of the opponent could also be used as a severity index for a possible crash [SUBW04]. Visibility can also easily be modeled in such a fuzzy rule-base system since this also effects risk assessment. E.g., the risk for an available time-gap in an intersection could be assessed higher for poor visibility than in very good weather conditions. The risk assessment takes the probabilities of the behavior prediction as weighting factors and computes a risk level for each possible conflict in the time and space domain. The results of the risk assessment module are different risk levels for all possible conflicts in the scene.

A fuzzy-logic [Zad65] approach was used in this work to judge the risk of a possible conflict for the intersection scenarios. Such a fuzzy-logic approach allows the formulation of the rules for risk assessment in a very natural and easy way. No widespread expert knowledge is needed in order to define the rules so that the resulting system can work properly. The concept of the inference system is based on B-spline membership functions and is similar to that presented in [ZK99]. Each input is uniformly covered by five membership functions. This is due to a natural human partitioning of a specific linguistic variable. The linguistic variable *speed* would therefore be represented by the linguistic terms *very slow*, *slow*, *medium*, *high* and *very high*. The risk computation is shown in Equation (1).

$$risk = \frac{\sum_{i_1=1}^{m_1} \cdots \sum_{i_n=1}^{m_n} (Y_{i_1,\ldots,i_n} \prod_{j=1}^{n} X_{i_j,k_j}^j(x_j))}{\sum_{i_1=1}^{m_1} \cdots \sum_{i_n=1}^{m_n} \prod_{j=1}^{n} X_{i_j,k_j}^j(x_j)} = \sum_{i_1=1}^{m_1} \cdots \sum_{i_n=1}^{m_n} (Y_{i_1,\ldots,i_n} \prod_{j=1}^{n} X_{i_j,k_j}^j(x_j)) \quad (1)$$

where x_j is the j-th input, k_j the order of the B-Spline basis function for x_j, X_{i_j,k_j}^j the i-th B-Spline membership function of x_j, $i_j = 1,\ldots,m_j$ the number of membership functions for the linguistic variable for x_j and $Y_{i_1 i_2 \ldots i_n}$ the fuzzy singleton for Rule$(i_1, i_2, \ldots, i_n)$.

This above risk assessment computation is performed for every conflict c which possibly can occur in the current situation. Since due to the number of the road users currently at the intersection and their predicted driving behavior which will be less than 100% most of the time, a lot of possible conflicts can occur. Therefore an additional weighting factor has to be added to the risk computation which influences the overall risk for a specific conflict. Assuming $\mathscr{C} = (c_1, \ldots, c_N)$ are the current conflicts for a specific situation, the most critical conflict is computed by:

$$\theta = \operatorname{argmax}_{c_l \in \mathscr{C}} \left[\omega_{c_l} \sum_{i_1=1}^{m_1} \cdots \sum_{i_n=1}^{m_n} \left(Y_{i_1,\ldots,i_n} \prod_{j=1}^{n} X_{i_j,k_j}^{j} (x_{j,c_l}) \right) \right],$$

where x_{j,c_l} is the j-th input and ω_{c_l} the weight for conflict c_l. Several procedures for the computation of the weight ω_{c_l} can be used. All are based on the probabilities calculated for the current conflict. The easiest way is to weight the risk computation simply by the probability for the conflict: $\omega_{c_l} = p(c_l)$. This has the effect that the risk changes if the probability for the conflict changes. If the risk should not change proportionally to the probabilities of the conflicts, the following weighting factor can be used:

$\omega_{c_l} = 1$ if $p(c_l) > \frac{1}{N}$, $\omega_{c_l} = 0$ otherwise, where N is the number of calculated possible conflicts.

The fuzzy-system approach introduced above can be extended with the ability for optimizing and generating rules by a machine learning approach. The practical suitability of this method was among others shown by the authors of this paper in the field of robotic grasp learning [ZR03]. The goal is to minimize the following squared error function: $E = \frac{1}{2}(risk_r - risk_d)^2$, where $risk_r$ and $risk_d$ are the current calculated risk and the desired outcome, respectively. The momentous risk level $risk_r$ is thereby calculated by Equation (1). In order to minimize the error function, the parameters $Y_{i_1,\ldots,i_n}$ of Equation (1) have to be adapted. For this purpose the gradient descent method is used: $\Delta Y_{i_1,\ldots,i_n} = \varepsilon \frac{\delta E}{\delta Y_{i_1,\ldots,i_n}} = \varepsilon (risk_r - risk_d) \prod_{j=1}^{n} X_{i_j,k_j}^{j} (x_j)$.

The automatic adaption of the proposed risk assessment by machine learning techniques offers additional enhancement. It is either done online in the vehicle or offline in a developed simulation. In both cases the adaption is used in order to adjust the parameters of the membership functions for the fuzzy rule base.

In the offline risk adaption, the parameters for the fuzzy rule base are generated automatically from scratch without designing the membership functions with expert knowledge. The idea is to simulate a lot of different situations which do or do not result in accidents. From the conflict situation (e.g. accident, near accident, no accident) corresponding feedback can be calculated and thus the parameters can be adopted. The measure for evaluating the risk is called Conflict Time Gap (CTG). For the definition of this measure the Time-to-Collision-Point (TTCP) is used as differentiation to the well-known term Time-to-Collision (TTC) (e.g. see [vdHH93]). For the TTC the time trajectories of two vehicles ($\mathscr{T}_h(x,y), \mathscr{T}_o(x,y)$) are intersecting exactly in one point $P = (x_c, y_c, t_c)$ in the time-space domain. Thus, the TTC is the same for both vehicles. This results in: $\text{TTC} = \mathscr{T}_h(x_c, y_c) = \mathscr{T}_o(x_c, y_c)$ The TTCP is defined as the time to a conflict point (within an intersection) where a collision would occur if the last equation would be true. For the TTCP both trajectories are not necessarily intersecting in the time-space domain but at least in the space domain, i.e. at $P = (x_c, y_c)$. This means that the TTCP is simply the time value of the time-space trajectory of the host vehicle h at a defined conflict point: $\text{TTCP}_h = \mathscr{T}_h(x_c, y_c)$. The TTCP for the host vehicle h

becomes the TTC if another vehicle o exists where $TTCP_o = TTCP_h$. Considering these two vehicles, the CTG is defined as follows: $CTG = abs(TTCP_h - TTCP_o)$. The CTG defines the time for a vehicle V_1 to reach a predefined point P after another vehicle V_2 has already crossed it. It is used to compute the risk of the situation and its conflict point: $risk_d = max(0., risk_{max} - \frac{CTG \cdot risk_{max}}{CTG_{max}})$, where $risk_{max}$ is the maximum number of the risk level and CTG_{max} the maximum CTG up to which a risk should be assigned.

The online risk adaption is performed in order to adjust the warning system to a specific driving behavior or driver's skill. Here, an initial parameter set is already given and the system is performing well in most situations. Just for some specific situations, where a driver reacts noticeably against the warning or recommendations of the assistance system, the risk assessment is adapted to the driver. Therefore, it is necessary to compare the computed risk of the system with the risk felt by the driver. So $risk_d$ becomes the felt risk of the current driver. The strategy introduced is as follows: if a driver always disregards the suggestion/warning of the assistance system in the car because from his point of view it is not suitable for his driving behavior, the automatic risk assessment adaption can adjust to his skills. This strategy can be explained by rules like "if the computed risk is high, but the driver passes the conflict point without stopping anyhow, then the risk is changed to a lower risk". Vice versa, "if the computed risk is low, but the driver stops in front of the conflict point anyhow, then the risk is changed to a high risk".

6 Results

The described behavior prediction and risk assessment algorithms were successfully implemented in the real demonstrator vehicle. A big challenge for humans while driving a car is to assess parameters like speed and distance of other approaching vehicles. Therefore, the developed HMI approach uses a warning interface that visualizes the computed risk level in a continuous manner for the time of a possible dangerous situation to the driver (see Fig. 4) In this way, the driver has a direct visual link to those parameters which are difficult to estimate.

Fig. 4. The used HMI for Risk Level Visualization in the Demonstrator Vehicle

6.1   System and User Test Results

System as well as user tests were carried out on a test intersection [FHO+07]. The system test evaluations were carried out based on the number and the rate of correct alarms, false alarms and missing alarms. The results of the test indicated that the system had a correct alarm rate of 93% in left turn scenarios and 100% in lateral traffic scenarios. For the user tests sixteen untrained subjects had been selected by taking their age, gender and driver experience into account. Each subject took around 2.5 hours to drive the demonstrator vehicles on the test intersection and assessed the performance of the systems. The subjects rated the ISS helpful and relieving. Further analysis showed that the subjects thought the ISS for left turn was more useful than for lateral traffic. They judged that such a system could have helped them in their daily driving and it was agreed that it would improve traffic safety.

7   Conclusion

Intersection Safety is a very hot research topic. Nearly every automobile manufacturer and also the suppliers have recognized that future advanced driver assistance systems have to deal to some extent with the topic of ISS. This is mainly due to the fact that intersections are a black spot in terms of road accidents. This work has shown a promising approach for all of the tasks that need to be solved in order to build a comprehensive ISS. A new approach was shown how to deal with the challenging topic of scenario interpretation and risk assessment in intersection safety systems. This approach was successfully implemented on a demonstrator vehicle and extensively tested in the European-funded project PReVENT-INTERSAFE.

References

[FHO+07]   K. Fürstenberg, M. Hopstock, M. A. Obojski, B. Rössler, J. Chen, S. Deutschle, C. Benson, J. Weingart, and A. de La Fortelle. D40.75 final report. INTERSAFE Deliverable, 2007.

[fS02]   International Organization for Standardization. *Intelligent transport systems - Geographic Data Files (GDF) - Overall dataspecification.* Draft International Standard ISO/DIS 14825. ISO, 2002.

[HST+05]   A. Heenan, C. Shooter, M. Tucker, K. Fuerstenberg, and T. Kluge. Feature-Level Map Building and Object Recognition for Intersection Safety Applications. In *9th International Forum on AMAA 2005*, 2005.

[RF06]   B. Rössler and K. Fürstenberg. Intersection Safety - the EC Project INTERSAFE. In *10th International Forum on Advanced Microsystems for Automotive Applications*, Berlin, April 2006.

[ROS+05]   B. Rössler, M. A. Obojski, M. Stanzel, D. Ehmanns, T. Kosch, M. Hopstock, C. Shooter, A. Heenan, P. Woolley, C. Benson, J. F. Boissou, Y. Martail, L. Serezat, Y. Page, C. Chauvel, K. Fürstenberg, J. Mousain, A. de La Fortelle, M. Parent, and S. Deutschle. D40.4 requirements for intersection safety applications. INTERSAFE Deliverable, 2005.

[SUBW04] D. Sun, S. Ukkusuri, R. F. Benekohal, and S. T. Waller. Fuzzy logic based online collision prediction system for signalized intersections. In *Advances in Transportation Studies an International Journal*, July 2004.

[vdHH93] R. van der Horst and Jeroen Hogema. Time-to-Collision and Collision Avoidance Systems. In *6th ICTCT Workshop*, Salzburg, 1993.

[Zad65] L. A. Zadeh. Fuzzy sets. In *Information and Control*, pages 338–353, 1965.

[ZK99]   J. Zhang and A. Knoll. Designing fuzzy controllers by rapid learning. In *Fuzzy Sets and Systems*, pages 287–301, January 1999.

[ZR03]   J. Zhang and B. Rössler. *Grasp Learning by Active Experimentation Using Continuous B-Spline Model*, chapter 3, pages 353–372. In Autonomous Robotic Systems - Soft Computing and hard Computing Methodologiesand Application. Physica-Verlag, 2003.

Transparente protokollierbare Kommunikation zwischen Funktionen kognitiver Systeme

Matthias Goebl und Georg Färber

Lehrstuhl für Realzeit-Computersysteme, Technische Universität München
{goebl,faerber}@rcs.ei.tum.de

Zusammenfassung. In kognitiven Systemen werden komplexe Entscheidungen getroffen, die ein umfassendes Umfeldverständnis erfordern. Technische Realisierungen sind meist datenintensiv und bestehen aus vielen Teilfunktionen. Um solche Systeme zu überwachen und neue Funktionen zu testen ist eine transparente und verfolgbare Kommunikation notwendig. Dieser Beitrag präsentiert einen datenzentrierten Ansatz zur Kommunikation und liefert eine Methode um alle Kommunikationsbeziehungen zu beobachten und ganzheitlich aufzuzeichnen. Ausgewählte Anwendungen demonstrieren die erzielten Ergebnisse.

1 Einleitung

Grundlage des Handelns kognitiver Systeme ist die Erkenntnis über die eigene Situation, die über die Wahrnehmung der Umwelt gewonnen wird. In der menschlichen Kognition wird das Umfeld vorwiegend visuell erfasst und beispielsweise das Verhalten anderer Menschen interpretiert. Aufgrund erlangter Erkenntnisse werden dann zielgerichtete Aktionen ausgeführt. Langfristig nähren diese Erkenntnisse einen Lernprozess, um das eigene Verhalten sukzessive zu optimieren.

Technische Realisierungen kognitiver Systeme sollen ihre Umwelt ebenso gut verstehen, sodass sie komplexe Entscheidungen treffen und selbständig mit ihr interagieren können. Dazu besitzen sie Sensoren zur Gewinnung von Umweltinformationen und Aktoren, um auf ihre Umgebung einzuwirken. In „Kognitiven Automobilen" [1,2] dienen u. a. Kameras und LIDAR-Sensoren der Umgebungserfassung. Die zu treffenden Entscheidung umfassen z. B. Spurwechsel, Überholen, Vorfahrtsgewährung und Wegplanung.

Ein gemeinsames Merkmal maschineller Kognition ist die notwendige Auswertung großer Datenmengen auf Sensorebene, die hin zur Wissensebene stark verdichtet werden. Durch die Umgebung werden meist enge Zeitbedingungen vorgegeben, sodass eine schritthaltende Reaktion notwendig ist. Die dafür eingesetzten Funktionen werden auf einem Rechnersystem gewöhnlich in einzelnen Modulen implementiert, die durch ein Framework miteinander verbunden sind. Werden auf unterschiedlichen Ebenen verschiedene Lösungen eingesetzt, besteht die Gefahr von harten Brüchen z. B. zwischen Wahrnehmung und Handlung.

Im Folgenden wird ein Ansatz zur Kommunikation zwischen den einzelnen kognitiven Funktionen vorgestellt, der sich durch Transparenz, Effizienz und Echtzeitfähigkeit auszeichnet und sämtlichen Datenfluss mitprotokollieren kann.

2 Stand der Technik

In der Robotik existiert ein großes Feld von Architekturen, deren Einsatztaug-
lichkeit für kognitive Systeme vom jeweiligen Anwendungsfeld abhängt. So setzen viele bestimmte Sensoren oder Aktoren voraus und legen den Datenfluss
fest. Damit ist die Integration zusätzlicher Sensoren wie einer aktiven Kameraplattform nicht ohne Weiteres möglich. Dafür bieten sie meist Funktionalitäten,
die weit über die hier betrachtete Kommunikation hinausgehen. Die Anforderungen an harter Echtzeit sind in der Robotik hingegen oft geringer als z. B.
bei kognitiven Kraftfahrzeugen. Kann eine Roboterplattform bei längeren Berechnungen kurzfristig angehalten werden, ist das bei der schnellen Fahrt eines
Fahrzeugs auf öffentlichen Straßen nicht möglich. Die Echtzeitanforderungen bei
der Durchführung von Ausweichmanövern sind dann höher.

CORBA (*Common Object Request Broker Architecture*) ist programmierspra-
chenunabhängig und plattformübergreifend. Die Interprozesskommunikation ge-
schieht sehr komfortabel durch den Zugriff auf verteilte Objekte. CORBA eignet
sich gut für größere verteilte Robotikanwendungen, bei denen die Speicheranfor-
derungen einer CORBA-Implementierung keine Rolle spielen.

OROCOS (*Open Robot Control Software*) [3] bietet umfangreiche Softwarebi-
bliotheken für Kinematik, Dynamik, Bayes-Filter, Steuerungskomponenten und
ein Echtzeitframework. Schwerpunkt sind Roboter und Industriemaschinen, es
kam auch im Fahrzeug „Spirit of Berlin" der FU Berlin zum Einsatz.

MCA2 (*Modular Controller Architecture*) [4] ist ein modulares Framework
zur Implementierung von komplexen echtzeitfähigen Regelungen. Ein- und Aus-
gangsdaten der einzelnen Softwaremodule können jederzeit von außen über das
graphische „MCAadmin"-Tool eingesehen und geändert werden. Regelalgorith-
men können in MCA2 auf Microcontroller verschoben werden und so sehr gut
Roboter mit vielen Freiheitsgraden geregelt werden.

EMS-Vision [5] wurde speziell für intelligente Fahrzeuge, die nach dem 4D-
Ansatz arbeiten, entwickelt. Jede Kommunikation zwischen zwei Modulen erfolgt
über eine *dynamische Objektdatenbasis* (DOB), die mit einem Systemtakt (*Zyklus*) synchronisiert wird.

Das *Agent NeTwork System* (*ANTS*) [6] ist eine Softwarearchitektur für verteilte Multi-Agentensysteme und wurde in Versuchsträgern für den Stadtverkehr
eingesetzt. Benötigte Daten werden in lokalen Datenbanken gespeichert, die re-
gelmäßig mit einer *Hauptdatenbank* abgeglichen werden.

In der Softwareinfrastruktur *Tartan Racing Urban Challenge Systems*
(*TRUCS*) des Gewinnerfahrzeugs „Boss" im DARPA Urban Challenge dient
SimpleComms [7] zur Interprozesskommunikation. Es nutzt das Konzept des
„Anonymous Publish/Subscribe" mit einem Ereignis-Bus. Es sorgt insbesondere
für die Nachrichtenverteilung zwischen Rechnern über dedizierte TCP/IP Ver-
bindungen. Es beinhaltet ein Aufzeichnungssystem, das 67 der 84 Kanäle mit
einer Gesamtdatenrate von ca. 17 MB/s durch jeweils einen Logging-Task in einzelne Dateien schreibt. Dabei wurde Verbesserungspotenzial bei der zeitlichen
Zuordnung der aufgezeichneten Daten festgestellt.

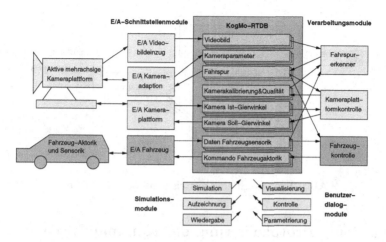

Abb. 1. Transparente Kommunikation in einem kognitiven Automobil

3 Transparente Kommunikation für kognitive Systeme

Wie gezeigt existieren eine Reihe von Softwarearchitekturen für kognitive Systeme, gerade aus dem Bereich der Robotik. Diese sind jedoch meist auf ein bestimmtes Anwendungsgebiet spezialisiert und legen grundsätzliche Strukturen des Systemaufbaus fest. Um jederzeit auch neuartige Strukturen zu realisieren, wurde eine leichtgewichtige generische Architektur entwickelt, die einheitliche Schnittstellen zur Integration aller Softwaremodule eines kognitiven Systems bietet und dabei harte Echtzeitanforderungen erfüllt [8,9].

Abb. 1 zeigt am Beispiel eines kognitiven Automobils, wie die Kommunikationsbeziehungen zwischen den einzelnen Funktionen aussehen. Im Zentrum befindet sich die *Realzeitdatenbasis für kognitive Automobile* (KogMo-RTDB) [10]. Alle Daten werden dort in RTDB-Objekten $\mathcal{D}$ strukturiert und mit genauen Zeitstempeln $t_{committed}$ und t_{data} versehen gespeichert. Aus einer objektindividuellen Kurzzeithistorie der Länge $T_{history,\mathcal{D}}$ können andere Module sogar vergangene Daten wieder abrufen. Zur Laufzeit können jederzeit neue Objekte angelegt und gelöscht werden. Sie bekommen eine eindeutige Identifikationsnummer OID.

Ein Objekt besteht aus einer vorgegebenen Menge statischer Informationen (Metadaten $\mathcal{M}$) und den frei definierbaren Nutzdaten $\mathcal{D}$, die laufend aktualisiert werden. Dabei darf die jeweils spezifizierte Maximalgröße $n_{bytes,max}$ nicht überschreiten werden. Da die einzige Kommunikationsverbindung zweier Module über die KogMo-RTDB besteht, ist deren Transparenz stets gewährleistet.

Damit an dieser Stelle keine Engpass entsteht, sorgen echtzeitfähige Methoden für einen effizienten Datenaustausch. Dabei werden Ringpuffer zur zeitlichen Entkopplung eingesetzt, die in Verbindung mit einem eigens entworfenen Schreib-/Leseprotokoll einen blockierungsfreien Datenfluss ermöglichen [10]. Die Architektur erlaubt zudem die Kooperation von Echtzeit- und Standardprozessen. In Anwendungen wurden gleichzeitig Datenobjekte mit >1 MB und sich schnell ändernde Objekte mit Aktualisierungsfrequenzen von >1 kHz bewältigt.

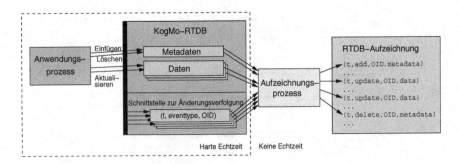

Abb. 2. Aufzeichnung mittels Änderungsverfolgung

4   Effiziente Protokollierung der Kommunikation

Die zentrale Datenhaltung der KogMo-RTDB eröffnet die Möglichkeit einer umfassenden Protokollierung aller Daten. Ein Aufzeichnungsprogramm (*RTDB-Recorder*) schreibt alle sichtbaren Änderungen in der KogMo-RTDB einschließlich des genauen Zeitpunkts in eine Datei. Dies umfasst alle Einfüge-, Schreib- und Löschoperationen, nicht jedoch die Leseoperationen, da diese an den Daten keine Änderungen verursachen.

Eine aufgezeichnete Datei kann mit einem Wiedergabeprogramm (*RTDB-Player*) wieder in eine KogMo-RTDB mit wählbarer Geschwindigkeit abgespielt werden. Die eingespielten Objekte können von allen Modulen ohne Modifikation oder Umkonfiguration genutzt werden.

4.1   Aufzeichnungsmethode

Im Konzept der KogMo-RTDB darf eine Aufzeichnung unter keinen Umständen die Echtzeitfähigkeit der Prozesse, deren Transaktionen protokolliert werden, beeinträchtigen. Dies schließt die naheliegende Lösung aus, die Protokollierung im Kontext des verursachenden Prozesses durchzuführen. Stattdessen wurde die in Abb. 2 gezeigte schlanke Schnittstelle zur Änderungsverfolgung (*trace tap*) entworfen. Durch konsequente Nutzung der RTDB-Historie minimiert sie den Rechenaufwand der protokollierten Prozesse. Im Kontext des Anwendungsprozesses wird lediglich das die jeweilige Transaktion eindeutig identifizierende Ereignistupel $EV = (t, eventtype, OID)$ in einen Ereignispuffer ausgekoppelt. Durch die Beschränkung auf diesen Ereignistupel EV ist die Erzeugungsdauer der Änderungsnachricht unabhängig von der individuellen Objektgröße n_{bytes} des geschriebenen RTDB-Objekts. Durch eine Erweiterung von EV um die redundanten Parameter $(\mathcal{M}_{slot}, \mathcal{D}_{slot})$, die auf die betroffenen Speicherplätze hinweisen, konnten die Lesezugriffe des Recorders zusätzlich optimiert werden.

Die Art des Ereignisses bestimmt die Belegung des Ereignistupels nach Tabelle 1. In Abhängigkeit von *eventtype* holt sich der Aufzeichnungsprozess die zum Zeitpunkt t_{event} aktuellen Daten bzw. Metadaten des Objektes mit der

Tabelle 1. Belegung des Ereignistupels EV

Ereignis	Betroffene Daten	t_{event}	eventtype	OID
Objekt erstellt	Metadaten	$t_{created}$	$CREATED$	neue OID
Objekt aktualisiert	Objektdaten	$t_{committed}$	$UPDATED$	aktuelle OID
Objekt gelöscht	Metadaten	$t_{deleted}$	$DELETED$	alte OID

Kennung OID durch die Standardmethoden der KogMo-RTDB aus dessen Historienspeicher und führt die Festplattenschreibzugriffe durch. Der Vorteil dieses Vorgehens ist die Reduzierung unnötigen Kopieraufwands für Objektdaten. Der Nachteil ist, dass dadurch Daten verloren gehen können, wenn die Zeitspanne zwischen der Protokollierung des Ereignisses t_{event} und dem Abrufen durch den Aufzeichnungsprozess $t_{read,recorder}$ größer als die gültige Historienlänge $T_{history}$ ist. Daher muss $T_{history}$ ausreichend (z.B. ≥ 3 s) dimensioniert werden.

4.2 Aufzeichnungsformat

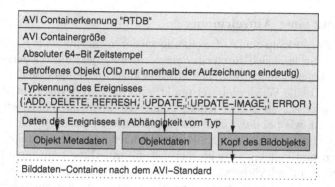

Abb. 3. AVI-kompatible Struktur eines aufgezeichneten RTDB-Ereignisses

Ein aufgezeichneter Datenstrom benötigt eine wohldefinierte Struktur, die flexibel und erweiterbar sein muss. Sie darf sich aber nach ihrer Etablierung nicht mehr ändern, sonst werden alte Aufzeichnungen wertlos. Um die Akzeptanz des KogMo-RTDB-Aufzeichnungsformats zu fördern, wurde das bekannte *AVI*-Multimediaformat (*audio video interleave*) so erweitert, dass andere AVI-Wiedergabeprogramme die enthaltenen umkomprimierten Videobildobjekte als Videofilm ohne vorherige Konvertierung abspielen können.

Ein aufzuzeichnendes Ereignis der KogMo-RTDB wird in einen AVI-kompatiblen Container verpackt, dessen Struktur Abb. 3 zeigt. Die gewählte Kennung (*four character code*) „RTDB" wird von der meisten AVI-Software wie beabsichtigt ignoriert. Jedes Element enthält den Zeitstempel t_{event}, der je nach verwendeter Rechnerhardware eine Genauigkeit bis zu einer Nanosekunde abbilden kann, die so für eine spätere Auswertung erhalten bleibt. Der verbleibende Inhalt des Containers enthält abhängig vom aufzuzeichnenden Ereignis die betroffenen Daten:

- Für ein neues Objekt werden die neuen Objekt-Metadaten angehängt.
- Die Metadaten eines gelöschten Objekts enthalten zusätzlich die Kennung $PID_{deleted}$ des löschenden Prozesses. Ein gelöschtes Objekt wird aus der KogMo-RTDB erst nach Ablauf von $T_{history}$ entfernt.
- Zu Aufzeichnungsbeginn erfolgt eine Zustandsaktualisierung aller Objekte.
- Bei einer Aktualisierung der Objektdaten werden die neuen Daten mit ihrer angegebenen Größe $n_{bytes,committed} \leq n_{bytes,max}$ geschrieben.
- Bei Videobild-Objekten wird nur deren Kopf im „RTDB"-Container protokolliert, auf den dann die eigentlichen Bilddaten als AVI-Bild folgen.

Sollten bei der Aufzeichnung Fehler auftreten, z.B. der Verlust einzelner Objekte oder Bilder, weil sie in ihrer Historie bereits überschrieben sind, wird eine Fehlermarkierung mit der Typenkennung „ERROR" in den Aufzeichnungsstrom eingefügt. So lässt sich später ein Maß für die Fehlerhaftigkeit angeben und eine fehlerfreie Aufzeichnung automatisch identifizieren. Das Design des strukturierten Datenstroms verhindert unnötige Kopfbewegungen der Festplatte, zudem kann er auch ohne Dateisystem auf einen Datenträger geschrieben werden.

4.3   Einsatz einer Aufzeichnung

Der *RTDB-Player* kann eine Aufzeichnung wieder in eine laufende KogMo-RTDB einspielen. Dabei lässt sich durch ein *Playercontrol*-Objekt die Wiedergabe anhalten, die Geschwindigkeit regeln, eine Position anspringen und eine Endlosschleife setzen. Der aktuelle Wiedergabezeitpunkt wird als *Playerstatus* veröffentlicht.

Das Festplattensystem des wiedergebenden Rechners muss mindestens so leistungsfähig sein, wie bei der Aufnahme, andernfalls ist eine Wiedergabe nur verlangsamt möglich. Es existiert jedoch ein Werkzeug, um eine Aufnahme zeitlich zu schneiden und beliebig Objekte herauszufiltern. Diese reduzierte Aufnahme lässt sich dann auf schwächeren Systemen in Echtzeit abspielen.

Aufzeichnungen können zum einen zur Dokumentation eingesetzt werden. Zum anderen dienen Sie zur Generierung von Testdatensätzen, anhand denen neue Algorithmen getestet und bewertet werden können. Abb. 4 zeigt ein Beispiel für den Einsatz von KogMo-RTDB-Aufzeichnungen:

- Auf dem Fahrzeugrechner eines kognitiven Automobils werden die Rohdaten aller Videokameras einschließlich der dazugehörigen aktuellen Kalibrierdaten der aktiven Kameraplattform aufgezeichnet.
- Beim Abspielen im Labor werden beispielsweise erkannte Objekte herausgefiltert und stattdessen die Bildrohdaten von mit einem verbesserten Algorithmus erneut analysiert. Das Ergebnis kann hierbei leicht mit den aufgezeichneten Resultaten verglichen werden.
- Um einen Algorithmus zur Situationserkennung anhand eingespielter Situationen zu trainieren, werden in RTDB #3 nur die dafür interessanten Objekte wiedergegeben. Die zusätzlichen Ergebnisse werden nun in einer zweiten Aufzeichnung festgehalten und können ebenfalls weitergeben werden.

Wie auch in Abb. 1 zu sehen, wird empfohlen, sämtliche Visualisierungselemente als eigenständige Module zu realisieren. So können sie ohne Modifikation zur späteren Visualisierung einer Aufzeichnung verwendet werden.

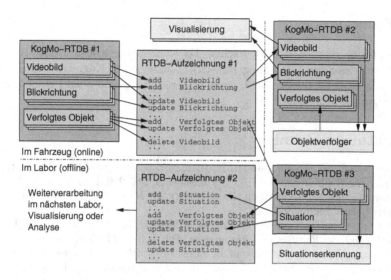

Abb. 4. Aufzeichnungen und Wiedergabe von KogMo-RTDB-Protokollen

5 Ergebnisse und Anwendungen

Die KogMo-RTDB dient als zentrales Kommunikationsframework auf den Rechnersystemen mehrerer kognitiver Automobile, wie einem autonomen Audi Q7 und dem autonomen VW Passat „AnnieWAY" [11], der ins Finale des *DARPA Urban Challenge 2007* kam. Dort werden gleichzeitig Objekte mit Sensorrohdaten wie HD-LIDAR (1.2MB, 10Hz), Kameras (300kB, 30Hz), Fahrzeugdaten (100 Bytes, 1kHz) und CAN-Frames (44 Bytes, 2.5kHz) zusammen mit den Objekten der Verhaltensentscheidung ausgetauscht und protokolliert.

Insgesamt wurden dabei > 60 MB/s mit $> 2 \cdot 10^4$ Ereignisse/s aufgezeichnet. Über die entwickelte Schnittstelle zur Änderungsverfolgung konnten ohne Festplattenzugriffe $> 5 \cdot 10^4$ Ereignisse/s verlustfrei erfasst werden.

Die Fahrzeuge besitzen einen Multinode-Multicore-Rechner [10]. Dort wird mit geringer Latenz auf den lokalen Speicher anderer Knoten zugegriffen, sodass auf ein Rechnernetz verzichtet werden kann. Zur Übertragung von Objekten zwischen mehreren Instanzen der KogMo-RTDB sind anwendungsspezifische Lösungen (z.B. Car2Car) entstanden.

Die präsentierte Lösung skaliert bis zu einem Minimalspeicherbedarf von lediglich 0.5 MB RAM und läuft auch auf einem 266 MHz ARM-Board. Dieses wird zur GPS-Positionsübermittlung eines nicht-autonomen Fahrzeugs über WLAN und als GPS-Logger eingesetzt.

Gerade die gesamtheitliche Aufzeichnungsfunktion, die sowohl Rohdaten als auch sämtliche Verarbeitungsergebnisse umfasst, hat sich für viele Projekte auch über den Automobilbereich hinaus [12,13] als äußerst nützlich erwiesen. Eine optionale Kompression der RTDB-Objekte ist in Arbeit. Für eigene Anwendungen steht die KogMo-RTDB unter [14] als OpenSource bereit.

6   Danksagung

Die Autoren danken der Deutschen Forschungsgemeinschaft (DFG) für die Förderung des Sonderforschungsbereich/Transregio 28 „Kognitive Automobile", Herrn Samarjit Chakraborty für seine Unterstützung und allen Projektpartnern für die gute Zusammenarbeit.

Literaturverzeichnis

1. STILLER, C., G. FÄRBER und S. KAMMEL: *Cooperative Cognitive Automobiles*. In: *Proc. IEEE Intelligent Vehicles Symposium*, S. 215–220, 2007.
2. SONDERFORSCHUNGSBEREICH TRANSREGIO 28: *Homepage Kognitive Automobile*. http://www.kognimobil.org.
3. BRUYNINCKX, H.: *Open Robot Control Software: The OROCOS Project*. In: *IEEE Intl. Conf. on Robotics and Automation*, Bd. 3, S. 2523–2528, 2001.
4. SCHOLL, K.-U., J. ALBIEZ und B. GASSMANN: *MCA - An Expandable Modular Controller Architecture*. In: *3rd Real-Time Linux Workshop*, Milano, Italy, 2001.
5. RIEDER, A.: *Multisensorielle Fahrzeugerkennung in einem verteilten Rechnersystem für autonome Fahrzeuge*. Doktorarbeit, Universität der Bundeswehr München, 2000.
6. GÖRZIG, S., A. GERN und P. LEVI: *Realzeitfähige Multiagentenarchitektur für autonome Fahrzeuge*. In: *Autonome Mobile Systeme 1999*, S. 44–55. Springer, 2000.
7. MCNAUGHTON, M., C. BAKER, T. GALATALI, B. SALESKY, C. URMSON und J. ZIGLAR: *Software Infrastructure for an Autonomous Ground Vehicle*. Journal of Aerospace Computing, Information, and Communication, 5(12):491–505, 2008.
8. GOEBL, M. und G. FÄRBER: *Eine realzeitfähige Softwarearchitektur für kognitive Automobile*. In: BERNS, K. und T. LUKSCH (Hrsg.): *Autonome Mobile Systeme 2007*, Informatik Aktuell, S. 198–204. Springer, 2007.
9. GOEBL, M. und G. FÄRBER: *Interfaces for Integrating Cognitive Functions into Intelligent Vehicles*. In: *Proc. IEEE Intelligent Vehicles Symposium*, S. 1093–1100. IEEE Press, 2008.
10. GOEBL, M. und G. FÄRBER: *A Real-Time-capable Hard- and Software Architecture for Joint Image and Knowledge Processing in Cognitive Automobiles*. In: *Proc. IEEE Intelligent Vehicles Symposium*, S. 734–740. IEEE Press, 2007.
11. KAMMEL, S., J. ZIEGLER, B. PITZER, M. WERLING, T. GINDELE, D. JAGZENT, J. SCHRÖDER, M. THUY, M. GOEBL, F. VON HUNDELSHAUSEN, O. PINK, C. FRESE und C. STILLER: *Team AnnieWAY's autonomous system for the DARPA Urban Challenge 2007*. In: *International Journal of Field Robotics Research*. John Wiley & Sons, Inc., 2008.
12. WALLHOFF, F., J. GAST, A. BANNAT, S. SCHWÄRZLER, G. RIGOLL, C. WENDT, S. SCHMIDT, M. POPP und B. FÄRBER: *Real-time Framework for On- and Off-line Multimodal Human-Human and Human-Robot Interaction*. In: *Proc. of the 1st Int. Workshop on Cognition for Technical Systems*, Munich, Germany, 2008.
13. LENZ, C., S. NAIR, M. RICKERT, A. KNOLL, W. ROSEL, J. GAST, A. BANNAT und F. WALLHOFF: *Joint-Action for Humans and Industrial Robots for Assembly Tasks*. In: *IEEE Intl. Symposium on Robot and Human Interactive Communication*, S. 130–135, 2008.
14. GOEBL, M.: *Homepage und Quellcode der Realzeitdatenbasis für kognitive Automobile (KogMo-RTDB)*. http://www.kogmo-rtdb.de.

Walking Humanoid Robot Lola
An Overview of Hard- and Software

Markus Schwienbacher, Valerio Favot,
Thomas Buschmann, Sebastian Lohmeier and Heinz Ulbrich*

Institute of Applied Mechanics, Technische Universität München,
Boltzmannstr. 15, 85748 Garching, Germany
{schwienbacher, favot, buschmann, lohmeier, ulbrich}@amm.mw.tu-muenchen.de

Abstract. Based on the experience gathered from the walking robot JOHNNIE the new performance enhanced 25-DoF humanoid robot LOLA was built. The goal of this project is to realize a fast, human-like walking. This paper presents different aspects of this complex mechatronic system. Besides the overall lightweight construction, custom build multi-sensory joint drives with high torque brush-less motors were crucial for reaching the performance goal. A decentralized electronics architecture is used for joint control and sensor data processing. A simulation environment serves as a testbed for the walking control, to minimize the risk of damaging the robot hardware during real world experiments.

1 Introduction

Many of the recent developments in enabling technologies such as biped walking control, mechatronics and computer technology have helped to make the realization of biped humanoid robots easier or even possible. Prominent examples are the TOYOTA PARTNER ROBOT [1], ASIMO [2], HRP-2 [3], HRP-3 [4] and WABIAN-2 [5]. Even if all robots achieve reliable dynamic walking —compared to a human being— high walking speeds and flexible motion generation still remain challenging. Many unresolved control problems still exist, e.g. fast walking and running [1], sudden turning motions, walking on rough terrain and trajectory generation in complex environments.

On the other hand, the robot hardware cannot be neglected. If designed carefully the robot hardware contributes significantly to overall system performance. Both robot hardware and software must be seen as tightly coupled parts of a highly integrated mechatronic system.

In the first part of this paper, the mechanical and electronics design is introduced. The second part outlines the simulation environment and deals with the real-time trajectory generation and stabilizing control.

---

* This work is supported by the "Deutsche Forschungsgemeinschaft" (grant UL 105/29).

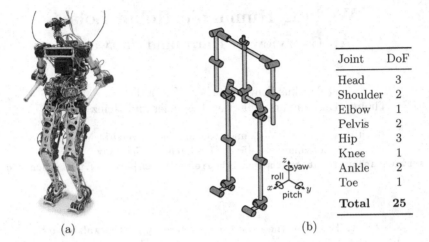

Joint	DoF
Head	3
Shoulder	2
Elbow	1
Pelvis	2
Hip	3
Knee	1
Ankle	2
Toe	1
Total	**25**

(a)   (b)

Fig. 1. (a) Photograph of the anthropomorphic walking robot LOLA. (b) Kinematic structure of the robot.

2   Mechanical and Electronics System Design

Based on the research experience with JOHNNIE, which was developed at our institute between 1998 and 2003 and achieved a maximum walking speed of 2.4 km/h, design considerations were derived towards a general improvement of the whole system [6,7]. The long term speed goal for LOLA is 5 km/h.

The presented robot LOLA is 180 cm tall and weighs 55 kg. The physical dimensions are based on anthropometric data. Fig. 1(a) shows a photograph of the fully assembled robot and Fig. 1(b) explains the kinematic configuration with 25 DoFs. Simulations and experiments have shown that additional redundant DoFs enable more natural and flexible gait patterns and extend the abilities of the robot in general. Therefore the legs have 7 DoFs each, the pelvis has 2 and each arm has 3 DoFs.

While most humanoid robots have 6 DoF legs with a rigid body foot, LOLA incorporates an additional actively driven 7th DoF, located between forefoot and heel, equivalent to the human toes. Other examples of humanoid robots with actuated toe joints are: H6, H7 [8] and the TOYOTA PARTNER ROBOT [1].

In addition to the pan/tilt unit of the stereo camera head, the convergence angle can be actively adjusted, which enables stereo vision of objects close to the robot's head.

2.1   Structural Components

The dimensioning of the robot hardware is an open ended iterative process of mechanical design and extensive multibody simulations (MBS). High priority design goals for the hardware are: (1) minimum overall mass, (2) sufficient structural stiffness, (3) high center of mass and (4) low moments of inertia of the leg links.

It is obvious that the overall mass should be minimized while a sufficient stiffness of the robot's structure must be maintained. Furthermore, the weight and the power of the joints must be balanced with the overall mass. Based on topology optimization results —produced with the finite element (FEM) program *Optistruct*[1]— both thigh and shank were designed as investment cast parts. This technology gives more freedom in the design process compared to traditional milling or welding parts. While making the mechatronics integration easier, it also facilitates a better stiffness to weight ratio of the structure. A more comprehensive description of the structural design is given in [6].

2.2   Joint Design

All actuators have a similar structure with the sizes of gear and motor adapted to the requirements of each link. We use high performance permanent magnet brushless synchronous motors (PMSM) from *Parker Bayside* [9] because of their superior torque and speed capabilities. By using kit motors, a space- and weight-saving integration of actuators and sensors becomes possible.

Except for the knee and ankle, all joints employ Harmonic Drive[2] (HD) gears as speed reducers. We use custom lightweight versions with a T-shaped Circular Spline which is, in our experience, the best tradeoff between weight and loading capacity. For the knee and ankle joints roller screw-based linear drives are employed, which —compared to the HD-based solution— leads to a better mass distribution in the hip-thigh area.

Fig. 2 illustrates the structure of a HD-based joint. Each joint contains an incremental rotary encoder, an absolute angular encoder used as link position sensor and a limit switch. The incremental rotary encoder mounted on the motor shaft is mainly used for motor control. The absolute angular encoder (resolution 17 bit, accuracy 0.1°) compensates elasticities and nonlinearities in the drive chain and eliminates the need for a homing routine, making startup faster and easier. To improve operational security and to prevent the robot from self-destruction each joint incorporates a limiting switch in the form of a light barrier.

2.3   Force/Torque Sensors

LOLA is equipped with two six-axes force/torque sensors which are designed as supporting elements of the foot structure. The required measurement range was determined for a walking speed of 5 km/h using our detailed multibody simulation model [10]. Based on these data and multiple iterations of FEM-analysis, an optimal design for the force-sensing members was developed (Fig. 2). The Maltese crossbar type sensor body is designed as a single milling aluminum part. The sensing members are equipped with two pairs of strain gauges that operate in a half bridge circuit for temperature compensation.

---

[1] from *Altair Engineering, Inc.* (www.altairhyperworks.com)

[2] from *Harmonic Drive AG* (www.harmonic-drive.de and www.harmonicdrive.aero)

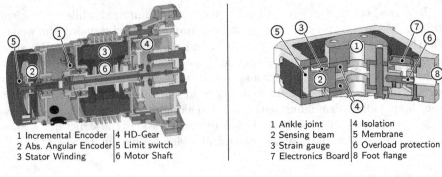

1 Incremental Encoder	4 HD-Gear
2 Abs. Angular Encoder	5 Limit switch
3 Stator Winding	6 Motor Shaft

1 Ankle joint	4 Isolation
2 Sensing beam	5 Membrane
3 Strain gauge	6 Overload protection
7 Electronics Board	8 Foot flange

Fig. 2. CAD sections through (left) hip yaw joint and (right) force/torque sensor.

An integrated overload protection protects the sensitive sensing members from damage in experiments. The calibration matrix was generated by evaluating more than 450 different load cases with the least squares method. At a total weight of 395 g the sensor includes all necessary electronics and provides a digital interface.

2.4   Inertial Measurement Unit

The inertial measurement unit (IMU) estimates the orientation and velocities of the upper body. Simulations and experimental results with the robot JOHN-NIE have shown that the precision of this sensor significantly determines the performance of the stabilizing controller. Therefore, the IMU must show high accuracy, signal quality (i. e. low noise) and bandwidth. Moreover, a low sensor bias results in a low long time drift and a reliable calibration. We are using the inertial measurement unit *iVRU-FC-C167*[3] in a custom made light weight version. The sensor consists of three open-loop fiber-optic gyroscopes and three MEMS[4] accelerometers. The sensor fusion comprises internal error models and is integrated into the sensor, which has a CAN interface.

2.5   Electronics Architecture

Fig. 3 shows a schematic overview of the electronics architecture. LOLA is control-led by a central control unit (CCU) mounted on the upper body and nine local controllers carrying out low-level tasks, such as joint control and sensor data processing. The local controllers are a custom development because of compact-ness and various sensor/actuator interfaces. Similar to hierarchical structures in biological systems, sensor data is preprocessed decentrally and only relevant information is forwarded to the CCU. Local controllers and CCU are connected via the Ethernet-based real-time communication system Sercos-III. The CCU is

---

[3] from *iMAR Navigation* (www.imar-navigation.de)
[4] short for: Microelectromechanical systems

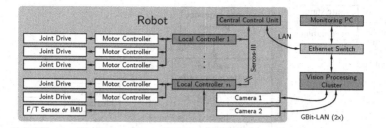

Fig. 3. Electronics architecture of LOLA

based on a PC platform (Intel Core 2 Duo Mobile, 2.33 GHz), running the QNX[5] real-time operating system. Gait pattern generation and stabilization control run on the on-board computer system without any support from outside except for power supply. An external PC is used only for monitoring purposes and to give basic operating commands if the robot is not connected to the vision system. Due to high computing power requirements, vision processing is done on an external PC cluster.

3 Simulation

The design of the robot's hardware and control algorithms are based on simulations of the closed-loop system. During the design stage both hardware and control software are refined iteratively based on simulations of the current hard- and software design. To facilitate such a design procedure we have implemented a modular simulation system that can be used to simulate various robot configurations. The simulation model includes rigid body mechanics, gear friction models, actuator dynamics and models for the unilateral, visco-elastic foot-ground contact. This leads to the following coupled dynamic systems:

$$M\ddot{q} + h = W_\lambda \lambda + W_\tau \tau \tag{1}$$

$$B\dot{d} + Kd = f \tag{2}$$

$$L\dot{I} + RI + k_M \omega_{\text{rot}} = U \tag{3}$$

Equation (1) represents the equations of motion (EoM) for the rigid body dynamics. The vector of generalized coordinates q consists of the model's degrees of freedom (cf. Fig. 1(b)), M is the mass matrix and h the vector of smooth forces. Finally, λ and τ are the contact and actuator forces, acting on the MBS via the Jacobian matrices W_λ and W_τ respectively.

Eq. (2) considers the contact forces f modeled as visco-elastic contact elements with the node displacements d. The damping and stiffness matrices B and K can be obtained by discretizing the contact element continuum using FEM.

---

[5] from *QNX Software Systems* (www.qnx.com)

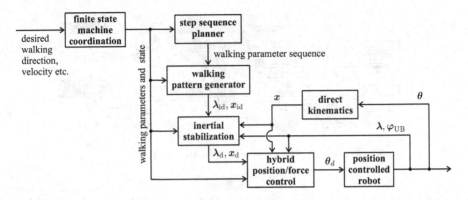

Fig. 4. Real-time walking control architecture

Drive dynamics —presented in eq. (3)— considers the HD friction, modeled as load dependent STRIBECK friction [10] and motor dynamics [11]. Here U is the armature voltage, I the current and ω_{rot} the rotor's angular velocity. Whereas L, R and k_M are the inductance, resistance and motor back EMF constants, respectively. Obviously, the components τ_i of the torque vector τ in eq. (2) depend on the gear used in the joint. For a HD-based actuator the torque results to $\tau_i = k_{M,i} I_i + \tau_{\text{HDgear},i}$, where i is the joint index and $\tau_{\text{HDgear},i}$ the friction torque model of the Harmonic Drive gear used.

By combining the components described above, different models of the robot are generated, satisfying either low calculation times or high accuracy. The simulation software has been validated against experiments with JOHNNIE [10].

4   Control Aspects

Fig. 4 shows an overview of the real-time walking control system. The concept is outlined in the following.

4.1   Trajectory Generation

From global inputs, such as the desired walking velocity and direction and a local map of obstacle positions and dimensions, the *walking pattern generator* calculates a trajectory for the following three steps at the beginning of each step. To facilitate real-time execution, we separate planning into smaller and simpler subtasks. First, constraints are calculated from given parameters such as average walking speed. Second, foot trajectories are planned in task space as fifth order polynomials. We then calculate reference torques $T_{i,\text{ref}}$ that minimize $\int \dot{T}_{i,\text{ref}}^2\,dt$, $i \in \{x,y\}$ and stay within the admissible range. By choosing a piecewise linear parametrization of $T_{i,\text{ref}}$ we obtain a quadratic programming problem with bound constraints, that can be solved efficiently. Finally, the robot's center of mass (CoM) trajectory is calculated based on the previous calculation steps [12].

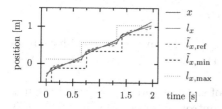
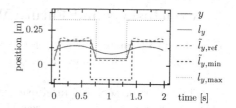

Fig. 5. Example solution using spline collocation with 30 equally spaced control points. $l_y := T_x/F_z$ is the center of pressure.

For real-time trajectory generation the robot is modeled using a modified *Inverted Pendulum Model* with one additional point-mass for each leg. The simplified EoM in the lateral y-z-plane is given by

$$m_b[z_b\ddot{y}_b - y_b(\ddot{z}_b + g)] = -T_x + m_l \sum_{i=1..2} [y_{l,i}(\ddot{z}_{l,i} + g) - z_{l,i}\ddot{y}_{l,i}] =: -\tilde{T}_x \quad (4)$$

where b denotes the body mass point, i is the foot index, T_x is the torque heading into forward direction, m_l is the mass of one foot mass point.

We solve eq. (4) as a boundary value problem (BVP) on the time interval $t \in [t_B, t_E]$ with the boundary values

$$\left(y_b(t_B), \dot{y}_b(t_B), y_b(t_E)\right)^T = \left(y_{b,B}, \dot{y}_{b,B}, y_{b,E}\right)^T, \quad (5)$$

where t_B denotes the begin time and t_E the end time. Thus connecting a stable CoM trajectory solution to the current trajectory with continuity in y and $\dot{y}$.

In order to solve the BVP numerically in real-time we have implemented a collocation method with cubic splines as basis functions (cf. [12]).

Fig. 5 shows a solution obtained by the proposed method for a periodic gait at 2.5 km/h using 46 cm steps and leg masses m_l equivalent to 8.2 % of the robot mass. We used 30 spline parameters for three walking steps. Evidently, the trajectories are smooth and the contact torques stay within the region prescribed by the sequence of support polygons.

4.2 Stabilizing Control

The basic idea is to stabilize the upper body inclination by controlling the contact torques at the feet. Similar concepts are used to control most of the existing full-size humanoid robots [13–15].

The task-space trajectories, obtained from the trajectory generator, are modified to satisfy stability criteria using sensor data from the 6-DoF force torque sensors in the feet and the IMU in the torso. The resulting trajectories are then mapped into joint space using a resolved motion rate control scheme [16] with nullspace optimization [17]. Finally, the joint trajectories are tracked using high-gain joint position control.

5   Conclusions and Future Work

Compared to humans, current biped walking robots are still slow and have limited autonomy. With our new developed humanoid robot LOLA we try to diminish this gap.

This paper presented a brief overview of some important aspects of the mechatronic hardware design and real-time control system of the robot. LOLA is 180 cm tall and weighs 55 kg (without batteries). The distinctive features are the extremely lightweight construction, and the redundant kinematic configuration.

Currently, LOLA has been fully assembled and we are performing initial experiments. Furthermore, the vision system is being developed for autonomous walking experiments.

References

1. Tajima, R. et al.: Fast Running Experiments Involving a Humanoid Robot. In: Proc. of the IEEE Intl Conf on Robotics & Automation (ICRA). (2009)
2. Hirai, K. et al.: The Development of Honda Humanoid Robot. In: Proc. ICRA, Leuven, Belgium (1998) 1321–1326
3. Kaneko, K. et al.: Humanoid Robot HRP-2. In: Proc. ICRA, New Orleans, USA (2004) 1083–1090
4. Kaneko, K. et al.: Humanoid Robot HRP-3. In: Proc. of the IEEE Intl Conf on Intelligent Robots & Systems (IROS). (2008) 2471–2478
5. Ogura, Y. et al.: Development of a Humanoid Robot WABIAN-2. In: Proc. ICRA. Orlando, Florida, USA (2006) 76–81
6. Lohmeier, S. et al.: Leg Design for a Humanoid Walking Robot. In: Proc. of the IEEE-RAS Intl Conf on Humanoid Robots (Humanoids). (2006) 536–541
7. Lohmeier, S. et al.: Modular joint Design for Performance Enhanced Humanoid Robot LOLA. In: Proc. ICRA. Orlando, Florida, USA (2006) 88–93
8. Nishiwaki, K. et al.: Toe Joints that enhance Bipedal and Fullbody Motion of Humanoid Robots. In: Proc. ICRA. Washington, DC, USA (2002) 3105–3110
9. Bayside Motion 27 Seaview Boulevard, Port Washington, NY: Product Manual: Frameless Kit Motors. (2008) Rev. 2.0 / 1100.
10. Buschmann, T. et al.: Dynamics Simulation for a Biped Robot: Modeling and Experimental Verification. In: Proc. ICRA. (2006) 2673–2678
11. Schröder, D.: Elektrische Antriebe - Grundlagen. Volume 1. Springer (2009)
12. Buschmann, T. et al.: A Collocation Method for Real-Time Walking Pattern Generation. In: Proc. Humanoids. (2007) 1–6
13. Kajita, S. et al.: A Running Controller of Humanoid Biped HRP-2LR. In: Proc. ICRA. (2005) 616–622
14. Löffler, M. et al.: Sensors and Control Concept of a Biped Robot. IEEE Trans. Ind. Electron. **51** (2004) 972–80
15. Takenaka, T.: Controller of Legged Mobile Robot. European Patent Application no. EP1475198A1 (2004)
16. Whitney, D.E.: Resolved Motion Rate Control of Manipulators and Human Prostheses. IEEE Transactions on Man Machine Systems **10** (1969) 47–53
17. Liégeois, A.: Automatic Supervisory Control of the Configuration and Behavior of Multibody Mechanisms. IEEE Intl. Transactions on Systems, Man, and Cybernetics **SMC-7** (1977) 63–71

Printing: Mercedes-Druck, Berlin
Binding: Stein+Lehmann, Berlin